THE BIRTH OF WHITENESS

THE BIRTH OF WHITENESS

Race and the Emergence of U.S. Cinema

Edited by Daniel Bernardi

RUTGERS UNIVERSITY PRESS
New Brunswick, New Jersey

Published by Rutgers University Press, New Brunswick, New Jersey

Manufactured in the United States of America

Library of Congress Cataloging-in-Publication Data

The birth of whiteness : race and the emergence of U.S. cinema / edited by Daniel Bernardi.
p. cm.
Includes bibliographical references and index.
ISBN 0-8135-2277-3 (cloth : alk. paper). — ISBN 0-8135-2276-5 (pbk. : alk. paper)
1. Minorities in motion pictures. 2. Racism in motion pictures. 3. Race relations in motion pictures. 4. Silent films—United States—History and criticism. I. Bernardi, Daniel, 1964–
PN1995.9.M56B57 1996
791.43'6520693—dc20 95-52727
CIP

British Cataloging-in-Publication information available

I dedicate this book to five teachers and friends who, while
I was a beginning graduate student at the University of Arizona,
had a lasting impact on my thinking, politics, and career:

Caren Deming, for her determination and foresight
José Colchado, for his confidence and dedication
Lynne Tronsdale, for her compassion and insight
Don Kirihara, for his rigor and honesty
Marietta Ciaccio, for her perseverance and kindness

Thank you.

Contents

Acknowledgments ix

Daniel Bernardi
Introduction: Race and the Emergence of U.S. Cinema 1

REPRESENTATION AND RESISTANCE(?)

Clyde Taylor
The Re-Birth of the Aesthetic in Cinema 15

Thomas Cripps
The Making of *The Birth of a Race*: The Emerging Politics of Identity in Silent Movies 38

Pearl Bowser and Louise Spence
Identity and Betrayal: *The Symbol of the Unconquered* and Oscar Micheaux's "Biographical Legend" 56

Donald Kirihara
The Accepted Idea Displaced: Stereotype and Sessue Hayakawa 81

WHITE NATIONALISM

Daniel Bernardi
The Voice of Whiteness: D. W. Griffith's Biograph Films (1908–1913) 103

Virginia Wright Wexman
The Family on the Land: Race and Nationhood in Silent Westerns 129

Dan Streible
Race and the Reception of Jack Johnson Fight Films 170

THE FEAR OF MISCEGENATION

Chon A. Noriega
Birth of the Southwest: Social Protest, Tourism, and D. W. Griffith's *Ramona* 203

Nick Browne
The Undoing of the *Other* Woman: Madame Butterfly in the Discourse of American Orientalism 227

Gina Marchetti
Tragic and Transcendent Love in *The Forbidden City* 257

THE COLONIAL IMAGINATION

Roberta E. Pearson
The Revenge of Rain-in-the-Face? or, Custers and Indians on the Silent Screen 273

Fatimah Tobing Rony
Robert Flaherty's *Nanook of the North*: The Politics of Taxidermy and Romantic Ethnography 300

Sumiko Higashi
Touring the Orient with Lafcadio Hearn and Cecil B. DeMille: Highbrow versus Lowbrow in a Consumer Culture 329

Selected Bibliography 355

Contributors 363

Index 367

Acknowledgments

I would like to thank the Institute of American Cultures and the American Indian Studies Center, University of California, Los Angeles, for providing me with two grants that enabled me to travel to the Library of Congress and the Museum of Modern Art to research and screen many of the films in this anthology, particularly those associated with my article on D. W. Griffith. In this regard, Donna Kuyiyesva was especially helpful in administering the funds.

I would also like to thank the UCLA Film and Television Archive, particularly Andrea Kalas, Manager, Research and Study Center, for screening several of the films in this book for me. Also, Sam Gill and Robert Cushman at the Academy of Motion Picture Arts and Sciences, Special Collections, provided thoughtful and professional help in tracking down production files and stills. Susanne Bieger, my good friend, helped check facts and citations for both my article and the bibliography.

Bob Rosen, Nick Browne, Vivian Sobchack, and Chon Noriega, faculty in the Department of Film and Television at UCLA, provided intellectual and moral support, and I cannot thank them enough. I consider them to be both mentors and friends, and I look forward to more debates and laughs. I would also like to thank my editor, Leslie Mitchner, for taking a chance on an unknown graduate student. She helped both conceptualize and edit this book, and, while I deserve all criticism, she shares in any praise. Finally and most importantly, I am especially indebted to Lahn S. Kim for all her support during a hectic, intense, and exciting time in our lives.

THE BIRTH OF WHITENESS

Daniel Bernardi

INTRODUCTION
Race and the Emergence of U.S. Cinema

"Race matters."

—*Cornel West*[1]

Is race a biological subdivision of human beings or is it merely an illusion? If it is a biological subdivision, what precisely is the defining criteria and what relevance does that criteria have for explaining culture or social life? If it is an illusion, what role does history play in its production and perpetuation? Any scholar, including film historians and critics, must in some way grapple with these questions when writing about race.

If scholars assume that race is a natural taxonomy of Homo sapiens, a biological subdivision or subspecies, then their work is linked with a tradition of essentializing and discriminatory discourse that extends from eugenics and social Darwinism to studies of gene pool variances and the inheritance of intelligence quotients (Figure 1). While scientific approaches such as these purport to be objective, the identification and interpretation of biological or innate differences and their subsequent relevance to individual and social history is imminently—and ominously—subjective.[2] Biological definitions of race all too often lead to a determinism that validates and promotes sociopolitical hierarchies. As Henry Louis Gates, Jr., remarks, "Race, in these (scientific) usages, pretends to be an objective term of classification, when in fact it is a dangerous trope."[3] This is not to suggest that there are no useful reasons for dividing humans into categories, but that the criteria for justifying those categories and their relevance for explaining social formation or cultural expression is more a product of knowledge and ideology than it is of "nature."

If scholars assume that race is merely an illusion or a fiction, then their work risks negating identity and social history. While arguments that characterize race in this way acknowledge the constructedness and thus the ideology of the term, they can fail to address fully the fact that race also names a profound sociocultural phenomenon. In other words, whether there are biological "races" or not (and I would argue there are

Fig. 1: "The Races of Men," drawn from a text of 1877.

none), there are historical "races"—or groups of individuals who share past and continuing experiences: from group solidarity and expression to forms of oppression and privilege. Thus, even if race is merely a fiction, it is a powerful fiction in that it systematically affects how we see the world, how we present ourselves to the world, who we associate with, and how we are conversely treated by people and by institutions.

One of the challenges in editing this anthology has been grappling with the various definitions and subsequent pitfalls of that "dangerous trope." In some ways, I have an intuitive understanding of race as both an identity worthy of pride and as a maker for discrimination. As a Puerto Rican/Italian with a second father who is African American, I grew to accept my "mixed racial make-up" as something to be proud of as well as something that separated me from dominant and so-called pure races. In grade school, I proudly wore the Puerto Rican flag on one shoulder and the Italian flag on another. In high school I was an actor for Ododo Theatre, an African American performing arts company in Tucson, Arizona. During these same years, "spick," "guinea," and "nigger lover" were slurs that I had occasionally to confront and deal with. Today, too many people assume I'm "white." Thanks to these somewhat unique and utterly historical experiences, I have come to understand race as that which is simultaneously a point of solidarity and dignity and that which is a symbol for cultural Otherness and social privilege. Any definition of race, it seems to me, must take into consideration these seemingly disparate experiences.

Much of the current debate about race in cultural studies centers on the notion of identity, an approach which aptly recognizes that where we come from, how we see ourselves, and how we express ourselves are essential elements in the construction of race.[4] Stuart Hall, a pioneer in theorizing the relationship between race and identity, has argued that identity is both real, in the sense of material and historical, as well as heterogeneous, or "crossed and recrossed" by such categories as gender, class, and ethnicity.[5] Moreover, Hall describes how identity ebbs and flows, undergoing constant change and alteration: "identities come from somewhere, have histories. But, like everything which is historical, they undergo constant transformation."[6] For example, Puerto Ricans, like most Latinos, are an amalgam of travelers, including Tiano Indians, former African slaves, and past and current European and North American conquerors and immigrants. Our identity is informed by all of these "presences," as well as by class, sexuality, and other formations. And, this historically specific and multifaceted identity continues to evolve, as it has with Nuyoricans (Puerto Ricans living in New York). Identity, as Hall explains, "is a matter of 'becoming' as well as 'being.' It belongs to the future as much as to the past."[7]

In studying and critically engaging the articulation of race in popular culture, particularly the ways in which cinema represents and narrates race, I have come to understand that this term also names a hegemonic way of knowing and seeing. Race is not only identity, but also a sociohistorical formation. In the United States, this amounts to what sociologists Michael Omi and Howard Winant call a "racial formation," a ubiquitous and enduring color-line based on cultural and physiognomic differences that inform and at times determine our access to institutions, our social organization, our self-perception and our self-expression. "From a racial formation perspective," the sociologists explain, "race is a matter of both social structure and cultural representation."[8]

Like identity, the racial formation shifts and changes with time and space. During the birth of cinema, for example, social Darwinian and eugenics paradigms dominated the meaning of race, promoting the notion of a natural hierarchy of human cultures and histories. At the top of the so-proscribed evolutionary ladder were people who counted as "Anglo-Saxons" and, then, the rest of the "Caucasians"; at the bottom: "Mongoloids" and "Negroids." Today, though biological determinism is still with us, few people agree that these racial—or, more appropriately, racist—classsifications actually exist.[9] The meaning of race has shifted away from a singularly biological taxonomy restricted to three subspecies of human beings.[10] This suggests, as Omi and Winant note, that the racial formation is a socio-historical process in which "racial categories are created, inhabited, transformed, and destroyed."[11]

While the forms and veracity of the racial formation have shifted over the last one hundred years, its trajectory has not been so radical that racism has ceased or been eradicated. What remains a constant in the United States, and indeed in the West, is what Ella Shohat and Robert Stam call Eurocentrism: "the procrustean forcing of cultural heterogeneity into a single paradigmatic perspective in which Europe is seen as the unique source of meaning, as the world's center of gravity, as ontological 'reality' to the rest of the world's shadow."[12] Although some forms of colonialism have ended, Eurocentrism is still with us, defining and shaping the significance and the direction of the racial formation. Shohat and Stam find that "as an ideological substratum common to colonialist, imperialist, and racist discourse, Eurocentricism is a form of vestigial thinking which permeates and structures *contemporary* practices and representations even after the formal end of colonialism."[13] Though the manifestation of this "vestigial thinking" are relatively distinct from country to country and from region to region, in the United States, the physiognomic, legal, and representational marks of Eurocentrism have consistently been the degree to which an individual or a group counts or doesn't count as "white." As I argue in my contribution to this anthology, people unable to count as white remain marginalized, exploited, and degraded by this enduring order of things.

Culture is one of the main terrains where the white order is alternately supported and contested. In film, arguably the most popular and profitable form of culture in the last one hundred years, racist practices dominate the industrial, representational, and narrational history of the medium. Indeed, U.S. cinema has consistently constructed whiteness, the representational and narrative form of Eurocentrism, as the norm by which all "Others" fail by comparison. People of color are generally represented as either deviant threats to white rule, thereby requiring civilizing or brutal punishment, or fetishized objects of exotic beauty, icons for a racist scopophilia. This anthology aims to contextualize and critically engage the forms of these and similar practices in early U.S. cinema, investigating and analyzing such diverse subjects as exhibition, genre, intertextuality, narrative, reception, stardom, and stereotyping.

Film Historiography

Irrespective of the definition of race a scholar chooses, the subject is both contentious and volatile. Write about it to someone's disliking, and you can be labeled politically correct or, worse, racist. Race is certainly not a safe or a straightforward subject for any scholar to grapple with. However, to bypass or ignore this term of differentiation is to bypass and ignore film history. The examples of racist representations are numerous, ranging from the *Chinese Laundry Scene* (1896) to *The Birth of a Nation* (1915), from *The Searchers* (1956) to the Latino drug and Vietnam revisionist films of the 1980s, among many others. Race has been and continues to be a fundamental part of U.S. cinema. And the fact remains that silence on this albeit contentious subject serves to perpetuate and enforce one of the dominate ways whiteness persists from historical period to historical period, and from film to film.

Though slow to tackle rigorously the racial practices that inform U.S. cinema, film studies, thanks largely to the impact of cultural studies, has begun systematically addressing this important issue. A significant work of the late 1970s is Thomas Cripps's *Slow Fade to Black*, which historicizes both the representation of African Americans and African American filmmaking from 1900 to 1942.[14] A sampling of just the books published in the last few years on African Americans include Cripps's *Making Movies Black*, Manthia Diawara's anthology, *Black American Cinema*, Ed Guerrero's *Framing Blackness: The African American Image in Film*, and Mark A. Reid's *Redefining Black Film*.[15] On Chicana/o cinema, there are Chon Noriega's *Chicanos and Film: Representation and Resistance* and Rosa Linda Fregoso's *The Bronze Screen: Chicana and Chicano Film Culture* and numerous articles and special issues of journals.[16] Eugene Franklin Wong's *On Visual Media Racism* was one of the first studies of

Asian Americans in cinema.[17] More recently, Kevin Brownlow's *Behind the Mask of Innocence*, Sumiko Higashi's *Cecil B. DeMille and American Culture: The Silent Era*, and Gina Marchetti's *Romance and the "Yellow Peril": Race, Sex, and Discursive Strategies in Hollywood Fiction* have contributed to this debate.[18] Though much more sporadic, there have been a few published studies of Native American images, including most notably Kevin Brownlow's *The War, the West, and the Wilderness*.[19] These and other publications are slowly helping to revise both the film canon and the arguments about the history of U.S. cinema.

Most of these scholarly works focus solely on either African Americans, Chicano/as, Asians and Asian Americans, or Native Americans. In fact, there are relatively few books that address the experiences and forms of race that all these groups share and commonly endure.[20] Unlike feminist research or even studies of class, film scholarship on race as a formation has yet to develop into a major critical movement. And, since the meaning of race constitutes a hegemonic formation in the United States that stretches beyond the experiences of any single group, this lack of scholarship is, in a word, problematic. While books that focus on specific racial groups are necessary and important, more historical, theoretical, and critical work on the meaning of race that these groups share is required.

While the aforementioned studies are beginning to make a difference, film books not devoted to the specificity of race, such as texts on aesthetics or the general history of cinema, have been negligent in addressing cinema's racism (or, for that matter, work by filmmakers of color). Shohat and Stam's *Unthinking Eurocentrism* is an exception. More common are books such as *Film Art*, *Film History: Theory and Practice*, *A History of Narrative Film*, *The Classical Hollywood Cinema: Film Style and Modes of Production to 1960*, among others, which either neglect a discussion of race almost entirely or relegate their references to a sentence, paragraph, or a small section of a chapter.[21] This silence and marginalization of race in film studies undermine both the impact that the racial formation has had on film history—from style to industry—and the impact that film history has had on the racial formation. More specifically, it directs attention away from whiteness, the underlining logic of cinematic racism. As Clyde Taylor argues in his essay for this anthology, "By segregating the issue of racism for bracketed attention, the real issue—White supremacy—is avoided."

In the last five years there has been a substantial growth in the critical and historical writings on early cinema. However, within this work there is surprisingly little attention given to the issue of race. There is not a single book on race in early cinema; there are only a few articles or book chapters (most of which deal with *The Birth of a Nation*). Yet, racial meanings are a significant, omnipresent part of the birth of cinema. Edwin S. Porter, D. W. Griffith, Oscar Micheaux, among other early filmmakers, employed race in both overt and implicit ways throughout their work. Genres such as the Western and the melodrama, and subgenres such as the Indian and "greaser" film, were very much about the "manifest destiny" of white civilization. Race marked the careers of such notable silent stars as Lillian Gish, Mary Pickford, Sessue Hayakawa, Al Jolson, Rudolph Valentino, Anna May Wong, to name just a few. Indeed, cinema's invention and early development coincided with the rise in power and prestige of biological determinism, with increased immigration and immigrant restriction laws, and with the United States' imperialist practices in the Caribbean and Asia. As the essays in this anthology point out, these and other sociopolitical practices insured that the articulation of race in early cinema crossed studios, authors, genres, and styles.

It is time to begin revising the revisionist, with an eye to expanding the history of U.S. cinema to uncover, deconstruct, or defamiliarize its racial practices. This anthology aims to do just that: to show how a discourse of race, one which was dominated by a white "ideal," significantly, even profoundly, informed the history of early cinema.

The first section of this anthology, "Representation and Resistance(?)," includes discussions that range from racist images and narratives to attempts to resist and subvert such images. Clyde Taylor's article, "The Re-Birth of the Aesthetic in Cinema," tackles the formal and epic qualities of white supremacy in D. W. Griffith's landmark film, *The Birth of a Nation*. Taking academic criticism to task for its "passive racism," Taylor contextualizes Griffith's "negrophobia" by focusing on the filmmaker's Southern background as well as his use of both minstrel show and lynching tropes. Thomas Cripps shows how a film like *The Birth of Race* (1918), though initially conceived as an antidote to the racist imagery of *The Birth of a Nation*, gets co-opted and reconfigured as a propaganda film supporting the United States' efforts in WWI. Pointing to such historical events as the sinking of the passenger ship Lusitania by a German submarine, the "cold feet" of liberal Hollywood financiers, and divisions within Black efforts to respond to Griffith's epic, Cripps unravels the racial politics that informed the making of this film. Next, Pearl Bowser and Louise Spence analyze the "biographical legend" of Oscar

Micheaux, focusing mainly on one of his extant films, *The Symbol of the Unconquered* (1920). In the process, they reveal and question the many ways in which the filmmaker engaged the origins of white-capping (or the KKK), the politics of interracial relationships, and the ideology of "uplifting the race." Finally, Donald Kirihara shows how Sessue Hayakawa struggled against the stereotypical nature of many of the characters that he portrayed. Kirihara's work is especially insightful for its focus on the narrative function of stereotypes.

The next section, "White Nationalism," engages the forms and functions of whiteness and nationalism in early cinema. In my contribution to this anthology, I attempt to reveal the relationship between narrativization and racial articulations in Griffith's Biograph films, showing how the racism in *The Birth of a Nation* and *Broken Blossoms* (1919) can be traced to the director's early work. I argue that Griffith's narrative system utilizes such stylistic techniques as mise-en-scène and editing to articulate an ideology of race that positions "whites" as normal and superior and "non-whites" as deviant and inferior. Next, Virginia Wright Wexman examines how Western tropes such as the body, the landscape, and the law are used to negotiate the racially based contradiction in early twentieth-century nationalism between an "imagined community" where all citizens enjoy parity and a community that supports a "hierarchy of group identities." For Wexman, the image of the "ideal family on the land" forms the cornerstone of the Western's contradictory and ambivalent articulation of the United State's national identity. Finally, Dan Streible looks at the reception of the Jack Johnson fight films, showing how biological determinism informed and even determined both the exhibition and the reception of early films. Streible's work on Johnson addresses representation, miscegenation, and the question of resistance, but perhaps best illustrates the machinations of American whiteness.

The third section, "The Fear of Miscegenation," focuses on a particular discursive strategy within early cinema's racial formation, that of interracial relationships. Chon Noriega investigates the various texts of *Romona*, from the novel by Helen Hunt Jackson (1884) to the film by D. W. Griffith (1910), showing how the discourses of race, gender, class, and nation shifted between the nineteenth and twentieth century. Nick Browne traces the intertextual history of *Madame Butterfly* (1915), focusing on Puccini's opera, the original novel, and contemporaneous military and ideological tensions between Japan and the United States. One of Browne's central points is that Madame Butterfly narratives, though shifting from novel and opera to film, are "sexed" in a complex of cultural difference particular to early twentieth-century American representation of Asia, and ultimately underline the impossibility of racial assimilation of the Japanese into American society. Next, Gina Marchetti takes on the trope of miscegenation as it is constructed in *The Forbidden City* (1918). An insightful close reading, the article shows how the use of parallel interracial love stories uphold and condemn the film's racial/sexual status quo.

The final section, "The Colonial Imagination," also looks at a particular discursive field in early cinema, that of colonialism. Roberta Pearson examines films featuring the character of George Armstrong Custer, the white man's martyr for "manifest destiny." Pearson reveals the contradictory ways in which Native Americans, Custer, and "Custer's last stand" were represented and narrativized. Next, Fatimah Tobing Rony focuses on the relationship between Flaherty's *Nanook of the North* (1922) and the discourse of authenticity surrounding it. Concerned with what this relationship can tell us about anthropological knowledge and the role of film in legitimating that knowledge, Rony reveals the interdependence of three hunts: "the hunt for representations of the Inuit for science and popular culture, the hunt for cinematic images of the Inuit for the film *Nanook*, and cinema's hunt for Flaherty as great artist and/or great liar." Finally, Sumiko Higashi considers the ways in which the literary texts of Lafcadio Hearn, an influential interpreter of Japanese culture for "highbrow" readers, informed the films of Cecil B. DeMille. Careful to contextualize her arguments by pointing to social and international practices, Higashi shows how DeMille used the icons and ideologies of highbrow culture both to legitimate cinema and to articulate "an unambiguous message about white supremacy."

These essays are an initial step in filling the gap in film studies on the enduring legacy of race and whiteness in U.S. cinema. However, the task is far from complete: There are gaps in this project. Not adequately addressed is the function of race in the earliest of film practices, what Tom Gunning refers to as the "cinema of attractions."[22] Nor is there an analysis of race in the silent comedies of Keaton or Chaplin, for instance. There is also a need for more focused attention on "greaser" films, a genre that was much more prolific during the development of early cinema than most accounts suggest. Further, while Jewish and Italian identities are broached by various contributors, no article specifically addresses the representation of ethnic immigrants—many of whom were considered "racial" Others at the turn of the century. Ideally, these and other subjects will be explored in subsequent projects.

What all the contributions to this study of race in early cinema have in common is the grounding of their analysis in history. Each contribution contextualizes the respective articulations of race that it addresses, linking this ideological practice to other forms of culture such as music and dime novels, to social and legal policy, to myths of nation and of evolution, to international politics and economic tensions. Though only a few address the workings of whiteness, they collectively reveal how race, and particularly racist practice, was very much a part of the birth of U.S. cinema.

Notes

I would like to thank Sumiko Higashi for her insightful comments and suggestions on an earlier draft of this introduction.

1. Cornel West, *Race Matters* (Boston: Beacon Press, 1993).

2. Several scholars, from the physical sciences to the social sciences, have refuted the science of race. See Stephen Jay Gould, *The Mismeasure of Man* (New York: W. W. Norton, 1981); Daniel J. Kevles, *In The Name of Eugenics: Genetics and the Uses of Human Heredity* (Berkeley and Los Angeles: University of California Press, 1985); and Sandra Harding, editor, *The "Racial" Economy of Science: Toward a Democratic Future* (Bloomington: Indiana University Press, 1993).

3. Henry Louis Gates, Jr., "Writing 'Race' and the Difference It Makes," in *"Race," Writing, and Difference*, ed. Henry Louis Gates, Jr. (Chicago: University of Chicago Press, 1986), p. 5.

4. The appearance of circularity in arguments that link race with identity is necessary, it seems to me, because to divorce the meaning of race from a consideration of identity is to take real people out of the equation, something that seems wholly inappropriate and potentially hypocritical given the history of racist practice.

5. Stuart Hall, "New Ethnicity," *ICA Documents* (1988): 28.

6. See Stuart Hall, "Cultural Identity and Cinematic Representation," *Framework*, no. 36 (1989): 70.

7. Ibid.

8. Michael Omi and Howard Winant, *Racial Formation in the United States: From the 1960s to the 1990s*, 2d ed. (New York: Routledge, 1994), p. 56.

9. See, for example, Richard J. Herrnstein and Charles Murray, *The Bell Curve: Intelligence and Class Structure in American Life* (New York: Free Press, 1994).

10. For discussions centering on the shifting meaning of race, see Thomas F. Gossett, *Race: The History of an Idea in America* (New York : Schocken Books, 1965); Peter Isaac Rose, *The Subject Is Race* (New York: Oxford University Press, 1968). For more contemporary debates about the meaning of race, see David Theo Goldberg, ed., *Anatomy of Racism* (Minneapolis: University of Minnesota Press, 1990); Omi and Winant, *Racial Formation in the United States*; Gates, ed., *"Race," Writing, and Difference*; Hall, "New Ethnicity"; and West, *Race Matters*.

11. Omi and Winant, *Racial Formations in the United States*, p. 55.

12. Ella Shohat and Robert Stam, *Unthinking Eurocentrism: Multiculturalism and the Media* (New York: Routledge, 1994), pp. 1–2.

13. Ibid., p. 2, authors' emphasis.

14. Thomas Cripps, *Slow Fade to Black: The Negro in American Film, 1900–1942* (New York: Oxford University Press, 1977).

15. Thomas Cripps, *Making Movies Black: The Hollywood Message Movie from World War II to the Civil Rights Era* (New York: Oxford University Press, 1993); Manthia Diawara, ed., *Black American Cinema: Aesthetics and Spectatorship* (New York: Routledge, 1993); Ed Guerrero, *Framing Blackness: The African American Image in Film* (Philadelphia: Temple University Press, 1993); Mark A. Reid, *Redefining Black Film* (Berkeley and Los Angeles: University of California Press, 1993). See also James Snead, *White Screens/ Black Images: Hollywood form the Dark Side*, ed. Colin MacCabe and Cornel West (New York: Routledge, 1994).

16. Chon Noriega, ed., *Chicanos and Film: Representation and Resistance* (Minneapolis: University of Minnesota Press, 1992); Rosa Linda Fregoso, *The Bronze Screen: Chicana and Chicano Film Culture* (Minneapolis: University of Minnesota Press, 1993); see also special issues on Chicana/o cinema in *Spectator* (Fall 1992) and in *Jump Cut* (June 1993; June 1994).

17. Eugene Franklin Wong, *On Visual Media Racism: Asians in the American Motion Pictures* (New York: Arno Press, 1978).

18. Kevin Brownlow, *Behind the Mask of Innocence* (New York: Alfred A. Knopf, 1990); Sumiko Higashi, *Cecil B. DeMille and American Culture: The Silent Era* (Berkeley and Los Angeles: University of California Press, 1994); Gina Marchetti, *Romance and the "Yellow Peril": Race, Sex, and Discursive Strategies in Hollywood Fiction* (Berkeley and Los Angeles: University of California Press, 1994).

19. Kevin Brownlow, *The War, The West and the Wilderness* (New York: Alfred A. Knopf, 1979).

20. A useful exception is Allen L. Woll and Randall M. Miller, *Ethnic and Racial Images in American Film and Television* (New York: Garland, 1987). Lester Friedman's anthology, *Unspeakable Images* (Urbana: University of Illinois Press, 1991), is a recent step, though most of the articles in this work deal more with ethnicity than with the specificity of race or whiteness.

21. David Bordwell and Kristen Thompson, *Film Art: An Introduction*, 4th ed. (New York: McGraw-Hill, Inc., 1993); Robert C. Allen and Douglas Gomery, *Film History: Theory and Practice* (New York: Alfred A. Knopf, 1985); David A. Cook, *A History of Narrative Film*, 2d ed. (New York: W. W. Norton, 1990); David Bordwell, et al., *The Classical Hollywood Cinema: Film Style and Modes of Production to 1960* (New York: Columbia University Press, 1985).

22. Tom Gunning, "The Cinema of Attractions: Early Film, Its Spectators, and the Avant-Garde," *Wide Angle* 8, nos. 3 and 4 (1986): 63–71.

REPRESENTATION AND RESISTANCE(?)

Clyde Taylor

THE RE-BIRTH OF THE AESTHETIC IN CINEMA

For obscure reasons, narrative works considered landmarks in American culture for technical innovation and/or popular success have often importantly involved the portrayal of African Americans. Consider, for example, *The Jazz Singer*, which is known as the "first" sound film; *Gone With the Wind*, which made history as a technicolor historical epic; *Song of the South*, which is believed to hold decisive historical attention for innovations in technicolor, feature-length animation, and the combined use of human and cartoon characters; and *Roots*, which had such a massive reception that it has been credited with ensuring the future of the mini-series as a television genre. Might it be that some affinity exists between breakthrough productions and national allegories in which the definition of national character simultaneously involves a co-defining anti-type?

This description would certainly apply to D. W. Griffith's *The Birth of a Nation*, one of the most popular turning-point films of all time. *The Birth of a Nation* represents two historical landmarks: an incomparable racial assault and a major breakthrough for subsequent filmmaking technique. The impact of the film on the art-culture system might best be summarized by quoting Lewis Jacob's observation that it "foreshadowed the best that was to come in cinema technique, earned for the screen its right to the status of art, and demonstrated with finality that the movie was one of the most potent social agencies in America"[1]—and, I might add, the modern world. *The Birth of a Nation* instantly became the object of compelling national and international attention for all classes at the same socio-historical moment. The outcry against the film's racism, led by African American activists, was also massive, as has been frequently observed.[2] Griffith's film became the center of the first media event of a type that complements the definition of mass culture (Figure 1).

Black activists and critics have generally taken a reactive stance toward films such as *The Birth of a Nation*, seeking redress in "positive

Fig. 1: The grandiose mythology of Griffith's reinterpretation of history made good advertising copy. (Courtesy of the Academy of Motion Picture Arts and Sciences)

images" to counterbalance negative ones. But this approach, which focuses on isolated characterizations within a given work, tends to bypass considerations of narrative, formal devices, motifs, and, most important of all, meaning. Mainstream cinema scholars and aestheticians, on the other hand, have kept the race issue at arm's length from their exploration of the film's technique, refusing to synthesize these two discussions. One explanation for this is an anxiety of influence. Because cinema studies has charted its historical claim from the starting point of Griffith's movie—almost a myth of origin—there is an inclination to unburden this grand originating moment from any discourse on race relations in the United States. As a probationary branch of the aesthetic, cinema studies can only be legitimated through the exercise of the fundamental act of the aesthetic: the establishment of its discourse as autonomous. Were the discussion of the social implications of Griffith's racist movie to intrude to the fullest impact possible, then the discipline of film studies might lose its status, might enact its own "undisciplining."

Because of the collision of these issues on a rather massive scale in the critical space surrounding *The Birth of a Nation*, the film poses a dramatic confrontation involving the validity of the aesthetic vis-à-vis other interpretive paradigms. My argument is that the aesthetic celebration of Griffith's blockbuster movie is another scene where the ideological determination of aesthetic discourse is at work—and that the aesthetic not only conceals its alliance with ideological motivations, as it always must, but that in the specific instance of Griffith's movie it works to suppress important social meanings which become clearer when seen within the framework of the politics of media representation.

Apologist film scholars for *The Birth of a Nation* take a passive attitude toward the film's racism, usually tempering its force on one of four grounds. Some simply accept Griffith's denial of racist intent. Some specify the "unconsciousness" of his racism. Others argue that Griffith's portrait of the Reconstruction era and the role of Black people in it is essentially accurate. The comment sometimes added—that Blacks had made considerable social progress of which Griffith was unaware—implies that Blacks of the Reconstruction era may have been just as savage and backward as Griffith portrays them, and stands in uneasy relation to the fourth defense frequently made: that Griffith's posture towards Blacks, and its easy acceptance by mass audiences, attests to the conventional racist thought of his time.

In satisfying itself with these pro forma arguments, the discourse of film studies in the United States makes its own compromise with racist ideology. It has become conventional to repeat these critical positions without interrogating their relation to each other or to the film as a whole. It is as though the film's many celebrated rhetorical achievements and its substantial defamation of Blacks were isolated issues, discussible as if they belonged to two separate films. Demonstrations of Griffith's artistic mastery in particular scenes are never connected to their role in denigrating Blacks. More importantly, the reflex interpretation avoids connection between the film's racist import and racism as a fact in American life. The passive racism of film studies has led it to neglect the meaning of Griffith's national allegory and the role of racism in it, in striking contrast to the subtle social analysis given other national allegories like the Western or the gangster movie. Nor has film studies crossed its self-constructed boundaries and examined the links between Griffith's racial characterization, certainly the most negative in U.S. film history, and the wider theme of Hollywood negrophobia, arguably the most massive racist assault in the history of mass communications.[3]

Gerald Mast's *A Short History of the Movies*, now in its fourth edition since 1971, is fairly representative of the film's treatment in standard college texts.[4] His approach to the issues of racism and aesthetics is to condemn the film's bigotry, but in a way that mitigates its severity, then turn from that subject as a troublesome intrusion to examine the film's artistic achievements as landmarks in "human" expression. Mast introduces the issue of racism indirectly, by reporting the response of liberals to the film upon its release in 1915. "The NAACP, the president of Harvard University, Jane Addams, and liberal politicians all damned the work for its bigoted racist portrayal of the Negro." He then outlines his rhetorical plan: "With all of the controversy over the film, it might be wise to look at Griffith's handling of the black man a bit more closely *before moving on* to the cinematic qualities of the film" (my emphasis).

Mast's "close examination" reveals that two of the film's three villains are mulattos, possessing qualities that Griffith had damned in White characters in earlier films. He argues, "That they were mulattos indicates that Griffith's main target was not blacks but miscegenation." This makes sense if one assumes that racist discourse always invents novel devices to attribute to its targets. Mast's attempt to distance Griffith's portrayal from ordinary racism by focusing on mulattos and miscegenation loses force, however, when he later acknowledges that Griffith indeed saw Blacks as inherently inferior to Whites. Mast's final reflection on racial portrayal in the film concerns the notorious legislature scene in which Black legislators with bare feet propped on desks swill liquor and carouse boisterously. "Griffith's treatment of these blacks is not an isolated expression of racial prejudice; it is a part of his whole system of the evil of social change and disruption." This distinction implies either that Griffith draws no particular association between this behavior and Blacks as Blacks, or that he could not have been ravening among racist caricature and opposing "social change and disruption" at the same time. "And," Mast concludes, "cinematically this legislature scene is a visual marvel!"

The intrusive issue of race out of the way, Mast's exploration of the movie's cinematic qualities follows familiar lines, but produces a striking iteration of a quality observed as "human." He finds that "though Griffith summarizes an entire historical era . . . his summarizing adopts a human focus," so that "human values—love, sincerity, natural affection—triumph over social movements and social reformers." (One might here ask whether Griffith's disdain for movements inconsistently excludes the Ku Klux Klan, and whether Mast's formulation does not echo his disdain for the social reformers who attacked the film.) Further, Mast insists, "Griffith never deserts his human focus. . . . [H]e cuts from the valiant human effort on the Union side to shots of a similar effort on the Confederate." Other celebrations of Griffith's humanism include the following: "Griffith's attention to human dramatic detail dominates the film"; "By capturing human motions in concrete visual images, Griffith successfully renders human feeling"; and "*The Birth of a Nation* is part mammoth spectacle and part touching human drama." Mast concludes his discussion of the film on this exhaustively prepared note: "The film remains solid as human drama and cinematic achievement, flimsy as abstract social theory."

The studied innocence and lack of penetration within canonical film studies in this crucial instance is reflected in the defense of the film's racial portrayals by one of its founding heroes, James Agee. Himself a Southerner, Agee defends Griffith and Southern legend at the same time: "Griffith went to almost preposterous lengths to be fair to the Negroes as he understood them, and he understood them as a good type of Southerner does. . . . Griffith's absolute desire to be fair, and understandable, is written all over the picture; so are degrees of understanding, honesty and compassion far beyond the capacity of his accusers. So, of course, are the salient facts of the so-called Reconstruction years."[5] As part of the discursive etiquette of his times, Agee speaks through a polite silence by leaving unsaid what is an unavoidable conclusion: If Griffith went to almost preposterous lengths to be fair to Negroes, then they were in actuality measurably worse than he depicted them, or not fully worth the lengths he went to in his portrayal.

Thorstein Veblen's comment on the film applies as well to the drift of its aesthetic reception: "Never before have I seen such concise misinformation." Concise misinformation is evident in Agee's summatory praise of the movie as "the one great epic, tragic film." The aesthetic masking of ideology is coined in this usage of "epic" and "tragic." These are, of course, generic designations linking the work to an ancient discussion of narrative art, to enshrined artifacts of the Western art-culture system. At the same time, no work can be appreciated as epic or tragic without acceptance or identification with its hero, its actions—in short, its ideological meaning. If the work is an epic, which means among other things that it elaborates a theme of national unity, then it goes without saying that this unity must rest on the basis of White values, particularly the hatred of miscegenation. If *The Birth of a Nation* is an epic, it is an epic of White supremacy.

Fig. 2: Griffith speaks of the introduction of the African as an American tragedy, but he omits the telling word "slavery." (Courtesy of the Academy of Motion Picture Arts and Sciences)

The bracketing of racist portrayal of Blacks protects the film's reception as an epic, a grand spectacle on the theme of national unity. If racism is the issue, then racism can be denounced and mitigated through sophistic rationalizations. By segregating the issue of racism for bracketed attention, the real issue—White supremacy—is avoided. "Epic" euphemistically masks a more cogent, less aesthetic designation—myth. As propaganda, *The Birth of a Nation* accomplished the significant feat of transposing the national myth of the South into terms congruent with the mythology of White American nationalism. In Griffith's inscription, this myth rehearses Christian eschatology in national terms. Its basic narrative rhythm is this: Eden established, lost, and restored. From the opening title, the Edenic scene is established, as well as its fundamental threat: "the introduction of the African to American shores laid the seeds of national tragedy" (Figure 2). This fundamental premise of Griffith's four-hour narrative is marvelously neglected in most commentaries, even those grappling with Griffith's attitude toward Blacks.[6]

The Arcadian visit of the Stonemans to the Camerons establishes the Edenic wholeness of the nation, as reflected in two idealized families (not a poor White is to be found speaking in the film), and at the same time uses the delighted presence of the Northerners to confirm the plantation myth of a "naturally" ordered Southern civilization in which Blacks are both happy and well behaved. The tragic flaw in this divinely chartered land is the Northerners' belief that Whites and Blacks can live together without Whites controlling and containing the sub-developed Black population. Stoneman's scheming, hissing, "mulatto" mistress is given as much weight as any other character in explaining how the North and South came to blows due to Northern misunderstanding of this principle. The Honorable Austin Stoneman is obviously modeled on Congressman Thaddeus Stevens, leader of the Radical Republicans in the U.S. Congress. He is shown to be manipulated through his passionate alliance with the scheming "leopardess" (so described in Thomas Dixon's novel about Stevens's affair with his Black housekeeper). Stoneman is the epical dark angel who, in his fall from grace, precipitates wider disaster by imposing a harsh Black Reconstruction regime on the defenseless White South after the war.

The Christlike martyrs in this mythic narrative include the soldiers who fall on the battlefield, Lincoln, little Flora Cameron, and the ravaged South itself. The Christlike redeemers are the "Little Colonel" and his cohorts in the Ku Klux Klan, which he is credited with organizing. (It is not always remembered that the KKK is a Christian secret society—the crosses on their robes and those they burn testify to an apocryphal, fundamentalist syncretism fusing the Bible with Scottish rites into American Christian fascism.) The spectral image of a superimposed Christ blessing the newly united Ben Cameron and Elsie Stoneman on their way to a New Jerusalem, a "city on the hill,"[7] often derided as a gratuitous, unrealistic intrusion into the text, is in fact perfectly consistent with the mythic fabric of the tale.

As a national epic, Griffith's film asks the spectator in the White subject position to perceive the essential scene of national development as the South instead of colonial New England or the Western frontier. It also asks this spectator to shift the core nationalizing experience from the land, and the taming thereof, to miscegenation, to Blacks, and the taming thereof. The issue of Black-White sexual relations, in fact, forms the spine of the text. If, in terms of action and excitement, the triple parallel chase scene at the end of the film is the narrative climax, thematically the most potent and emotionally charged moment is the "Black" trooper Gus stalking the hapless Flora "tigerlike" to her death leap over a precipice in order to avoid dishonor. This moment triggers the explosion of the racial resentments smoldering in the pre-coding scenes. The later sequence in which Lynch, the upstart mulatto carpetbagger politician, salaciously entraps Elsie Stoneman, serves to communalize the threat that by Gus's action alone might be taken as individual aberration.

The problem of this classic film may be summed up: Its great power in manipulating formal strategies has won it voluminous attention and respect as an aesthetic achievement. Its blatant racist portrayal of Blacks as threat to the national civilization has engendered another passionate discussion, in which the introduction of African Americans to the politics of representation in mass media can be historically traced. If, as I contend, the central theme of the work is the unification of national sentiment around the theme of miscegenation as a threat to "civilization," then the neglect of this theme in the aesthetic dialogue surrounding the film amounts to a curious evasion of the question of meaning.

This indifference to meaning explains an extraordinary lapse in the worshipful exegesis of the film's cinematic innovations. It goes unnoticed that virtually all of the film's formal achievements—its editing, close-ups, iris shots, manipulation of crowds, camera movements, scenic setups, literary titles, etc.—are deployed in the cause of aestheticizing and sentimentalizing the principal characters as White people. Gerald Mast's celebration of the "human" qualities of the film can be recast as investing White American representations with ennobling virtues, articulating their personalities with individualizing, endearing details, and placing their dreams and visions within grand confirming visual contexts. When such humanizing delineation is directed to non-White or politically variant characters, mainstream critics call it "sentimentality." Mast's "'humanist" aesthetic takes advantage, consciously or not, of the narrative equation of "human" with the White bourgeoisie. He subtly excludes Black representation and expression from the "human" articulation. In fine scope, Mast encapsulates the hidden racial particularity of "humanist" discourse in general.

This becomes all the more clear when we see that Blacks in the film are not involved in this aestheticization, but are consistently incorporated within contra-aesthetic film language. This separate and unaesthetic representation of Blacks does more than provide grounds for complaints of stereotypic imagery. The divide between the aesthetic portrayal of Whites and un-aesthetic portrayal of Blacks reveals a "crack" through which the artistic overlay of the film can be penetrated, its meaning more fully clarified. Once penetrated, the crack provides an excellent illustration of the way in which aestheticism can cast a shadow over ideological meaning.

Cheryl Chisolm locates the crack in the surface of the film in the way in which its celebrated pictorial realism is crudely interrupted by the representation of Blacks, particularly by the convention of casting Black roles with White actors in burnt cork. She observes that this contributes a surreal dimension to the film—one that, despite a general accommodation for distorted racial representation, should be seen as a striking and anomalous directorial intervention.[8] The poetic realism with which Griffith depicts his White characters stands in opposition to the anti- or sub-poetic "realism" he fashions for Blacks. Seeing this, we are better able to grapple with the murky grotesqueness of the humanoid figures dimly lit by the reverse of the fire that brightens his aureoled White figures. This alternative sub-poetics is consistent with the manichean cultural symbolism Griffith marshaled throughout his life.

The contradictory and overdetermined use of White actors in blackface opens our perception to Griffith's personal stake in the making of the film. Richard Schickel, Griffith's most thorough biographer, has cleared new ground that should help move interpretation beyond its twin-sided myopia. One anecdote highlighted by Schickel from the largely self-made Griffith legend seems to augur the authorial elements behind the controversial labors of the film.

It seems that Griffith's first love was "a slim, nut-brown maid with curling chestnut tresses" with whom he played a tag game. In one version, he is never able to catch her; in another, he does catch her, after which she coyly tells him that she allowed him to do so.[9] Griffith pursued this fantasy figure, whom he called his "first star," through a number of imaginative exertions. He wrote a short story about the girl, whose name he could not remember, entitled "It Never Happened." The story included, according to Schickel, gossip about a father-daughter incest relation and suggestions of masturbatory fantasies about his dream girl.

Griffith apparently fell prey to the idea that only unattained desire can keep romantic love alive. He could not, in Schickel's interpretation, find resolution to his lifelong division of women "between the virgin whom one somehow could not tag and the wanton who both titillated and appalled."[10] Much the ladies' man, Griffith plowed through a number of aspiring and working actresses and admirers, but found himself impotent or emotionally inhibited with the few women who captured his image of the ideal. This *femme ideal*, imperiled by a beast-rapist with dishonor so deep as to make death a superior alternative, apparently served as the *auteur* of his film corpus, showing up not only in the guise of Flora in *The Birth of a Nation*. Indeed, the villain-rapist in *War*, a play Griffith wrote in 1907, prefigures not only Gus, but menacing counterparts in *Hearts of the World, Broken Blossoms*, and *America*, "to name only a few of his lustful sadists."[11]

So captivated by this dream motif was Griffith that he dragged it unfashionably into the 1920s and 1930s, and thereby doomed his comeback opportunities as a director. On this point Schickel sums up:

> But if it was not clear before, it became self-evident at this late date [1933]: with Griffith we are dealing not so much with racial prejudice, but rather with a deep and permanent sexual obsession. Indeed, the thought recurs that blackness was almost incidental to the obsession, a convenient visual aid in symbolizing the ugliest and most rapacious of male impulses, but not perhaps to be taken personally by blacks. As he had proved in so many films after *Birth*, color was not entirely necessary to the working out of his great, sordid theme, that theme that thrilled him to the deepest, darkest (and entirely unacknowledged) recesses of his being. In any event, he could no more abandon it in his work than he could abandon the pursuit of underage girls in life. It is saddening and infuriating, for one is hard-pressed to think of any other major figure, in films or for that matter in any of the arts, who so single-mindedly kept circling back on this particular pathology. And to find him still in thrall to it when he needed to prove that he could move on to other matters is particularly distressing.[12]

Searching for the etiology of Griffith's psychic dilemma, Schickel considers the uncertain grasp he had on his parents' love, particularly his war-adventuring father. First of all, Griffith had no model for interaction with women other than his father's remoteness toward them. More pressingly, Griffith's obsession-formation seems to have transferred his father's obsession with macho courage to a culturally more elevated theme, a staple of the Confederate mythic code: the ideal, unattainable symbol of Womanhood and the valor necessary to protect it.

Should we be surprised that Thomas Dixon, the former preacher turned racist novelist who wrote the book and plays later adapted as *The Birth of a Nation*, held a kindred obsession with the same virginal child-woman auteur who dominated Griffith's imaginative life? Except that, as interpreted by historian Joel Williamson, Dixon's psyche was locked into

Fig. 3: Gus, obviously a white actor in blackface, faces retribution from the KKK.

a more classically Oedipal absorption with his mother. Dixon's consciousness was torn by the suffering he imagined his mother endured as a thirteen-year-old bride. The decisive trauma apparently occurred during the final collapse of his mother's health, with her deliriously mumbling references to her untimely marriage and he—a boy of twelve, overwhelmed by the medical and emotional responsibilities of caring for her—blaming her illness on this early marriage. Dixon's writing of *The Leopard's Spots*, his first Ku Klux Klan novel, is portrayed by Williamson as an effort at psychic self-cure. As such, "it was a brilliant, disingenuous performance in which, in brief, Southern White maidenhood substituted for his mother, the black beast rapist was a surrogate for her never named violater, and the violater in the person of the black beast was horribly punished" (Figure 3).[13]

Griffith's racism *was* unconscious—but then all racism, as a group psychosis, is unconscious, at least of its motivating sources. His negrophobia differs from Dixon's mainly in that it played a smaller role in his biography. Griffith's later gestures of amends and less vicious depictions of

Blacks have been rightly dismissed as paltry in offsetting the damage of *The Birth of a Nation*, but they do establish that he did not continually need to resort to the Negro-beast image. His obsession as well as Dixon's, so much alike despite their Oedipal variations, reached for nourishment into a largely unconscious collective cultural symbolism.[14] If myth, as Lévi-Strauss argues, is a mechanism for resolving the contradictions of group experience and knowledge, then ideological rationales must similarly bear the strain of masking and concealing alternate and incongruous perceptions.

Griffith's modus operandi, as that of an instinctive auteur improviser for whom Black people did not really exist, offers the most fascinating glimpse of this cultural symbolism at work. His reason for rejecting Black actors in favor of White actors in burnt cork was that he could not find any qualified Negro actors in the Los Angeles area and, further, that he wanted to cast from his own company. These were familiar Hollywood excuses, but they obviously papered over other needs. He was casting a private/cultural psychic drama in which the identifiabilty of Whiteness beneath the surface bestiality of Blackness was a libidinal requirement. As Silas Lynch, the half-caste upstart importuning Elsie Stoneman—a character played by Lillian Gish, who was one of Griffith's idealized romantic attachments—he cast his chief assistant and man of all work, an actor described as "sensitive to Griffith's every whim." The newcomer Gish was given her major role because, as she explained it, "one day while we were rehearsing the scene where the colored man picks up the Northern girl gorilla-fashion, my hair, which was very blond, fell below my waist and Griffith, seeing the contrast in the two figures, assigned me to play Elsie Stoneman."[15]

The spectacular oddness of the Blacks in Griffith's Civil War drama arises from his deployment of the theatrical and psychic license of the blackface minstrel show in the middle of an otherwise realist-poetic rhetorical mode. The minstrel show's function of producing comedy and laughter obscures our recognition that Griffith used its crucial masking mechanism for similar but more hard-nosed purposes. By having his foregrounded Black characters played by Whites in blackface, he exploited the same emotional dynamics that made White minstrel audiences love to see their fellows in burnt cork. Under the mask of racial and moral darkness, hidden desires could be exercised and indulged in public performance, even glamorized and applauded. With the violence supplied by Dixon's narratives, Griffith carried the minstrel trope one step further.

Using as spiritual ballast a Victorian religious morality so desperate as to endorse the racial religiosity of the KKK, Griffith fashioned a drama of the id in which he could re-enact the deflowering of Nordic nymphets—those virgins who most completely embodied the tribal idea one must live and die for—and then experience the chastisement of this deepest of imaginative sins in the lynching of a Black alter ego who performed the desired sacrilege for his vicarious satisfaction.

By its extraordinary fusion of the two basic racial rituals of the post-bellum South—the minstrel show and the lynching—the movie exposes the essential kinship between them. Some of the fantastic gratification White men got from witnessing a lynching came from the purgation of incestuous guilt through the transfer of their inadmissible desires to the immolated Black victim. The minstrel mechanism, we can see, is one instance in which the ideological masking of unspeakable knowledge requires an actual mask. It is ideological masking elevated to a ritual level.

What name should be given this psycho-social phenomenon? Negro-fetishism? That term might easily be confused with anthropological characterizations of African traditional religions. A more descriptive name would be negrophobia, understanding its complex fusion of desire and aversion, projection and concealment. Negrophilia is most lavishly displayed in the minstrel show. Contemporary witnesses testify to the essential good-naturedness and friendliness toward the Negro that was present in the minstrel tent. The carnival gaiety and circus atmosphere surrounding lynching is also richly documented (Figure 4).

The heart of negrophilia is bared in that curious erotic ritual in which a White male heightens sexual pleasure by witnessing his wife having intercourse with a Black man—sometimes while he has sex with another partner. The White man's pleasure derives from identifying with the erotic experience and performance of his Black surrogate. His wife, if cooperative, says and does with the surrogate partner whatever most erotically arouses her legitimate mate. Freudian analysis offers the accurate designation for this psychological maneuver as displacement. Fetishism is also involved, inasmuch as the obsessive object is not worshipped for itself but for the transcendental values it is believed to represent.[16]

This radical displacement—including the obliteration of the actual presence of the Black partner in order to obtain the satisfying use of his fantastical image—is necessary to recognize, since it explains several otherwise curious displacements in the way Blacks are portrayed through fantasy in otherwise realistic representation, not excluding Hollywood

Fig. 4: The smiling faces of the spectators are not the faces of people who have seen justice fulfilled, but rather the faces of those who have experienced a pleasurable event. (Courtesy of Schomburg Center for Research in Black Culture)

movies. A relevant displacement of this secondary kind is Griffith's insistence that he meant no insult to the Negro race in his portrayal of Blacks in his film. We can read this as meaning that he never thought about actual Negroes, so caught up was he with them as auxiliary, fetish instruments for his private reveries.

The point of exploring Griffith's personal, erotic obsessions is to document his real but hidden purpose as he and Dixon manipulate White cultural symbolism while laying the foundation of popular, classical cinema. The vast popularity of Griffith's blockbuster movie suggests that he was lucky enough to find autobiographical impulses that coalesced with transindividual symbolic needs, not only among his contemporaries but also among successive generations of American cineasts.

The minstrel show and the lynching formed twin theaters of this American symbolic order as seen from its underbelly. Both forms of ritual entertainment were extremely popular in the North, the minstrel show without rivalry. The inventive contribution of Dixon and Griffith was to disassemble and reorganize the symbolic values of these familiar, conventional rituals into a grand mythic design in which they were discoverable afresh. These symbolic values were redistributed within a fabric of pseudo-historical pageantry in which their truth-value was reconfigured through narrative agencies such as suspenseful action moving inevitably toward a stirring climax. On a small scale the lynching and castration of Gus (the last deleted from the film in most versions), clearly a White actor in blackface, skillfully fused these two apparently contrary rituals. On a larger scale, the ingenuity of the epic-mythical design lies in the recombination of the minstrel-lynching sign system, the Southern plantation myth, and the familiar fable of White Southern degradation under Reconstruction, with more broadly national iconographies in the framework of a national allegory.

In order to do this, Griffith not only biblicized his story, he also activated in it the racist European concept of the great chain of being; this extended from the playful puppies and birds that validate the domesticated Eden of the White Southern home and hearth to the Negroes most like those lovable pets when given the protection of White stewardship, but animalized as tiger/gorilla/serpent-like when unleashed by misguided leadership, and was carried through the decent and pure White Southern gentry who invent the Klan right up to the Nordicized Christ who blesses the triumph over the Northern antichrist gentry at the end.

Sergei Eisenstein forcefully analyzed his own cinematic rhetoric as dialectical, as opposed to Griffith's innovations, which had profoundly influenced him. By contrast to Eisenstein's dialectics, the strategy of Griffith's rhetorical organization is manichean—indeed, manichean dualism provides the key to understanding much of Griffith's cinematic rhetoric. He opposes peace to war in the first half of the film, preparing his viewer to accept the opposition of White to Black in the second.

And since Western cognitive grammar is oriented toward oppositional dualities, the play of this manicheanism in Griffith's "aesthetic" successfully masks its ideological bearings. The Eurocentric bias of aestheticism explains why criticism has largely failed to recognize *The Birth of a Nation*'s epic quality as White supremacist myth,[17] or the catharsis of its tragedy as pseudo-erotic release or exorcism brought on by witnessing a well-orchestrated lynching of fetishized Black reality. So it is not surprising that this criticism has overlooked one of the film's fascinating distinctions. It is clearly the most powerful evocation of fascism among classics of the cinemateque, not excluding *Triumph of the Will*. To embellish this impression of American fascism in this work, Griffith expressed mutual admiration for Italian fascists under Mussolini in 1924. After a lionized tour of Italy during which he considered representing the Italian film industry, Griffith found himself "mad about Mussolini" and projected a biography of Il Duce: "I believe that anything may happen as a result of this fascism. I should like to put into a film the remarkable spirit of the fascist."[18]

(I have been slow to recognize that the largely unconscious cultural symbolism of *The Birth of a Nation* is equally expressive on the level of gender as of race, about the way rape is constructed as a constituent of culture. The sexual fascism to which Griffith's symbolism attests, which may also be perceived as a sadistic patriarchalism, relies on a dynamic in which a rape culture justifies its unspoken commitment to rape through the symbolism of protection against a primitive, rapacious Other. The powerful cinematography of Griffith's film has also extended this legacy into our contemporary film culture. The seductiveness of this theme among major American auteurs can be followed through John Ford's *The Searchers* into a number of other major films, including Martin Scorsese's *Taxi Driver*, where the manner in which the theme is simultaneously reproached and celebrated is typical of the double-speak of this pathological discourse.[19] The imminent violation of a White woman has played so large a role in American cinema compared to others as to seem an American obsession. As such, it is a component of the American fascism articulated in Grifffith's national allegory, a latent and incipient social pathology always awaiting exploitation by opportunistic politicians and filmmakers. When American fascism is finally understood, it will be found, I believe, that *The Birth of a Nation* is its archetypal text.)

Let me return once more to the common assertion that Griffith's racism was largely unconscious. What does that mean? The assertion is made as if to bracket Griffith's racist attitudes from further analyses. To say that his racism was unconscious is also to say that it was ideological, that he was little more racist than his historical times, whose bigotry he was merely reflecting in his films. The better observation is that he was no more racist than other Hollywood functionaries; had he not made this one symbolically hate-filled movie, he would never have called attention to his bigotry. But the notion that *The Birth of a Nation* merely reflected contemporary racial prejudice is another way of bracketing the phenomenon of the film from wider significance in our understanding of American culture and media.

Richard Schickel's description of Griffith's racism elaborates this bracketed perception without, finally, dissolving the brackets. Throughout most of his life, Schickel observes, Griffith subscribed to a traditional Southern view of African Americans as "Pre-moral children" of whom moral understanding was not to be expected: "This view of the blacks, which did not preclude (at least in theory) their coming after the passage of time to a true state of equality with whites was and remained until very recent time the conventional wisdom of 'enlightened' Southerners."[20] Schickel makes use of a favored trope in his discussion of American racism, that of a mobile and advancing time boundary, "the very recent past," beyond which the pathologies of U.S. racist attitudes are framed as artifacts in a museum.

Williamson presents a sharper, more penetrating historical analysis of racial attitudes in the post–Civil War South, one that gives background to Griffith's views. According to Williamson, White perceptions of Blacks after the Civil War fell among three predominant positions. The Conservative view—the central, most entrenched one—sought to conserve the Negro by defining and protecting his place as an inferior in society. The Liberal view, held by a minority, was that the Negro's capacity to rise to a position closer to that of Whites had not been tested and was open to social experimentation that might validate an optimistic outlook for the future of Negro uplift.[21] This is where Schickel mistakenly places Griffith and *The Birth of a Nation.* The opposite extreme of the Conservative position was held by the racial Radicals, who flourished from 1889 until 1915. Radicalism was alarmed by the vision of a "new" Negro released from the wise controls of slavery into a freedom beyond his moral capacity and rapidly retrogressing toward his natural state of savagery and bestiality. The economic crises of the South during those years, according to Williamson, diminished the role of White Southern manhood as breadwinner; hence that role shifted to defender of White womanhood from the threat of unsupervised Negroes roving through the Southern countryside. The Radicals saw no future for the Negro in the United States and looked for his eventual elimination.

Race Radicalism went into decline about 1915, according to this analysis, because of the inadequacies of its alarmist vision; instead of degenerating and disappearing, Blacks were visibly advancing numerically and somewhat socially. Ironically, then, *The Birth of a Nation* stands as the swan song of Radicalism as a major, acceptable position, a position whose fervor Dixon, one of its most passionate ideologues, passed on to his suddenly inspired convert, D. W. Griffith. The Southern Conservative center recovered ground lost to the Radicals, freezing racial perception of Blacks at a level very close to that drawn by the Radicals for the next half century.

One contribution of Williamson's analysis is the restoration of variety, dynamism, and historical mobility to racialist representations. From this standpoint, *The Birth of a Nation*, like the sensational Radicalism that conceived it, reflects a virulent episode in Southern consciousness, more than an aberration but less than a permanent fixture. On the level of representation occupied by cinema, at least, *The Birth of a Nation* brought the ensuing ideological conflict to a head. The singularly trenchant counterattack on the movie by Black libertarians and their progressive White allies represented an unprecedented new force of resistance that demonstrated an altered historical terrain in which racial Radicalism was removed further from the center and placed on the defensive.

Mainstream filmmaking in the United States never again fashioned a portrait of Blacks massed in menace against White society or being mowed down in droves, in a style reserved for darker hordes of Indians in the westward trek, Mexican banditos or federales, and for other non-Western pagans. Yet the struggle pictured by Williamson between a dominant, centralizing Conservatism working to maintain a fixed place for Blacks, viewed as childlike, aspiring wards of White civilization on the one hand and the Race Radicalism that saw them as brute, menacing savages on the other, was to be replayed on American screens for the half century following Griffith's supremacist epic and longer. The attitudes nurtured by his movie and its parent movement left enduring legacies and shaped psychic postures that would recur as themes in later episodes of national symbolic thought.

It is transparent, looking back, that the doctrine of the neutrality of the aesthetic and the later Kantian assertion of its disinterestedness were essential maneuvers for establishing its identity and integrity as a distinctive and separate activity and a ground for autonomous rules and criteria. This maneuver was necessary on several counts, all of them lying within the crises and local circumstances of Occidental history. The many recent schools and movements of criticism that have attempted to modify this central doctrine, arguing that the work cannot be interpreted and understood apart from its social, historical, and political contexts, have, sometimes laughably, failed to confront the fact that the serious inclusion of these contexts violates and invalidates the identifying claims of the aesthetic itself.

These very sound contextualist arguments work to mitigate the confusions of the aesthetic and, as I have argued, to abrogate its effect almost entirely in major regions of contemporary critical discussion. Nevertheless, vast social, political, and economic interests have accumulated around the aesthetic as an institutionalized discursive history, much of it around the site of the established art-culture system. These interests manage to keep the aesthetic in operation, very much like a politics against political clarity, a mystifying ideology of autonomous art. In denying the political resonance of cultural works, this discourse in effect throws protective skirts around all sorts of political ideologies and nostrums couched within the representational form of "art," not simply because it loves them, but because it must protect them in order to protect its own authority. *The Birth of a Nation* is an arresting case in point.

The danger faced by aesthetic discourse is that the delegitimation of the political representations it protects may also dispel its aura of authority.

I have spoken of Griffith's work as a radical and evil work. This raises a question that deserves a postscript. If one grants that *The Birth of a Nation* may be an evil work, one injurious to the social fabric and retarding the effort to articulate the human, then the grounds of discussion have shifted. Whereas before the tension arose between the film's aesthetic reception versus its social-historical interpretation, now we are looking at its aesthetic versus its moral interpretation. Griffith's film confronts us with the possibility of a work being powerfully persuasive, affecting and aesthetically rewarding, while at the same time saturated with noxious conceits and ideas: beautiful yet evil. Cinema has established this possibility more vocally than other forms. The subject of evil art does appear in literature, as in Thomas Mann's "Mario the Magician" and *Doctor Faustus*. The dilemmas raised by this prospect nevertheless remain an isolated sidebar in aesthetic discourse. It should be clear by now that human skills, artistic or otherwise, can not only serve both negative and positive ends, but can serve each just as easily as the other. As one of the Japanese American women who happened to be in Hiroshima as a child when the nuclear bomb detonated over the city describes the event in the documentary film, *The Survivors*: "It was the most beautiful thing I ever saw."

Canonical reception of films like *The Birth of a Nation* and *Triumph of the Will* foregrounds their formal accomplishments while bracketing their intended meanings as vicious material whose poison is no longer active or transparent to the historical observer. This is not the same as the ancient and intelligent realization that a work may be artful and pernicious at the same time. Instead, it hedges these considerations by reflecting on them only when the work in question holds no immanent threat to the values of the art-culture formation directing the aesthetic at a given historical moment.

More revealing is the aestheticist response to a work it finds ideologically or morally threatening as "not art at all." This maneuver clearly betrays the intent to protect the definition of art as contribution to "civilization," meaning canonized art of course. The obscurantist confusion over evil art arose at the point when art was redefined beyond its traditional significance as skill or craft and embodied with idealized, transcendental qualities as an autonomous realm of human experience, replacing the declining hegemony of Christian religion. Hence the exaggerated claims for art, such as Keats's assertion that "Truth is beauty, beauty truth," can be recognized as propaganda for this radical reorganization of knowledge and experience.

Set beside the medieval order of knowledge that the new concept of art helped displace, the mystifications of the new paradigm allow us to surmise that it too is a gross superstition. Moreover, whatever was superstitious in medievalism from the point of view of an enlightened humanist view was not its concept of art but the religious hierarchy that concept sometimes served. This leads to the paradox that the new concept, relying on displaced mystery, may be more superstitious and hackwork—and certainly more superstitious—than the paradigm it subverted. It is this mystifying aura orchestrated by the art-culture system that has deterred the recognition of *The Birth of a Nation* as one of the most accomplished articulations of fascism, of twentieth-century evil.

The confluence noted earlier of major, "liberating" American narrative texts and deposits of what Toni Morrison calls Africanisms—configurations of the African presence in American fiction—appears at once more and less strange when examined in *The Birth of a Nation*. The parasitic nature of American identity in relation to the apparition of Blackness should no longer evoke surprise. But what might intensify reflection is the silence maintained by criticism and theory when faced with this asymmetrical coupling of cultural symbolism. This silence testifies to the location of this parasitic relationship at the crux, rather than the margin, of American cultural practice. This location is further certified when we perceive the fateful confluence as one between the aesthetic and the Amero-European racial consciousness.

In what sense, to be more specific, did Griffith rebirth the aesthetic in cinema? Not merely by installing unity, balance, decorum, or other such values that were available to and availed by Edwin S. Porter and other early directors of European descent. Nor was it in unleashing the technical facilities of close-ups, continuity editing, composition, iris shots, night photography, etc. For while this was a brilliant achievement, it was of the order of the discovery of one grammar of cinema. It is on the rhetorical level, where meaning is encountered, that we can watch the aesthetic being reborn in his film.

Like the aesthetic inaugurated by eighteenth-century European philosophers, Griffith's film aesthetic promises and delivers sentiment beyond considerations of craft—large, ennobling sentiments of a sensory/moral gestalt transcending any particular place or any given art-piece. But whereas the architects of aesthetic theory based their modular vision of beauty and perfection in ancient Greece, Griffith turned to the homier epiphany of racialized Christianity. We may remark that in both cases the inscription of higher aesthetic values was also an inscription of the Aryan self as civilized ideal.

Since Griffith brings us to this point of recognition, it is fair that he bring us to another. The values encoded by the aesthetic—beauty, disinterestedness, purity, vitality—which have undergone change at historic crossroads, are nevertheless always the values by which Occidental imagination conceives of itself in its highest forms. If Griffith gave a new birth to the aesthetic in cinema, it was necessarily as the apotheosis of Caucasian perfection.

This aspect of the aesthetic, its celebration of the collective self, might not be in itself alarming or objectionable. It must be clear that most if not all cultures cling to a hierarchy of values that confer identity, and perhaps also distinction. Where this celebratory commitment becomes problematic is in the constitution of the aesthetic as a supra-ethnic cognitive grid, as a universal configuration. So canonized, it becomes a mythic construct, assuredly of great force and power, but of the sort that requires massive repressions along with its massive assertions. In this, the aesthetic operates simultaneously and harmoniously with a kindred ideology, that of western racial superiority. What *The Birth of a Nation* alludes to on the level of aesthetic theory, amid structures of denial, is the priority of its staged transcendence over the common psychological mechanism of displacement and projection.

The critical and theoretical apparatus of film studies has inherited this unholy marriage of parasitic group fantasy—the wedding between transcendental Whiteness and aesthetic theory—as a double bind. It must persist in a willful critical blindness, which becomes more easily, casually willed as its blindness becomes conventional. Or, by perceiving the doubled, contradictory meanings of its monological aesthetic discourse, it must begin to rid itself of its founding false consciousness. And the longer it delays taking this second course, the more violent will be the traumas inflicted on its self-definitions and basic assumptions.

Notes

This essay was completed with the assistance of a Rockefeller Foundation-Whitney Fellowship, for which I wish to express my gratitude.

1. Lewis Jacobs, *The Rise of the American Film*, 4th ed. (New York: Teachers College Press, 1939, 1968), p. 171.

2. Lary May, *Screening Out the Past: The Birth of Mass Culture and the Motion Picture Industry* (New York: Oxford University Press, 1980), chapter 4.

3. A much favored option is to defer this subject by referring without further examination to three specialized texts: Donald Bogle, *Toms, Coons, Mulattos, & Bucks: An Interpretive History of Blacks in American Films*, rev. ed. (New York: Continuum, 1973, 1989); Daniel J. Leab, *From Sambo to Superspade: The Black Experience in Motion Pictures* (Boston: Houghton Mifflin, 1976); Thomas Cripps, *Slow Fade to Black: The Negro in American Film* (New York: Oxford University Press, 1977). A rather ironic example of this scholarly casualness, considering its title, is Garth Jowett's *Film: The Democratic Art Form* (New York: William Morrow, 1976), which devotes one page to Black representation in American movies, and is largely a synopsis of these three texts. An important exception to this cavalier approach is Michael Ryan and Douglas Keiner, *Camera Politica: The Politics and Ideology of Contemporary Hollywood Film* (Bloomington: Indiana University Press, 1988), which makes original and insightful forays into Black representation.

4. Gerald Mast, *A Short History of the Movies*, 4th ed. (New York: Macmillan, 1986). All quotations are from pages 63–69.

5. James Agee, "David Wark Griffith," in Fred Silva, ed., *Focus on "The Birth of a Nation"* (Englewood, N.J.: Prentice-Hall, 1971), p. 17.

6. Gerald Mast's commentary does not ignore this statement, but rephrases it, making a crucial substitution: "*The Birth of a Nation* recognizes the institution of slavery as the poisonous seed from which a social evil grew." Griffith had taken rhetorical pains to avoid the convenient term save as cause of the national ills in order to protect vital threads of Southern history and culture. Mast's reassertion of this most obvious word choice almost makes Griffith a post facto abolitionist.

7. This apocalyptic image is analyzed in the richly interpretive essay of Michael Rogin as it figures not only in *The Birth of a Nation* but also the presidential imagery of Ronald Reagan. See Michael Rogin, *Ronald Reagan, The Movie* (Berkeley and Los Angeles: University of California Press, 1987).

8. Cheryl Chisolm, unpublished seminar paper, UCLA.

9. Richard Schickel, *D. W. Griffith: An American Life* (New York: Simon & Schuster, 1984), pp. 33–34.

10. Ibid.

11. Ibid., p. 89.

12. Ibid., p. 578.

13. Joel Williamson, *The Crucible of Race: Black–White Relations in the American South since Emancipation* (New York: Oxford University Press, 1984), p. 165.

14. I have in mind the collective consciousness of the sort invoked by Frantz Fanon, releasing the biological determinism of Carl Jung. See Patrick Taylor, *The Narrative of Liberation: Perspectives on Afro-Caribbean Literature, Popular Culture and Politics* (Ithaca, N.Y.: Cornell University Press, 1989), pp. 38, 42.

15. Jacobs, *The Rise of the American Film*, p. 173.

16. This ritual is alluded to in Ralph Ellison's novel *Invisible Man*, in the scene where the protagonist is in bed with a seductive matron and her husband returns to the apartment from a business trip and passes through the bedroom, greeting his wife as if she were alone. It is also alluded to in the film *American Gigolo*, where the male prostitute played by Richard Gere is hired for such an evening's entertainment. Gere's identification as a white male reminds us that this ritual of surrogate eroticism can and does use White male surrogates as well as Black. However, the use of a Black male surrogate may be seen as a higher delicacy in this form of erotic consumerism. Moreover, an interesting case could be made that *American Gigolo* would make more sense as a film if Gere's role as protagonist were reread as a Black man. I would argue that cinematic enunciation frequently uses displacement of racial identity to take advantage of the force of subterranean desires without acknowledging them dinnly. This strategy would be similar to the displacement of gender identities in movies where a heterosexual relationship or a same-sex friendship is coded as a surrogate for the homoerotic expression implanted in the narrative. For one example, Gore Vidal has described the relationship between Ben Hur (Charleton Heston) and his boyhood friend Messala (Stephen Lloyd) in the 1959 remake of *Ben Hur*, which he scripted, as such a displaced homoerotic attraction. See Vito Russo, *The Celluloid Closet: Homosexuality in the Movies* (New York: Harper & Row, 1981), pp. 76–78.

17. I am consciously using the term in a wider sense than as an 1890s art movement.

18. Schickel, *D. W. Griffith: An American Life*, p. 496. Schickel adds: "in his defense, it should be noted that Griffith was not the first nor the last foreign observer to come from Italy with glowing reports of a new spirit in these early days of sascism." However, I believe that Griffith's openness to particular currents of American fascism in different periods of his life prepared his enthusiasm for Mussolini's variety.

19. One cannot fully explore this issue without digesting Brian Henderson's "*The Searchers*: An American Dilemma," reprinted in Bill Nichols, ed., *Movies and Methods, Vol. II* (Berkeley and Los Angeles: University of California Press, 1985), pp. 429–449. I have also interpreted the *Star Wars* series as a rewriting of *The Birth of a Nation* in "The Master Text and the Jedi Doctrine," *Screen* (Autumn 1988), pp. 96–104.

20. Schickel, *D. W. Griffith: An American Life*, p. 235.

21. Williamson, *The Crucible of Race: Black and White Race Relations in the American South Since Emancipation*, p. 165.

Thomas Cripps

THE MAKING OF *THE BIRTH OF A RACE*

The Emerging Politics of Identity in Silent Movies

Historians in recent years have found it a commonplace to argue that African Americans have constituted an out-group, an "Other" that was *in* but not *of* the American polity. Indeed, such a social construction formed the basis of the antebellum system of slavery. Early on, after the post–Civil War Reconstruction, the white South attempted to perpetuate this notion of the black as outsider, as "Other," by means of the icons of popular culture, particularly in that form of performance art known as minstrelsy and in advertising and other forms of graphic art, and finally, when all else failed, by terrorism in the form of nightriding by masked vigilantes, political disfranchisement, and legalized social segregation.

But with the turn of the twentieth century, as African Americans moved off Southern ground toward cities, they effectively formed a new black polity that successfully contended for a new place within American society. One of the most bitterly contested grounds in this struggle centered in American cities, particularly on the eve of the Golden Anniversary of the Civil War and the ensuing years up to the release of D. W. Griffith's celebrated movie, *The Birth of a Nation* (1915).

Griffith's movie, apart from its stature as a benchmark of the cinema art and a synthesis of the rhetoric of the filmmaking technique of its day, was calculatedly offered to its audience as racial propaganda. Indeed, African Americans correctly inferred this and used its inflammatory advertising as a catalytic moment that set in motion black countercampaigning that grew from isolated "branches" of the National Association for the Advancement of Colored People (NAACP) into a nationwide movement of blacks and their white allies for whom Griffith's artistry was not only beside the point but in fact a weapon aimed at black well-being.[1]

Historians have used the resulting ideological conflict as their own occasion for studying the ideology of popular culture. Was ideology no more than a blunt instrument wielded from above by the ruling classes as a means of cowing the benighted lower orders? Or was ideology a residue of the conflict between countervailing, albeit often unequal, forces, in an unending contest for political sway? Oddly, there has been a scholarly tendency, particularly on the left, to characterize the formation of ideology as though handed down by an invisible source so omnipotent as to allow the renowned Frankfurt social critic, Theodor Adorno, to find that popular culture "always" reflects the status quo. If this puppeteer seems purposelessly dominant, the more recent Marxist critic, Louis Althusser, gives thrust to the process, arguing that "the *social function* [my italics] of ideology is to constitute . . . subjects." In much the same way, the contemporary critic Fredric Jameson finds ideology so pervasively embedded in "narrative itself, or story-telling in general" as to constitute a form of "programming" for its readers.[2]

Not to deny the wisdom of these scholars whose work spans a half century of cultural criticism, I wish this present history of *The Birth of a Race* to also reflect the role of chance, accident, and contentiousness in this process. Critics of both the Marxist and liberal left have each expressed a hope that ideology has been the outcome of struggle. For Antonio Gramsci, a founder of the Italian Communist Party, the struggle at its most fruitful occurred during crises when "organic" leaders of the oppressed emerged to challenge an already threatened establishment. In his *American Capitalism* (1955), John Kenneth Galbraith thought of such contests between "countervailing" interests as more normative and thus more persistently an influence upon political and cultural history—a history, therefore, that acted itself out not as an inexorable flow of events along a path toward "progress" but rather a form of change over time that chaotically blundered in fits and starts. Indeed, this sense of history as inchoate forms its central identity as a discipline. "The supreme duty of the historian is to write history," said Steven Runiciman, the student of Byzantium, "and not to reduce history to a series of economic or sociological laws." For him history, then, is a cast of actors who contend for power, never quite winning or losing, but ever-reforming into countervailing camps, schools, sects, and parties.[3]

It is with this in mind that I should like to take up the making of the movie *The Birth of a Race* (1918) as an African American antidote to *The Birth of a Nation*, justly remembered as the most eloquent formulator of a black dramatic figure meant to terrify white viewers with the assertion of a black malevolent "Otherness" that, if unchecked, threatened white "civilization."

At the outset, it must be said that *The Birth of a Nation* was not merely a Southern white conceit that somehow slipped through a Yankee customhouse of ideas. As John Hope Franklin, the historian of the South, has pointed out, the sentiments expressed in Thomas Dixon's books, The *Leopard's Spots* and *The Clansman*, upon which *The Birth of a Nation* was based, were shared by many Northerners. Both sections admitted of a "Negro problem" and differed mainly over which solutions to embrace, a Northern, benign, paternal progressivism grounded in black "self-help" or the Southern right-wing view that the purity of its Victorian values was so threatened by "black brutes" that even lynching was included in its arsenal of defenses. *The Birth of a Nation* differed from hundreds of shorter, less well-mounted vehicles only in its bringing to the screen the "black brutes" whose behavior was meant to justify Southern lynching to Northern audiences. So said Thomas Dixon in his wish "to teach the North what it has never known," the awful suffering of the white South at the hands of the black South during Reconstruction. In other words, the legendary uses of Griffith's movie as a Ku Klux Klan recruiting device are beside the point; more to the point is the fact that Thomas Dixon's racial attitudes were shared by most Americans—not merely Southerners. Indeed, long before the splash of *The Birth of a Nation*, Dixon had outgrown his native North Carolina, traveled a national lecture circuit, and for a time enjoyed preaching to the largest flock of parishioners in all of New York City. Moreover, as Franklin discovered, remnants of Dixon's politics could be found not only in almost any American high school history book of the post–World War II era, but also in E. M. Coulter's history of Reconstruction in the distinguished ten-volume Louisiana State University history of the South.[4]

There was yet another context in which African Americans took up the project that became *The Birth of a Race*. Not only had Griffith's movie eloquently defined blacks as a malevolent Other whose credibility as a historical figure was confirmed by on-screen references to Woodrow Wilson's much admired history of America, but he had succeeded in previewing the movie in the White House where Wilson himself exclaimed that it was "history written in lightning and it is all so terribly true" (said Dixon in his now-lost memoir).[5]

Furthermore, such unprecedented celebrity came at the end of an era of African American history so shattering in its impact on blacks that the historian Rayford Logan labeled it "the nadir" years. For blacks, this era from the end of Reconstruction in 1877 to the eve of World War I was a lost generation not so much for its rise in the incidence of lynching, or the grinding poverty of its peonage and sharecropping, or its resort to political disfranchisement and segregation. Rather it was the sense of abandonment by the Republican Party, "the party of Lincoln," the ship when all else was the sea, as the black abolitionist Frederick Douglass had put it. After 1890, "the Mississippi plan" for constitutionally disfranchising blacks was adopted by all the states of the old Confederacy; in 1898 in the Spanish War, Southern soldiers rejoined the Army in droves, most famous among them Theodore Roosevelt's own "Rough Riders"; in the same year, the Republican President William McKinley treated a North Carolina race riot as a local matter over which he had no jurisdiction; in 1901, President Roosevelt coyly denied to the press that Booker T. Washington had dined at the White House, characterizing it instead as an impromptu luncheon; in 1906, Secretary of War Taft spoke to the "lily white" wing of the North Carolina Republican convention, thereby lending it the prestige of the White House; in the same year, Roosevelt discharged without honor an entire company of veteran black soldiers in the aftermath of a shoot-out by unidentified nightriders in Brownsville, Texas; and in 1912, the capstone of the era, the election brought to the White House a Southerner and only the second Democrat since before the Civil War.[6]

Save for an occasional Northern newspaper editorial assault on some Southern "outrage"—the cant word for lynching—this leaching of Southern culture into American public life permeated the national popular culture. Books from Thomas Nelson Page's *Two Little Confederates*, to John Esten Cooke's novels of life in the saddle, to Joel Chandler Harris's *Uncle Remus*; minstrel shows that played the breadth of the nation; graphic caricatures of African Americans in postcards and advertising artwork; and, of course, the scores of movie versions of avaricious colored preachers, jackleg lawyers, unctuous toms, and rascally colored scamps—all of these reached a fevered pitch in the hundreds of Civil War movies that dominated popular culture between 1910 and 1915.

Meanwhile, within black circles the objective social data that popular culture had caricatured—the Southern, rural, sharecropping, disfranchised black society that emerged from the abandonment of blacks after Reconstruction—had itself changed. At the turn of the century blacks not only began to move to cities but also formed a rigorous political culture and a dense community life. Leadership passed from that of Booker T. Washington's sort of rural self-help to an urban activism. To take only one instance, a largely white movement, the Constitution League, and a largely black group, the Niagara Movement, merged into the eventually nationwide NAACP.[7] It was this culture that first protested *The Birth of a Nation* and first proposed an antidote to it in what became *The Birth of a Race*.

Thus the agenda of racial politics in this era was set by Griffith and Dixon in separate creative courses that reached a confluence in *The Birth of a Nation*. For both men, the post–Civil War Reconstruction had been a defining moment, albeit if only as residual legend told around their youthful hearth fires, a legend in which vengeful black brutes threatened innocent white women and their "faithful" black retainers, thereby rendering the rise of the Ku Klux Klan a historical necessity.

At this point, the clash of two cultures—white and black—seemed sharply etched. *The Birth of a Nation* opened in mid-February 1915 in Los Angeles, in New York in early spring, and finally in April in Boston where organized blacks mounted a stand against it. At issue in these Northern African American circles was Griffith's retelling of the old tales of white scalawags and carpetbaggers and their ignorant black dupes, the truculent black soldiers and their pushiness toward their former masters (and mistresses), and the loudly dressed, smelly, booze-swilling black legislators who passed "forced marriage" laws and looted the Southern state treasuries. For years, distinguished historians such as James Ford Rhodes, Woodrow Wilson, and the students of W. A. Dunning at Columbia brought to their work a newly professionalized discipline, yet allowed these tales to pass unchallenged into the nation's collective memory. But by 1915, Major John R. Lynch, who had been a participant in Reconstruction, had written *The Facts of Reconstruction*, and W.E.B. Du Bois had written on "the benefits of Reconstruction" in the prestigious *American Historical Review*. So the black communities of East Coast cities possessed ideological ammunition with which to challenge Griffith and to demand revision of his movie.[8] It was an easy step for them to imagine a movie of their own that would trace *The Birth of a Race* from ancient times in Africa to its "progress" after slavery.

Then on May 7, 1915, a German submarine sank the *Lusitania*, a passenger ship bound for Liverpool from New York. Hundreds of American lives were lost, stirring a hawkish temper that resulted in the resignation of the pacifist Williams Jennings Bryan from Wilson's Cabinet. Thereafter, the terms of the debate muddled in subtle ways. Throughout the spring, *The Birth of a Nation* had characterized African Americans as a baleful Other (save for the "faithful souls," those blacks who knew their place as dutiful servants). Opposing the movie were those Northern black activists who challenged the notion of blacks as mere Others and insisted on a constitutionally protected place in the American polity. "It would be ideal if it could be suppressed altogether," wrote May Childs Nerney of the NAACP, knowing that white allies would not join her in suppressing free speech. So during the spring and summer of 1915, the Boston NAACP took up two conflicting lines of argument, allowing the threat of war to comingle the two discrete issues of "racial antagonism" and the world's "longing for peace."[9]

The Griffith group quickly drove a wedge between Northern and Southern wings of black opinion by offering to tack on an epilogue purporting to reveal the "progress" of African Americans since Emancipation. Washington quietly joined Northern blacks in denying Griffith the use of footage of Tuskegee, but his alma mater, Hampton Institute, once a preeminent black academy but, by that time, eclipsed by Tuskegee, agreed to supply actual footage of the half century of black "progress." At issue among blacks was the nature of progress and the fear of having it defined by paternalistic whites—whitewashing cabins, digging privies, and such—as against social and political activism. In the end Nerney at NAACP thought it was "really adding insult to injury," and by summer's end the secretary of Hampton's board went to New York to plead for the removal of the Hampton scenes.[10]

Meanwhile, Nerney, having concluded that NAACP protests in various cities "have gotten nowhere," decided "that this picture has a political significance" that compelled blacks to "create a powerful public opinion against this [outmoded] idea of the Negro and we cannot create it except in some such spectacular way [as movies]." Parallel to this NAACP initiative, Booker T. Washington entered his own idea into the stakes—his autobiography, *Up from Slavery*, which according to "friends," "might quite properly be used as a counter-irritant [to *The Birth of a Nation*]." At least one black advocate of movies as a weapon, George William Cook of Howard University, even imagined that "such a thing will pay," particularly if concocted into a thriller.[11]

Only dimly seen was the outline of the eventual impact of the *Lusitania*'s sinking on the proceedings. Between May 1915 when the ship went down and November 1916 when Wilson was reelected in part by riding the slogan "He kept us out of war," American diplomacy took a tortured turn from pacifism to belligerence—and left blacks in its wake. In the spring of 1917, after the Americans entered the war, politicians of all persuasions turned about and became apologists for "the war to make the world safe for democracy." Unavoidably, whatever ideological formulations that African Americans chose as a sort of platform would surely be altered by the nation's oscillating entry into a war on foreign soil.

Besides, blacks split over what to say to white people. On the one hand, they wished to reach beyond Washington's personal rise "up from slavery," but on the other they could agree on no clear-cut means of breaking with its Horatio Alger line of argument. The NAACP's writing partner, Elaine Sterne, liked the idea of engaging white attention by defining black aspiration as *Lincoln's Dream.* At the same time, the scholar among the membership, the Harvard historian Albert Bushnell Hart opened his private library for her research, possibly seeking a revised account of Reconstruction. But early on, the NAACP's ranking black intellectual, W.E.B. Du Bois, withdrew his support in favor of his own project, a "pageant of Negro history and some plays of my own and in moving pictures based on them." And Mary White Ovington, one of the urban liberal founders of the NAACP, aimed for the sort of broad audience that any Hollywood studio might have wished for: She called for a tale of black "sufferings and strivings" that would "meet with favor from conservative and radical alike."[12]

The almost unavoidable result was cold feet on the part of their one Hollywood connection. Carl Laemmle had only just moved his IMP studio to California, renamed it Universal, and begun operations at the center of his vast real estate investment, Universal City. Perhaps cash-poor as a result, he offered the NAACP his services provided they contributed a daunting $10,000 in front money to his nut of $60,000. But as the NAACP waffled through the summer and autumn, he gradually withdrew, first by cutting the proposed twelve reels to five, then by confessing to an NAACP angel, Jacob Schiff, that "we have not yet decided," and finally, so Ovington heard, by trimming "parts favorable to the Negro" at the behest of "Southern" members of Laemmle's firm.[13]

With the fading of the NAACP's hopes for its own challenge to *The Birth of a Nation*, the way was open for a project that actually survived long enough to face the warping that followed from the fate of *Lusitania*. Moreover, sad to say for its black ambitions, the little engine that drove it was that of Emmett J. Scott, Washington's amanuensis at Tuskegee, and an ex-newspaperman rather than a scholar. More worldly than most players in this game, he might be expected to fix an eye on the main chance and to compromise with the devil, even to the point of adapting *Up from Slavery* to whatever situation war or white people brought to the table.

In any case, he signed no less than three contracts and their codicils, in each of which he sought greater precision in defining his royalties and perquisites than in sketching the nature of the product. This meant that as the nation drifted from pacifism to a war footing and from parochialism to internationalism, no black consciousness intruded on the process.[14] Moreover, by drawing his inspiration from Washington's black puritan Horatio Algerism, he effectively denied his colleagues any alternative black identity—neither the black socialism that Du Bois would later take up, nor the Pan Africanism of Edward Wilmot Blyden, nor the cultural nationalism of the young Marcus Garvey.

In this sense, he played into the hands of his white angels for whom the proposed movie had become a binary organism capable of making money while putting forth a universalism into which the black Other was invited in the role of tamed exotic. Thus, it transformed the focus from a story of black "progress" into a neutrally shaded universal "progress." William Selig best phrased the link between money and universalism. "It should make a great deal of money," wrote this first of several prospective directors. "It will impress and encourage all races and nationalities." Such sentiments became the running theme of the promotional brochures. "'Up from Slavery' is the background," wrote Edwin Barker, their main tub-thumper. "Into it are being woven the many-colored threads of . . . a story of interest and value to all races."[15]

Their notion of a sprawling universal history of human progress had come down to their era through the post–Renaissance Italian writer Giambattista Vico, whose essays on cyclical history had caught the attention of both Marx and nationalist historians such as Leopold von Ranke, author of *Universal History*. With the coming of movies, the movement began to pass into popular culture in the form of the historical novels of Henryk Sienkiewicz (for which he won a Nobel in 1905), Griffith's own movie, *Intolerance* (1916), and eventually the two long-term bestsellers, H. G. Wells's *Outline of History* (1920) and Hendrik Willem van Loon's *The Story of Mankind* (1921). Thus for Scott, or any other black presence on the scene, it must have seemed a marvelous opportunity to integrate African Americans into the story of mankind. What could go wrong?

But then the unraveling began. *Lusitania* was only the beginning of a veering away from a specifically black angle. The war fever that it generated not only shouldered aside the pacifism that had been a thread running through the early story conferences, but diverted many pro-black activists away from their campaigns. Oswald Garrison Villard, the descendant of abolitionists, for example, broke off working on behalf of *Lincoln's Dream* because, as Nerney reported, "he has been kept in Washington by the *Lusitania* crisis."[16] Moreover, the *revanchist* sentiments generated by the sinking of the ship and by the ensuing American entry into the war gradually warped the universalism into a jingoistic plea for the defense of "civilization" against "the Hun."

The most scandalous loss of black influence over the project befell them beginning in December 1916 and ran through the early spring of 1918. At first, it only seemed a matter of a zealous promoter, Giles P. Cory, promising too much to a group of black prospective stockholders in the firm: He all but guaranteed that "all risk is practically eliminated" because the participation of Julius Rosenwald, the first Jewish vice president of Sears-Roebuck, served as a form of underwriting. The enraged Rosenwald—who indeed had offered his warm approval, if not his capital—quickly drew away from the project despite Barker's promise that "we are not taking anything away from the story of the Negro" by shifting the angle to "the great melting pot of America." Thereafter, the smell of money seemed to tinge their every act. Cory, their broker in Chicago, for example, pointed out the differing profit to be made from "a picture so broad that it will appeal to millions" as against "narrow, commonplace pictures that appeal only to thousands." In a single stroke, the firm then "by mutual consent" dumped Scott (and *Up from Slavery*) along with Selig, whom they replaced with the Broadway impresario Daniel Frohman, whose "organization" seemed up to "the tremendous scope" of the evolving movie.[17]

By the spring of 1918, with their "nut" all but spent, a new and unfamiliar team assembled, and what must have been an absurdly ecumenical mess of footage in the can, they set out for Tampa where they had found a public park graced with mock-Egyptian architecture. Here they shot the last sequence, an Old Testament struggle between Pharaoh's Nubian army and the fleeing Children of Israel. The local *Tampa Tribune* played it as a feature-page lark in which they portrayed the African American extras as though the reporters were composing racially comic postcards: "Well worth a trip to the [Sulphur] springs," in order to see "a gang of darkies . . . dressed up in a pocket handkerchief and nothing else" as they fought the fleeing Jews. As to the message of the movie, the *Tribune*'s reporter garbled it beyond comprehension. "This [the Jews' flight] marked the beginning of the ascendancy of the white race and the decline of the brown," he wrote, "—all due to prejudice and the oppres-

Fig. 1: The ambitious title card promised more than the film offered.

sion which followed it."[18] Clearly, in the writer's view the movie seemed to be about the precise opposite politics from that with which the project began: with the exodus of an essentially European people from Africa, the blacks who were left behind became, self-evidently, iconic non-European Others.

In the bargain, of course, they also committed a worse crime, at least in show-business circles—they produced a flop (Figure 1). Precisely in cadence with the end of the Great War in November 1918, when surely war movies would have become "box office poison," they released their tangle of biblical universalism, residual pacifism, a non sequitur sequence of Columbus's first voyage, a stately Lincoln—perhaps a survival of the pages of *Lincoln's Dream*—emancipating the slaves, sprawling stockshots of serried ranks of marching armies, and though they no longer survive, sequences in which a German family, like Griffith's brothers in *The Birth of a Nation*, is divided by the pull of clashing loyalties toward either the Kaiser or their new American home.

Apart from the black reviewers who had scant choice but to wish it well—"truly great," they wrote—the few journalists who gave it the time of day hazed it as a "grotesque cinema chimera" whose "preachment went glimmering" among its tangled threads of subplots. Robert Russa Moton, Washington's successor at Tuskegee, heard that "there is very little showing the progress of the colored people." A black Omaha mailman, George P. Johnson, an acerbic critic of race movies who started his own Lincoln Motion Picture Company in order to enter the game where *The Birth of a Race* had stumbled, caught the sense of the entire story in a single sentence: "Owing to War conditions . . . ," he wrote, "the advancement of the Negro was dropped out [while] the second part was converted into a modern war drama."[19]

In any case, at every turn the movie reflected the ambiguities thrust upon it by circumstance. As whites were divided by differing economics and politics, so blacks were divided by the wish to make either great art or great profits. As surely as Barker and Rosenwald were different sorts of white people with clashing hopes for black fortunes, so Washington, Du Bois, Scott, and the NAACP spoke for clashing, self-negating black ambitions.[20]

At least by then, in the fall of 1918, they knew how *not* to do it. To locate the roots of human progress in biblical times inevitably led to the portrayal of Jews as the victims of the Pharaoh's black army. To carry the story to the birth of Christianity just as surely centered the movie on an eventually European religion, thereby rendering Africans as outsiders. In a night sequence meant to urge "harmony" upon humankind, it is the *black* tribe that invades the white, an event Noah characterizes as rooted in "living apart" and its resulting "prejudice" (as the titlecards say), as though these failings were black traits. Moreover, as these themes are traced, the blacks grow distinctly, even startlingly, *darker*.[21]

In Part II of the movie, mainly a synthesis of the Gospels, this racial separatism is carried forward in the person of Jesus done up in the mode of white American Sunday School posters, complete with aquiline nose. He preaches to a multiracial world beset by "doubt and prejudice," once again linking discord with blackness. The only black figure possessed of an identity is Simon the Cyrene who, according to Renaissance painterly convention, was rendered as black (Figure 2). Of all the anonymous black faces depicted, only he exhibits the compassion that by default had seemed a white trait.

Here their harried cutter, working against a deadline imposed by an optimistic lease of the imposing Blackstone Theatre in Chicago's Loop, made a startling leap across the centuries. Partly, of course, he was also driven by their straitened circumstances: an exhausted nut, an almost

Fig. 2: Early on the image of Simon the Cyrene falsely promised that African Americans would have a role throughout human history.

certain lack of insurance shots of historical events, and a wish to prod the storyline closer to the Great War that had begun to consume American attention. Just as the expository title frames point up Jesus's messages of "equality instead of slavery" along with "peace and humanity" (a residual sentiment from Wilson's first term), a cut carries the viewer to Columbus's first voyage, thence in seconds to Paul Revere's ride, and onward to the constitutional convention in Philadelphia where, says a titlecard, at last the human family formed a government based upon "equality." In yet another tableau of fabled American history, Lincoln forges "the last link" to "the torch of freedom," a trope that allows him to emancipate the slaves without actually mentioning slavery. In a final survival of the pacifist mood of Wilson's first term, Lincoln on his deathbed wishes for "peace."

But as the director—by then the veteran John W. Noble—knew, the American Expeditionary Force had reached the Western Front and the nation's newspapers were filled with stories of Chateau Thierry, St. Mihiel, and the Argonne Forest. And so the ideological voice shifted to a higher pitch as it embraced the notion of a "just war" in the defense of "civilization." Thus the movie that had begun as apologist and defense counsel for African Americans drifted into a pre-*Lusitania* pacifism, unctuously flattered its mass white audience for its centuries of "progress," then easily betrayed all of its germinal sentiments by resorting to a rousing martial coda that celebrated the American entry into the war.

Here we cannot know the sequence of the images as they appeared in the release print. Only a few shards of this segment—which might have been as many as two hours long in 1918—survive: a vast montage of serried ranks of marching men, infantry charges across the desolate moonscapes of the Western Front, and a curiously compelling dramatization of black and white farmers volunteering for service in the army. In addition to the fragmented footage, a music cue sheet also survives and proves informative because it ties the musicians' cues to images on the screen that are described in one-line phrases. From this we can infer at least the subjects of some of the shots, and thus can sense the political thrust of the final reels.[22]

Clearly discernible in the cues is a storyline that renders the Great War on a human scale while at the same time breaking with the pacifist thread of previous sequences. In the end, the war and America's share of victory are seen together as an apogee of human progress, an achievement that, it must be said, African Americans have taken part in.

This message is given dramatic energy in the form of a German American family who must choose between their old country and the new. To affirm this moral choice as crucial to the survival of civilization, the music cues introduce it as the establishing shots of the movie so that the vast story of mankind is seen as a flashback that gives moral urgency to the decision. Indeed, that this was the sense of the original cut may be seen in the form of a "visitor arguing with the Kaiser" that is laid in between Jesus's crucifixion and Columbus's voyage and again after Lincoln's death scene when the Kaiser is shown in "council."

At this moment, the cue sheet calls for the first of two intermissions, suggesting that the surviving historical footage is but one-third of the released movie. The entire middle segment is taken up with the choice between war and peace as faced by both the United States and its German immigrants. Of all the Germans, George Schmidt seems to have his heart in the right place: He protests the German invasion of Belgium while in the midst of his family circle. On the other hand, a Herr "Von H.," perhaps a relative, is seen saluting the Kaiser, perhaps possessed of an Iron Cross, and probably an agent active in stirring industrial strikes in America. No *Lusitania* appears, but other less clear outrages compel Wilson to declare war, thereby sending the film into a sequence of troopships sailing for France and life in the trenches, and a dramatic sequence in which a cash reward is offered for the capture of "boche" prisoners. Here, with the war raging full tilt, the second intermission breaks off the story. In the final segment, the debate is resolved and the decision to fight on the side of the United States and of Civilization is given moral authority. Mainly, this seems to have been done by portraying the different styles of combat chosen by the two sides. Amid the shots of trench warfare and heroic soldiers, titlecards cry out: "Look at those French soldiers" and "See those Negroes," while the Germans raid an Allied hospital. "Hun raid on hospital," says the cuesheet. The heroism of Schmidt in making the right choice is seen by intercutting his heroism with shots of the German enemy and eventually to shots of Schmidt in closeup, falling in combat. The last music cue calls for "Stars and Stripes Forever."

Clearly, these last two-thirds of the movie warrant the complaints of African Americans that their investment in the movie amounted to nothing. And yet, a surviving sequence in the film itself, along with a one-line music cue, suggests an African American centrality that would have been uncommon in American movies either before or since *The Birth of a Race*. Moreover, the sequence echoed a commonly embraced African American ideology that rested on the principle of enhanced social status in return for service to the nation, an idea that both armies employed as early as the War of the Revolution.[23] In any case, in this latter third of *The Birth of a Race*, in a fleeting moment a black man following his mule and plow pauses, drops the plow handles, walks across the furrows and, along with a similarly portrayed white farmer, dissolves into the campaign uniform of the AEF, and both men march shoulder to shoulder out of the frame (and into the war) (Figures 3 and 4). For any African American viewer who had read George Washington Williams's *The History of the Negro Race in America from 1619 to 1880* (1882), the message was clear: If the Great War were in defense of Civilization against the Hun, then black soldiers were being asked not only to join the ranks, but implicitly the promise of a better lot in life seemed to follow from the enlistment.

At this writing we cannot know the details of the internal struggle over control of *The Birth of a Race* nor can we know the extent to which

Figs. 3 and 4: Black and White farmers dissolve into Black and White soldiers.

the surviving film represents the conscious intentions of its makers. But at least we may infer from the surviving evidence that African Americans had initiated a massive propaganda project on their own behalf; had stood as a countervailing force against white presumption; had drawn upon the cultural inventory that was open to them, such as the idea of progress and of enhanced status in return for service; had used an international crisis and war as the occasion for renegotiating some of the worst conditions that oppressed them; had countered *The Birth of a Nation*, the most racist assault that had ever been directed against them; had marshaled the NAACP into a national voice and force; had entered the ranks of moviemakers with such vigor (and bungling) as to inspire other black firms, first among them the Lincoln Motion Picture Company, to take up "race movies" designed to speak to black audiences unmediated by Hollywood stereotypes; and had re-learned at great cost the art of bargaining with white people, both their presumed enemies and putative friends.

That all of this resulted in scant short-term gain testifies more to the intransigence of American racial culture than to the blacks' own considerable failings at the still youthful art of moviemaking. And yet, white culture had been split by the conflict into Griffith/Dixon conservatives and Rosenwald progressives, a configuration that would persist through the twentieth century. Moreover, the conservatives had been made to retreat from their favored black stereotype, the black Other lurking under the veneer of civilization. Coincidentally, the progressives won their own iconic point: the decent black who wished to ally with "the best" whites, an image that in *The Birth of a Race* ranged from Simon the Cyrene to the black farmer who dissolved into an AEF uniform. That is, the progressives contested the conservative pool of negative black images by drawing upon their own pool that included both Western painterly images and Frederick Douglass's famous Civil War speech, "Men of Color, to Arms!" As for African Americans in search of a black aesthetic, or at least a black imagery unmediated by cultural bargaining with white people, their cause must have seemed surely lost. Yet by the close of the decade of the Great War, they had begun in earnest the cinematic form that would come to be known as "race movies." Far from caring about whether blacks seemed worthy in white eyes, they stood apart from the emerging cinematic mainstream and, even as their work was half-formed by its evolving conventions, strove for, as Emmet Scott once wrote, "that indefatigable something which I shall call *the colored man's viewpoint*."[24]

Notes

1. Thomas Cripps, "The Reaction of the Negro to the Motion Picture, 'The Birth of a Nation,'" *Historian* 25 (1963): 344–362.

2. Fredric Jameson, *Signatures of the Visible* (New York and London: Routledge, 1990), p. 165; Althusser quoted in Stephen Heath, *Questions of Cinema* (Bloomington: Indiana University Press, 1981), p. 103. Not all students regard ideology as a sort of blunt, unopposed instrument. Jameson himself has elsewhere urged "always historicize," as though granting that history provides circumstances that create inventories of choice within cultures whose traits may permit or even partially shape such choices. See Patrick Colm Hogan, *The Politics of Interpretation: Ideology, Professionalism, and the Study of Literature* (New York: Oxford University Press, 1990), p. 175.

3. Galbraith, *American Capitalism: The Concept of Countervailing Power* (Boston: Houghton Mifflin Co. 1972); Stuart Hall, "Gramsci's Relevance for the Study of Race and Ethnicity," *Journal of Communication Inquiry* 10 (Summer 1986): 5–27; David Plante, "Profiles: History," *New Yorker* (Nov. 3, 1986): 63–90.

4. Dixon's curtain speech on the opening night of *The Clansman*, quoted in Raymond Allen Cook, *Fire from the Flint: The Amazing Careers of Thomas Dixon* (Winston-Salem, N.C.: John F. Blair, 1968), p. 140; John Hope Franklin, "*The Birth of a Nation*—Propaganda as History," *Massachusetts Review* 20 (1979): 417–434.

5. Dixon told Joseph Tumulty, Wilson's spokesman, of his hope that the movie would "revolutionize Northern sentiments," thereby turning "every man who comes out of one of our theatres [into] a Southern partisan for life." See Arthur S. Link, *Wilson: The New Freedom* (Princeton, N.J.: Princeton University Press, 1965), p. 253.

6. This political account is told from a black angle in Louis R. Harlan, *Booker T. Washington: The Wizard of Tuskegee. 1901–1915* (New York: Oxford University Press, 1983), *passim*.

7. See Charles Flint Kellogg, *NAACP: A History of the National Association for the Advancement of Colored People*, Vol. I, *1909–1920* (Baltimore: Johns Hopkins University Press, 1967), chapter 1.

8. Lynch's *The Facts of Reconstruction* appeared in 1913 (reprint, Indianapolis: Bobbs-Merrill, 1970); and Du Bois, "Reconstruction and Its Benefits," *American Historical Review* 15 (1910): 781–799; see also Lynch's "Some Historical Errors of John Ford Rhodes," *Journal of Negro History* 2 (1917): 345–368.

9. May Childs Nerney to John E. Barnett, April 22, 1915; NAACP resolution of June 8, 1915, in NAACP Records, Library of Congress (hereafter, NRLC).

10. Nerney to Barnett, April 22, 1915, NRLC; Thomas Cripps, "The Birth of a Race Company: An Early Stride Toward a Black Cinema," *Journal of Negro History* 59 (1974): 38–50 (see 32). See also Nickie Fleener, "Answering Film with Film: The Hampton Epilogue, a Positive Alternative to the Negative Black Stereotypes in *The Birth of a Nation*," *Journal of Popular Film and Television* 7 (1980): 400–425.

11. Nerney to Charles Bentley, Chicago, June 6, 1915, NRLC; Booker T. Washington to C. R. Miller, copy, Oct. 26, 1915, in Washington Papers, Library of Congress, hereafter BTWLC; George William Cook to Nerney, May 11, 1915, NRLC.

12. Du Bois to Committee, May 12, 1915; and Mary White Ovington circular, Oct. 27, 1915, in NRLC.

13. Carl Laemmle to Jacob Schiff, copy, Nov. 2, 1915; and Mary White Ovington to

Ernest Poole, Nov. 11, 1915, in NRLC. For fiscal matters, see Cripps,"The Birth of a Race Company," p. 33.

14. Scott's contracts, dated Dec. 20, 1915, June 27, 1916, and Sept. 22, 1917, in Scott Papers, Soper Library, Morgan State University, hereafter EJSSL.

15. William N. Selig to Birth of a Race Company, Oct. 3, 1916; and [Barker] in *Birth of a Race News*, Oct. 1916, in Julius Rosenwald Papers, Regenstein Library, University of Chicago, hereafter JRRL.

16. Nerney to Joseph P. Loud, May 17, 1915, NRLC.

17. William C. Graves to Edwin L. Barker, Dec. 20, 1916 (quoted); see also Carter H. Hayes to John Byrne, copy, Nov. 14, 1917, JRRL, an apparent private investigator's report on Giles P. Cory's "blue sky" promises of Rosenwald's participation. Barker to Graves, Jan. 10, 1917 (quoted); and Barker to Graves, Jan. 22, 1917, an apology, JRRL. Cory quoted in *Birth of a Race News*, July 1917; and on Frohman, see *Birth of a Race News*, Oct. 1917, all in JRRL. For trade paper coverage of the finances, see *Billboard*, March 25, 1918; and *Variety*, June 21, 1918.

18. *Tampa Tribune*, Jan. 21, 1918, on "darkies;" and Dec. 21, 1917, on "prejudice," both in Tampa Public Library.

19. Chicago press quoted in Cripps, "The Birth of a Race Company," p. 36; Moton quoted in George Frederic Wheeler to Emmett J. Scott, Feb. 6, 1920, EJSSL; Johnson quoted in his memorandum-for-file in Johnson Papers, Research Library, UCLA.

20. Wheeler to Scott, Feb. 6, 1920, in EJSSL. George Frederic Wheeler, one of the original writers, inquired as to the copyright status of *Up From Slavery* and added Du Bois's *The Quest for the Silver Fleece* and Charles Waddell Chesnutt's *The House Beyond the Cedars* to his list of prospective movies "worthy of the race."

21. The *Birth of a Race* described here is from the incomplete print in the Library of Congress. For its provenance, see Thomas Cripps, "*The Birth of a Race:* A Lost Film Rediscovered in Texas," *Texas Humanist* 5 (1983): 11–12.

22. "Conductor's piano score," music cues for the moment provide the only clues from which to infer the images of Part III of the film.

23. On the origins of the idea of enhanced status in return for national service, see Benjamin Quarles, *The Negro in the Making of America* (New York: Collier Books, 1964), particularly its last chapter.

24. Scott to Barker, Oct. 18, 1915, and Nov. 6, 1915, in EJSSL.

Pearl Bowser and Louise Spence

IDENTITY AND BETRAYAL

The Symbol of the Unconquered and Oscar Micheaux's "Biographical Legend"

"The Symbol of the Unconquered, *the latest and the best of the Micheaux productions, will open a six day showing at the Vendome Theater on Monday January 10th [1921]. This feature has been creating a wonderful amount of comment all over the East and is one which should be seen by everybody. The story is a clean-cut one and the action is full of speed, interesting and exciting. It tells of the struggles of a young man to retain possession of a piece of valuable oil land against tremendous odds, which includes [sic] everything from intimidation at the hand of his neighbors to a narrow escape from death for him at the hands of the Ku Klux Klan. A love story of beautiful texture lends added interest and some red-blooded scrapping and hard, hard riding furnishes the picture with the amount of exciting action required to make the blood tingle through your veins at high speed.*"

—The Chicago Defender, *1/8/21*

"*It is claimed the touch of the romance woven in* The Homesteader *is coincident with the author's own life but this is still a matter of conjecture.*"

—The Half-Century Magazine, *April 1919*

"*My color shrouds me in. . . .*"

—*Countee Cullen*

Seventy-two years after its 1920 premiere at the Vaudette Theater in Detroit, a print of *The Symbol of the Unconquered*, Oscar Micheaux's tale of mistaken identity, romance, and adventure in the West, was repatriated to the United States from the Belgium national film archives (Cinémathèque Royale/ Koninklijk Filmarchief) with French and Flemish intertitles. *The Symbol of the Unconquered* is one of only three of Micheaux's silent films that have "survived" thus far.[1] Though his career spanned thirty years, approximately twenty-five features—more than half of his total output—were produced in the first decade (1918–1929). These films were tools to express his personal view of the African

American experience. In his desire to have his life be an example for others, Micheaux fostered certain aspects of his personal vision, made artistic use of his personal history, and dramatized particular motifs. He created a biographical persona composed of selected actual and imaginary events that continues to exist and exert influence today, even though many of his films are lost and forgotten.

In his silent films, Micheaux chose themes that were contentious or explosive in their time. By responding to such contemporary social issues as concubinage, rape, miscegenation, peonage, and lynching, he created a textured and layered expressive response to the social crises that circumscribed African American life. *Within Our Gates*, for example, unveils the lynch mob, exposing its members as ordinary townfolk: men, women, and even children who participate in hunting down and hanging a Black family. *The Symbol of the Unconquered* unmasks the Ku Klux Klan. In *The Gunsaulus Mystery* (1921), a reworking of the Leo M. Frank case, a man is wrongfully accused of the murder of a white woman.[2] Promotion for *The Dungeon* (1922) touted the film as dealing with the then-pending Dyer anti-lynching bill. *The Brute* (1920) condemned racketeering and the abuse of women. Passing is the central theme of *The House Behind the Cedars* (1925); *Body and Soul* confronts hypocrisy and corruption in the ministry; and racially restrictive real estate covenants are challenged in *Birthright* (1924).

These films generated heated debate and were subject to censorship by official censor boards, community groups, and individuals such as local sheriffs and theater owners. For instance, a police captain in New Orleans ordered a Race theater to discontinue showing *Within Our Gates* because in his opinion the lynching scenes would incite a riot.[3] The Virginia State Board of Motion Picture Censors rejected the full version of *The House Behind the Cedars* for "presenting the grievances of the negro in very unpleasant terms and even touching on dangerous ground, intermarriage between the races."[4]

Micheaux sometimes defied the censor board by showing a film without submitting it for a license or without eliminating offensive passages[5] and, on occasion, would use the controversy over a film in one town to promote it in other locations, advertising, for example, the "complete version" of *Within Our Gates*. For its run in Omaha, an article in a local newspaper announced the forthcoming showing as "the Race film production that created a sensation in Chicago" and "required two solid months to get by the censor board."[6] Censorship became the plot of his 1921 film *Deceit*.

Fig. 1: Portrait of Oscar Micheaux from his first novel, *The Conquest* (1913).

The silent features now extant (*Within Our Gates* [1920], *The Symbol of the Unconquered* [1920], and *Body and Soul* [1925]), along with his novels, promotional materials, and personal papers, illuminate the degree to which Micheaux used his self-constructed social identity, political point of view, and status as African American entrepreneur to create, promote, and shape the reception of his works. This "biographical legend," to borrow from Boris Tomashevsky,[7] was not only the way that Micheaux made expressive use of his biography, it also validated the racial experiences of his audiences and gave credibility to his role as a successful filmmaker and novelist. During the first decade of his career, Micheaux developed a public persona as an aggressive and successful businessman and a controversial and confident maverick producer—an image that was to sustain him for the next twenty years, although little of the work after his first sound picture, *The Exile* in 1931, would seem to justify it.[8]

Micheaux, son of former slaves, was the product of a generation of African American migrants who left the land in search of "the freedom of life and limb, the freedom to work and think, the freedom to love and aspire."[9] In his semi-autobiographical novels *The Conquest: The Story of a Negro Pioneer by the Pioneer* (1913) and *The Homesteader* (1917), he tells of venturing forth from his home in southern Illinois in 1901, in search of a career at the age of seventeen. Heading north to Chicago, he supported himself at odd jobs, shining shoes, bailing water in a coal mine, laboring in a factory, the stockyards, and as a Pullman porter. While working as a porter, Micheaux was able to save enough money to set up an agrarian enterprise, a homestead on the Rosebud Reservation in Winner, South Dakota.[10] His novels suggest that, like many of his white immigrant neighbors who made land purchases based on the prospects of the railroad extending westward, he hoped to turn a profit on the value of his holdings. However, in order to acquire title to the land, it was necessary to build a house on it and till the soil. He wrote of preferring selling the family crop to working in the fields as a boy and knowing little about farming. Undeterred by lack of experience, he taught himself the rudiments of Great Plains farming, a process he described in painful detail, including purchasing mules, getting the right equipment to break the prairie, and turning the sod over day after day.[11] He also reflected on the need, as the only "colored man" engaged in agriculture on the Reservation,[12] to demonstrate to his neighbors that he was an honest, hardworking Negro determined to succeed. Bent on disproving the widely held belief that "the negro," when faced with the hardships of homesteading, would opt for the "ease and comfort" of the city, Micheaux broke-out three times as many acres as his neighbors.[13]

Working hard for five years, Micheaux amassed more than five hundred acres by the time he was twenty-five. He approached homesteading with the same philosophy he was later to apply to his book and movie businesses: independence, persistence, and a willingness to take risks. One chapter of *The Conquest*, in a writing style that differs from the rest of the novel,[14] digresses to report the history of two towns, detailing the townsfolk's speculation on the routes of the railroad's expansion. Although the "objective reporting" of the details and key players obviously attempts to distance Micheaux from those speculators, it is given such prominence in an otherwise personal story that one cannot help but wonder what role he had in the scheme. Indeed, the image of Micheaux as land speculator seems more in tune with Micheaux-the-entrepreneur than with Micheaux-the-homesteader. In his own words, he "was possessed with a business turn of mind."[15] In *The Homesteader*, for example, he boasts about how, after writing "his life story" and having a publisher reject it, he financed *The Conquest* himself. With borrowed money for a suit and a trip to Nebraska, he struck a deal with a printer there and then raised money for the first payment by preselling copies of the book to his neighbors in South Dakota.

Although Micheaux acquired a large holding and claimed to have been successful at farming wheat and flax,[16] his career as a farmer ended sometime between 1912 and 1913. He tells of liens on his homestead and struggling to pay interest and taxes so he would not lose his land. Many homesteaders who had settled with great optimism were forced to abandon their claims because of a prolonged drought. Foreclosures were so common, they "occasioned no comment."[17] In his next novel, *The Forged Note* (1915), he refers nostalgically to the Rosebud Reservation and returning to the land.[18] By 1916 Micheaux had moved to Sioux City, Iowa, where he published a third novel, *The Homesteader*, and sold his earlier works through his firm, The Western Book Supply Company.

In 1918 George P. Johnson, general booking manager of the Lincoln Motion Picture Company of Los Angeles, initiated a correspondence with Oscar Micheaux, now an author, publishing his own books and selling them door-to-door. Johnson wrote to The Western Book Supply Company about his discovery of *The Homesteader* in a *Chicago Defender* advertisement and inquired into the film rights to the book.[19] His brother and founder of the company, the actor Noble Johnson, reviewed Micheaux's novel and suggested that parts of it—the interracial romance, most likely—were too controversial for them to deal with, adding, "It is a little too advanced on certain subjects for us yet and unless we would change [it] so decidedly that it would hardly be recognizable, we could not expect much support from white houses."[20]

There followed a rapid exchange of correspondence over three months between Micheaux and George P. Johnson, with Johnson initially trying to convince Micheaux that he had more expertise in "the movie game" and promising that he could mold it "into a first-class feature." Micheaux, just as he had approached learning to farm by inquiring from others, was probing for information from the Johnsons. At the same time, he was already constructing a grandiose persona by maintaining that his 500-page novel should be a big picture, at least six reels, not the Lincoln Company's usual two- or three-reel product.[21] He was also apparently convinced that, far from being a detriment to profitability, the controversial nature of such themes as interracial marriage was a very good selling device and should be exploited: "Nothing would make more people as anxious to see a picture than a litho reading: SHALL RACES INTERMARRY?"[22]

With no movie experience at all, Micheaux ultimately decided to produce *The Homesteader* himself, incorporating under the name of Micheaux Book and Film Company. Bragging to Lincoln that he was able to raise $5,000 through a stock subscription in less than two weeks,[23] he went on to produce an eight-reeler, the longest African American film at that time, and advertised it as "Oscar Micheaux's Mammoth Photoplay." The theatrical debut of the film was promoted as "Passed by the Censor Board despite the protests of three Chicago ministers who claimed that it was based upon the supposed hypocritical actions of a prominent colored preacher of the city!"[24]

With the release of *The Homesteader* in February of 1919, Micheaux joined the growing number of small companies producing films exclusively for African American audiences. By the end of 1920, Micheaux had released his fourth feature, *The Symbol of the Unconquered*, "A Stirring Tale of Love and Adventure in the Great Northwest," like *The Homesteader*, a wilderness story. The frontier, for Micheaux, is the mythic space of moral drama and the site of opportunities seemingly free of the restrictive and discriminatory laws and social arrangements of the rural South and the urban metropolis, where the characteristic model of economic expansion is entrepreneurship. His first novel, *The Conquest*, set in Gregory County, South Dakota, celebrates the enterprising individuals: homesteaders, merchants, bankers, and real estate dealers involved in commercial clubs, land booms, and speculating on the route of the railroad. The hero of *The Symbol of the Unconquered*, a man of the frontier, self-willed and self-motivated, is another articulation of Oscar Micheaux's biographical legend. Accumulating wealth through hard work and self-denial, he is almost a metaphor for the spirit of individualism. In a 1910 article in *The Chicago Defender*, Micheaux quoted Horace Greeley, "Go west young man and grow up with the country," and although he wrote about openings for doctors, lawyers, laborers, and mechanics, he posited the future of the West with agricultural possibilities, calling farmlands "the bosses of wealth." For Micheaux, the land openings along the Frontier provided the opportune moment for the

Negro to "do something for himself." Detailing the participation of the Race in agriculture, he wrote of fewer than "300 Negro farmers in the ten states of the Northwest [and] more opportunities than young men to grasp them."[25] Although such an image made him seem unique, enlarging his legend as a "Negro pioneer," Micheaux was one of many thousands of African Americans, since emancipation, who saw the frontier as the land of hope where one could realize one's own destiny.[26]

The appeal of the West spoke strongly to many Americans as both a symbolic and actual place offering an unspoiled environment in "the hollow of God's hand"[27] for individuals to fill with their own virtue, where social conventions and distinctions prove less important than natural ability, inner goodness, and individual achievement. Real estate promoters, railroad advertisements, news stories, dime novels, traveling shows, and movies mythologized the frontier as the site of freedom, wealth, and independence, capturing the imagination of a multitude of African Americans determined to put the residues of slavery and racial barriers behind them. Micheaux's hero in *The Symbol of the Unconquered*, Van Allen, a gentlemanly frontiersman in a buckboard riding the prairies of South Dakota, embodied the Western hero, self-sufficient and calmly rugged. Race theaters, not unlike white houses, featured Westerns as an important part of the programming in the late teens and twenties. Edward Henry, a projectionist throughout the 1920s in a Black theater in Jackson, Mississippi, recalled, "When you go back, William S. Hart was one of the big men. . . . All you had to do was just put his name out there; [you] didn't have to put any pictures or anything, just William S. Hart, Wednesday, and they'd be coming. . . . William S. Hart, Tom Mix . . . as I say, just open the door and stand back. The crowds'll come in."[28]

The great antagonist in *The Symbol of the Unconquered*, however, was not hostile elements, menacing outlaws, or "savage" Indians, as in most white Westerns, but the Ku Klux Klan. And Micheaux capitalized on that. Despite a climate of racial violence and intimidation, he advertised the film's premiere in Detroit as, "SEE THE KU KLUX KLAN IN ACTION AND THEIR ANNIHILATION!"[29] When it played in Baltimore, the *Afro-American* ad exhorted, "SEE THE MURDEROUS RIDE OF THE INSIDIOUS KU KLUX KLAN in their effort to drive a BLACK BOY off of valuable Oil Lands—and the wonderful heroism of a traveler to save him!"[30] Another reference to the KKK (apparently quoting from Micheaux's press release) appears in *The Chicago Whip*: "night riders rode down upon [the hero] like ghosts with firey torches intent upon revenge."[31] And a

New York Age review headlined, "KKK Put to Rout in PhotoPlay to be Shown at the Lafayette [Theatre]," called attention to "[t]he viciousness and un-Americanism of the Ku-Klux-Klan which . . . is beginning to manifest itself again in certain parts of the United States. . . . [The film] is regarded as quite timely in view of the present attempt to organize night riders in this country for the express purpose of holding back the advancement of the Negro."[32]

Promotion for *The Symbol of the Unconquered* addressed the Black spectator and underscored the protest nature of the film. However, to think of the Klan as the singular antagonist is to reduce the complexity of Micheaux's representation. The hero, the homesteader Hugh Van Allen (played by Walter Thompson), is echoed by Driscoll (played by Lawrence Chenault), the villain who is also out to improve his lot. Both characters are speculators who have migrated to the Northwest in pursuit of bigger and better opportunities. Although Driscoll is motivated by the same drives as the hero (indeed, as Micheaux himself), he acts in unscrupulous ways. He advances his standing, not by hard work and self-denial, but through coercion and deception. Through Driscoll and his cohorts, Micheaux exposes the economic origins of whitecapping; Driscoll, a light-skinned man passing for White, is the leader of a gang of greedy misfits plotting to intimidate Van Allen and drive him off his valuable oil lands. It is Driscoll's participation in the Klan, his use of the same forces of intimidation that he would experience if his true racial identity were known, that disturbs the equilibrium of any clear-cut binary opposition.

Why does Micheaux superimpose the image of the KKK over an interracial band of thieves, swindlers, and connivers (including a former clergyman)? Is Driscoll the resurrected Eph from *Within Our Gates*, a betrayer, albeit in a more complex form? Driscoll's racial ambiguity allows him to pass, but the darker complected Eph must rely on a charade of obsequious behavior to gain white acceptance. Micheaux appropriated the stereotype to comment on the aspirations and social behavior of those who kowtow to Whites. Eph's wearing of the servile mask and his loyalty to his master represents his way of negotiating racism; however, as the mob turns on him, it is clear that his shield is precarious; in the end, he is just another "nigger."[33] Driscoll, on the other hand, not only wants to be White, but in order to achieve whiteness, he assumes the posture of the oppressor; in order to ward off the terror of the other, Driscoll himself becomes a terrorist. He counters racism with hatred, turns that hatred on the Race and, by extension, on himself. Both Eph and Driscoll deny their solidarity with the group. Eph in trying to secure his own "privileged" position among the Whites in the big house, separates himself and betrays a fellow Negro.[34] Driscoll, by internalizing negative perceptions of blackness, isolates himself and betrays the Race.[35] Micheaux criticized the social behavior of both characters and both get their just desserts.

Van Allen's triumph over hatred is even sweeter because he has overcome Driscoll's "self-hate," as well as the nightriders, the symbol of racial oppression and intimidation. The unmasking of hatred is as much a part of the film as the violence perpetrated in the name of hatred.

We think of Van Allen as Micheaux's surrogate, and in the character of Van Allen, Micheaux was dreaming and redreaming his own ambitions and desires. In the epilogue, Van Allen's good deeds are rewarded: He becomes prosperous from the oil on his land and discovers that Eve Mason (played by Iris Hall), a neighboring homesteader, is, despite her looks, really a Black woman, and thus a suitable wife. In *The Conquest*, Micheaux writes of his experiences homesteading and falling in love with his neighbor's daughter, an unnamed young Scottish woman of strong character and "anxious to improve her mind," attributes he clearly admired.[36] One of the least verifiable facts of the author's life, this interracial romance is a recurring theme and rhetorical trope in his films and novels. Micheaux replays this love, or the possibility of it, in much of his work. In *The Conquest*, although he never acts on his feelings, he conveys a sense of anxiety about even considering it: To pursue an interracial relationship would be to call into question his loyalty to the Race.

This type of titillation—and concession to popular mores—is more developed in his novel *The Homesteader*. The main character, the Negro pioneer Jean Baptiste, deciding not to marry the woman he loves (whom he believes to be Caucasian), cites, "*The Custom Of The Country, and its law*," and goes on to note that such a marriage "would be the most unpopular thing he could do . . . he would be condemned, he would be despised by the race that was his."[37] However, in this book (and in his later films and novels) Micheaux provided a happier ending: The hero discovers that his love is not White after all and marriage becomes possible.

Clues to the true racial identity of the woman, who seems to be an inappropriate love interest for the hero, emerge in different ways in these works. In *The Exile* (1931), for example, the heroine is described as a White woman by another character early in the film. The audience gets essential narrative information as she does: We share her curiosity when she examines her physical appearance before a mirror, but do not know for certain that she is Black until the heroine does, in a final scene.

On the other hand, the audience knows more than the characters do in *The Betrayal* (1948), the film version of Micheaux's 1943 novel, *The Wind from Nowhere* (another reworking of his biographical legend). The film opens with a scene of an elderly Black man explaining his granddaughter's lineage; however, the heroine is not present in that scene and does not know that the gentleman is her grandfather.[38] By carefully tracing the character's origins, Micheaux informs the audience that the heroine herself is unaware of her true racial identity and therefore is neither deceitful nor disloyal. Consistently in all these works, it is the Micheaux-like male hero who struggles for much of the story with the political and moral dilemmas of such a marriage.[39] His is the noble fight. In *Thirty Years Later* (1928), it is the man who is unaware of his ancestry; however, he *also* fights the noble fight, and when he finds out his origins, the hero becomes proud of the Race and marries his love.[40]

Micheaux's treatment of miscegenation in such films as *The Homesteader*, *Within Our Gates*, *The Symbol of the Unconquered*, *A Son of Satan*, *The House Behind the Cedars*, *Thirty Years Later*, *Birthright*, *The Exile*, *Veiled Aristocrats*, *God's Stepchildren*, *The Betrayal*, and all seven of his novels, are ambitious reworkings of the conventions of melodrama from a point of view within the Black community—a resourceful reconfiguration of the genre. By centering the African American experience, he offered a bold critique of American society. To understand the scope and complexity of this critique, we must see it as a political enterprise that both codified the values of the time and attempted to mold them.[41]

Although mistaken identity was a common convention of nineteenth- and early twentieth-century melodrama—the ill-suited lover who turns out not to be ill-suited after all (not a sibling, a pauper, a moral indigent, etc.)—the reversals in Micheaux's stories more often involve the potential transgression of the social taboos and legal prohibitions against miscegenation.

Miscegenation threatens definitions of race, challenging the idea that racial identity might be "knowable." By blurring the dichotomy on which whiteness depends, miscegenation throws into disarray the basis of white supremacy, Black "inferiority." As Toni Morrison has pointed out, it is by imagining blackness that whiteness "knows itself as not enslaved, but free, not repulsive, but desirable, not helpless, but licensed and powerful."[42]

Rather than suggesting a radical new way of seeing or attempting to create a new narrative space for representation, in *The Symbol of the Unconquered* (as in much of his other early work), Micheaux worked within the hardened conventions and presuppositions of "the Negro problem" text, melding the plots and conventions of the sentimental melodrama with Western settings and characters. He was "crafting a voice out of tight places," as Houston Baker wrote of Booker T. Washington's use of minstrelsy.[43] Often invoking the novel *Uncle Tom's Cabin* in his promotional material (print ads, trailers, etc.), Micheaux seems to have admired not only the enormous social impact (and commercial success) of Harriet Beecher Stowe's work, but also its evangelical piety and moral commitment.[44]

Many of his characters represent sociological and moral forces rather than psychologically individuated people, and function as models to prove what can be accomplished through hard work and industry. At the beginning of his career, striking out on his own and settling on the land, Micheaux was influenced by Booker T. Washington's philosophy, "not of destruction, but of construction; not of defense, but of aggression; . . . not of hostility or surrender, but of friendship and advance"; where self-help, one's "own efforts," and "usefulness in the community" were the "surest and most potent protection."[45] *The Conquest*, a success and adventure story about a Black pioneer in the West, was dedicated to "The Honorable Booker T. Washington," and many of his other books and movies aimed to galvanize the spirit of success through examples of individual achievement. In *Body and Soul*, Micheaux used Washington's image as a visual tag to identify characterological traits. Sylvester, the industrious inventor, is introduced in a shot that frames him with a portrait of Booker T. Washington.[46] In the 1910 *Defender* article referred to earlier, Micheaux wrote that he was "not trying to offer a solution to the Negro problem, for I don't feel that there is any problem further than the future of anything, whether it be a town, state or race. . . . It depends first on individual achievement, and I am at a loss to see a brilliant future for the young colored man unless he first does something for himself." The hero of his film *The Millionaire* (1927), a soldier of fortune, who as a youth possessed "great initiative and definite purpose," returns to the community as a rich man. Explaining why Jean Baptiste foreswears marriage with his White neighbor in *The Homesteader*, Micheaux wrote, "He had set himself in this new land to succeed; he had worked and slaved to that end. He liked his people; he wanted to help them. Examples they needed and such he was glad to have become; but if he married now the one he loved, the example was lost."[47] Micheaux stated in *The Conquest* that one of his greatest tasks in life was "to convince a certain class of my racial acquaintances that a colored man can be anything."[48] Mildred Latham, the love interest of the homesteader, author, and itinerant book peddler in *The Forged Note*, admires the hero as "a Negro pioneer . . . [who] blaze[d] the way for others."[49]

However, Micheaux's racial uplift, which was so important to counter accusations of "inferiority," challenged White definitions of race without changing the terms. Others in this period—Sterling Brown, Langston Hughes, and Zora Neale Hurston, for example—questioned those very terms, demanding new definitions of Race from within Black America. Hurston's work recodifies both language and story by bringing out the richness of oral culture, the African American vernacular, and folk tales. Hughes wrote of his own use of Black culture, "Jazz to me is one of the inherent expressions of Negro life in America: the eternal tom-tom beating in the Negro soul—the tom-tom of revolt against weariness in a white world, a world of subway trains and work, work, work; the tom-tom of joy and laughter, and pain swallowed in a smile."[50] Hurston and Hughes, and other New Negroes, saw themselves as reclaiming images of blackness, an attempt, as Alain Locke put it, to build Americanism on Race values.[51]

Like Hurston, Hughes, and Brown, Micheaux spoke as a Negro; the "blackness" of the author is a strong presence. However, because of his sense of personal responsibility and uplift, he saw himself as an instructive voice and an empowering interpreter of Black life *for* the community. Van Allen in *The Symbol of the Unconquered*, as the title implies, is an expression of Oscar Micheaux's optimism for the Race. Like Micheaux's biographical legend, Van Allen is the adventurous entrepreneur, an achiever, loyal to the Race, persistent and brave in the face of adversities.

Ironically, however, today Van Allen is one of the least provocative characters! Driscoll, on the other hand, is so overdrawn that he borders on the horrific—almost uncanny. "Uncanny" because he is at once so evil and so familiar. The act of passing is not uncommon or automatically condemned by the Black community. Rather, it is Driscoll's attitude of superiority, seeing Blacks as subhuman and taking pleasure in their misfortune, that is so wicked and well known—both a betrayal and a surrender. In his hotel, he refuses a room to Abraham, a Black traveling salesman (played by E. G. Tatum), and leads him to the barn. When Eve arrives from a long journey exhausted and hungry, Driscoll at first thinks the light-skinned woman is White; but, as she is about to register, he looks into her eyes and "sees" her true identity. His initially genial behavior turns to hatred; he denies her a bed in his hotel, sending her to the hayloft. During the night, Eve, awakened by a storm and frightened when discovering that there is someone else in the barn, falls from the loft and runs out into a driving rain. Driscoll, watching from his bedroom window as she struggles in the storm, takes sinister joy in her suffering. Surrounded by an aura of shimmering whiteness (in white nightshirt and sheets, lit as if he were aglow), he thrashes his arms in triumph.

What is so disturbing about Driscoll is his assumption of the posture of the oppressor *and* his terror of discovery. He sees both his true identity in Eve's pale face and the possibility of being unmasked. In *The Conquest*, invoking a story from his experiences as a homesteader in South Dakota, Micheaux wrote about the children of a wealthy mixed-race family who were passing and lived in fear of other members of the Race, dreading "that moment of racial recognition."[52] Driscoll's own racial identity is exposed early in the film by his mother, a darker skinned lady, as he is proposing to a White woman. In this scene, the terror of racial recognition and the odiousness of racial terror come together as Driscoll attacks his own mother because she is Black.

Later, in a barroom scene, there is a fist fight between Van Allen and Driscoll, supposedly over a horse deal turned sour. The fight scene is introduced by a close shot of both Driscoll and Van Allen framed in a mirror. Driscoll looks up and recognizes Van Allen. Perhaps he sees Van Allen as the horse-trade victim he has been mocking. Or is this that moment of racial recognition? Perhaps Driscoll sees his despised self in Van Allen, his own blackness. Driscoll pulls a gun threatening Van Allen; but Van Allen wrestles the gun away from him and they fight. After being beaten by Van Allen and declaring, "I'll get my revenge!," Driscoll is thrown out of the bar with a swift kick in the butt by the same traveling salesman whom he had refused to serve in his hotel. Is this a matter of a Black man getting the better of a "White" man[53] or is it intra-racial censure?

Lawrence Chenault's performance style throughout the film—his chalky makeup; outlined eyes; arched eyebrows; tense, often flailing, arms and hunched shoulders; the rigidity of his body and the vehemence of his gestures—expresses a man driven by fear. Driscoll's self-loathing and terror of discovery provoke his attack on Van Allen; having failed, he uses the Klan as a personal instrument of revenge. It is because his life is so tenuous that he is so vicious. Reflecting on the South Dakota mixed-race family, Micheaux wrote, "What worried me most, however, even frightened me, was, that after marriage and when their children had grown to manhood and womanhood, they . . . had a terror of their race."[54] They looked upon other Blacks with a dread of discovery. Such a discovery would expose not only their racial identity, but also a life of deception, threatening social and psychological upheaval. For Driscoll, race is the unspeakable, the stranger entering the gate, menacing his whiteness. Identity, to borrow from James Baldwin, "would seem to be the garment with which [he] covers the nakedness of the self."[55]

The Competitor magazine praised *The Symbol of the Unconquered* as making a significant thrust at the "more than 500,000 people" in America who are "passing for white."[56] *The Daily Ohio State Journal* in 1909 wrote of thousands of people passing in Washington, D.C. alone: "Those who just occasionally pass for white, simply to secure just recognition, and the privileges the laws vouchsafe an American citizen, should not be censured harshly. An unjust discrimination, a forced and ungodly segregation drives them to practice deception. . . . But it is an awful experience to pass for white. At all times fear—the fear of detection—haunts one. . . . Those who turn their backs upon their own color, own race and own relatives to live a life of fear, of dread, and almost isolation just to pass for white seven days in the week, while regarded with utter contempt by their colored race, really ought to be pitied, when it is known how heavy is the burden they carry, and how much they suffer in silence."[57]

Micheaux exploited these concerns in the script for the 1938 film, *God's Stepchildren*. Andrew, the white husband of the young woman who is passing, upon discovering his wife's "streak" says, "You aren't the first to try this, Naomi. No, it has been tried since the days of slavery and even before that; but they can't get away with it, so you see you can't get away with it, for sooner or later, somewhere, some time after a life of fear and exemption you will be found out, and when you are they'll turn on you, loath you, despise you, even spit in your face and call you by your right name—Naomi, Negress."[58]

The Black press often covered both well-known interracial marriages and court cases of people attempting to prove that they were Negro in order to counter charges of miscegenation.[59] Stories of Whites not being able to discern what is obvious to a Black person were part of the popular discourses of the time. It was thought quite funny that for Whites, race was not so much a matter of color and appearance as mannerisms and deportment. Helen M. Chesnutt, in her biography of her father, tells of the family entering a restaurant while traveling and after being seated, seeing the manager "bearing down" upon their table; they immediately began speaking French . . . and the man retreated.[60]

Lester Walton, in an article entitled "When is a Negro a Negro to a Caucasian?," asked, "[B]y what standard do they differentiate as to when is a Negro a Negro?" and laughed about vaudevillian John Hodges ("Any colored person can tell what John Hodges is") trying to eat at a restaurant and telling the waiter that he is not a Negro, but an English Jew, and getting served.[61] In another article, Walton tells the story of the White manager and cashier at the Fifty-ninth Street Theatre in New York who were discharged because "they mistook a young lady of color to be of the white race and proceeded to speak disrespectfully of their ebony-hued employer [William Mack Felton]." Walton mused, "One of the amusing features of the so-called Negro problem is the inability of the white people to recognize hundreds and hundreds of colored people who have gone on the other side of the color line. To us there is nothing so ludicrous as to observe one known as a violent Negro hater walking arm-in-arm or sitting at a table eating with a person of color, the radical Caucasian indulging in an erratic outburst of abuse on the Negro to the unconcealed delight of the colored person."[62]

In 1925, the wealthy White New York socialite, Leonard "Kip" Rhinelander, took his new wife, Alice Jones Rhinelander, to court to dissolve their marriage when he found out that she had "Negro ancestry and concealed the fact from him during their courtship."[63] Mrs. Rhinelander denied any deception, insisting that anyone could tell she was a Negro. The trial made the front pages of the Black weeklies. Micheaux used the notoriety of the Rhinelander case to promote *The House Behind the Cedars*, his 1925 adaptation of Chesnutt's story of passing.[64] But even without mentioning it in his ads, such popular discourses on crossing the "color line" certainly would have influenced the way audiences understood Micheaux's films. Press coverage, folk sayings, blues songs, verbal exchanges are all part of the spectatorial experience. As Tony Bennett and Janet Woollacott put it, "a text . . . is never 'there' except in forms in which it is also and always other than 'just itself,' always-already humming with reading possibilities which derive from outside its covers."[65]

Because Driscoll's true racial identity is established early in the film, audiences watch his vileness, knowing he is Black. In his mask, he so rejects blackness that, turning his anger on the Race, he becomes an assault on the audience. The defeat of the vengeful character at the end of the film must have given the audience a moment of relief and joy—an assault on the oppressor. Likewise, the scene in the bar where he is kicked in the butt by the traveling salesman, one of the gestures that clustered around the "Tom" character in minstrelsy, offers vicarious pleasure in his humiliation. Driscoll's downfall and the apocalyptic renewal of the ending is a victory not only for Van Allen, but for the audience as well, putting to rest notions of Black "inferiority." What visions of their own radical anger and omnipotence might the audience have experienced through the hero!

Driscoll is both a vehicle to explore interracial relations and, as a person of mixed blood (the product of historical miscegenation), an expression of those relations. The question of color is a recurring interest for Micheaux. However, it's not a simple infatuation with color, nor is it simply a narrative contrivance—that is, the melodramatic trope of someone being not what he or she seems. It's far more complex than that. Although he was often accused of casting by color,[66] he criticized the color-caste system within the community as destructive social behavior. And although he created a star system of fair-skinned performers (Iris Hall, Shingzie Howard, Evelyn Preer, Lawrence Chenault, Carman Newsome, Lorenzo Tucker, etc.) chosen for their "look" and potential appeal to audiences, he didn't necessarily associate these "looks" with certain qualities, such as "goodness." In *Body and Soul*, Paul Robeson plays both the hero and the villain with no change of make-up, and the scoundrel, Yellow Curley, is played by Lawrence Chenault (who also plays villains in other films where the shade of one's skin is not part of the story).[67] In *The Symbol of the Unconquered*, Walter Thompson playing the hero, a rugged outdoorsman, acquires his swarthy complexion with dark make-up. Carl Mahon, who did not think of himself as an actor, felt that Micheaux cast him in romantic leads because of his "exotic looks," the combination of dark skin and straight hair.[68] In several of Micheaux's films—*The Symbol of the Unconquered, The House Behind the Cedars*, and *God's Stepchildren*, for examples—we would argue that he is not reproducing "color prejudice," but criticizing it.

For Micheaux the problem of miscegenation is not the mixing of the races but the disloyalty that comes from trying to hide one's racial identity. Sylvia, in *Within Our Gates*, who is the offspring of the plantation owner's brother, is adopted by Black sharecroppers and is raised as one of their own. She sees herself as a Black woman. As a person of mixed blood, Sylvia is not automatically an outsider, someone different, a point of division. In a medium long shot of her family around a table, there are a variety of skin colors. The storyline is not "about" skin color per se; it is "about" the rape of Black women by White men.

Although much of Eve's backstory in the only surviving print of *The Symbol of the Unconquered* seems to be missing,[69] Eve, like Sylvia, is comfortable with who she is and is not trying to pass. In an interview around the time of the film's release, Micheaux said, "There is one thing aside from [making] the story interesting that I strive to demonstrate in all my pictures and that is, it makes no difference what may be a person's color, or from where a person comes, if the heart is right, that's what counts, and success is sure."[70] Eve is not only a Black woman but a Race woman. It is through a letter commending her for her service to the Race that Van Allen discovers her true identity.

In *The Betrayal*, Micheaux's final film, Martin Eden (the character's name, like Eve's, associates him with a pastoral innocence)[71] tells the story of a mixed-race family in South Dakota with many children who would pass their father off as an "old colored servant who helped to raise them" when visitors came to call. One of the brothers was dark. Drafted into the army and assigned to a colored unit, unhappy with being unable to serve in a White regiment, "he stood before a mirror in his tent one night, took a German Luger that he had acquired—and blew his brains out."[72]

Although some contemporary critics have accused Micheaux of "Race hatred,"[73] it might be more fruitful to look at his work as adamantly depicting the diversity of Black life as he saw it. His works criticized certain attitudes, behavior, and conduct as detrimental to the future of the Race. Among the great diversity of characters criticized are gamblers, womanizers, people without ambition, and blind followers of the faith. As bell hooks put it, "[H]e was not concerned with the simple reduction of black representation to a 'positive' image."[74] In his 1946 novel *The Story of Dorothy Stanfield*, Micheaux described his surrogate, the book publisher and motion picture producer Sidney Wyeth with the following: "Wyeth is an intense race man; and while he can and does criticize the Negro in his books . . . , he is for his people at all times, regardless the circumstances."[75]

There are characters who hate the Race—Driscoll in *The Symbol of the Unconquered* is a clear example; Naomi in *God's Stepchildren* is another. Like Driscoll, Naomi abandoned her family in order to pass for White. The scene of discovery is once again a scene of maternal devotion; however, contrary to Driscoll's, Naomi's is a scene of love not hate.

It is her pained reaction upon seeing her small son on the street that gives her away.[76] Driscoll has no loving ties to anyone; Naomi is defeated by both her love and her self-loathing. Condemned by her betrayal, she quietly sinks into the murky river to end her suffering. In the film's final shot, the words "As ye sow, so shall ye reap" are superimposed over her hat floating on the surface of the water.

The most Micheaux-like character in *God's Stepchildren* is Jimmy, Naomi's morally upright foster brother. Like Micheaux, Jimmy worked as a railroad porter and saved money to buy a farm. In a scene where he tells his fiancée Eva his plans, she asks, "Why is it that so many, most all of our men, when they go into business it's got to be a crap game, a numbers bank or a policy shop? Why can't they go into some legitimate business, like white people?" Jimmy replies, "They could, but they made no study of economics. Their idea of success is to seek the line of least resistance. The Negro hates to think. He's a stranger to planning. . . . For that is the failure of our group. For we *are* a failure, you know. . . . [I]t seems that we should go right back to the beginning and start all over again. That's what I've decided to do. . . . I'm going to buy a farm and start at the beginning." A similar pastoral image appears in Booker T. Washington's *Up from Slavery* where he wrote about wishing he could "remove the great bulk of . . . people into the country districts and plant them upon the soil, upon the solid and never deceptive foundation of Mother Nature, where all nations and races that have ever succeeded have gotten their start—a start that at first may be slow and toilsome, but one that nevertheless is real."[77] If one accepts Jimmy as a voice of Micheaux, Micheaux is once again adapting Booker T. Washington's attachment to the land, philosophy of meritorious work, and proving one's self to the outside world. Twenty-five years before Jimmy's speech, Micheaux declared his own decision to seek a homestead, going West to "the land of real beginning."[78]

However, unlike Washington, Jimmy's criticism of the work attitudes of urban Blacks suggests an acceptance of the mythical figure of the shiftless "coon," incapable of learning or achieving, holding the Race down. In the 1910 *Defender* article quoted earlier, Micheaux himself confessed, "I return from Chicago each trip I make, more discouraged year after year with the hopelessness of [the young Negro's lack of] foresight. His inability to use common sense in looking into his future is truly discouraging. . . . The trouble with the men of our race is that they want something for nothing."

In his biographical legend, Micheaux was working to disprove these kinds of stereotypes. The portrait he paints of himself is one of ambitious well-laid plans, initiative, and persistent hard work. In *The Conquest* he comments on planting more acres than than his neighbors: "At first I was regarded as an object of curiosity, which changed to admiration. I was not called a free-go-easy coon, but a genuine booster for Calais and the Little Crow."[79] It is almost as though Micheaux felt that in order for him to rise, he had to uplift the Race, and a criticism of negative behavior would help to advance his cause. Although not an essentialist position (Micheaux clearly felt that, with education and guidance, people could change), the rub is, of course, that the character on whose back he builds his own legend of success must be held in contempt for the comparison to work.[80]

Jean Baptiste, in *The Homesteader*, a more clearly autobiographical character than Jimmy, "had confidence in education uplifting people; it made them more observing. It helped them morally":

> He had studied his race . . . , unfortunately as a whole their standard of morals were not so high as it should be. Of course he understood that the same began back in the time of slavery. They had not been brought up to a regard of morality in a higher sense and they were possessed with certain weaknesses. He was aware that in the days of slavery the Negro to begin with had had, as a rule only what he could steal, therefore stealing became a virtue. When accused as he naturally was sure to be, he had resorted to the subtle art of lying. . . . So with freedom his race had not gotten away from these loose practices. They were given still to lustful, undependable habits, which he at times became very impatient with. His version was that a race could not rise higher than their morals.[81]

With the arrogance of the self-taught and self-made, Micheaux projects himself as upright and highly moral; he also sets himself apart from others as a superior and righteous person. Part of the means by which he built the appearance of success included singling out those of the Race whom he characterized as immoral or without ambition and perseverance and censuring them for impeding the progress of the Race, and therefore holding *him* back. When he says there's no Negro problem, just the problem of individuals, he was acting on the premise that individual acts affect the entire group, a dynamic imposed by a racist system. That was his "burden of Race." By setting himself up as a model of one who had risen above the prevalent notion of the Negro as "inferior," he was inadvertedly reinforcing the very attitude he imagined he was overcoming—the notion that the morality, ambition, and abilities of the

Negro was "the problem." Col. Hubert Fauntleroy Julian, associate producer of two of Micheaux's films, was still using these same discourses in 1940. Describing *Lying Lips* in *Time* magazine, he said, "It's about a beautiful girl who is lead astray because she wants beautiful things. . . . You see, I am trying to build up the morals of my race."[82]

The Symbol of the Unconquered sets up a moral opposition between individual attitudes and behavior (such as the denial of racial identity in order to assert personal power and privilege) and the well-being of the group. Driscoll is the moral instrument through which Micheaux offers direction on social aspirations. Van Allen is both a stand-in for Oscar Micheaux and a means through which Micheaux builds his biographical legend, his legend of success. The working title of *The Symbol of the Unconquered* was *The Wilderness Trail*.[83] The name change is both affirming and challenging, a call to collective consciousness—very much like the title and long patriotic speech at the end of *Within Our Gates*. These films are a part of a continuous recoding and reshaping of Racial identity, African American solidarity, and the individual.

Notes

The material in this essay is part of the authors' forthcoming book, *In Search of Oscar Micheaux*, Rutgers University Press, 1997.

1. This was the second of Micheaux silent films to be returned in the past several years. *La Negra/Within Our Gates*, was repatriated from La Filmoteca Nacional de España, the National Film Archive of Spain, in 1990. The politics of what is "lost, stolen, or strayed," to quote Bill Cosby, is an important area of research and speculation. What motivates the "discovery" of a film in an archive? Why only three of at least twenty-five? Although we do not know how many prints of *The Symbol of the Unconquered* were struck, Micheaux claimed to have had nine prints of *The Brute* (also 1920) circulating; yet none have surfaced, so far. Letter, Swan Micheaux to George P. Johnson, 10/27/20, George P. Johnson Collection, Powell Library, University of California, Los Angeles.

2. Frank, a Jewish man convicted of the rape and murder of a young White woman, was lynched by a mob in Marietta, Georgia, in 1915. The Black press covered the case extensively, partially because a Black witness was allowed to testify against a White. See Joel Williamson, *The Crucible of Race: Black–White Relations in the American South since Emancipation*. (New York: Oxford University Press, 1984), pp. 168–172.

3. Letter to Frank T. Monney, Superintendent of Police, from Theodore A. Ray, Captain, Special to the Superintendent, March 19, 1920, George P. Johnson Collection, UCLA.

4. 2/4/30, Commonwealth of Virginia, Department of Law, Division of Motion Picture Censorship, list of films rejected in toto since 8/1/22, Virginia State Library and Archives. In his 1925 review of *The House Behind the Cedars*, the board's chair, Evan Chesterman, wrote that the film "contravenes the spirit of the recently enacted anti-

miscegination law which has put Virginia in the forefront as a pioneer in legislation aimed to preserve the integrity of the white race."

5. Letter, Micheaux to Virginia State Board of Censors, 10/14/24, Virginia Division of Motion Picture Censorship, Virginia State Library and Archives.

6. "Race Problem Play Comes to Omaha," clipping file, George P. Johnson Collection, UCLA, no date. The film was to play at the Loyal Theater beginning 8/9/20. This article seems to be based on Micheaux's promotional material; the same wording appeared in an article in *The Chicago Defender* for the January run of the film at the Vendome Theater.

7. "Thus the biography that is useful for the literary historian is not the author's curriculum vitae or the investigator's account of his life. What the literary historian really needs is the biographical legend created by the author himself." See Boris Tomasevskij's [Tomashevsky] "Literature and Biography" in *Readings in Russian Poetics: Formalist and Structuralist Views*, Ladislav Matejka and Krystyna Pomorska, eds. (Ann Arbor: University of Michigan Press, 1978), p. 55.

8. A previous film, *Daughter of the Congo*, 1930, was billed by Micheaux as a "talking, singing and dancing" picture; however, the sound sequence, according to one reviewer, John Mack Brown, was confined to "one short and unnecessary scene." [Norfolk] *Journal and Guide*, 4/12/30.

9. *The Souls of Black Folk* in *W. E. B. Du Bois Writings*, Nathan Huggins, ed. (New York: The Library of America, 1986), p. 370.

10. *The Conquest: The Story of a Negro Pioneer, by the Pioneer* (Lincoln, Nebraska: The Woodruff Press, 1913) p. 47. Richard Slotkin (in *The Fatal Environment: The Myth of the Frontier in the Age of Industrialization, 1800–1890* [New York: Atheneum, 1985] pp. 284–285) suggests that the Homestead legislation that divided Indian lands into homestead-type allotments was planned as both a safety valve for urban discontent and a way to integrate native Americans into "civilized society" by making them into yeoman farmers. However, "unlike homesteading in the well-watered and forested Middle West, plains farming required considerable investment of capital and a larger scale of operations to make it profitable. . . . Indeed, the greatest beneficiaries of the Homestead legislation were railroad, banking, and landholding corporations; and thirty years after the first Homestead Act, land ownership in the Great Plains states was being steadily consolidated in fewer and fewer hands."

11. Ibid., pp. 74–85.

12. Ibid., p. 145.

13. Ibid., pp. 98–99.

14. Pp. 104–107. In a biographical note from the "Publishers" that prefaces *The Homesteader*, Micheaux is described as having written articles for newspapers and magazines.

15. *The Homesteader* (McGrath Publishing Company Reprint, 1969 [1917]), p. 407.

16. *The Chicago Defender*, 10/28/11.

17. Ibid., pp. 400–401. In his novels, he also writes of having lost some land due to marital difficulties.

18. (Lincoln, Nebraska: Western Book Supply Company, 1915), p. 541.

19. 5/7/18, George P. Johnson Collection, UCLA.

20. Noble Johnson to George Johnson, no date (this letter seems to be from the end of May 1918, immediately before George Johnson's 5/31/18 letter to Micheaux), George P.

Johnson Collection, UCLA. The handwritten letter goes on to say, "and as I said before I for myself will not make [indistinguishable] my/any living/thing catering to our people." (Noble did not take any salary from the Lincoln Company.)

21. See, for example, letters 5/13/18, 5/15/18, 5/31/18, and 6/25/18, George P. Johnson Collection, UCLA.

22. In a letter from Micheaux to the Lincoln Motion Picture Company, 6/25/18, George P. Johnson Collection, UCLA; capitalization and punctuation thus in original. Micheaux certainly was cognizant of the public attention brought to the interracial marriage of the champion boxer Jack Johnson and the government's attempt to legally entrap him.

23. Letters to Clarence A. Brooks, 8/11/18 and 8/13/18, George P. Johnson Collection, UCLA. The stock offering budgeted $15,000 for the total cost of the film, including four prints, overhead, and advertising lithos.

24. Vendome Theater, *The Chicago Defender*, 3/1/19.

25. "Where the Negro Fails," *The Chicago Defender*, 3/19/10.

26. Nell Irvin Painter's *Exodusters: Black Migration to Kansas after Reconstruction* is a study of one such group of homesteaders (New York: W.W. Norton, 1992). Micheaux's own family had migrated West from Southern Illinois to Kansas, and later, Colorado and California (interview with Verna Crowe, Micheaux's niece, Los Angeles, California, 1/29/91).

27. Micheaux used this phrase in *The Homesteader*, p. 25, and, again, in *The Wind from Nowhere* (New York: Book Supply Company, 1943), p. 133.

28. Interview, Jackson, Mississippi, 6/18/93; Mr. Henry worked at Race theaters in Jackson from 1919 to 1977 and trained several other African American operators.

29. *The Chicago Defender*, 11/20/20.

30. *Afro-American*, 12/31/20.

31. *Whip*, 1/15/21.

32. Unsigned, *The New York Age*, 12/25/20.

33. See the authors' presentations, "'I may be crazy, but I ain't no fool': The Strategic Use of Stereotypes in Oscar Micheaux's *Within Our Gate*," at the Modern Language Association, San Diego, December 1994, and the revised and expanded version at the Society of Cinema Studies Conference, New York, March 1995.

34. Eph is a peripheral character, living on the edges of both Black and White society. He is never shown in the same space or frame with other Blacks.

35. This is interesting in contrast to the mulattos in C. W. Chesnutt's works, characters who continue to have ties to the community (in, for example, the short story, "The Wife of His Youth" in *The Wife of His Youth and Other Stories of the Color Line* [Boston: Houghton, Mifflin and Company, 1899]) or who have affection for and the support of their family, even though they are bitterly missed (*The House Behind the Cedars* [Boston: Houghton, Mifflin and Company, 1900]).

36. Pp. 153–154.

37. P. 147. Italics and capitalization thus in original.

38. Script, The Motion Picture Commission of the State of New York, New York State Archives, Albany, New York.

39. South Dakota did not have an anti-miscegination law until 1909.

40. Bernard L. Peterson, Jr., *Early Black American Playwrights and Dramatic Writers: A Biographical Directory and Catalogue of Plays, Films, and Broadcasting Scripts* (Westport,

Connecticut: Greenwood Press, 1990), p. 139. According to Peterson, the story is based on *The Racial Triangle* by Henry Francis Downing.

41. See Jane Tompkins's "Sentimental Power: *Uncle Tom's Cabin* and the Politics of Literary History," in *The New Feminist Criticism: Essays on Women, Literature and Theory*, Elaine Showalter, ed. (New York: Pantheon, 1985), p. 85.

42. *Playing in the Dark: Whiteness and the Literary Imagination*. (Cambridge, Massachusetts: Harvard University Press, 1992), p. 52.

43. Houston A. Baker, Jr., *Modernism and the Harlem Renaissance* (Chicago: University of Chicago Press, 1987), p. 33.

44. *Within Our Gates*, for example, was advertised as "the most sensational story of the race question since Uncle Tom's Cabin." He described *Birthright* as "a grim, gripping story of Negro life in the South today, more crowded with action, thrills, romance, comedy and suspense than any story on this subject since *Uncle Tom's Cabin*." His 1947 novelization of *Veiled Aristocrats* and *The House Behind the Cedars*, *The Masquerade* (New York: Book Supply Company) opens with a reference to Stowe's book.

45. *World's Work*, November 1910, reprinted in Herbert Aptheker's *A Documentary History of the Negro People in the United States, 1910–1932*. (New York: Citadel Press, 1973), pp. 3–15.

46. A portrait of Washington also appears on the wall of Eve's grandfather's frontier cabin in *The Symbol of the Unconquered*.

47. P. 147.

48. P. 145.

49. P. 48.

50. "The Negro Artist and the Racial Mountain," *The Nation*, 6/23/26.

51. *The New Negro: An Interpretation*. (New York: A. and C. Boni, 1925), p. 12.

52. Pp. 160–162. However, in what appears to be a contradiction, the Black romantic lead, in order to meet the demands of melodrama, must be blind to the race of his beloved until the moment of utopian revelation. A review of the film in *The New York Age* (1/1/21) noted, "As in nine cases out of ten Negroes instinctively recognize one of their own, some are apt to wonder why he did not learn the truth sooner. However, the raising of such a point does not in anyway detract form the general excellence of the picture."

53. Boxer Jack Johnson's defeat of his White opponent broke a social taboo of the period, and films of his bouts were banned from interstate commerce. See Dan Streible's "A History of the Boxing Film, 1894–1915: Social Control and Social Reform in the Progressive Era," *Film History* 3, no. 3 (1989).

54. *The Conquest*, p. 162.

55. *The Devil Finds Work* (New York: Dell, 1990), p. 93.

56. January–February 1921.

57. Quoted in *The New York Age*, 10/16/09.

58. New York State Archives; script copyrighted 1937. There exists no record of the determination of the Motion Picture Commission of the State of New York; however, this scene does not exist in the print currently in circulation. The author's preface to the script declares that "all the characters appearing herein, regardless how bright in color they may seem, are members of the Negro Race." In a film that deals with the sensitive subject of an interracial marriage, Micheaux seems to be assuring the censors, and perhaps even his distributors, that the cast is all Black.

59. See, for one example, the front page of the *The New York Age*, 8/21/13. In one article, "Can't Tell Who's Who: Denver Authorities Think Woman Married to Coal Black Negro is White," Mrs. Nora Harrington Frazier offers samples of her blood to prove that she is Black. The article also discusses several tests that the woman submitted to in order to convince the marriage licence bureau clerk to give her a licence, including looking for dark blotches at the root of her hair and pressing her finger nails. Just below that notice is a piece "Gives up all for Negro: Pretty Daughter of Wealthy White Farmer Marries Samuel De Frees Against the Wishes of Her Parents" about a Ringwood, New Jersey, couple.

60. *Charles Waddell Chesnutt: Pioneer of the Color Line* (Chapel Hill: University of North Carolina Press, 1952), p. 274.

61. 4/22/09.

62. *The New York Age*, 5/1/13. The theatre, near a neighborhood known as San Juan Hill, catered to the residents of the vicinity, both Black and White.

63. [Norfolk] *Journal and Guide*, 11/28/15. During the proceedings, Mrs. Rhinelander was asked to bare her back to the jury, so that they could tell how dark her skin was.

64. See, for example, "The Parallel of the Rhinelander Case" (*Amsterdam News*, 3/4/25).

65. *Bond and Beyond: The Political Career of a Popular Hero* (London: Methuen, 1987), pp. 90–91.

66. See Theophilus Lewis, *The New York Age*, 4/16/30, for example. Speaking of *Daughter of the Congo*, Lewis accused Micheaux of associating "nobility with lightness and villainy with blackness."

67. Richard Grupenhoff in *The Black Valentino: The Stage and Screen Career of Lorenzo Tucker* (Metutchen, N.J.: Scarecrow Press, 1988, pp. 61–81) discusses Tucker playing both romantic leads and gangsters in Micheaux's films.

68. Interview, 10/18/71, Julius Lester's *Free Time* (PBS). Mahon was a New York City school teacher with good diction, but no dramatic training.

69. Since the only extant print is 3,852 feet (the Museum of Modern Art print), a little more than half of the 7 reels advertised in 1920, it is difficult to determine exactly how Micheaux developed much of the story, characters, and themes.

70. Quoted in *The Competitor*, Jan.–Feb. 1921, p. 61. Micheaux's thoughts here seem similar to Washington's: "Every persecuted individual and race should get much consolation out of the great human law, which is universal and eternal, that merit, no matter under what skin found, is in the long run, recognized and rewarded." *Up From Slavery: An Autobiography* (Garden City, New York: Doubleday, 1963 [1901]), p. 29.

71. The name seems to have been borrowed from or an homage to Jack London's 1909 semi-autobiography, *Martin Eden*; Micheaux also used the title of Gertrude Sanborn's 1923 novel, *Veiled Aristocrats*, for his sound remake of C. W. Chesnutt's *The House Behind the Cedars*.

72. Script, New York State Archive.

73. See, for example, Joseph A. Young's *Black Novelist as White Racist: The Myth of Black Inferiority in the Novels of Oscar Micheaux*. (Westport, Connecticut: Greenwood Press, 1989). J. Ronald Green and Horace Neal, Jr.'s "Oscar Micheaux and Racial Slur: A Response to 'The Rediscovery of Oscar Micheaux" (*Journal of Film and Video* 40, no. 4 [Fall 1988]) raises questions on how Micheaux used racial stereotypes and "slurs" and their effects. Jane Gaines discusses the debate over Micheaux's class position and

Race hatred in "Fire and Desire: Race, Melodrama, and Oscar Micheaux," in *Black Cinema: History, Theory, Criticism*, Manthia Diawara, ed. (New York: Routledge and Chapman, Hall/American Film Institute, 1993).

74. "Micheaux: Celebrating Blackness," in *Black Looks: Race and Representation*. (Boston: South End Press, 1992), p. 133.

75. *The Story of Dorothy Stanfield* (New York: Book Supply Company, 1946), p. 85.

76. The script submitted to The Motion Picture Commission of the State of New York indicates that her husband sees her reaction and begins to suspect that she has been passing. He grabs her and says, "Let me look straight into your eyes. That's where I've been seeing something that I could never understand; but I'm going to now, so stand still woman and let me look into those eyes. So that's it. That's what I have been seeing all the time, and could never understand. You have got a streak. . . ." Although this scene is not in the print currently in distribution, it is in one of the trailers. It is interesting that Micheaux used the controversal out-takes for the trailer. Was this a question of economy? His taste for promotion by the use of controversy? Or perhaps a way to give his audience important information that is not going to make it to the film?

77. P. 77. This idea is developed further in the utopian ending of Micheaux's novel *The Wind From Nowhere*, pp. 422–423. However, whereas Washington found hope in the South, Micheaux saw fresher prospects in the Northern Great Plains (which he refers to as the Great Northwest).

78. *The Conquest*, p. 47.

79. Pp. 98–99; Micheaux's fictional Little Crow is the Rosebud Reservation and Calais, Dallas, S. D.

80. His somewhat outdated ideas offended some of his audience. The film was protested in New York and Boston, as Beatrice Goodloe of the Young Communist League explained, "because it slandered Negroes, holding them up to ridicule" and set "light-skinned Negroes against their darker brothers." See Clyde Taylor's "Crossed Over and Can't Get Black," *Black Film Review* 7, no. 4 (1993): p. 25.

81. Pp. 160–161.

82. 1/28/40.

83. A Tom Mix film with the same name opened in July 1919.

Donald Kirihara

THE ACCEPTED IDEA DISPLACED
Stereotype and Sessue Hayakawa

There is nothing more difficult to eradicate than the obvious.
—*Ruth Amossy*[1]

Sessue Hayakawa is probably best known for his role as the Japanese prison camp commandant in *The Bridge on the River Kwai* (1957), for which he earned an Academy Award nomination. In recent years, film scholars have noted Hayakawa's contribution to the modernity of *The Cheat* (1915). In many ways, these two films make his reputation today, but in a manner somewhat different from how they made his reputation in 1957 and 1915. Today he is largely remembered as a villain: handsome, violent, inscrutable, and a figure whose power is secured through his position or his money.[2]

But Hayakawa's earlier silent film career, particularly from 1914 to 1918, challenges this image in several respects. Despite his modern reputation as an "Oriental" actor limited by the roles and characterizations offered to him, Hayakawa's silent career is a surprisingly varied and somewhat contradictory one. The success of *The Cheat* and the critical praise of his performance in that film gave Hayakawa the opportunity to play a series of romantic leads in melodramas produced by the Jesse L. Lasky studios from 1916 to 1918. In some of these films he woos the woman he loves, and some of these women are white. In some of these films he batters, rapes, and attempts to kill the woman he covets, and some of these women are white. In all of these films he is clearly marked as a foreigner, although in many that foreignness is seen as the basis not of the character's inferiority, but of his dilemma.

What I wish to suggest in this essay is that Hayakawa's early popularity is built upon the ability to exploit this contradictory image in his films, helped by his distinctive performance style and by the development of a classical narrational mode that used stereotypes in specific ways. I also wish to suggest that one reason why Hayakawa's characterizations seem to rise above the stock caricatures of the time is their deployment of and sensitivity toward cultural mediations in ways that displace stereotypic reduction.

This is not to say that Hayakawa's roles overcame stereotypes. My point is that his career is built around popular commonplaces about race and ethnicity. It is worth noting here that the period under review, 1914 to 1918, is within an era when there was growing suspicion toward the collective categorizations and alienating potential that stereotypes represent.[3] It was not until 1922, after the release of most of the films that I examine here, that Walter Lippmann provided a crystallization of the term that recognized both its cognitive (as a way to quickly sift through a mass of data) and naturalizing (to legitimate the status quo) functions; "pictures in our heads" is what Lippmann called them.[4]

Although most recent studies of stereotypes in film have either attempted to construct a typology of images or focused upon stereotypes as ideological phenomena,[5] I am less interested in the interpretations of stereotypes here than in their involvement and function in a narrational process and their usefulness as cultural norms. A stereotype is at once a collection of recognizable traits useful to the plot and dependent upon the relativity of the viewer's previous knowledge. As collections of recognizable traits we can examine stereotypes in terms of their functions: How do they participate in the elaboration of narration as a process, or in the revision—or defamiliarization—of the commonplace? How are they part of the activity between film and viewer? What role do they play in the strategies of narration and viewing? All the above questions assume that the stereotype cannot be "fixed" in an ahistorical zone, for not only will each period define its own stereotypes, but it will also offer tactics for their unveiling.

The stereotype, as Ruth Amossy puts it, "is necessarily reductive. . . . This does not, however, mean that it is always involved in reductive enterprises or that it is only used for purposes of schematization. The value of the stereotype depends on the role it plays in the strategies of text and reading: it cannot be fixed once and for all."[6] Hayakawa's films participate in a narration of hope and fear that works to problematize the patterns that we associate with stereotypes. The films do so partly by seeking to revise the patterns themselves, at a transitional point in the development of classical narration. Many of his films were about prejudice, discrimination, miscegenation, and acculturation, told within a framework that asks the viewer to accommodate the actions within existing societal norms. His characters were not limited to villains or stoic eunuchs or martyrs who never found love at the end of the story. His films, characterizations, and reputation are cogent instances of how stereotypes operate, as Joep Leerseen puts it, in the overlapping area between the spheres of the formal conventions of texts and the social conventions of that text's audience.[7]

It is in the interaction of viewer and film in narration that the stereotype is granted its scope as well as its limits, and Hayakawa's films exhibit a tendency to problematize the prefabricated patterns that we associate with stereotypes.[8] For all the reasons above, Hayakawa makes an interesting study in this period, positioned as he is in the midst of a dynamic affecting performance, racial representation, and classical narration, all of which were changing in fundamental ways.

I wish to briefly suggest how we might reconstruct the circumstances in which Hayakawa's work was produced and seen, and in doing so not only review some films which are, I think, quite underrated in their handling of social themes, but also review the importance of commonplace stereotypes for their implications in the functions of character in early classical film and the representation of race in those films. I am mainly interested here in Hayakawa's work from 1914 to 1918, when he worked for the Ince and Lasky studios.

Mediating the Image of the Yellow Peril

In our eagerness to condemn the stereotypes, we may find in old films it is easy to overlook the fact that our stereotypes today may not have been those of eighty years ago. Accepted ideas about individuals, groups, or institutions may quickly fade from the scene or mutate into a variant that is distinct from the original. Although Hayakawa presents a figure that initially seems an anomaly—an early film star whose ethnicity is undeniable in a period of growing nativism—the contradictions may be explained by examining some of the relevant discourses of his age. Jan Mukařovský proposed that we can study personality as a component of artistic development, but only as a figure that appears when everything has been "prepared for a turn."[9] How is the stage set for Hayakawa's appearance in 1914?

It can be said that the "orient" did not lack for topicality in the 1910s. The efforts around the turn of the century to deny Chinese and Japanese immigrants equal protection under American laws and eventually to prevent their legal entry and citizenship entirely has been well documented, and only a brief overview is necessary here.[10] After allowing the organized immigration of Chinese laborers in the 1860s and 1870s to speed western expansion, the U.S. government faced demands to limit immigration in order to prevent the further growth of the Chinese population, a group that many advocates of such legislation considered unassimilable with Anglo cultures. In 1882, Congress passed an immigration law effectively barring the entry of Chinese to the United States. From the 1890s to the early 1900s, Japanese immigration increased, again in response to demands for low wage laborers, and again highly organized by foreign and American entrepreneurs. Agitation against this wave of immigrants grew, peaking in 1906 when, in response to the Japanese government's protest of a segregated school for Chinese, Japanese, and Korean children in San Francisco, President Theodore Roosevelt negotiated a "gentleman's agreement" limiting Japanese emigration to the United States. The urgency of a diplomatic settlement was dictated by the international stature Japan had attained in its battlefield victories over China (in 1895) and Russia (in 1905). After Roosevelt's intervention, speculation of a Pacific war between Japan and the United States flourished in books and venues such as the Hearst newspapers.

Because it seems to dominate Americans' consciousness of the Pacific in this period, it is tempting to typify American attitudes toward Japanese in the first decade of the twentieth century in terms of a "yellow peril." The subject's literature—predicting imminent conflict between East and West—focused popular interest on Asia and Asian immigration at several levels, and also formed an obvious background for filmmakers to exploit. But here some care must be taken not to exaggerate its impact or its usefulness for filmmakers. Gregory Waller has indicated how what he calls "Japan films" were made in significant numbers before World War I (his period of study is 1909–1915), spurred by this interest in Japan's military successes and by the anti-Japanese incidents on the West Coast.[11] But Waller also observes that the more sensational examples of this discourse—that is, outright xenophobia—formed only a minor part of film productions. The worst excesses of xenophobia were likely mediated by the commercial needs of the film industry at this time. Not only were American filmmakers in this period increasingly seeking a wider audience for their product, but a more upscale one as well.[12]

Instead, Waller notes the variety of uses that were made of Japanese imagery. Nonfictional forms stressed the quaintness of a culture "out there"—a land of pagodas, kimono, and cherry blossoms, seemingly disconnected with the belligerent Japan of newspaper headlines. These scenics contributed to the special place that Japan held in American culture in the late nineteenth century, expressed, as Neil Harris puts it, in Japanese culture's "tension between the pull of modernization and the antiquity of native traditions."[13] Writers and filmmakers could mine from these films—as well as other opportunities for spectacle such as international expositions—images that became the commonplace version of what Japan must be like. Thus, one reviewer of the two-reel drama *The Courtship of O San* (1914) could compliment the film for meeting an existing standard of verisimilitude: "There is enough real Japanese atmosphere in the sets to keep up the illusion and this is heightened by the typical Japanese ceremonies, tea drinking, formal calling, at weddings and the like, with all of which the average spectator has become familiar from tropical pictures of Japan."[14]

The genre that dominated fictional films, on the other hand, was melodrama. A great influence was undoubtedly the success of *Madame Butterfly*, an 1898 short story by John Luther Long, a 1900 New York stage production by David Belasco, a Puccini opera in 1904, and a Mary Pickford film in 1915.[15] This story of an American officer who loves and abandons a native during his stationing in Japan is crossed by so many possible lines of conflict and exploitation (gender, class, ethnic, and imperialist, to name a few), that it could be repeated again and again in many different forms with only slight changes in emphasis.

But besides offering a template for innumerable future plots, *Madame Butterfly* also offers strategies in which the yellow peril may be mediated in art. Here again, the richness of the text offers many interpretations, but one component of *Madame Butterfly* worth consideration is what James Moy calls the "death of Asia" on stage, or "the rather troubling tendency for Asians (both female and male) to find death on the American field of representation" a tendency that he links to Western colonialist activity toward the end of the nineteenth century.[16] It is not just death that this gesture seeks, but the death of mystified figures worthy of it: selfless actions by individuals, martyrdom for a cause, and the irreconcilable differences between "east" and "west." Indeed, the death of Asia serves as a continuing motif in serious portrayals of the East in Western culture of the early twentieth century and frames in important ways how Hayakawa enters the popular consciousness. His first feature appearance came with *The Typhoon*, a 1914 film produced by Thomas Ince, in a role originally performed on the New York stage by a white actor.[17]

The play on which *The Typhoon* is based exploits the expectation that non-Western culture is something worth dying for. Written by the Hungarian playwright Menyhért Lengyel, it was staged in New York in March 1912, and ran for ninety-six performances. The play follows a Japanese man of letters who goes to Europe to write a book on European civilization to aid Japan's Westernization (referencing a phenomenon of the time: Japanese sent abroad to study Western industry and culture). The stage version contrasts the scholar's personality with that of his undisciplined white lover. Present in the play, as one writer puts it, are the "popularly recognized Oriental mannerisms, such as the repression of emotions, excessive politeness, secretiveness, and a suppression of individual inclinations for the good of the state."[18] The scholar strangles her in the second of three acts, leaving most of the play to depict the man's disintegration as he is torn between duty to country and what is presented as the tainted individualism of the West. At the end, patronized by his countrymen and unable to live with the murder, he commits suicide.

Changes in the film version retain the irreconcilability between East and West while they underplay the theme of the West's corrupting influence on the Japanese. Instead of opening *in medias res*, for instance on the murder, and then reconstructing the events leading up to the crime (a strategy followed by the American novelization of the play, published in 1912),[19] the film adds a long prologue set in Japan, focusing on the student émigré who will later accept blame for the murder. The added prologue delays the introduction of the protagonist, using the film's initial scenes to set up the basis for cultural differences rather than an individual's personal trauma. The mise-en-scène also helps to underscore the foreignness of the culture in these initial scenes. For instance, as the student embarks on his journey to the United States, he and his sponsors walk through a carefully sculpted garden to a waiting rickshaw (Figures 1 and 2). The framing of the shot emphasizes the garden, not the figures walking through it, referencing the scenic films of Japan and deferring interest in the individuals to interest in the cultural accoutrements associated with a quaint Japan. In addition, the film changes the scholar to a chargé d'affaires working on a military report to better capitalize on American fears in 1915 of a belligerent Japan in the Pacific and to motivate the protagonist's interests in a narrower fashion. Finally, the film's long trial scene (in the original play but eliminated in the New York stage version) not only offers the opportunity for spectacle but also directs attention to the suspense surrounding the verdict while it diverts the narration from the conflict within the murderer.

These choices are not indicative of some white conspiracy, but are consistent with the narrational tendencies of films during the transitional period between "primitive" and "classical" style—roughly 1913 to 1917—when the creation of individualized characters was one choice

Figs. 1 and 2: The Typhoon (courtesy of George Eastman House).

in unifying the feature-length film.[20] Rather than moving in the direction of greater character subjectivity invited by the play's tormented protagonist—a "classical" choice—the film's makers instead chose to move toward the greater schematization offered by an East-West dichotomy. Thus, intercultural (or intracultural) contradictions in the film are subsumed under a single dominating impression, what Vachel Lindsay called "patriotic splendor," in which the drama of an individual becomes the drama of a type. The diplomat is a loyal bureaucrat when introduced, when he kills, and when he dies, and there is a consistency in his characterization that Lindsay calls attention to: "The one impression of the play is that Japanese patriotism is a peculiar and fearful thing."[21]

The initial impressions of what it means to be Japanese in the stage version of *The Typhoon* are challenged by events of the play's unfolding, so that the Japanese scholar must reflect at the end—of his life and of the play—upon what it means to be Japanese in a foreign culture. But in the film, the relative poverty of detail at the outset, the repetition of the patriotic pattern through the film, and the downplaying of traits that seriously challenge the initial characterization work to fix the character in place, and the overall effect is a static one.

Still, the death of Asia was but one familiar pattern that could be utilized by film stories, and in some ways it was an awkward (as indicated in the efforts to motivate the protagonist's suicide in the film version of *The Typhoon*) and excessively morbid alternative to staging ethnic allegiances. Other storylines were available as well which allowed race to enter in a variety of guises. For example, Amy Ling has recorded the remarkable popularity of Winnifred Eaton's romance novels published from 1901 to 1916. Writing under the pseudonym Onoto Watanna, she crafted stories set in Japan, with Japanese or Eurasian heroines. Formulaic and commercial by her own admission, Eaton's novels constitute models of narrative economy and bourgeois ideology coveted by the developing classical cinema of the time:

> all have the same narrative structure and form: they are invariably short works that can be read easily; they are escapist in plot and exotic in setting; they prolong the separation and estrangement between two potential lovers; and they end happily. Following the meeting of girl and boy there is an initial obstacle to love: a difference in class, a previous engagement, opposing families, parties, or religions. The initial obstacle overcome, love develops only to be met by another obstacle: war, meddling third parties, misunderstanding, duty elsewhere. This second obstacle is followed by prolonged separation during which both lovers suffer either mental anguish or physical hardship and illness. Finally, with the aid of mutual friends, with the passage of time, by chance and by fate, the lovers are reunited at the novel's end.[22]

Although Eaton's novels frequently incorporated miscegenationist storylines—usually between a Japanese or Eurasian woman and a Western man—they form a significant alternative to the pathos of *Madame Butterfly*. In their "stairstep" structure of obstacles overcome to reach a goal, their character-centered narrative catalysts and final closure, and their dependence upon psychological motivation, her novels seem much more conducive to the developing needs of classical cinema. One novel, *A Japanese Nightingale*, was produced onstage in 1903 and as a film in 1918, but plotlines and devices similar to those found in Eaton's stories made their way into such Hayakawa vehicles as *Alien Souls* (1916) and *The Honorable Friend* (1916).

Another mediation of the yellow peril originated in the response of some groups that opposed anti-immigrant agitation of the period. John Modell has chronicled how the cohesive, well-organized Japanese-American community in California sided with the Japanese government and what he terms "a prestigious group of white Japanophiles: churchmen, educators, and international businessmen" to counter discrimination during the 1910s.[23] They presented an image of an accommodating ethnic group—hard-working, self-censoring, and willing to settle for defined niches in the economy (like produce growing and marketing). The accommodationist strategies pursued by these groups persisted through World War I and the nativist debates of the postwar period.

A literary offshoot of this accommodationist thinking was Wallace Irwin's *Letters of a Japanese Schoolboy*, originally serialized in *Collier's* and published in book form in 1909, followed by sequels in 1913 and 1914. The ethnic humor surrounding Irwin's character, Hashimura Togo, portrays a figure struggling to remake his image in an unfamiliar culture while earnestly looking for work to survive. The situation offered ample opportunity to satirize not only popular attitudes toward immigrants but also the self-interested nature of xenophobia. Of the yellow peril Togo opins: "I have given some brain-study to this Yellow Peril to make sure it is a bad blessing for these Uniteds State. It is. But should we Americans of all-colour enjoy fear of such? Answer is, No! Coreans, Chinese, & Hindus is Yellow Peril. All Japanese can defeat these easily with club-stick. We have been there to try it."[24] Overall, the portrait of Togo is not unsympathetic, simultaneously conveying the sense of wonder and loss of a new immigrant. As Modell puts it, "A sense of melancholy, of the cost of eagerness thwarted, and of human dignity challenged is present beneath the buffoonery required by the literary conventions of a racial stereotype."[25]

Irwin's writings furnished not only the mannerisms, but also the goals for many of Hayakawa's characters in the mid- to late-1910s (and the actor even starred in a movie version of Irwin's writings in 1917 entitled *Hashimura Togo*). His characters could be more fully clothed with motives and desires, as immigrants who work hard toward objectives of acceptance and acculturation in the new land, and as emigrants who work to dignify the traditions of their past and justify the flight from their homeland. A model like Hashimura Togo, even as it used pidgin English and circular logic as the basis for much of its humor, also offered

Fig. 3: Production still from *The Bravest Way* (courtesy of the Academy of Motion Picture Arts and Sciences).

characteristics of earnestness and cleverness, and a nostalgia for the past. These were all useable narrational goals that could define a character quickly and drive him across a feature-length film, and they were also material that could be used to challenge the poverty of previous stereotypes.

Several of Hayakawa's films made at the Lasky studio forward characters in keeping with accommodationist behavior and goals. For instance, in *The Bravest Way*, Hayakawa's immigrant aspires to be a professional landscape gardener in America (one of the few professions open to Japanese at the time) and marry the woman he loves, a "half-caste" Japanese-American kindergarten teacher (played by Florence Vidor). Through hard work and selfless actions his aspirations are fulfilled by the end of the film. The scenario's epilogue, left out of the eventual film, would have provided a visualization of the American Dream: a dissolve from a sketch of the immigrant's dream home to the completed home, with father, mother, and three adopted Japanese children on the porch (Figure 3).[26]

Accommodationist assumptions like those used in Irwin's stories help us understand some of the continuities in Hayakawa's silent film career: what differentiated his appeal from that of other actors and how his characterizations often urged nuance and subtlety on existing stereotypes. Like the death of Asia and "Onoto Watanna's" picturesque romances, accommodationist narratives provide the background against which Hayakawa's characterizations were seen and the materials from which those characterizations were drawn. They indicate some of the ways that the discourse on the yellow peril was mediated by the popular art of the period. But there remains for consideration the impact that Hayakawa had on these developments. What comes from his appearance, when things are prepared for a turn?

A Melancholy Threat

> *Hayakawa dominates the crowd through his melancholy. . . . It is not his cat-like, implacable cruelty, his mysterious brutality, his hatred of anyone who resists, or his contempt for anyone who submits; that is not what impresses us, and yet that is all we can talk about.*
>
> —*Louis Delluc*[27]

Although today there is a tendency to think that Hayakawa only had recourse to villainous roles due to a myopic overemphasis on *The Cheat*, Hayakawa seldom played the incarnation of the yellow peril in his silent career. Delluc's comments—on Hayakawa's performance in *Alien Souls* (1916)—refer to the actor's ability to elicit sympathy in a stereotypic role or situation. Part of this certainly involves Hayakawa's skill in the developing art of film performance. But here I would like to examine how stardom and narrational strategies—two other important components of film acting—contributed to his reception and how the cultural norms I have already discussed were interwoven into this process.

The fact that Hayakawa had a variety of roles in his development as a leading man should not be too surprising. One reason for this was the nature of the star system as it developed in the motion picture industry after 1908. Charles Musser has observed that viewers quickly came to appreciate stars who could play a wide range of roles, including diverse ethnic roles, in a period when many immigrant audience members were themselves undergoing daily trials in forging new identities.[28] Thus, Hayakawa's early feature roles at Lasky from 1915 to 1918 encompassed a range of characterizations, from the sadistically brutal authority (*The Cheat*, *The Jaguar's Claws* [1917]), to the accommodating immigrant (*The Honorable Friend* [1916], *Forbidden Paths* [1917], *The Bravest Way* [1918]), to the temporary foreign student or worker who intends to return home (*Hashimura Togo* [1917], *The City of Dim Faces* [1918]), to the native defending Western encroachments upon his homeland (*The Call of the East* [1917], *The White Man's Law* [1918], *Hidden Pearls* [1918]). Hayakawa also portrayed a variety of ethnic and racial types: Japanese, Chinese, Mexican, Asian Indian, and Arab. While modern observers may view this as an example of how limited Hayakawa's opportunities were, it indicates the diversity of non-villainous leading roles open to the actor and a foundation for Hayakawa's reputation as a versatile and accomplished film actor.

The star system also aided in the narrational process as feature-length narratives began to dominate film production after 1915. Stardom offered a set of traits associated with an actor that could be carried over from one film to the next, creating opportunities for scenarists to better unify their stories and to motivate action more efficiently.[29] This "star personality" represents a transtextual discourse that viewers may draw upon in their engagement with the narrational process of an individual film. But the star system as it developed simultaneously with Hayakawa's popularity after 1914 also demanded that he move Asian stereotypes beyond their frozen state in order to gain attention and develop his career. Like other actors, had Hayakawa been no more than a victim of a stereotype, had he not been able to differentiate himself from the simplicity of an accepted idea, he likely would not have enjoyed the success that he did.

The traits that Hayakawa's stardom was founded upon drew from many of the mediations on the yellow peril that I have already described. The most distinctive quality has been described by Gaylyn Studlar as a "combination of refinement with the dangerous or 'barbaric,'" and where it erupts most spectacularly is in the romantic byplay between Hayakawa's character and a (usually white) woman.[30]

The best-known example of this is of course Hayakawa's characterization of a wealthy Japanese trader in *The Cheat* (1915), but *The Typhoon* (1914) predates that film in several senses. The most sensational scene in *The Typhoon* occurs when the Japanese chargé has spurned his French lover and she begs his forgiveness. He momentarily weakens, tempted to forsake his principles and return to her arms. But she turns and repudiates him, berating and insulting him (title: "I am going back to Bernisky and laugh with him at you—you whining yellow rat—and at your Japan, a dirty yellow blot upon the face of the earth."). Enraged (Figure 4), he strangles her. The film provides the visualization of a refined diplomat transformed into an unthinking monster. But earlier, the novelization (published in 1912) provided detailed direction on how to stage the scene:

> Gone was the carefully taught self-control of generations! Gone was the thin varnish of culture that hid the fighting, yellow savage of the Pacific! The long schooled features were twisted into a horrible grimace of anguish and rage. The dark eyes flamed with a maniacal fire. He crouched forward like a beast about to spring. His strong fingers were crooked like the talons of a carrion bird and his breath escaped through the clenched teeth with a hissing, rattling sound.[31]

There is one other aspect added in the scene worth noting for its contribution to the character's monstrousness and as another indication of *The Typhoon*'s transitional status in this pre-classical period. The scene is intercut with shots of the chargé's Japanese colleagues, laughing in an office far from the couple (Figure 5). This is not an innovative device; Tom Gunning notes that a "contrast" pattern of editing like the comparison between the Wheat King and the poor in *A Corner in Wheat* (1909) and other Griffith Biographs was a convention well before 1914.[32] It is also set up earlier in *The Typhoon* through parallel editing implying simultaneity between the chargé and the woman dallying and the colleagues discussing his dissipation (Figures 6 and 7). I note the cutaway to the laughing men here as a moment of self-conscious omniscience that undercuts the individual's torment (for it is not presented as an interior "fantasy" or similar point-of-view device), substituting instead a "chorus effect," commenting upon the drama and restating the irreconcilability of East and West that is the film's center. It seems, again, an "unclassical" choice in this transitional film, and one which reinforces the stereotypical nature of the chargé's barbarism.

The image of a thin veil of civility shrouding the menacing beast would remain part of Hayakawa's star personality throughout his career. But this characteristic is not enough to explain Hayakawa's impression upon observers like Delluc. The "melancholy" that he cites refers to more than the suave intimidation Hayakawa's characters carry through a film. Indeed, Hayakawa's "type" as it develops at the Lasky studio retains the combination of refinement and barbarism while it integrates other characteristics drawn from accommodationist narratives like *Letters of a Japanese Schoolboy* and miscegenationist romances like those of

Figs. 4 and 5: The Typhoon (courtesy of George Eastman House).

Winnifred Eaton. The later films amplify the notion of a figure caught between cultures—usually but not always signified as races. This is one motivation for much of the action in *The Typhoon*, although as we have seen, the contradictions of that situation are largely undercut by the film's "patriotic splendor." Also, increasingly after *The Cheat* romance usually serves as the test of this accommodationist quandary.

Thus, in *The Call of the East* (1917), Hayakawa plays a Japanese noble in Japan who falls in love with a woman that he (and she) believes is white. However, unlike *The Typhoon, The Call of the East* demonstrates a more facile hierarchy of knowledge in order to reconcile disparate cultures. Although the characters believe East is East and West is West, the viewer knows otherwise, because in the first scene of the film it is revealed that her mother was actually Japanese, although this has been kept from her. The melodramatic force of the narration depends upon

Figs. 6 and 7: The Typhoon (courtesy of George Eastman House).

waiting for the lovers to find out what we already know. In this way the film presents a romance that the characters believe forbidden, but the viewer knows is not. At the end of the film, the "strange attraction" to the Japanese referenced in the film's title is explained to her, and she remains with him. In the last shot of the film, in a remarkable turn-about from the initial scene of secretive shame, the Japanese character wakes to find the woman next to his bed, saying, "I am a woman of your own people—lord!"[33] Here the narration introduces a miscegenationist stereotype of shame and fear at the outset, but in the course of the narrative introduces elements that disrupt its homogeneity. The woman is reluctantly drawn to the handsome and charming Hayakawa character. The narration's omniscience—and the woman's relative lack of knowledgeability—frees the viewer to construct a desirable character that cannot be reconciled with the stereotype's frozen form.

This is somewhat more complex than simply saying that the film reinforces dominant ideology by revealing the woman is not white. It is the narrational process that is of interest here: the development of a classical mode of narration that can sustain viewer interest through informational gaps, delays, and reversals.[34] This is also not to say that these miscegenationist narratives present characters who change in a fundamental way or that the traits of the Hayakawa character in *The Call of the East* are universally positive (indeed, the refined barbarism of Hayakawa's star personality continues in this film). Classical narration provides characters with traits and goals, but the traits are organized toward the goals and seldom reverse or contradict themselves. Rather, the narration of *The Call of the East* reveals or conceals traits as they become necessary to motivate a move in the story or a realistic effect. The repetition of those traits across several films helped to build a "personality" for Hayakawa that formed a basis for viewer expectations.

The personality that Hayakawa would most stress after leaving the Lasky studio in 1918 combined these qualities into the figure of a man caught between two cultures, attempting to act out an accommodationist ethic through occasionally violent means. In doing so, the actor participated in the process of building the expectations—the accepted ideas—that were at the service of the film viewer's stereotypes.

After working at Lasky for three years, Hayakawa established his own production company, Haworth Pictures, in 1918. There, five of the first six productions utilized some variation on the contradictory ties the Japanese characters have with the culture of the homeland and the culture in which they "come of age." In early 1922, Hayakawa suddenly left Hollywood for a film and stage career that would take him to Europe, Japan, and, at the end of the decade, back to Hollywood. Until his death in 1973, he would shuttle between three continents, teaching and performing on stage, in films, and on television, exploiting in various ways the stereotypes that he helped to forge in the 1910s and 1920s in American films.

Notes

For their comments on portions of this essay, I would like to thank the members of my graduate seminar on race and film narration, conducted at The University of Arizona in 1994: Allan Campbell, Betsie Gross, Jay Kirby, Robert Loomis, Ellen Riordan, Robert Ritter, Andrea Rock, and Tani Sanchez. I would also like to thank Angela Record for her library skills. For providing support for some of the work that resulted in this essay, I thank the Vice President for Research at The University of Arizona, Michael Cusanovich.

1. Ruth Amossy, "Commonplace Knowledge and Innovation," *SubStance*, no. 62/63 (1990): 145.

2. On Hayakawa's career, see Stephen Gong, "Zen and the Art of Motion Picture Making," *Bridge* 8, no. 2 (Winter 1982–83): 37–41; DeWitt Bodeen, "Sessue Hayakawa: First International Japanese Film Star," *Films in Review* 27, no. 4 (April 1976): 193–208; Elaine Mancini, "Sessue Hayakawa," *The International Dictionary of Films and Filmmakers*, Vol. 3, *Actors and Actresses*, ed. James Vinson (Chicago: St. James Press, 1986), pp. 295–296.

3. Amossy, "Commonplace Knowledge," pp. 145–148.

4. Walter Lippmann, *Public Opinion* (New York: Macmillan, 1922). For the later implications of this duality for social science and mass media research, see Ellen Seiter, "Stereotypes and the Media: A Re-Evaluation," *Journal of Communication* 36, no. 2 (Spring 1986): 14–26.

5. For the latter, see especially T. E. Perkins, "Rethinking Stereotypes," *Ideology and Cultural Production*, eds. Michele Barrett, et.al. (New York: St. Martin's Press, 1979), pp. 135–159, and Richard Dyer, "Stereotyping," in *Gays and Film*, ed. Richard Dyer (London: BFI Publishing, 1977), pp. 27–39, and "The Role of Stereotypes," in *The Matter of Images: Essays on Representations* (London: Routledge, 1993), pp. 11–18.

6. Ruth Amossy, "Stereotypes and Representation in Fiction," *Poetics Today* 5, no. 4 (1984): 700. See also Ruth Amossy, *Les idées reçues: Sémiologie du stéréotype* (Paris: Nathan, 1991).

7. Joep Leerssen, "Mimesis and Stereotype," in *National Identity: Symbol and Representation*, Yearbook of European Studies no. 4 (Amsterdam: Rodopi, 1991), p. 175.

8. Amossy, "Stereotypes and Representation": 697.

9. Jan Mukařovský, "The Individual and Literary Development," in *The Word and Verbal Art: Selected Essays by Jan Mukařovský*, trans. and ed. John Burbank and Peter Steiner (New Haven: Yale University Press, 1977), p. 170.

10. The standard work on this subject is John Higham, *Strangers in the Land: Patterns of American Nativism, 1860–1925* (New Brunswick, N.J.: Rutgers University Press, 1955). See also Ronald Takagi, *Iron Cages: Race and Culture in Nineteenth-Century America* (New York: Knopf, 1979). On the formation of American attitudes toward Asians at the turn of the century, see Stuart Creighton Miller, *The Unwelcome Immigrant: The American Image of the Chinese, 1785–1882* (Berkeley: University of California Press, 1969); Harold R. Isaacs, *Scratches on Our Minds: American Images of China and India* (New York: John Day Co., 1958), and Akira Iriye, "Japan as a Competitor, 1895–1917," in *Mutual Images: Essays in American-Japanese Relations* (Cambridge: Harvard University Press, 1975), pp. 73–99. On the debate over Japanese immigration after World War I, see Roger Daniels, *The Politics of Prejudice: The Anti-Japanese Movement in California and the Struggle for Japanese Exclusion* (Berkeley: University of California Press, 1962), and Yuji Ichioka, *The Issei: The World of First Generation Japanese Immigrants, 1885–1924* (New York: The Free Press, 1988), pp. 176–254.

11. Gregory Waller, "Historicizing, a Test Case: Japan on American Screens, 1909–1915," unpublished paper. On yellow peril literature, see William F. Wu, *The Yellow Peril: Chinese Americans in American Fiction, 1850–1940* (Hamden Conn.: Archon Books,

1982). On Asian stereotypes in film, see Eugene Franklin Wong, *On Visual Media Racism: Asians in the American Motion Pictures* (New York: Arno, 1978); Richard A. Oehling, "The Yellow Menace: Asian Images in American Film" in *The Kaleidoscopic Lens: How Hollywood Views Ethnic Groups*, ed. Randall M. Miller (Englewood, N.J.: Jerome S. Ozer, 1980), pp. 182–206, and Kevin Brownlow, *Behind the Mask of Innocence* (Berkeley: University of California Press, 1990). On the durability of Asian caricatures in the 1930s and 1940s, see John W. Dower, *War Without Mercy: Race and Power in the Pacific War* (New York: Pantheon, 1986), esp. chapter 7. Although it deals with the longevity of yellow peril imagery in American films from the early silents to the present day, Gina Marchetti's *Romance and the "Yellow Peril": Race, Sex, and Discourse Strategies in Hollywood Fiction* (Berkeley: University of California Press, 1993) focuses exclusively on that imagery as it relates to the depiction of interracial romance. She does acknowledge the existence of other yellow peril scenarios, as well as alternative romances without a yellow peril basis (pp. 1–4).

12. On the materialist strivings of film studios in this period, particularly as they relate to the Lasky studio, see Sumiko Higashi, *Cecil B. DeMille and American Culture: The Silent Era* (Berkeley: University of California Press, 1994).

13. Neil Harris, "All the World a Melting Pot? Japan at American Fairs, 1896–1904," in *Mutual Images*, p. 24.

14. "Comments on the Films" (The Courtship of O San), *Moving Picture World*, 28 Feb. 1914, p. 1090.

15. Kevin Brownlow also notes the influence of the stage production of *East Is West* in 1919. Brownlow, *Behind the Mask*, p. 322. See also Nick Browne's essay on *Madame Butterfly* elsewhere in this collection, and Marchetti, chapter 5.

16. James S. Moy, *Marginal Sights: Staging the Chinese in America* (Iowa City: University of Iowa Press, 1993), pp. 82–94.

17. The actor was Walker Whiteside. "Whiteside to Make Patriotic Picture," *Moving Picture World*, 22 June 1918, p. 1,700.

18. Emro Joseph Gergely, *Hungarian Drama in New York: American Adaptations, 1908–1940* (Philadelphia: University of Pennsylvania Press, 1947), p. 76. The original Hungarian version locates the action in Berlin, but the German, New York, and London versions use Paris. The New York version is three acts, but most of the other versions have four.

19. J. W. McConaughy, *The Typhoon: A Story of New Japan* (New York: H. K. Fly Co., 1912).

20. See Kristin Thompson, "The Formulation of the Classical Narrative," in *The Classical Hollywood Cinema: Film Style and Mode of Production to 1960*, by David Bordwell, Janet Staiger, and Kristin Thompson (New York: Columbia University Press, 1985), pp. 174–183, 189–193.

21. Quoted in Brownlow, *Behind the Mask*, p. 346. The original passage is Vachel Lindsay, *The Art of the Moving Picture* (New York: Liveright, 1970), p. 80. See also Nick Browne, "Orientalism as an Ideological Form: American Film Theory in the Silent Period," *Wide Angle* 11, no. 4 (1989): 23–31.

22. Amy Ling, *Between Worlds: Women Writers of Chinese Ancestry* (New York: Pergammon, 1990), p. 49. See also Amy Ling, "Winnifred Eaton: Ethnic Chameleon and Popular Success," *MELUS* 11, no. 3 (Fall 1984): 5–15. Eaton later worked in Hollywood as a scenarist for Universal.

23. John Modell, *The Economics and Politics of Racial Accommodation: The Japanese of Los Angeles, 1900–1942* (Urbana: University of Illinois Press, 1977), p. 11.

24. Wallace Irwin, *Letters of a Japanese Schoolboy* (London: Hodder & Stoughton, 1909), p. 21.

25. Modell, *Economics*, p. 3.

26. "The Bravest Way" continuity (Folder 191), Paramount Pictures Corporation Collection, Margaret Herrick Library, Academy of Motion Picture Arts and Sciences, Beverly Hills, California.

27. Louis Delluc, "Beauty in the Cinema," quoted in Richard Abel, *French Film Theory and Criticism: A History/Anthology, 1907–1939*, Vol. 1: 1907–1929 (Princeton: Princeton University Press, 1988), p. 139. Originally published as "La Beauté au cinéma," *Le Film* 73 (6 Aug. 1917): 4–5.

28. Charles Musser, "Ethnicity, Role-playing, and American Film Comedy: From *Chinese Laundry Scene* to *Whoopee* (1894–1930)," *Unspeakable Images: Ethnicity and the American Cinema* (Urbana: University of Illinois Press, 1991), pp. 54–55. Critical praise for Hayakawa's versatility resembles in some ways that of his contemporary, Henry Walthall. See Roberta Pearson, *Eloquent Gestures: The Transformation of Performance Style in the Griffith Biograph Films* (Berkeley: University of California Press, 1992), pp. 99–104.

29. See Richard deCordova, *Picture Personalities: The Emergence of the Star System in America* (Urbana: University of Illinois Press, 1990).

30. Gaylyn Studlar, "Valentino, 'Optic Intoxication,' and Dance Madness," in *Screening the Male: Exploring Masculinities in Hollywood Cinema*, eds. Steven Cohan and Ina Rae Hark (London: Routledge, 1993), p. 29, 41.

31. McConaughy, *The Typhoon*, p. 168.

32. Tom Gunning, "Weaving a Narrative: Style and Economic Background in Griffith's Biograph Films," in *Early Cinema: Space, Frame, Narrative*, ed. Thomas Elsaesser and Adam Barker (London: BFI Publishing, 1990), pp. 341–346.

33. "The Call of the East" continuity (Folder 226), Paramount Pictures Corporation Collection.

34. For film narration generally, see David Bordwell, *Narration in the Fiction Film* (Madison: University of Wisconsin Press, 1985).

WHITE NATIONALISM

Daniel Bernardi

THE VOICE OF WHITENESS
D. W. Griffith's Biograph Films (1908–1913)

In order to understand Griffith, one must visualize an America made up of more than visions of speeding automobiles, streamlined trains, racing ticker tape, inexorable conveyor-belts. One is obliged to comprehend this second side of America as well—America, the traditional, the patriarchal, the provincial.

—*Sergei Eisenstein*[1]

Many scholars of D. W. Griffith have focused on the filmmaker's role in the transformation of film into art. While recent revisionist historians downplay Griffith's impact on film history, most nonetheless agree that the filmmaker, though clearly not the inventor of such techniques as the close-up and parallel editing, was an important innovator in the emergence of what came to be known as the Hollywood style. Tom Gunning's recent book, *D. W. Griffith and the Origins of American Narrative Film: The Early Years*, is a thoroughly researched example, as he argues that Griffith was a pioneer in the transformation of early cinema from a system of attractions, or the displaying of film as a curiosity, to a system of narration, or the use of film for storytelling.[2]

In assessing Griffith's role in film history, many scholars have also focused their efforts on the ideologically divisive aspects of the filmmaker's work. Sergei Eisenstein, very much concerned with the rhetoric of Griffith's filmic technique, was one of the first to discuss his "provincial" side when he wrote that "among the most repellent elements in his films (and there are such) we see Griffith as an open apologist for racism, erecting a celluloid monument to the Ku Klux Klan, and joining their attack on Negroes in *The Birth of a Nation*."[3] More recently, Thomas Cripps, Robert Lang, Julia Lesage, Michael Rogin, Clyde Taylor, among others, have followed Eisenstein's lead and centered their investigations on the racist practices found in Griffith's work.[4] These scholars usually concentrate on the filmmaker's post-Biograph films, with special emphasis given to *The Birth of a Nation* (1915) and *Broken Blossoms* (1919), films in which the meaning of race—or, more appropriately, racism—has overt representational and narrative functions. Of course, such emphasis on these films is warranted considering their impact both on filmic technique and the politics of representation.

There is, however, a lack of scholarship on the racist practices in Griffith's Biograph films, especially in recent revisionist writings. Tom Gunning's book, although addressing class and gender, neglects a discussion of race almost entirely.[5] Yet, throughout the over 450 Biograph films directed by or under the direct supervision of Griffith, racism is a consistent and often explicit formation. Griffith is a pioneer of "narrative integration," to use Gunning's term,[6] not only because he helped develop parallel editing and other stylistic techniques in support of storytelling, but also because he perpetuated a discourse supported by racist practices—which is to say that Griffith's articulations of style and of race are involved in the same cinematic and discursive processes; pragmatically, they co-constitute the filmmaker's narrative system.

This essay attempts to uncover the relationship between narrativization and racial articulations in Griffith's Biograph films, showing how the racism in *The Birth of a Nation* and *Broken Blossoms* can be traced to the director's Biograph work. To ground my analysis of race in these films, I first attempt to specify what I mean by whiteness, a discourse that I feel best describes and explains the enduring color-line in the United States. Next, I show how whiteness informs the earliest of filmmaking practices, especially pre-Griffith cinema. My goal here is to reveal the genealogy of whiteness, showing how it goes beyond Griffith the actual filmmaker.[7] After laying this groundwork, I attempt to show how Griffith's narrative integration utilizes stylistic techniques—from composition to editing—to articulate an ideology of race that positions "whites" as normal and superior and "non-whites" as deviant and inferior.

The Discourse of Whiteness

The discourse of whiteness refers to the persistence of racial hierarchies that, in the United States, have systematically privileged those who count as white—generally European Americans—at the expense of those who do not count as white—generally non-European Americans.[8] Rationalized on the basis of physiognomic and cultural differences, ranging from skin color to tastes to mannerisms, whiteness gains its power and legitimacy from the politico-scientific myth that "whites" are innately superior, the ultimate result of divine intervention, natural selection, or cultural preeminence. Like all myths, white superiority legitimizes the ideological as biblical or evolutionary: the right of the chosen/survival of the fittest. Of course, the power of this myth is that it rests on the reciprocal ideology that people who do not count as white are divinely, biologically, or culturally inferior.

Masking ideology as nature, the myth of white superiority earns historical determinacy from a hegemony of racist practices that position those beyond the white "ideal" in economically, politically, and ideologically exploitive and degrading conditions. Supporting the political economy of United States capitalism, these conditions include the genocide of Native Americans, the enslavement of African Americans, the colonialization of Mexico, Puerto Rico, and other Latino countries as well as the systematic exclusion of Asian Americans—to name some of the more obvious examples. And, it seems clear, people who count as white have been most responsible for and privileged by this legacy. As sociologists Michael Omi and Howard Winant note: "With the rule of Europeans and their descendants . . . went a highly flexible and adaptive, but nevertheless inexorable 'color code,' a system of racial distinctions that was [usually] effective in reinforcing colonial domination."[9]

While the material benefactors of racist practices are those who count as white, whiteness does not describe or explain the totality of European American identity and experience. On the contrary, whiteness is a historical formation; European Americans are a heterogeneous collective of people who often—but certainly not universally—pass as white. The implication here is that the term 'white,' as with the term 'race,' does not refer to a biological classification of people—e.g., the pseudoscientific notion of "Caucasoid"—but, rather, to a historically specific formation of meanings that characterize social, political, and individual experiences.[10] Like 'race,' 'white' as a category of human beings is determined by history. This clarification is important to emphasize because it specifies that there is no essential—divine, genetic, or cultural—identity to European Americans (or any collective of people).[11]

Though present since the founding of the Republic, the discourse of whiteness is nonetheless historical: a shifting and reforming system of meanings that, while consistently hierarchizing physiognomic and cultural difference, moves collectives of people up and down the racial privilege ladder. Early in the history of the United States, German and Irish Americans, though in a much different way than, say, Native Americans or African Americans, were often considered "racial" inferiors, less worthy of the "rights of man."[12] At the turn of the century, eugenics and the social-Darwinian paradigms, supported by those fearful of new immigrant populations and subsequent labor competition, divided "Caucasians" into hierarchical subdivisions, including Anglo-Saxons, Southern Europeans, and Jews.[13] Eventually, "white" and "Caucasian" would become synonymous racial categories, as can be seen with recent government classifications that lump all European Americans under the heading of "white."[14] In short, an enduring aspect of whiteness is that it consistently moves various groups up and down the racial ladder—including the section at the top reserved for "Caucasians."

While a diverse collective of peoples with distinct histories have been excluded from the privileges of whiteness at any given moment in United States history, I want to emphasize that the discourse has consistently relegated Native, Latino, Asian, and African Americans to the very bottom of the racial privilege ladder. For one thing, European immigrants and their descendants have, for the most part, assimilated into the status of whiteness, usually after losing cultural signifiers, such as dress and accents, and, in many cases, by participating in white racism. However, the so-proscribed colored Other—an otherwise heterogeneous collective of groups and individuals—have, for the most part, not assimilated: U.S. history has yet to stop perpetuating the Otherness ascribed to physiognomic difference. Thus, African, Asian, Latino, and Native Americans, among other groups that signify color, have at least one historical formation in common: whiteness.

In film studies, Richard Dyer has analyzed the representation of whiteness. For Dyer, white domination colonizes the standard of "normal," leaving blackness as something that is particular, a mark of Otherness. He writes, "In the realm of categories, black is always marked as a colour (as the term 'coloured' egregiously acknowledges), and is always particularizing; whereas white is not anything really, not an identity, not a particularizing quality, because it is everything—white is no colour because it is all colours.[15] The invisibility of whiteness, he writes, "secures white power by making it hard, especially for white people and their media, to 'see' whiteness." Due to this invisibility, or the "everything and nothing" of whiteness, Dyer concludes that "white people—not there as a category and everywhere as a fact—are difficult, if not impossible, to analyze *qua* white. The subject seems to fall apart in your hands as soon as you begin."[16]

While I agree with Dyer that whiteness is hard to "see," I do not think this is because of the discourse's representational or narrative properties (or lack thereof). On the contrary, whiteness is not "everything and nothing," as he posits, but a very particular something: a representational and narrative construction with identifiable properties and a specific history.[17] Representations of blackness, redness, yellowness, and browness are intermediate clues to the constructedness and particularity of whiteness, as Dyer recognizes, if only because this discourse dominates both the production and reception of these racial categories. When we write about race we are always in some way also writing about whiteness. More specifically, however, whiteness, though coyly masking itself as normal, is also recognizable and analyzable "qua white." In early cinema, the particularity of this discourse ranges from the representational—where whiteface becomes an enduring image—to the narrational—where stories of non-white servitude, of colonial love, and of the divine centrality and virtue of the white family/white woman dominate countless films.

A Brief History of Whiteness

The meaning of race was very much imbricated with white superiority immediately before and during the era of Griffith's tenure at Biograph. The turn of the century, a period when the director was entering adulthood and struggling with a fledgling theatre career, was marked by a Supreme Court which, finding itself unable to "eradicate racial instincts," institutionalized and legitimized Jim Crow exclusionism in such infamous court decisions as *Plessy* v. *Ferguson* (1896) and *Williams* v. *Mississippi* (1898). The imperialistic and propagandistic practices of the United States in Hawaii, the Philippine Islands, Guam, and the Caribbean islands of Cuba and Puerto Rico both before and during the Spanish-American war ensured that those who counted as non-white included more than African Americans. Most of these and similar practices were legitimized by the intellectual and academic community as a brand of Social Darwinism—one that supported the notion that Anglo Saxons, first, and the rest of Caucasians, second, were superior to all other "races"—became a pervasive paradigm.

The rise of Democrats to Congressional power in 1910 and, later, the presidency of Woodrow Wilson beginning in 1912 brought a return of Southern patriarchal and racist beliefs and practices to political prominence. This shift in political power, coupled with growing anxiety over the influx of Southern European and Jewish immigrants and the migration of African Americans to Northern cities, was used by various politicians and community leaders to support both de jure and de facto separate and unequal practices. Indeed, this was the period that saw numerous urban protests as well as the founding of the NAACP and the Urban League, two political projects specifically organized to combat the growing menace of what C. Vann Woodward labeled the "capitulation to racism."[18]

This brief sketch of the social and political factors that informed early filmmaking corresponds with the transformations taking place in the film industry during Griffith's tenure at Biograph. As Tom Gunning notes, "1908 is a year not so much of innovation as of crystallization. It is not the year of the first story film, or of the first full reel [1,000-foot] or the first film exchanges or nickelodeons. Rather, it is the year when the film industry tried to knit all these developments into a stable industry."[19] In the year of Griffith's directorial debut with *The Adventures of Dollie* (1908), both the Motion Picture Patents Company (MPPC) and the National Board of Review, the industry's censorship apparatus, were established by the major patent holders and film manufacturers to stabilize and control the film market.

Both the MPPC and the National Board of Review, supported by industry trades and the critical press, attempted to "upgrade" the actual decor and safety of movie houses as well as "uplift" the audience to a respectable, more bourgeois level. The logic was that upgrading and uplifting would minimize censorship and ensure market stability. Mass attendance was key to increased profits. Yet, while sexual explicitness, violence, and other such "vulgar" representations were practices upon which the industry cracked down, issues of white racism were not. It was not a censurable problem to depict non-whites as bloodthirsty or noble-yet-inferior savages, or to consistently show them as devious, wanton threats to white society, white families, and white women. For the most part, blackface, brownface, redface, and yellowface were not deemed unacceptable or immoral. Instead, censorship came in the form of excluding of African Americans and others who did not count as white from acting roles as well as restricting their admittance into theaters or relegating them to the balconies.

While racist representations and narratives did not require "upgrading," depictions of non-whites as somehow equal or superior to whites did. The social Darwinian paradigm of the period precluded any evidence contrary to the order of so-labeled Anglo Saxon and "Caucasian" superiority. This can be seen in the case of Jack Johnson, an African American boxer who defeated European American boxers at a rate much too fast for community and industry leaders. Johnson's boxing victories produced a tension in the racial "order of things" that forced various communities and the film industry to censor his films.[20]

Gunning's research also shows that the industrial move toward upgrading cinema and uplifting the audience put pressure on filmmakers of the period to improve upon narrative legibility. He notes that "filmmakers like Griffith had to respond to the challenge of balancing new cultural pretension with the need to make films which were narratively comprehensible to the broadly based nickelodeon audience."[21] In Griffith's films of the period, this translated into a systematic emphasis on suspense, character psychology, and moral judgment. Gunning provides a concise summation: "The desire to imitate respectable forms of art and to counter allegations of obscenity provided a spur for the creation of a filmic rhetoric that could convey the mental life of characters and preach a sermon of morality."[22] Thus, the move to upgrade and uplift resulted in the narrator system, a bourgeois, patriarchal, and, as I will show, white system of narrative integration.

Of course, racist practice was a part of the industry before its movement to upgrade and uplift. Moreover, Griffith's films were not the only participants: Whiteness found its way into film at the hands of a number of studios and filmmakers. Along with cat and dog shows, racial caricatures were one of the more popular attractions in a disturbingly "primitive" cinema. For instance, a Chinese caricature is chased about in *The Chinese Laundry Scene* (1894), a so-called actuality that reportedly received high exhibition for the period. Around the same year, Buffalo Bill's Wild West Show, another popular attraction, brought the Indian, trained like a loyal horse by a white man, to early film shorts in such Edison works as *Buffalo Bill*, *Sioux Ghost Dance*, *Buffalo Dance*, and *Indian War Council*.[23]

As early cinema became more concerned with narrative continuity, films like *A Mexican's Gratitude* (1909), released by Essanay, and *The Poisoned Flume* (1911), released by the American Film Manufacturing Company, brought caricatures of the villainous "greaser" and loyal brownface to the silver screen. In the first film, a "good" Mexican is one that is depicted as loyal to the white man. In the second film, a vindictive brownface who lusts for a white woman is killed for his inter-racial desires.[24]

Along with Asian and Latino Americans, African Americans were a group systematically associated with natural or primitive inferiority in pre-Griffith cinema. For example, in 1902 and 1903 William Selig, who had worked in early minstrel shows, produced a number of racist shorts, including *Interrupted Crap Game*, a film of "darkies" who neglect their game to pursue a chicken, *Prize Fight in Coontown*, depicting "two bad coons," and *A Night in Blackville*, a short showing "two coons" dancing with their "best babies."[25] Lubin films also contributed to whiteness, particularly with their popular "watermelon pictures." As the Lubin catalogue explains, "The demand for a new watermelon picture had induced us to pose two colored women in which they are portrayed, ravenously getting on the outside of a number of melons, much to the amusement of the onlookers."[26] Crescent films, a partnership between William Paley and William F. Steiner, made several racist shorts. One such film, *Avenging a Crime* (1904), depicts a blackface caricature, who has killed a white woman, being chased and subsequently lynched by a squad of whites.[27] In many films like this, caricatures coded as black males are seen as child- or animal-like, requiring either supervision or bondage. In comparison, characters coded as white males are depicted as natural leaders, the rightful disciplinarians.

Edwin S. Porter and the Edison Manufacturing Company produced a number of films before 1908 that also helped integrate whiteness into the narrator system. This is especially the case with blackface, which dominated almost all representations of African Americans in Porter's films; indeed, even African Americans who played "darkies" in these films often had to wear blackface. Porter's "screen entertainment," as Charles Musser has labeled it,[28] included the stereotype of a shiftless, lazy, watermelon-eating, dancing "darkie," a caricature that would find its way into Griffith's films.

Janet Staiger's research on *Uncle Tom's Cabin* (1903) shows that the articulation of race in the film had a clear intertextual history, including not only Harriet Beecher Stowe's best-selling novel (1852) but also George L. Aiken's popular stage version (which Staiger notes ran for over ninety years in the United States).[29] Thus, audience knowledge of the film's "moral and abolitionist" plot, or its liberal coding of African Americans as loyal-yet-inferior, was a likely factor in its popularity. What this suggests is that whiteness is very much genealogical, even tied to the patterns and complexities of reception.

Musser's research on *The Watermelon Patch* (1905) shows how Porter's use of filmic technique, particularly sight gags and mise-en-scène, worked to cement the function of the black caricature as, above all, threatening to white civilization. The "race" of the caricatures is implicitly offered by the film as a causal explanation for their crime. The film tells the story of twenty blackface thieves stealing watermelons, then subsequently chased for their crime by a small group of whites. The caricatures eventually find refuge in a small shack, where they dance and partake of their spoils. The white vigilantes inevitably find them and plug up the chimney of the house, causing soot to fall on the caricatures' faces—a blatant racial sight gag, as Musser points out. Moreover, the shots of the numerous blackface caricatures in the shack juxtaposed with the whites outside the shack show the blackfaces as "pygmies," dwarfed by their ability to all fit into a tiny shack, and the whites as giants. Mise-en-scène becomes one of the means by which whiteness is enunciated in this Porter film.[30]

Porter's *Life of a Cowboy* (1906) demonstrates that non-whites included more than African Americans, as a brownface greaser, redface savages, and loyal Indians all function to support the myth of the heroic whiteface cowboy. The film shows a greaser lusting after a white woman and a band of renegade Indians threatening the white community, here metaphorically depicted as a stagecoach. The greaser and his band of renegade Indians capture a white girl, who is eventually saved by the white cowboy—a common narrative resolution. As the story comes to an end, the greaser sneaks up on the reunited white couple in revenge, gun poised, only to be shot by a loyal Indian girl. The spectator of this film is entertained not only by the traditional caricaturing of Mexican Americans as greasers, but also by the established dichotomy between the noble savages, loyal to the white man, and the renegade Indians, a horde of bestial creatures threatening white civilization and white women.

These examples show that there is no single or even dominant individual or film company responsible for integrating whiteness into United States cinema. In fact, many Biograph films before Griffith show instances of racist practice. For instance, Biograph's *Nigger in the Woodpile* (1904) portrays caricatures of African Americans as shiftless, criminal and lazy.[31] Another film, *The Chicken Thief* (1904), depicts chicken stealing "darkies" chased by whites, and is essentially a forerunner to Porter's *The Watermelon Patch.*[32] The discourse of whiteness, then, had numerous socio-political, industrial, and individual proponents.

Griffith's Narrative System

My analysis of whiteness in Griffith's narrative system relies on the framework laid out by Gunning, who synthesizes the literary structuralism of Gérard Gennette and Tzvetan Todorov with a historical methodology. While it is not in the scope of this article to explain the subtleties of this approach, I do want to stress that, like Gunning, I am concerned with "the telling of a story" that is found in Griffith's work. This involves an investigation into what Gunning terms narrative discourse: "Narrative discourse is precisely the text itself—the actual arrangement of signifiers that communicate the story—words in literature, moving images and written titles in silent films. It is only through this means of expression that we come in contact with either story or the act of narrating."[33]

A study of storytelling in Griffith's Biograph films thus requires a close analysis of the textual properties that comprise a story film: What Gunning, borrowing from Gennette, specifies as tense, mood, and voice. First, "tense" refers to the temporal relationship between shots. This includes flashbacks, ellipses, and, most prominently in Griffith's narrative system, temporal continuity across spatial set-ups. The articulation of time is coherent in the filmmaker's work, making his stories highly legible. Second, 'mood' refers to "the narration's perspective of the story told," or what American literary criticism usually refers to as "point of view."[34] In Griffith's narrative system, this is primarily achieved through characterization, which is visible through casting, performance, and, of course, make-up. Finally, and central to the discourse of whiteness, "voice" "refers to the traces of telling left in the text through which we sense a storyteller addressing an implied or real audience."[35] Voice is essentially the ideology of the "narrator," an intervening force visible in the juxtaposition of shots, or editing, and through story structure (hence Todorov). All these properties of storytelling, most prominently mood and voice, integrate whiteness into Griffith's Biograph films.

The voice of whiteness in Griffith's narrative system circulates within three intermixed genres: 1) stories of non-white servitude; 2) stories of colonial love, or turn-of-the-century jungle fever; and 3) stories of the divinity of the white family and serenity of the white woman. Intermixed with the more common genres Griffith worked in—"Greaser" films, Indian films, Civil War films, and, the most inter-generic form, Melodramas—these three types of stories work out Griffith's contemporaneous concern with the politics and ideology of white supremacy. More specifically, Griffith's films employ cinematic techniques—from characterization to editing—to tell the story of the inability of non-whites to fully assimilate into white culture and society, and ultimately provide a justification for their servitude, segregation, and punishment. Through stories of servitude, colonial love, and the white family/white women, the filmmaker—his voice—perpetuated a discourse that cast non-whites as the metonymic and metaphoric threat to the normality and superiority of whiteness.

Stories of Non-White Servitude

Many of Griffith's Biograph films narrativize the social and political status of non-whites in white society. The segregating voice of whiteness always intervenes in these films, as story resolution regularly maintains the superiority of whites—their economic and moral privilege within the diegesis—at the expense of non-whites. At the center of these stories is a non-white character, usually a male, who struggles and sacrifices in order to better serve the clean and civilized space of white society. This character is usually de-masculinized in a way that rationalizes and justifies his service as well as ensures that his motivations are not read as sexually transgressive or miscegenetic. Ultimately at issue, then, is the desire of the non-white male to faithfully serve the white family and, by extension, white society, both of which are held as glorified spaces culturally and morally inaccessible to those marked as colored.

In *That Chink at Golden Gulch* (1910), Griffith constructs a narrative around a Chinese character, Charlie Lee, who sacrifices his cultural identity in order to serve his white benefactors. The story progresses toward resolution through the actions of characters coded as white, except when the non-white character is serving whiteness. Early in the film, Charlie Lee is pushed, kicked, and his queue is pulled by a white cowboy, the Dandy, while other cowboys laugh and shoot their pistols at his feet. Eventually, Charlie Lee is saved from the threatening whites by a white woman, the ultimate insult in patriarchal Westerns. Grateful, he kneels in gratitude and then follows her to her fiancée, pledging his loyalty to both. The yellowface character soon overhears the Dandy planning a robbery, and decides to follow him. After the scene in which the Dandy commits the robbery and subsequently takes a nap, Charlie Lee cuts off his queue (Figure 1), using it as a makeshift rope to tie the robber's hands. He then returns the stolen loot and his captured thief to the authorities, recovering a modest reward for his efforts. Ever the faithful servant, Charlie Lee gives the reward money to the white couple. An intertitle card, cued as a poorly written letter from Charlie Lee, ensures audience comprehension of both the Chinese character's motivations and the voice of the narrative: "Missie, Dean alsame Bud Miller too—Charlie Lee wishee much glad you two when alsame one. Hope take

Fig. 1: The "Chink," a white actor in yellowface, recognizes the supreme sacrifice he must make to capture the Dandy. (Courtesy of the Library of Congress)

money for blidel present—goodby. Charlie have went away." Thanks to Charlie Lee's metaphorical self-castration, the white couple is free to live happily ever after.

Charlie Lee is a character ascribed with racial signifiers that code and rationalize the hierarchy of whiteness. Characters are the primary movers of plot in Griffith's films; they are also the primary mechanisms by which mood and voice participate in whiteness. This is clearly the case with the "Chink," whose representational and narrative functions go beyond the histrionic, or theatrical, acting style of the period. In most of the scenes that feature Charlie Lee, he is crouching in the background, head down, arms across his stomach and walking in a bow-legged manner. He shuffles his feet as if his shoelaces were tied together. This is not the case with white characters, who perform in the verisimilitude style, a style which codes behavior and physicality as natural and normal.[36] Less a character and more a caricature, the Chink is de-masculinized in a way that justifies his eventual servitude and ensures that his intentions are not read as sexually transgressive. In the scene after he cuts off his queue, the realization of what he has done causes him to run screaming off in a panic. He frantically moves from the background to the foreground of the shot, his arms and hands waving uncontrollably in the air. Intensified by the character's movement into a close-up, this emotional performance codes the figure as strange, weak, and, in the tradition of misogynistic practices, "feminized"—worthy only of servitude.

Similar to *That Chink at Golden Gulch*, *His Trust* and *His Trust Fulfilled* (1910), Griffith's first two-part/two-reel narrative, tell the story of a slave, George, who sacrifices his meager savings and ties to black culture in order to faithfully serve the values of Southern whiteness. In the beginning of the two-part film, the patriarch of the Southern white family goes off to fight the North and is quickly killed, initiating George's lifelong devotion to the widowed wife and daughter. The Southern patriarch's presence is nonetheless maintained throughout the film in the figure of his military sword, which is returned to the family after his death. George places the sword on the living room mantle, enabling the icon to mediate his narrative and spatial proximity to the white mother and daughter.

Soon, drunken Northern soldiers ransack and burn the family plantation. George risks losing his life to save not only the little girl who was left inside, but the sword. Eventually, George gives the white mother and her child his shack, sleeping outside to ensure both their safety from the now free slaves and, as with the Chinese caricature in *That Chink at Golden Gulch*, that his intentions are not read as miscegenistic. He hangs the sword prominently on one of the shack's walls, allowing the voice of the white patriarch to remain a screen dominant.

Mise-en-scène in this two-part film is markedly segregated, as George is systematically restricted from the immediate space of white females. One primary exception to this pattern is in the beginning of the film, when he is "play" acting as a horse for the white girl to ride. In most scenes, George is spatially segregated. In shots where the slave and the white mother are featured in the same frame, they are generally positioned in different planes. George is almost always in the background, even if narrative logic would otherwise suggest that he belongs in the foreground. In the few scenes in which they are shown on the same plane, a white male or the sword usually mediates their proximity. Thus, the voice of the narrative utilizes spatial segregation in order to restrict blackface caricatures from the literal space of white women, as there must be no sexual associations between servants and masters if the nonwhite is to fit the racist ideals of whiteness.

Fig. 2: George gets a handshake from a white man for his lifelong devotion.

In a melodramatic twist of Southern romanticism, the widow eventually dies of depression, life without her husband and with George having apparently overwhelmed her. George faithfully continues to take care of the little girl, eventually sacrificing his meager savings to secretly send her to private school—an ironic and particularly disturbing plot twist given that the restriction of African Americans from education was a tool used to maintain slavery and segregation. When he runs out of money, George steals from a white man in hopes of paying her remaining school costs. Though caught trying to return the money—George is forever faithful to the laws of white society—he explains his dilemma and is forgiven. The young woman is eventually saved by a white cousin who agrees to marry her. For his self-sacrificing service, George receives a single handshake from the cousin (Figure 2).[37] The film ends with a shot of George, in his shack, clutching his master's sword—his trust fulfilled.

Clearly, the sword is a prominent symbol of George's devotion and loyalty to the values and ideals of both the South and the white patriarch. It is a phallic icon with a particularly white and patriarchal charge. In the possession of George, however, the sword is not a phallus: It does not, in other words, confer power on the domesticated slave. In fact, once put in charge of the sword, George loses everything—his shack, his money, and all ties to black culture—making him more a slave after the North's victory than before. Instead, the long and shiny sword empowers the myth of an honorable and romantic South where "good" slaves sacrificed their freedom and any sexual desire for the honor and virtue of Southern whiteness. The icon becomes a symbol of George's perpetual servitude.

Stories of Colonial Love

Race and sexuality are either pointedly segregated or linked as something that is immoral and prurient in Griffith's narrative discourse. Moreover, while non-white male desire for white females is almost always motivated by an intent to rape and while white females only desire white males, white male desire for non-white females is loosely sanctioned in Griffith's narrative system. There are many instances in his work in which white males seduce non-white females, particularly Native American "squaws." Essential to the voice in these films is the overdetermined articulation that the white male is motivated by loneliness and lust and that the non-white female is motivated by love and the desire to assimilate.[38] In what amounts to colonial love, films from this genre culminate in characterizations and narrative resolutions that maintain and advocate segregation. While a white male can have his way with an Indian female in Griffith's films, their union always ends with the Indian back on the reservation. The narrative in these stories goes out of its way to educate the desiring Other, and the audience, in keeping the races separate.

A Romance of the Western Hills (1910) tells the story of a white male who shares his affections with both an Indian female and a white female. The film begins with the Indian girl among her own people. After being introduced to a "book of civilization," she rejects the affections of an Indian suitor. Not unlike the sword in *His Trust* and *His Trust Fulfilled*, the book serves as an icon of white enlightenment and power. The Indian girl is eventually adopted by an elderly white couple, who take her from the wild into civilization. Her adulation of whiteness is enforced by a shot that shows her being overly impressed with the home and material possessions of her adoptive parents.

Soon, a nephew of her new parents charms the young Indian girl. "This the little girl assumes is love for her," an intertitle continues, and she "confides in him." The Indian girl eventually finds out that the nephew has a white fiancée and thus does not intend to marry her, and runs to inform her adoptive parents. In a medium shot, Griffith has the white mother shaking her finger at the Indian girl as if she ought to have known better. The voice in this scene scoffs at the Indian girl's desire to marry the white nephew. Eventually, her Indian boyfriend returns and takes the Indian girl back to the reservation, ostensibly where she belongs. Thus, narrative resolution is reached when the Indian girl returns to her tribe, validating Griffith's point that assimilation should only go so far.

Much like *A Romance of the Western Hills* (1910), *The Call of the Wild* (1908) tells the story of a Griffith Indian who falls in love with a white person. In this film, however, the Indian is a male, George Redfeather, who, having done all he can to assimilate into white culture, such as going to a military school and giving up his traditional clothing, finds out that his status within civilization is contingent upon his not seeking the love of a white girl. No matter how successful Redfeather is at passing, he is ultimately prohibited from marrying into whiteness. The Biograph Bulletin advertising the film provides a reliable synopsis of the story and of the ideology of whiteness: "Civilization and education cannot bleach his tawny epidermis, and that will always prove an insurmountable barrier to social distinction. He may be lauded and even lionized for deeds of valor and heroism, or excellence in scientifics, but when it comes to the social circle—never." In the film, Redfeather meets Gladys, the daughter of the military officer in charge of the school, and falls in love. "You may be sure he is indignantly repulsed by Gladys," the Bulletin continues, "and ordered from the house for his presumption by her father." The Bulletin, as with the film, affirms that acceptance into the circle of whiteness is, however sad, inaccessible to the Indian. "Lo, the poor Indian," the Bulletin concludes, "his condition is indeed deplorable; elevated to intellectual supremacy only to more fully realize his extreme commonality."[39]

This story of colonial love, or the colonial rejection of Indian-male love, clearly affirms segregation by rejecting and punishing the "interracial" affections of the Indian male. The voice of whiteness seeks to make this clear by emphasizing the myth that the nature of the Indian is savage. Here, the mood of the narrative constructs Redfeather as overly emotional and more primitive than civilized. For instance, after Gladys and her father make it clear that Redfeather's love is unacceptable, we see, in a long take, the rejected Indian fervently tearing off the whiteman's clothes and donning his traditional Indian garb replete with head feathers. He then drinks wildly from a bottle of whiskey and, like a gorilla, beats his chest with his fists. Once in his traditional clothing, he no longer performs "civilized" but barbaric. The voice of whiteness seems to be saying: you can take the Indian out of the forest, but you can't take the forest out of the Indian. The characterization of the Indian in this way rationalizes and validates his exclusion from the favors of white women.

The voice of whiteness is further expressed through both editing, specifically in the famous chase sequence, and composition, especially in the ending. On the rampage, Redfeather eventually meets up with his fellow Indians, all of whom are drunk and similarly acting barbarically. Redfeather orders his fellow Indians to join him in chasing down and kidnapping Gladys, who is out riding her horse. Crosscutting across parallel actions of Redfeather and his fellow renegades during the chase rhetorically enforces the representation of the Indian as imminent threat to white women. Within this single sequence, we see the white girl fleeing for her safety and the renegades in lustful pursuit. Griffith actually speeds up the tempo of the sequence by progressively shortening the length of the shots as the chasing Indians grow closer to the fleeing girl, thereby making the threat that much more intense. Eventually Griffith's Indian captures Gladys, who, in a medium shot, appeals to God for her salvation. The medium shot enables us to better see the character's fear. Of course, Redfeather's conscience overcomes his vengeful and savage intentions. He stops his fellow renegades from accosting the divine Gladys and sets her free. Though savage, Redfeather is no longer wild like his cohorts. Civilization, though not powerful enough to bleach his "tawny epidermis," has made him "humane." The final shot of the film shows Redfeather sitting upon his horse, dejected, with no place to go. He moves slowly toward the camera, eventually into a medium view. Clutching Gladys's handkerchief, another one of Griffith's icons of whiteness, he disappears into the mountains and becomes a noble savage.

The White Family/White Women

The third type of Griffith story involves what Nick Browne has labeled the "Griffith family discourse." Browne recognizes that the family in Griffith's films is often threatened with "dismemberment either by loss of a child or by the death, separation, or violation of a parent."[40] More specifically, Browne argues that "the structure of the drama is usually an attack on and defense of the integrity, should I say the virtue, of the woman, and on the social codes and prohibitions which enable her to maintain her place."[41] The woman in these films is positioned in an economy of desire and possession in which the divinity of patriarchy is protected and affirmed. As Browne shows, male control over both the family and women is ultimately at stake in many of Griffith's films.

When the family in Griffith's story is coded as white, the threat to its dismemberment comes from a savage and lustful non-white male. Indeed, stories of the family almost always involve a racial component that casts non-white males as a threat to the divinity and superiority of white patriarchy. Gentile virtue and femininity as well as white male masculinity and dominance are at stake in what amounts to Griffith's *white* family discourse. The aim in such stories, of course, is to segregate the "races" and bring the threatening non-white character under control in the hopes of maintaining the unity of the family, the purity of the white woman, and the power and divinity of white patriarchy.

The discourse of the white family can be seen operating in stories of colonial love, where the union of a non-white and white ends in separation and segregation. Interracial families fail in Griffith's Biograph films. The discourse can also be seen in stories of non-white servitude, where, in the examples I have highlighted, the Chink and George are ultimately concerned with sacrificing their "manhood" in order to serve a white family. In these stories, the slave and the female master must not be associated with racially transgressive sexual desire. In stories of the white family, however, sexual transgression is foregrounded as savage, as non-white males are positioned as deviant and violent predators.

The Zulu's Heart (1908), which Gunning primarily recognizes for the emotional resonance of its pictorial landscapes,[42] is one of several Griffith films that tell the story of a white family attacked by, as the Biograph Bulletin reads, "merciless black brutes." Set in South Africa, a nation Griffith seemed to think was not unlike like the Old South, the narrative has a Zulu tribe attacking a Boer family, specifically a father, mother, and daughter. As with the filmmaker's Westerns, the natives are the invaders in this story. Early in the film, a brief crosscut sequence, consisting of shots of the white family in a wagon happily traversing a rural trial and shots of the Zulu coming down from the hillside in pursuit, heightens the suspense and mood of the story. Eventually, the Zulu attackers catch up to the white wagon, killing the father in a dramatic and violent battle. In a performance style similar to that of the Indians in *The Call of the*

Wild, the Zulu tribesmen enter in a swarm-like fashion, continually waving their arms about and swinging their heads side to side. "Up rush the prancing, jibbing, gibbering barbarians," the Biograph Bulletin reads.[43]

The rest of the narrative involves an elaborate chase sequence that rhetorically draws the viewer into the didacticism of Griffith's moral voice. After the father has been killed, the next shot shows the mother, having sought refuge in the hills, hiding her daughter among the rocks. In the same shot, the Zulu attackers find the mother, taking her away but leaving one Zulu behind. The remaining Zulu eventually stumbles upon the little girl. Just as the Zulu is poised to cut the girl's throat, she pulls out her doll. The Zulu, enthralled with the doll, immediately has a change of heart, and, instead of killing the girl, hugs and kisses her. Thus, a horde of menacing and deviant non-whites is balanced by a loyal and serving—noble—non-white. The juxtaposition of what amounts to "good" savage and "bad" savage enforces the ideology that there are non-whites who serve, i.e., those who are "good," and non-whites who attack, i.e., those who are "bad." Griffith's voice in this regard is that simple.

The chase continues, further shedding light on the dual nature of the Zulu. After the "good" Zulu hides the little girl among the rocks, he starts chasing the "bad" Zulu. Griffith then cuts to a shot of the mother at the Zulu camp. Surrounded by the Zulu, she falls to her knees in fright and desperation. Using the psychology of characters to enforce the voice of whiteness, the Zulu captors stick their chests out and continue to wave their arms frantically in the air. Their plans are foiled, however, as the "good" Zulu recaptures the white mother, taking her to her daughter.

Always aware of the suspense of a chase, Griffith cuts to a shot of three Zulu attackers finding the little girl. To further emphasize the barbaric nature of the Zulu brutes, the voice of whiteness has the caricatures physically abuse the little girl in a manner difficult for even present-day viewers to stomach. Zulu attackers are shown kicking and dragging the little girl; one of them cuts at her with his knife. The performance is chilling and brutal; the psychology of the characters is clear: They are beasts.

Soon the "good" Zulu enters and defeats the "bad" Zulu. In the last shot of the film, the "good" Zulu, the mother, and the daughter stand against a "pictorial landscape." The noble savage points to the direction the mother and daughter must travel to get home. Segregation is key to narrative resolution; the Zulu and white woman must not and cannot remain in the same space. Before leaving the scene, the daughter gives the Zulu her doll. The Zulu holds and kisses the doll, much like he did in the early scene with the girl, and then looks to the sky in prayer. With segregation established and the attacking non-whites punished, the end shot effectively summarizes the voice of whiteness: The white family and white woman are divine, worthy of sacrifice and servitude.

Unlike *The Zulu's Heart*, *The Girls and Daddy* (1909) constructs a blackface caricature as an outright sexual predator, a wanton threat to two angelic white girls. The film tells the story of two burglars, one white and the other a "lowdown Negro" who, unaware of each other, burglarize a white man's house.[44] Inside the house are two young women serenely sleeping, their angelic vulnerability specifically foregrounded. Unlike the white burglar, the blackface caricature decides to lustfully chase the women. In the end, the white burglar, faithful to his race, saves the white girl by capturing the blackface burglar and turning him over to the police. Narrative resolution is achieved when the threatening non-white is captured and punished, the virtue of the white girls retained (thanks to a white male), and the white family safe and secure.

What is particularly compelling about this film is that cinematic style explicitly functions to highlight the psychology of the characters and, ultimately, the racial morality of whiteness. For instance, after the girls become aware of the presence of the blackface burglar in their home, they quickly move to impede his deviant advances. We see shots of the girls clutching each other in fear, followed by shots of the blackface caricature in pursuit. Meanwhile, the blackface caricature's physical movements and facial expression connote a savage psychology, foreshadowing Gus's performance in *The Birth of a Nation*. We also see a long shot of the colored caricature frantically jumping over and through chairs that have been placed in front of a locked door. The camera pans, revealing that behind the door are the two girls, one of whom sacrifices herself by staying so that the other can escape. The movement of the camera in this way functions quite similarly to a parallel edit, rhetorically linking the pursuit of the blackface burglar with the fright and virtue of the white girls (Figure 3).

Non-whites are universally constructed as threats to whites in Griffith's narrative system. In *Leather Stockings* (1909), *A Mohawk's Way* (1910), and *The Thread of Destiny* (1910), Indians attack and brutalize white families, particularly women and children. *The Last Drop of Water* (1911) tells the story of a white wagon train full of white families in pursuit of manifest destiny being attacked by bloodthirsty Indians. Chi-

Fig. 3: The blackface burglar, a forerunner to Gus of *The Birth of a Nation*, chases daddy's girls. (Courtesy of the Library of Congress, Kemp Niver Collection)

Fig. 4: Brownface "greaser" cowers in the background. (Courtesy of the Library of Congress, Kemp Niver Collection)

nese caricatures, though more often feminized servants than sexual or savage threats,[45] are also used in this way. For instance, *The Fatal Hour* (1908) tells the story of "A Stirring Incident of the Chinese White-Slave Traffic."[46] Mexicans are also represented as threats to the white family and white women. *A Temporary Truce* (1908) tells the story of a vengeful "greaser," as an intertitle in the film describes the character, who kidnaps and accosts the wife of a whiteface cowboy. Eventually the cowboy catches up with the greaser and his wife, only to be attacked by a horde of Indians. In this scene, the white man defends himself and his wife as the greaser cowers in the background (Figure 4).[47]

Toward a Conclusion

The socio-political institutionalization and resistance to Jim Crow laws and imperialistic practices and paradigms, the industrial determinants such as the MPPC and the National Board of Review, and, finally, the influence of such filmmakers and companies as Selig, Lubin, Paley,

Porter, the American Biograph Company, and the Edison Manufacturing Company—not to mention the numerous other film companies and filmmakers—can be seen as causal factors behind the cinematic categorizing of non-whites as inferior and whites as superior in early U.S. cinema. They are among the many institutions and decision-makers who inform and contextualize the racist practices supporting whiteness in Griffith's Biograph films.

Griffith's stories of whiteness eventually come to moral resolution with non-whites serving white society, white society safely segregated, white families secure in their homes, and white males atop the sexual and moral ladder. Griffith's stories are ultimately about white male masculinity—their divine and natural right to judge and punish. In the filmmaker's narrative system, dominance over non-whites is required to maintain the privilege of white men and the angelic essence of white women. The degradation and brutilization of non-white characters and their culture is required to enforce the role of the narrator's voice, Griffith's moral turpitude, and Southern chivalry.

Griffith systematically integrated whiteness into the narrative system. Methodological correctness aside, his innovations in style and storytelling cannot—should not—be abstracted from his punitive racism. In practice, both articulations collude to advance what came to be known as the Hollywood style.

Notes

Many thanks to George Lipsitz and Linda Williams for their insightful comments and suggestions on earlier drafts of this paper. Thanks also to the Motion Picture Division of the Library of Congress, especially Rosemary Hanes and Madeline Matz, the Museum of Modern Art, especially Charles Silver, and the UCLA Film and Television Archive for screening Griffith's Biograph films in both a professional and a comfortable environment.

1. Sergei Eisenstein, "Dickens, Griffith and the Film Today," in *Film Form*, ed. and trans. Jay Leyda (New York: HBI, 1949), p. 198.

2. Tom Gunning, *D.W. Griffith and the Origins of American Narrative Film: The Early Years* (Urbana and Chicago: University of Illinois Press, 1991); See also Tom Gunning, "The Cinema of Attraction: Early Film, Its Spectator and the Avant-Garde," *Wide Angle* 8, nos. 3&4 (1986): 63–70.

3. Eisenstein, "Dickens, Griffith and Film Today," p. 234.

4. See Thomas Cripps, *Slow Fade to Black: The Negro in American Film, 1900–1942* (New York: Oxford University Press, 1977); Robert Lang, "Introduction," *The Birth of a Nation: D. W. Griffith, Director*, ed. Robert Lang (New Brunswick, N. J.: Rutgers University Press, 1994). Julia Lesage, "*Broken Blossoms*: Artful Racism, Artful Rape," *Jump Cut* 26 (December 1981): 51–55; Michael Rogin, "'The Sword Became a Flashing Vision': D. W. Griffith's *The Birth of a Nation*," *Representations* 9 (Winter 1985): 150–195

(reprinted in Lang); Clyde Taylor, "The Re-Birth of the Aesthetic in Cinema," in this anthology.

5. This is also the case with Charlie Keil, "Transition through Tension: Stylistic Diversity in the Late Griffith Biographs," *Cinema Journal.* 28, no. 3 (Spring 1989): 22–40, as well as Joyce E. Jesionowski, *Thinking in Pictures: Dramatic Structure in D. W. Griffith's Biograph Films* (Berkeley: University of California Press, 1987).

Scott Simmon addresses the function of race and anti-Semitism in Griffith's Biograph work, especially in relation to the filmmaker's urban dramas. See *The Films of D. W. Griffith* (New York: Cambridge University Press, 1993), pp. 47- 49.

6. For Gunning, "narrative integration" characterizes the highly legible stories of early cinema roughly after 1910, including Griffith's later Biograph work, where film style—close-ups, parallel editing, etc.—is consistently subordinated to the development of characters and stories. To characterize Griffith's earlier Biograph films, Gunning uses the notion of the "narrator system," which involves a more experimental step toward narrative integration. Gunning provides a concise description: "the particularity of the narrator system comes less from its deviations from the norms of cinema of narrative integration than from its extreme expression of them." The distinction between the two narrative styles is not essential to my project, as the discourse of whiteness is central throughout Griffith's Biograph work (including the first two years of Griffith's tenure at Biograph, the years Gunning concentrates upon). As such, I will generally use the notion of narrative integration or narra*tive* system to characterize the body of Griffith's Biograph work. See *D. W. Griffith and the Origins of American Narrative Film*, pp. 25–26.

7. In referring to the Biograph films from 1908 to 1913 as being "authored" by Griffith, I assume Foucault's notion of the author as a function of discourse. In brief, the author-function implies the socio-political and institutional structures informing texts, such as Jim Crow exclusions and the machinations of the Biograph company. Related to this, Griffith as author refers to the actual agents who made decisions affecting the production of the Biograph films. This would include Griffith as well as other decision makers, such as Billy Blitzer, Griffith's cameraman. Moreover, the author-function implies the *voice* of the author, the author-in-the-text, which comes across as the film's moral judgment. This fictionalized author is enunciated in Griffith's films through various filmic devices ranging from caricaturing to parallel editing. Finally, Griffith as author-function implies the numerous subject positions offered by the narrative discourse, which is eventually determined—taken up or rejected—by a heterogeneous audience. See Michel Foucault, "What is an Author," *The Foucault Reader*, ed. Paul Rabinow (New York: Pantheon Books, 1984), pp. 101–120.

8. My elaboration of the notion of whiteness is informed by the analysis and historization of it by such scholars as Alexander Saxton, David Roediger, Ruth Frankenberg, and Toni Morrison. These scholars have sought to uncover the politics and culture of whiteness in the nineteenth century (Saxton), the class consciousness of whiteness in United States labor history (Roediger), the racial identity of "white" women (Frankenberg), and the forms and functions of whiteness in the literary imagination (Morrison). See Alexander Saxton, *The Rise and Fall of the White Republic: Class Politics and Mass Culture in Nineteenth-Century America* (New York: Verso, 1990); David R. Roediger, *The Wages of Whiteness: Race and the Making of the American Working Class* (New York: Verso, 1991); Ruth Frankenberg, *White Women, Race Matters: The Social Construction of Whiteness* (Minneapolis: University of Minnesota Press, 1993); Toni Morrison, *Play-*

ing in the Dark: Whiteness and the Literary Imagination (Cambridge: Harvard University Press, 1992).

9. Michael Omi and Howard Winant, *Racial Formation in the United States: From the 1960s to the 1990s*, 2d ed. (New York: Routledge, 1994), p. 49.

10. In defining 'race' as a historical formation, I am drawing on the work of Omi and Winant, who write: "The effort must be made to understand race as an unstable and 'decentered' complex of social meanings. . . . race is a concept which signifies and symbolizes social conflict and interests by referring to different types of human bodies." *Racial Formation in the United States*, p. 55. See also my introduction to this anthology.

11. Grounding race in history also allows room for change, or praxis. This is an important point, not only as a counter to the inherent fatalism of biological paradigms, but as a sign of hope that challenges to the hegemony of whiteness are worthwhile.

12. See Michael H. Hunt, *Ideology and U.S. Foreign Policy* (New Haven, Conn.: Yale University Press, 1987), especially his chapter "The Hierarchy of Race."

13. For a history of the Eugenics and Social Darwinian paradigms, see Daniel J. Kevles, *In The Name of Eugenics: Genetics and the Uses of Human Heredity* (New York: Knopf, 1985); Stephen J. Gould, *The Mismeasure of Man* (New York: W.W. Norton & Company, 1981). There is also a useful anthology on science and race: Sandra Harding, ed., *The "Racial" Economy of Science: Toward a Democratic Future* (Bloomington: Indiana University Press, 1993).

14. See Directive No. 15, "Race and Ethnic Standards for Federal Statistics and Administrative Reporting," Office of Management and Budget, May 12, 1977.

15. Richard Dyer, "White," *Screen* 29, no. 4 (Autumn 1988): 45.

16. Ibid., 46.

17. Dyer makes some headway in identifying the particularity of whiteness, specifically in relation to lighting and gender, in "The Colour of Virtue: Lillian Gish, Whiteness and Femininity," in *Women and Film: A Sight and Sound Reader* (Philadelphia: Temple University Press, 1993).

18. C. Vann Woodward, *The Strange Career of Jim Crow*, 3rd ed. (New York: Oxford University Press, 1974), pp. 67–109.

19. Tom Gunning, "Weaving a Narrative: Style and Economic Background in Griffith's Biograph Films," *Quarterly Review of Film Studies* 6, no. 1 (Winter 1981): 12.

20. For a history of early boxing films and the case of Jack Johnson, see Dan Streible, "A History of the Boxing Film, 1894–1915: Social Control and Social Reform in the Progressive Era," *Film History* 3, no. 3 (1987): 235–257, as well as his article in this volume.

21. Gunning, *D. W. Griffith and the Origins of American Narrative Film*, pp. 147–148.

22. Ibid., p. 183.

23. See Charles Musser, *Before the Nickelodeon: Edwin S. Porter and the Edison Manufacturing Company* (Berkeley and Los Angeles: University of California Press, 1991), p. 50.

24. Quoted in Blain P. Lamb, "The Convenient Villain: The Early Cinema Views the Mexican-American," *Journal of the West* 14, no. 4 (October 1975): 75–81.

25. Quoted in Cripps, *Slow Fade to Black*, p. 13. See also Musser, *The Emergence of Cinema: The American Screen to 1907* (New York: Charles Scribner's Sons, 1990), p. 292.

26. Quoted in Musser, *The Emergence of Cinema*, p. 331.

27. Ibid., p. 402.

28. Ibid., pp. 1–11.

29. Janet Staiger, *Interpreting Films: Studies in the Historical Reception of American Cinema* (Princeton, N. J.: Princeton University Press, 1992), pp. 105–123.

30. Musser, *Before the Nickelodeon*, p. 313.

31. Musser, *History of the American Cinema*, p. 380.

32. Musser's research shows that the similar articulations of race in *The Chicken Thief* and *The Watermelon Patch* can be partially tied to Wallace McCutchenson, a filmmaker who worked on both of the films and, thus, for both Biograph and Edison. *Before the Nickelodeon*, p. 314.

33. Gunning, *D. W. Griffith and the Origins of American Narrative Film*, p. 15.

34. Ibid.

35. Ibid., p.16.

36. For an insightful discussion of performance in Griffith's Biograph film, see Roberta Pearson, *Eloquent Gestures: The Transformation of Performance Style in the Griffith Biograph Films* (Berkeley: University of California Press, 1992).

37. Cripps makes this point in *Slow Fade to Black*, p. 29.

38. In only a few films does the white man force the Indian woman to be with him, as can be seen in *The Redman's View* (1909) and *The Indian Runner's Romance* (1909). In such films, the voice of whiteness ultimately condemns the brutalization, with narrative stasis ending when a "good" white man helps return the woman to her own kind. These stories are less about colonial love than they are about white brutality/white virtue. Nonetheless, they also end in segregation.

39. American Mutoscope & Biograph Co., Bulletin No. 182. Quoted in Eileen Bowser, *The Biograph Bulletins: 1908–1912* (New York: Farrar Strauss and Giroux, 1973), p. 59.

40. This phrase is generally attributed to President Woodrow Wilson, who reportedly made it after a screening of *Birth of a Nation* at the White House.

41. Nick Browne, "Griffith's Family Discourse: Griffith and Freud," *Quarterly Review of Film Studies* 6, no. 1 (Winter 1981): 68.

42. Ibid., 72.

43. Gunning, *D. W. Griffith and the Origins of American Narrative Film*, p. 108.

44. Bulletin No. 170, *The Biograph Bulletins*, p. 25.

45. Bulletin No. 210, ibid., p. 59.

46. Other than *That Chink at Golden Gulch*, Chinese caricatures function as feminized servants in such films as *The Call of the Wild*, *The Greaser's Gauntlet* (1908), *The Road to the Heart* (1909) and *The Chief's Daughter* (1911).

47. Bulletin No. 162, *The Biograph Bulletins*, p. 11.

Virginia Wright Wexman

THE FAMILY ON THE LAND

Race and Nationhood in Silent Westerns

The essence of a nation is that all individuals have many things in common, and also that they have forgotten many things.

—*Ernest Renan*

[T]he first law of private property is a simple one. There is no such thing as "empty" land.

—*Jean-Jacques Rousseau*

The Indians were fierce savages, whose occupation was war. . . . To leave them in possession of their country was to leave the country a wilderness.

—*Chief Justice Charles F. Wilkerson*

From its earliest days, the Western has been steeped in sentiments associated with American patriotism. D. W. Griffith's 1911 *Last Drop of Water*, in which Indians devastate a wagon train, is introduced as "a story of the great American desert." *The Deserter*, a 1912 Bison 101 production about a cavalry officer who saves his fort from a surprise Indian offensive, concludes with a funeral in which the soldier's body is prominently displayed draped in the American colors. *Fighting Blood*, made in 1911, depicts a Civil War veteran instilling a spirit of American loyalty in young people by marching them around behind the flag. Though an Indian attack briefly interrupts this exercise, the arrival of the cavalry quickly reasserts the national theme.

Patriotic motifs overwhelm the sense of violence and exclusion implicit in such scenarios by appealing to a mythology of American national origin centered on the sanctity of the image of the family farm.[1] Americanist Philip Fisher has characterized this ideal as follows: "The farm, particularly the Jeffersonian ideal of a nation of independent, small, self-sufficient, family farms, is a setting that represents an ideal stability. A nation of free democratic individuals who are satisfied and therefore not driven to increase their holdings or to seek ever-greater profits makes possible an unchanging balance between man and nature and between man and his fellow citizens" (12). This Jeffersonian standard embodies deeply held American principles concerning the value of private property widely distributed among the people.[2] It provided a rationale for the European immigrants to found a new social order distinct from that of Europe, and also, and perhaps more significantly, it justified the Anglo settlers' seizure of the domains of indigenous groups who did not conceptualize land in this way.[3]

The ideal of the family farm, while particular to the nationalist sentiments of the United States, invokes a theme common to all national ideologies in which the interrelation of groups within a common culture is contested. On the one hand, nations are, in Benedict Anderson's much-cited phrase, "imagined communities" where all citizens enjoy parity in the conduct of national life. On the other hand, nationalist discourse involves, as Ellis Cashmore has phrased it, a "hierarchy of group identities," in which a dominant segment of the population is designated as the repositors of the national language and appearance. While the principle of equality for all plays an especially prominent role in the nationalist sentiments of the United States, Americans also look to the image of one particular national type who can represent the amalgamation of the wide diversity of groups that make up the American citizenry.[4] As a myth of national origin, the Western focuses on this contradiction in American nationalist discourse, representing it in terms of a struggle over the model structure of the family farm and its corollary principles of endogamy and inheritance.[5]

Nationalist ideology as portrayed in Westerns is wedded to the ideal of the romantic couple.[6] The couple, put forward as a blandly apolitical norm in these films, is actually constructed from the intersection of a multifarious skein of discourses related to racial difference.[7] The definition of the romantic pair as Anglos is a function of their relationship to the land and, in particular, to the image of the family farm. Unlike some other Hollywood genres, Westerns often construe marriage as an economic rather than a romantic union. The concept of the family farm involves a marriage system that can be termed "dynastic" because it is built around the concept of land inheritance and the obligation to conserve this patrimony through group intermarriage.[8] Pierre Bourdieu has characterized the illusion of free choice in such economically charged conditions as the product of what he terms "habitus," a state of emotional preconditioning through which people internalize social attitudes as personal desires. "Socially approved love, or love predisposed to succeed," he writes, "is nothing other than love of one's own social destiny that brings socially predestined partners together along the apparently random paths of free choice" (160). The source of these predilections, according to Bourdieu, lies in materialist concerns involving endogamy and inheritance. He states, "Marriage strategies are inseparable from . . . the whole set of strategies for biological, cultural and social reproduction that every group implements in order to transmit the inherited powers and privileges, maintained or enhanced, to the next generation" (160).

It was during the silent era that Westerns took on the project of delineating a myth of national origin. Though Western lore of the nineteenth century, such as Buffalo Bill Cody's Wild West, surrounded itself with a mantle of authenticity, early filmed Westerns commonly constructed a mise-en-scène which featured anachronistic contemporary clothing and "modern" looking settings. William S. Hart, however, insisted on verisimilitude and vociferously attacked Western films that failed to meet this standard. In response to such criticisms, Western productions self-consciously affected a period look which connoted historicity. Westerns thus came to be seen as representing a privileged vision of America's past. Ward Churchill has argued that the Western's historical settings function ideologically to displace the issue of racial difference onto the past, thereby eliding the ongoing—and remediable—oppression of native peoples that continues to this day.

The Western's aura of verisimilitude, most notably cultivated in its construction of star personas and its tradition of location shooting, has obscured the way these productions address the contradiction in nationalist ideology I have described. One reason for studying the silent Western is that our temporal and cultural distance from these films renders their rhetorical contrivances more transparent. In this essay I will examine the ways in which some silent Westerns use tropes of the body, the landscape, and the law to negotiate the racially based contradiction in American nationalist ideology contained in the ideal of the family on the land.[9] My discussion is not limited to matters of plot, character, and dialogue, but encompasses more suppressed and pervasive representational strategies that support—or sometimes substitute for—these features as discourses which both construct and subvert racially based dominance. My argument responds to Ella Shohat's call for a textually based multicultural analysis that reads ethnicity as a structuring absence or what Edward Said has referred to as a structure of attitudes and reference. In addition, I have rejected the formula of binary oppositions, which has characterized most work on the Western up to now, in favor of a model of what Homi K. Bhabha terms hybridity, in which a wide dispersion of fragmented cultural motifs is related to the complex operations of power and resistance. My object is to draw on these modes of analysis to examine the way in which Hollywood's production of Westerns during the silent period encodes a mythology of national origin.

The Body: Imagined Communities and the Blood Pyramid

Anthropologist George Stocking has summarized the prevailing views on race at the turn of the century in terms of the widely used term "blood" to signify group identification. Though the term "blood" was used as a synonym for race and implied characteristics that were inherited rather than environmental, the strong Lamarkian bias of the day permitted people to assume that environmentally induced characteristics could also be inherited. This confusion, still present to be sure in prevailing social attitudes towards the topic, was more pronounced before the popularization of genetics made a sharper distinction in the public's mind between hereditary and environmental factors in the constitution of human beings. The result was a blurring of the distinction often cited in anthropological writings between class and caste in which the former concept connotes a malleable identity that would lend itself to assimilation while the latter implies an ineluctable difference that called for subordination or extermination.[10] Though the views most widely voiced during the period I am concerned with did not articulate clear principles that would define the nature of this distinction, they typically grouped Homo sapiens according to some form of pyramidal hierarchy that placed Northern Europeans at the pinnacle and other groups at varying distances from this elevated position. This scheme understood intermarriage between Anglos and Indians as a greater threat to the purity of Anglo blood than intermarriage between Anglos and Southern Europeans, who were seen as a class rather than a caste and thus as more readily assimilable into the world of Anglo privilege. Mestizo Mexicans, as part Southern European and part Indian, ranked somewhere near the middle of the hierarchy.[11] Heavily influenced by Darwin, the "blood pyramid" also typically included an evolutionary dimension, with animals at the lowest level. Although the concept of the blood pyramid was useful for establishing a national type, it was at odds with the ideal of an imagined community of equals. Writers like Theordore Roosevelt attempted to circumvent this contradiction by advocating the benefits of a judicious blending of Teutonic blood (Roosevelt's ideal type) with that of closely related groups to insure the continued revitalization of the Teutonic stock.[12]

Westerns were quick to adopt this popular discourse in their early days. For example, William S. Hart's 1916 *The Dawn Maker*, which features Hart as a half-breed, depicts him as torn between his two "bloods." Ultimately, he sacrifices himself to save the Anglo woman he loves from afar, who bears the overdetermined name of Blanche White. Similarly, the prologue to the 1923 Western *The Covered Wagon* reads: "The Blood of America is the Blood of pioneers—the Blood of lion-hearted men and women who carved a splendid civilization out of an uncharted wilderness." While this sentiment refers most obviously to the suffering undergone by the Anglo settlers, it also implies a "bloodline" of pioneer stock.

In early Westerns, this clouded rhetoric is most fully expressed in the persona of the cowboy hero. The image of authenticity associated with these figures concealed a message of blood. From the days of Buffalo Bill and other dime-novel heroes, Western stars were often seen as "real" historical personages. In the movies, cowboy heroes like William S. Hart, Al Jennings, and Tim McCoy claimed to have lived through versions of many of the events they enacted on screen. For others like Tom Mix and Ken Maynard, acting consisted largely of displays of the cowboy skills they had developed on the rodeo and Wild West circuit. Many played characters whose first names were the same as their own or, as in the case of Broncho Billy Anderson, they changed their names to those of the characters they played.[13] Richard Slotkin and Jane Tompkins identify these figures as Anglo. However, Western heroes are also importantly associated with the devalued groups whose land is being invaded. The cowboy's costume, for example, typically features the beading and fringe characteristic of Indian attire, and he often travels with Indian companions who teach him the secrets of the land. The hero's double identification with Anglo privilege and Indian ways allows him to express both the hierarchy of racial privilege and the egalitarian values of imagined community. He is depicted as occupying the pinnacle of the blood pyramid at the same time as he is seen as a model of egalitarianism.

The double meaning contained in the hero's persona may function in complicated ways. Consider, for example, two star-driven features of the mid-1920s, *The Great K and A Train Robbery* (1926), with Tom Mix, and *Red Raiders* (1927), with Ken Maynard. Both films poke fun at members of ethnic groups unfavorably ranked on the blood pyramid, yet both also construct subtle discourses that portray their heroes as champions of equality. While the conclusion of both narratives consists of an endogamous union between the hero and an Anglo woman, the films' rhetorical strategies allow for crucial equivocations on the issue of race.

Fig. 1

The Great K and A Train Robbery features a black porter called Snowball ("one of the few dark clouds without a silver lining"), whose terror at the threat of train robbers makes him the subject of a good deal of the film's low humor. Snowball has devised a scheme to insure his safety by mounting a gun on the back of his belt under his white jacket which he can "draw" by pulling on a string in the front. The figure of Snowball, with his firearm protruding from the back of his jacket, is frequently featured for comic effect (Figure 1).[14] As might be expected, the gun goes off accidentally at one point causing the black porter much consternation.

In contrast to its portrait of the grotesque and risible body of Snowball, *The Great K and A Train Robbery* presents the athletic Tom Gordon (Mix), who is introduced dangling from a rope over an immense gorge. Mix's agility is showcased throughout the narrative, which calls upon him to perform such stunts as conducting fistfights on the top of the train, jumping his horse off a balcony, and mounting the horse from the train. The virtuosity of these feats attests to Mix's right to occupy a position at the top of the blood pyramid. At the same time, however, his relationship with his horse attests to his character's egalitarian values. The horse, Tony, who famously appeared in all Mix's films, is initially described as a creature "whose human intelligence aids his master in his perilous work." In this spirit, Gordon speaks to and about Tony as though he were human. ("Tony thinks he has to go where I go," Gordon confides to his friend DeLuxe Harry.) As if to emphasize this point, the film associates the horse and the black man, for if Tony's name seems more appropriate for a human than for an animal, Snowball's name is one often selected for horses. Further, the image of Snowball with his gun cocked at his rear gives the distinct impression of being equipped with a tail. By such strategies the film depicts its hero as a privileged being who is nonetheless committed to an ideal of imagined community—even if this community must include people who are best viewed as animals.

Red Raiders employs many similar devices in a more highly elaborated form. The ethnic humor here concerns Irish and Jewish stereotypes in the lower ranks of the cavalry rather than a black porter. At one point the Irish sergeant exclaims, "Holy saints! With all ye furriners, what's the army comin' to?" As the film's hero John Scott, Ken Maynard displays the superiority of his body to the admiring ethnics in even greater shows of physical agility than Mix indulges in, relying, as does Mix, on a liberal use of undercranking to speed up the action of stunts such as boarding a runaway stage and riding a bucking bronco. (A contemporary review calls Mix's production "the fastest picture ever filmed" [quoted in Birchard 200].) Maynard's feats are rewarded at the film's conclusion when he wins the favor a white woman who is co-owner of a ranch.

The film's eponymous "Red Raiders," played by actual Crow Indians, are referred to as "frenzied—swooping—demons! Shrilling their savage war cry!" The hero's sentiments, however, place him squarely on the Indians' side; Scott pointedly states that he agrees with the government policy of granting them reservations. But egalitarianism is suggested in another way as well. In one of the production's most unfortunate lapses into ethnic stereotyping, Isadore Eisenstein, the Jewish private, tries to sell junk to the Indians by donning Indian attire and attempting to speak to them in sign language (Figure 2). This incident finds a curious echo later when Maynard also dons Indian clothing and pretends to be a medicine man as part of a strategy for infiltrating the enemy camp. Though he does not use sign language, he does attempt a war dance. These rhyming vignettes convey the strong suggestion that ethnic identity is superficial and mutable. As if to reinforce this reading, at one point Isadore calls the Indians "the lost tribes of Israel—mine pipple"; and the Sergeant explains Eisenstein's ability to communicate with "the savages" in sign language by stating, "Sure, they taught it to the Indians." At the

Fig. 2

most obvious level, of course, these comments are meant as comic attacks on Isadore. However, given the repetition of the Jewish private's accommodating behavior by the film's Anglo hero, such sentiments gain a certain credibility. The concluding intertitle, "White Man and Red to share the heritage of the West," reinforces the integrationst theme. The film seems to argue that, while Anglo males are physically superior to all others, at some level members of different groups can be understood as participating in what Ella Shohat has termed "cultural syncretism" (229).

John Ford's 1924 epic *The Iron Horse* displays a similar equivocation. Here Irish and Southern European railroad workers are the objects of the film's ethnic humor. At the conclusion, when the two transcontinental railroads meet, everyone comes together in a spirit of community as one Italian worker proclaims, "Me—I Irish now, too. I marry Nora Hogan" and another examines the pigtail of a Chinese worker. Even the hostile Indians are humanized in the film's last battle sequence when Ford's camera lingers over a fallen brave mourned by his dog.

Despite these gestures of communal harmony, however, the film speaks another language in which the body represents an ineluctable statement of difference. The story's villain Bauman is ultimately revealed as a white man who has caused trouble by masquerading as an Indian. Through most of the film he is able to suppress this link with the film's

Fig. 3

racial others by wearing a moustache and a bulky fur coat that conceals his body (Figure 3). His efforts are constricted, however, by a physical anomaly: he has only two fingers on his right hand (Figure 4). Whatever his disguises, this unalterable physical trait marks Bauman as irrevocably "other."

If the "lack" suggested by Bauman's missing fingers is understood as marking a deficiency of masculine potency, some of Ford's comic business involving the film's ethnic workers becomes significant. In a comic interlude two Irish workers, Sergeant Slattery and Corporal Casey, take a third, Private Mackay, to the dentist to have a tooth extracted. As this scene suggests, the ethnic male body is seen as malleable; it readily submits to rituals in which its integrity may be transgressed. Like Bauman, but in a more benignly comic manner, the ethnics possess bodies in which lack may replace inviolable masculine potency.

By contrast, the depiction of the story's hero Davey Brandon speaks of a truth contained in the body of an Anglo male which counters the film's spirit of egalitarianism with a claim about the justice of racial hierarchies. The film focuses on the muscularity of the male physique, an unusual strategy for its day. In Davey's climactic fistfight with Bauman, both combatants contrive to lose their shirts during the altercation (Figure 5). If visual evidence is to be credited, Davey's victory over his

Figs. 4 and 5

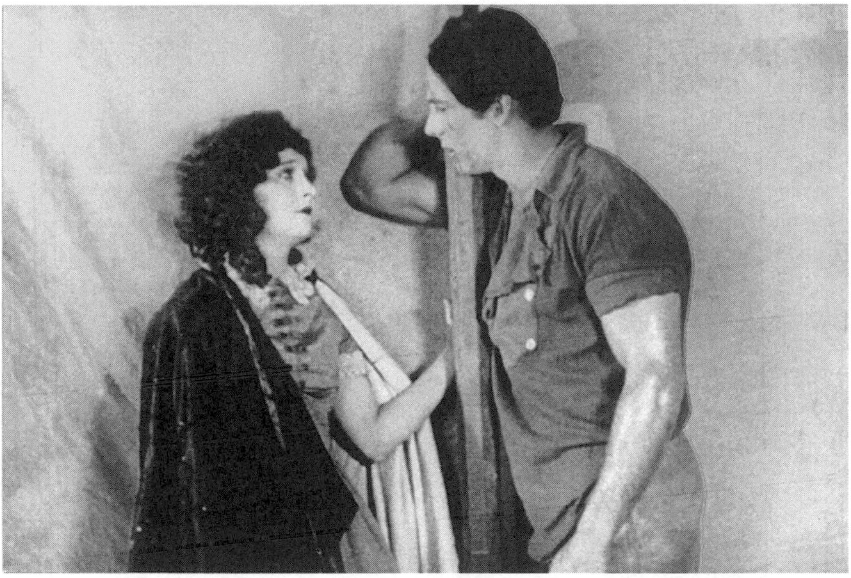

Fig. 6

nemesis in this scene is to be construed as the result of a superior anatomy rather than superior fighting skills. Davey's body thus functions as an advertisement for the right of Anglo males to rule those associated with racial others. Though Davey's friendship with the rustic ethnics allows him to participate in the communal spirit that characterizes *The Iron Horse*'s conclusion, his muscular unclothed body attests to his unquestionable right to a position at the pinnacle of the blood pyramid.

Each of these films features a conclusion in which the hero is united with an Anglo woman for whom he proves himself worthy by demonstrating his physical superiority. As if to emphasize this point, one of Davey Brandon's encounters with Miriam Marsh, the love interest of *The Iron Horse*, again exposes his bulging biceps, thereby graphically representing his strength (Figure 6). The heroes of all three films must win out over romantic competitors who are seen as unworthy not only because of their unscrupulous behavior but also because of their visible lack of masculine prowess. In *The Great K and A Train Robbery*, for example, Tom Mix's unsuccessful rival is introduced in an intertitle that states, "If he went to college, it must have been Vassar." The unhappy fate of this would-be suitor is further signaled near the end of the film when he

Fig. 7

appears clad in a woman's nightgown (Figure 7). The stories thus construct their protagonists as worthy husbands both because they occupy a position at the pinnacle of the blood pyramid and because their clear physical superiority to their intended spouses appears to necessitate their assuming a paternalistic role as protectors of women.

The Landscape: Imperialism and Resistance

Scenery lies at the heart of the Western's appeal. The success of *The Great Train Robbery* with its outdoor setting spurred moviemakers' searches for suitable Western locales and was a major factor in the industry's relocation to Hollywood. In 1910 Bison Films purchased eighteen thousand acres in the Santa Ynez Canyon and joined forces with the 101 Ranch Wild West Show based there to create Bison 101, which became a prolific producer of Westerns shot on location in Southern California. Other production companies quickly joined the search for "authentic" outdoor locations.

The verisimilitude of location photography, however, should not be taken at face value. Edward Buscombe has shown that traditions in American painting wielded a powerful influence over the nascent art of cinema in the early years of the century and has traced the influence

Fig. 8: Thomas Cole, "A scene from 'The Last of the Mohicans,' Cora kneeling at the feet of Tamenund." (Reprinted with permission of the Wadsworth Atheneum, Hartford. Bequest of Alfred Smith)

of Frederic Remington and other painters of vivid action on the imagery of Western films. The nationalist sentiment associated with visual representations of American landscape was by then an entrenched tradition, most strongly associated with Thomas Cole and the Hudson River School and later with Alfred Bierstadt and the Rocky Mountain School (Figure 8).[15]

In a broader consideration of the traditions of landscape painting, W.J.T. Mitchell has understood representations of scenery as exemplifying a complicated commentary on imperialist aspiration. Mitchell writes, "Landscape might be seen . . . as something like the 'dreamwork' of imperialism, unfolding its own movement in time and space from a central point of origin and folding back on itself to disclose both utopian fantasies of the perfected imperial prospect and fractured images of unresolved ambivalence and unsuppressed resistance" (10). This approach to representations of landscape encompasses what others have labeled "the imperial gaze" of the would-be colonizer while also comprehending imagery of what Mitchell calls "ambivalence" and "resistance." These latter phenomena arise when the vision of nature that forms the subject of such works cannot be apprehended unproblematically but rather bears traces of an indigenous presence whose perceptions of the landscape betray an otherness which cannot be easily assimilated. Paintings of the wilderness do not always indicate such an awareness, but in some cases works of this kind can be read as commentaries on what Mary Louise Pratt has called "the contact zone."[16]

The visual imagery of Western movies, for the most part, represents the family farm as the goal toward which the story moves. However, the modest, egalitarian implications of this ideal are typically countered by the genre's predilection for grandiose views of scenic panoramas and expansive vistas—the wide open spaces associated with the cowboy protagonist. The implications of such visions of vast territories embraced in a single possessive gaze is far from egalitarian; they rather suggest the more hierarchical, dominating dimension of American imperialist aspirations. At the same time, visions of the landscape may also be associated with the Indians, who frequently appear as wilderness guides or naturalist teachers. What is tacitly understood in such representations is the alien quality of the Indians' relationship to the land for, unlike the Anglos, their societies were not based on the principle of private property. As one commentator puts it: "The Indian . . . saw the land as supernaturally provided for man's use and not subject to sale or individual ownership" (Jacobs 11).[17] In sum, if the grandeur of the Western landscape offers itself up as a seductive spectacle bespeaking dominion and superiority, it may also imply the view of an other who may read the same topography quite differently. The Western's rendering of the modest and idealized image of the family farm is continually undermined by these competing visions.

The contested aspect of the Western's nature imagery implied by this description customarily remains submerged. The lavish 1923 production of *The Covered Wagon*, the most financially successful example of the genre during the silent period, illustrates the way in which Westerns are capable of managing the contradictions inherent in their representations of the land through a discourse of heroic national purpose. *The Covered Wagon* was conceived primarily as a spectacle centered on nature. It featured no major stars, but Paramount trumpeted its expenditures in the process of filming a large wagon train navigating the Oregon trail while on location at the Baker Ranch in Snake Valley, Nevada. The resulting narrative, in which hundreds of people, animals, and covered wagons traversed the great plains, was sold to the public as a national epic, with numerous comparisons to that earlier production having the most valid claim to this title—*The Birth of a Nation*. Paramount's attempt to persuade audiences that *The Covered Wagon* represented the ultimate embodiment of national sentiment is apparent in the film's original program book, which quoted reviews that proclaimed it "the great American picture," "an eloquent document on Americanization," and "sweeping in its power to stimulate patriotism. . . . a living, throbbing page from history." One critic is quoted as claiming that "no-one can sit through a showing of this picture without leaving the theater a better American." These testimonials were followed up by the subsequent commentary of a professor who, after attending the film with his history class, wrote: "another teacher of history enters the field—namely the motion picture. . . . [the filmmakers] have unquestionably caught the spiritual significance of our great Westward movement" (*Covered Wagon* clipping file).

To make its statement on national purpose, the film employs the image of the plow, which recurs in various contexts throughout the story, to signify the sanctity of the family farm. The director James Cruze makes a point of dramatizing the wrongheadedness of some pioneers who commit themselves to an uncertain future in the California gold fields by focusing his camera on the discarded plows they leave behind. Echoing the film's nationalist theme, the leader of the wagon train warns these miscreants: "The pick and shovel never built a country. You've got to have a plow." In keeping with its championship of husbandry, the story concludes with a shot of Will Banion and Molly Wingate, the Anglo romantic couple around whom the plot revolves, before a fenced farmyard that looks almost suburban (Figure 9).[18] By contrast, the film's prevailing images of Indians portray them beside makeshift teepees, and they are literally marginalized in the frame (Figure 10). Further, their hostility toward what the plow represents is made explicit. One intertitle represents the Indian sentiments toward the whites thus: "With him he brings this monster weapon [i.e., the plow] that will bury the buffalo—uproot the forest—and level the mountains."

The film's magnificent scenic displays are constructed as recurring obstacles which the European settlers must overcome in their quest for arable land near America's western border. The dominant visual trope depicts the wagon train piercing the seemingly boundless plains as it winds westward toward Oregon (Figure 11). In addition, many of the story's striking set pieces, such as the crossing of the Platte River and the trek through the Rocky Mountain snowfields, are built around the pioneers' struggle to conquer formidable natural barriers.[19] To a great

Figs. 9 and 10

Fig. 11

extent, Indians are represented as simply part of the hostile natural phenomena that must be overcome to make way for the pioneers' plows. The Shoshones' major attack is staged from the top of a mesa that curves majestically around the canyon where the wagon train has camped; in terms of scale and drama, this setting surrounds the Anglos far more effectively than the Indians could hope to do (Figure 12). In addition, the Shoshones approach their white enemies from behind evergreen branches they have cut for the purpose, thereby further positioning themselves as part of nature. By such strategies the film creates its native antagonists as an extension of the hostile landscape which the pioneers must domesticate and suppresses a more ambivalent view that could recognize the otherness of an alien perspective on the land. At one point in the story, the heroine's mother objects to the removal of a bureau from her wagon, protesting that it contains "rose cuttin's an' flower seeds" brought from the old country. This statement, which goes unchallenged, makes reference to the Edenic garden imagery that permeates the Western while making overt the Eurocentric world view that animates this project.

Fig. 12

The link between the pioneers and the Indians takes the form of two frontiersmen, Bill Jackson and Jim Bridger, both of whom are based on actual historical personages. These two old men demonstrate deep knowledge of and affinities for Indian ways; Bridger even has two Indian wives. Both men are featured in the film's most memorable set piece, the buffalo hunt, where their riding and hunting skills are showcased. In the Indian manner, Jackson hunts the buffalo shirtless and shoots them with bow and arrow. He is also seen triumphantly skinning a buffalo he has slaughtered. In these two figures the threat the Indians represent is domesticated and Anglicized. Moreover, the age of the frontiersmen connects them with an earlier time, thereby suggesting a temporal continuum in which the "primitive" Indians are tied to a past that has gradually given way to an Anglo-dominated present. Further, the image of the buffalo stampeding over the plain integrates animals and scenery. As an endangered species soon to become all but extinct, the buffalo position the threat represented by nature itself as part of the past.

If *The Covered Wagon* exemplifies the degree to which the race-related contradictions of American nationalist ideology can be effectively contained in the Western's depiction of landscape, two films made in the same

Fig. 13

decade, *Last of the Mohicans* (1920) and *The Vanishing American* (1925), foreground the conflicting perspectives on the land more overtly. Significantly, both films deal with the problematic subject of miscegenation, portraying ill-fated romances between white women and Indian men.[20] Both dramatize their tragic stories against a background of spectacular scenery: *Last of the Mohicans* is set in the Hudson River Valley and *The Vanishing American* in Monument Valley.[21] These sublime settings feature craggy peaks and precipitous drops, which the stories exploit by building to climaxes in which major characters plunge off precipices to their deaths (Figures 13 and 14). Human beings thus appear insignificant and fragile in the face of the awesome forces of nature. The landscape in these cases functions less as a challenging obstacle to be overcome than as an overarching force capable of crushing all human aspiration. *The Vanishing American* makes this thesis explicit in its final title, which reads: "For races of men come, live their hour and go, but the mighty stage remains."

In sharp contrast to these spectacles of the awe-inspiring power of nature, the scenes depicting the "forbidden" romances occur in enclosed spaces that are conspicuously bound by framing elements. In *Last of the*

Fig. 14

Mohicans the budding attraction between the Mohican brave Uncas and Cora Munro, the daughter of an Anglo general, takes place in a cave.[22] The film's director Maurice Tourneur frames the young woman's initial admiring gaze at the Indian man as he stands by the tunnel opening (Figures 15 and 16). Later the two have a tryst framed by a window sill as Cora stands in a small room where she has been imprisoned while Uncas is kept without (Figure 17). Similarly, in *The Vanishing American* director George B. Seitz cements the romantic bond between the Indian Nophaie and Marian Warner, the Anglo schoolteacher, when the Indian rescues the white woman from an attempted rape by a white man after witnessing her danger through the window of the schoolhouse (Figure 18).[23] In all of these instances the framing strategies separate the two lovers, visually denying the Indian access to the protected interior spaces that connote safe domesticity. In addition, by reproducing the frame of the film itself, they function self-reflexively to distance the audience from the emotions being portrayed. Finally, by virtue of the contrast they present to the awesome scenery that dominates the action as a whole, these restricted spaces and the emotions that occur within them are made to seem inconsequential and easily overcome.

Figs. 15 and 16

Figs. 17 and 18

If the subject of miscegenation calls up these dramatic visual strategies, it also brings to the foreground implications that the portrayal of landscape in Westerns represents fissures in American nationalist ideology. For while the grandiose mise-en-scène of both of these films is designed to speak to nationalist pride, it also appears as an image of resistance. The overwhelming quality of the landscape represents an immovable object against which the irresistable force of Euroamerican expansionism is powerless. Further, through its association with the films' stories of doomed interracial love, this impasse becomes a metaphor for the incompatibility between the American ideal of egalitarianism and the contrary value of a hierarchical system in which endogamy conserves the privileged position of the dominant group. *The Covered Wagon* never admits to such inconsistencies in its rendering of landscape; instead, it represents Indian culture as a natural force which the heroic pioneers are destined to overcome. Thus, its portrait of the national landscape, though resplendent, is never animated by the traces of heteroglossic voices that could speak of America's diverse cultures.

The Law: Due Process and Property Rights

"In America, the law is king," Thomas Paine once wrote. In no movie genre is this adage more self-evident than in the Western, where matters of legality and ethics are endlessly debated and tested. The fascination with jurisprudence in these films is yet another aspect of their exploration of the race-related contradiction in American nationalist ideology. Two aspects of the law were particularly clear-cut in the productions of the silent era: the conflict over the principle of due process and the opposition of land and money in relation to the law.

It is stating the obvious to assert that the Western's depiction of legal matters is characterized by confusion and conflict. Received wisdom has it that this state of affairs is a byproduct of the genre's setting on the frontier, where civilized values are not firmly entrenched. However, the clashes of legal doctrine that repeatedly surface in such stories may be seen as signs of incommensurable juridical regimes. These, in turn, represent the battle for cultural dominance with which Westerns are concerned. It is not simply that law is slow in coming to the frontier, but that the frontier is a place where American legal ideology must be validated in the face of rival models. In keeping with his status as an archetypal American, the Western hero stands at the center of this conflict.

The significance of due process in the history of American law is attested to by Robert Ferguson, who writes, "Judicial review would become the cultural paradigm for the lawyer's scrutiny" (22).[24] Legal systems in other parts of the world, by contrast, are not wedded to this principle. In an essay comparing judicial practices of diverse cultures, Clifford Geertz characterizes the Indic legal system as one concerned more with judgments than with process. Quoting previous work by David Engel, he writes, "The essence of [traditional Indic] justice is not the fairness of its procedures in sifting through the evidence of particular wrongs, but rather the aptness of final judgments as to the total value of an individual's existence" (20). This system has similarities to that of American Indian society, as described by John Wunder. "For native peoples," writes Wunder, "rights are found in rules and outcomes; for non-natives, rights come from the courts upholding them and the institutions enforcing them against societal or individual wishes" (6). In the larger framework of Indic law, according to Geertz, "right and obligation are seen as relative to position in the social order. . . . Status is substance" (198). The Indic system thus described is organized according to a principle of hierarchy, just as the American system of due process is egalitarian in the sense that it is designed to insure that every case is treated equally.[25]

"Status is substance" could also describe the workings of Western narratives, where the question of guilt or innocence is rarely put at issue and the courtroom appears most often as a place of buffoonery and corruption. Instead, the hero acts as judge and executioner of the "bad guys," whose emblematic black hats signify their status as unregenerate persons. The hero's code "A man's gotta do what a man's gotta do" attests to his loyalty to a way of thinking that will preserve his place on the hierarchy as a (white) male in an environment where cultural supremacy is being contested. This credo, typically stated to an Anglo woman, is intended as an assurance that the speaker is committed to upholding European dominance in the face of challenges from other groups, even as he appropriates the modes of legal thought identified with these groups for the purpose.

The woman, who may be a schoolteacher or, especially in these early films, the daughter of a judge or minister, is customarily thought to stand for civilized values; but the values she represents are more particularized, having to do with the relationship between law and Anglo tradition. Specifically, she is associated with the legal principle of due process in which the written word spells out the mechanism by which the violence inherent in legal punishment is tempered by a commitment to abstract and unvarying juridical precedents and procedures. The authority of the written word in relation to this principle is signified by the films' reverence for books, and, especially in silent Westerns, the Bible, which is seen as the ultimate written statement of incontestable law. In the immensely popular 1912 production *Broncho Billy and the Baby*, for example, the proof of the criminal-protagonist's reform is that he reads the Bible given to him by a beneficent woman. In Westerns this reverence for writing is linked with the European tradition and opposed to the oral cultures of the New World.[26]

The 1923 film version of Owen Wister's canonical Western novel *The Virginian* provides a revealing illustration of the way in which these differing principles animate many Western plots.[27] The story's major conflict concerns the irreconcilable views on the law held by the eponymous hero and an Eastern-bred schoolteacher called Molly Wood, whom he eventually marries. Molly's ire is sparked when the Virginian supervises the lynching of a band of cattle rustlers. Even after the two are married, Molly is further incensed when her new husband agrees to a shootout with the film's villain Trampas. In response to her pleas that due process be observed, the Virginian protests: "Can't you see how it must be with a man?" Molly, however, retains her attitude of stern disapproval until, after the showdown, the Virginian returns to her. At that point an intertitle explains, "Molly's New England conscience surrendered to love." To appreciate the significance of this final appeal to love, it is necessary to view it in the context of the film's submerged representation of cultural struggle.

Like many Westerns, *The Virginian* tries to repress evidence of the presence of a group whose social mores could challenge those of the Anglos. However, the film does not entirely succeed in this project, for it reveals traces of a disturbing vision of otherness. Though Trampas, the story's chief antagonist, is white, he is in league with a group of criminals who are initially identified in relation to a Mexican cattle rustler called Spanish Ed. Spanish Ed, who is described as "one of the unbranded mavericks," is thus positioned metonymically as the malignant influence whose spirit contaminates the Anglos who join him.[28] That Spanish Ed operates under an alien system of values is made clear in the superstitious anxiety he falls prey to in the face of omens such as a broken horseshoe and a full moon. The prophetic quality the film attaches to the portentous prognostications Ed makes on recognizing these signs suggests that there may be some validity to his beliefs; Ed's values could not be entirely without merit if they enable him to make accurate predictions. By presenting Ed's beliefs as superstition, the film attempts to position them as "primitive" and unsystematic. Nonetheless, they are also portrayed as revelatory and thus reality-based, even if their power is restricted to their ability to predict Ed's inevitable doom. Thus, they pose an implict challenge to the film's depiction of Anglo law as the only law.

At the same time Spanish Ed's exotic beliefs are made to seem disturbingly potent, Molly's quintessentially European convictions are called into question. The Virginian connects her concept of the law to her overly rigid notions of Old World etiquette, which he terms "childish." The belief in due process which lies at the center of Anglo-American legal thought thus appears in danger of trivialization. In such a contested setting, the authority of received European tradition appears shaky, and opposing systems of belief gain a certain plausibility. With this situation as a background, Molly's landlady argues that the Virginian must act as he does "to make this country safe for such as you to teach our children in." In other words, hierarchy must be established before equality can be preached. Anglo civilization must establish itself as *the* civilization before its law can establish itself as *the* law.

The audience, presumably predisposed to side with Molly's position rather than that of the Virginian, is nonetheless led to read the hero's vigilante actions sympathetically by the emphasis the story places on the extreme provocations that lead him to act as he does. He supervises the lynching of his friend Steve at the behest of his employer, the ranch owner Judge Henry, whose title is certainly significant in this context. Further, an intertitle lays the blame on Trampas for the deaths of Steve and Shorty, the two cowboys the villain has led into criminality. "Trampas did this," the Virginian states to his companion on discovering Shorty's body, "but we can't prove it—any more than we can prove he led the rustlers. Steve and Shorty—two reasons why I have to follow this trail alone." Since the audience has witnessed Trampas's culpable actions, there is no reason to doubt the validity of the inferences contained in the Virginian's judgment of him. Sympathy for the hero is further developed through the film's discreet presentation of the violence he perpetrates. In the lynching scene, the strung-up bodies are never depicted, and the shootout is presented entirely in a long shot. Any quality such representations might convey of bloodthirsty vengefulness on the protagonist's part is thus minimalized.

The association between Molly's convictions about the law and the written word is rendered obliquely in a few telling references to writing associated with the Virginian's friends Steve and Shorty, whom Trampas

Fig. 19

has corrupted. Both of these characters are depicted in terms of failed attempts to cement their relationship to the Anglo community through printed representations. Steve scrawls a note in pencil on the top of a newspaper bidding goodbye to the Virginian just before he is lynched (Figure 19). Shorty carries a printed advertisement in his hat which describes an accordion he wants to buy so that he can play at community dances (Figure 20). These printed messages, so critical to the characters who are associated with them, are nonetheless too frail to carry any social weight. It is only by the merest chance that the Virginian discovers the newspaper on which Steve has written his poignant farewell. Shorty's advertisement is scoffed at by Trampas, and when Shorty attempts to create an atmosphere of conviviality between himself and his outlaw companion by playing the paltry instrument he does possess, a mouth organ, Trampas, the film's symbol of antisocial behavior, becomes annoyed by the noise and kills him.

Such motifs suggest a cultural moment when the printed word had yet to achieve the authority that would allow it to legislate the terms by which a cohesive and ordered society could operate. The sense of the fragility of the printed word these incidents convey is reinforced by a

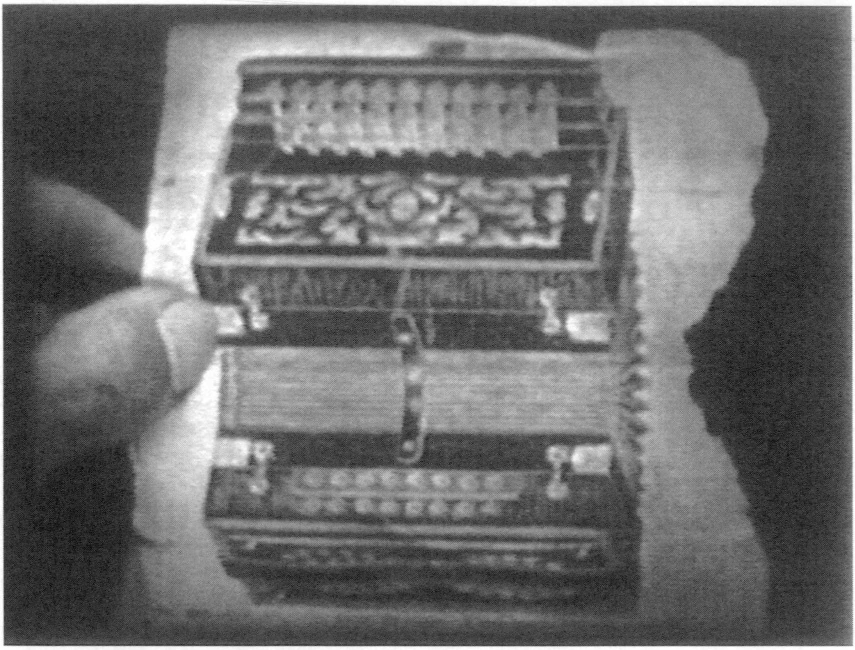

Fig. 20

vivid allusion to the existence of a still-powerful oral tradition associated with the indigenous New World peoples in which face-to-face interaction is subject to continual renegotiation. *The Virginian* is the film in which the hero utters the famous line, "When you call me that—SMILE!" This admonition implies that statements are to be read in the context of factors such as intonation and body language, a mode of communication impossible in cultures like those of Europe in which writing prevails.

These threats to the dominance of writing and the principle of due process it enables are countered by a third piece of paper which appears later in the action: a note to the Virginian from Judge Henry as the hero embarks on his honeymoon. "When you come back," the note reads, "you will find a parcel of land waiting for you" (Figure 21). Though this handwritten note is as flimsy as the other printed materials in the film, it refers to a more solid entity, namely land. It promises that by marrying the hero, Molly will become the wife of a landowner. The Virginian's commitment to his "duty as a man" over due process brings about this resolution and insures that his group—and especially the family he is in the process of founding—will be able to enjoy the spoils of conquest.

and when you come back you
will find a parcel of land waiting
for you
God bless you both
The Judge

Fig. 21

Only after the disposition of the land is securely established in favor of the European settlers is the country seen as being "safe" for the education of children in the democratic principles of egalitarian due process. Molly may "love" the Virginian, but the inevitability of her doing so is a function of what Bourdieu calls her "love of her own social destiny."

The Western genre's passionate involvement with land is a function of its larger concern with the sanctity of private property and its relation to the law. Outlaws are typically defined by their crimes against property rather than persons: cattle rustling, robberies of trains and banks, and inheritance swindles are the most common punishable offenses in these films.[29] In matters of law, Westerns grant land a privileged position in relationship to other forms of property, opposing it to a more modern capitalist money economy.

The significance of this valuation and its relation to the Anglo-American legal system has been explored by political theorist J.G.A. Pocock, who states: "English law is built on notions of property and attendant rights" (335). Under this system of property right, land occupies a preferential place. Pocock connects this model of land privilege with an Englightenment view of the integrated self inasmuch as the permanence and solidity of land can be seen as attesting to the wholeness and stability of the person who owns it. By contrast, the newer money economy is thought to spawn personalities characterized by dispersed allegiances and inconsistent values whose attachment to insubstantial commodities announces their inability to act rationally in the interests of the common good.[30]

In Westerns the values of law-abiding people are represented in terms of their commitment to a Lockean conception of land, and the town is seen as fostering a corrupt money economy in the form of crooked bankers and rigged poker games. This perspective looks back to an older system in which land rather than money formed the basis of an individual's worth. The genre manages to join this conservative economic outlook with its racist bias by associating the new money economy with the racial others (especially Mexicans) whose traditional cultures are being supplanted in these stories. To recognize the land-based economies of these marginalized groups would be to invalidate the argument that the Anglos possessed the only lawful claim to the land because they were the only group with a coherent philosophy governing its use.[31] Thus the money culture of the saloon is associated with dance-hall girls who are often Mexican, and the itinerant lifestyles of Mexican bandido figures attest to their reliance on a cash-based economy.

Western movies handle this opposition in a variety of ways. Most of D. W. Griffith's early Westerns are distinguished by their lack of attention to the rights of Anglo landowners, possibly because, as a Southerner, Griffith associated the image of the family homestead with plantation culture rather than with the Western pioneers. Though the plot of William S. Hart's last film *Tumbleweeds* (1924) concerns the Anglo struggle for land acquisition on the Cherokee strip, his earlier Westerns focus on the new, urban money economy and its corrupting influences, typically referring to landowning only inferentially. Hart's 1916 *Hell's Hinges*, for example, is entirely set in the town referred to in its title. There an Eastern-bred minister readily falls prey to the wiles of a Mexican saloon girl while the good-badman played by Hart wins the heart of the minister's pure sister. In this film as in his others, Hart's cowboy attire and its association with work on the land helps to construct his character as a down-to-earth figure whose basic goodness will triumph in the end. Hart's films also drew on the widespread publicity about the ranch in Newhall, California, where the star himself resided to anchor such fictions to a land-centered value system.

John Ford's first feature-length film, the 1917 *Straight Shooting*, consti-

Fig. 22

tutes an exemplary instance of the nature of the opposition between money and land cultures and their connection to the law and to racial others. The film's main conflict occurs between ranchers and farmers. The imperialistic overreaching of the ranchers in relation to the land is stressed at the outset when an intertitle describes "[t]he ranchers' *empire*, a vast grazing land. A once endless territory now divided and cut by farmers' fences" (italics added). The legality of the farmers' cause is similarly emphasized early in the story, when a subtitle describing the movie's central figure reads: "For years Sweet Water Sims has fought for his *right* to plow the plains" (italics added). The mediating figure in this struggle over the land is Cheyenne Harry (Harry Carey), an outlaw hired by the ranchers who is turned away from his nefarious purpose by the sight of Sims and his daughter mourning at the grave of the farmer's son, murdered by the ranchers.

Harry's conversion to the farmers' cause is built around a much admired point of view shot in which Ford depicts the misty-eyed outlaw's contemplation of the scene of the bereaved family through a blurred lens (Figures 22 and 23). This blurring of vision soon leads Harry to adopt a new perspective, and, after discussing the situation with Sims and his

Fig. 23

daughter, he announces, "Now I can see those boys [the ranchers] as they really are. Thank you for opening my eyes." "Things as they really are" thus comes to signify the justice of the farmers' position, and the blurring of the camera's lens invites the spectator to share in Harry's re-vision of the situation and to see it as "opening my eyes" rather than as a revised political alliance.

The integrity of purpose associated with the farmers' land-based culture is contrasted with the inconsistency and insubstantiality of saloon life, where Harry can be drinking buddies with a rancher at one moment and deadly enemies with the same man at another, and where the sheriff cowers in the face of the ranchers' power and is easily corrupted by their bribes. Though Harry is able to rouse his itinerant outlaw gang in the defense of the farmers, their noble action is later compromised when we witness a Mexican member of the band gratuitously stealing a jar of jam from the Sims's larder. Not being farmers, the outlaws lack respect for personal property.

Harry ultimately rejects Sims's offer to "be my son" and inherit the farm, concluding that "I belong on the range." This decision expresses the irresolvable nature of the contradictory values the film has associated

Fig. 24

with him.[32] In particular, his relationship to Mexicans, the film's racial others, is portrayed as a sign of both his egalitarianism and his moral weakness. In addition, Harry is identified with the wide open spaces of the Western landscape. Despite their steadfast religious piety and legitimate claim to land rights, farmers lack the heroic grandeur associated with this landscape. Ford makes this grandeur palpable in the many commanding views of vast herds of cattle grazing on expansive mountain plateaus he provides in the course of his portrayal of the ranchers and the outlaws (Figure 24). Thus, if *Straight Shooting* ratifies the rights of family farmers to hold jurisdiction over the land by dividing it up into small, equal parts, it also regrets the loss of Anglo dominance this democratic principle implies. It comprehends not only the virtue of a modest republic but also the desire for a boundless empire. In the withdrawal of its main character at the end of the story and his refusal to participate in the project of family farming, the film recognizes the impossibility of resolving these conflicting impulses.

In *The Virginian* and *Straight Shooting*, conflicts inherent in the American legal system are worked through in a highly elaborated manner. However, the issues they raise are common to the genre as a whole.

The threat of indigenous cultures on the one hand and modernity on the other strain the values implied by the concept of "the law of the land" in many directions. Westerns register these strains through equivocation: Though they believe in due process, they are attracted to vigilantism; though they believe in the family farm, they are attracted to visions of empire. In these films, the mandate to support both equality and superiority is the subject of perpetual struggle.

Conclusion

In William S. Hart's 1916 production *The Return of Draw Egan*, the hero courts the heroine by taking her to the top of a hill to view the "beautiful scenery." Such a moment, offered up as an innocuous respite from the serious concerns of the film's action-filled plot, is actually central to the project of this, as of all other Westerns. Far from constituting an empty space around which significant issues are gathered, the romantic couple in these films is saturated with meaning, for the couple forms the cornerstone of the genre's image of the family on the land. This image, in turn, is built up out of myriad discourses concerning the body, the landscape, and the law. If the race-related ideology that informs each of these discourses is a conflicted one, this conflict reflects the ambivalent rhetoric embedded in America's language of national identity. It should not be surprising, then, if these films, like those that followed them, failed to adjudicate an issue that has been left unresolved in the life of the nation itself.

Notes

I would like to thank the UIC Humanities Research Institute for granting funds for the reproduction of frame enlargements for this essay. I am also grateful to Paul Morrissey, who photographed frames from *The Iron Horse*, *Red Raiders*, and *The Great K and A Train Robbery*. I would also like to thank Maxine Ducey of the Wisconsin Film Archives, Mary Carbine of the University of Chicago Film Archives, Sam Gill of the Margaret Herrick Library of the Motion Picture Academy, Errol Stephens of the Seaver Center of Western Literature, and Kevin Mulroy of the Gene Autry Western Heritage Museum for their help in locating films and other materials for this essay.

1. I use the term mythology in the sense specified by Malinowski, who states: "myth acts as a charter for the present-day social order; it supplies a retrospective pattern of moral values, sociological order, and magical beliefs, the function of which is to strengthen tradition and endow it with a greater value and presige by tracing it back to a higher, better, more supernational reality of initial events" (quoted in Worseley 5).

2. This principle is ultimately traceable to John Locke, whose two treatises on government deeply influenced the formation of American values.

3. Given the changing meanings and connotations of the terminology used to signify cultural differences, it is perhaps well to note that I have adopted a somewhat ad hoc approach in this essay in the interests of clear, varied communication. I follow the practice of the films themselves in referring to the indigenous peoples of the New World as Indians. I also use the terms "Anglo," "European," and "white" interchangeably to designate the Northern European pioneers. Finally, I employ the term "race" loosely as a synonym for cultural difference, again referring to the conventions of popular usage as a guide.

4. A pronounced emphasis on the latter aspect of this contradiction is often termed "ethnonationalism." The nature of the contradiction itself has been explored by Balibar, "Racism and Nationalism"; Chatterjee; and Wallerstein. Renato Rosaldo has invoked the concept of second class citizenship to account for the way in which the contradiction in nationalist discourse is negotiated.

5. Two widely discussed recent books on the Western, Richard Slotkin's *Gunfighter Nation* and Jane Tompkins's *West of Everything*, also see the genre as a discourse that defines American values. However, Slotkin focuses on the formula's depiction of race and its connection with the American predilection for violence, while Tompkins stresses the issue of gender. The argument I put forward in my book *Creating the Couple* understands both race and gender as pivotal to the cultural work undertaken by Westerns by virtue of the relationship of these terms to the genre's concept of private property, and in particular the ideal of the family farm. The present essay represents a development of some of the ideas in my book. To avoid redundancy, I have not cited the secondary sources used there.

6. This image of heterosexual love was especially favored during the silent era. As Edward Buscombe has noted, "Those who assume that the Western hero traditionally preferred horses to women may be unprepared for the frequency with which romantic love turns the mechanism of the plot in these early films" (*BFI Companion* 26). Though, as Tag Gallagher pointed out in his essay "Shootout at the Genre Corral," early Westerns have received scant critical attention up to now; such commentary as does exist tends to downplay or even ignore the central role played by the romantic couple in creating the genre's ideological meaning.

7. A similar project of exploring "how the norm is constructed" has been undertaken by Richard Dyer in his essay "White." Also germane in this context is Stuart Hall's definition of inferential racism as "those apparently naturalized representations whose ethnocentric and racist propositions are inscribed in them as a set of unquestioned assumptions" (36–37).

8. The custom of group intermarriage is a more general rule of traditional cultures, where individuals operate on the principle of "respect for lineage and ancestry, in the concept of oneself as a trustee for the handing on of blood, property and tradition" (Stone 683–684). In European societies, however, property is closely held among a restricted group rather than widely distributed, as in the American model.

9. Because I am not concerned here with matters of genre definition, I have felt free to discuss any film customarily called a Western, even though, like *Last of the Mohicans*, it might not fit some descriptions of the formula. For more complete histories of the Western during the silent era, see Brownlow; Fenin and Everson; Garfield; and Buscombe, *The BFI Companion to the Western*. For filmographies, see Langman, Leutrat, and Pitts.

10. For a discussion of this distinction, see Goody.

Discriminations between caste and class do not necessarily rest on genetic determinants. In an essay on neo-racism, Etienne Balibar has argued that the prevalent form of contemporary prejudice "is a racism whose dominant theme is not biological heredity but the insurmountability of cultural differences, a racism which, at first sight, does not postulate the superiority of certain groups or peoples in relation to others but 'only' the harmfulness of abolishing frontiers, the incompatibility of lifestyles and traditions . . . [placing people] a priori into a genealogy, into a determinism that is immutable and intangible in origin" (21–22).

11. In the 1920s the Mexican government placed an embargo on the then-popular "greaser films," thereby leading Hollywood to drastically cut down on its production of movies featuring objectionable Mexican stereotypes (Woll 28). In his essay on villains in early Westerns, Peter Stanfield comments, "While the Indian in his noble guise is at least given some positive traits, the Mexican, as these films demonstrate, tends to be depicted in a wholly negative manner" (107). With few exceptions, this generalization is borne out by my own viewing of silent Westerns. The cause may lie in the greater threat posed by Mexicans to Anglo land claims during the period in question.

12. Richard Slotkin, who argues that Roosevelt's ideas on race heavily influenced the American national agenda in general and the ideology of Westerns in particular, also stresses the discourse of "blood" in Roosevelt's writings. For another perspective on Roosevelt's influence on the development of the Western, see Buscombe, "Painting the Legend." Philip Durham describes Roosevelt's close friendship with Owen Wister, author of the seminal Western novel *The Virginian*, and traces Roosevelt's direct influence on Wister's book.

13. The claims made by these stars were as often as not exaggerated or simply false. Here is Kevin Brownlow on Tom Mix: "In his desire to make an impact, and thus make money, he retold his life as it might have been written for the screen. In autobiographical articles—no doubt ghostwritten—he told haphazard tales of adventures so wild that his career eclipsed for sheer action and breathless pace the first few chapters of the Bible" (300–301).

For a discussion of the construction of the personas of Hart and others, see Slotkin, pages 242–245 et passim.

14. The frame enlargements that illustrate various points of my argument are reproduced from 16mm prints and videos. Because of the poor quality of the available prints of several of the films I discuss, some of the images have been computer enhanced.

15. For discussions of these schools in relation to the development of American nationalism, see Boime, Miller, Nash, Novak, Snyder, and Wilson. For classic analyses of the more general significance of land in American culture, see Marx and Smith.

16. Neil Whitehead and Brian Ferguson employ the term "tribal zone" to indicate a similar phenomenon.

17. Vine DeLoria and Clifford Lytle have also commented on the place of property in tradition Indian culture: "People felt free to use other people's property within reason and only a continuous and careless use of property invoked any kind of social sanction" (162).

18. In Westerns, fences signify the privately held domain of the family farm, as I argue in some detail in *Creating the Couple*.

19. Yet another such sequence in which the pioneers battle a prairie fire set by the

Indians was removed for reasons of length before the film was released (*Covered Wagon* clipping file).

20. The origin of American miscegenation laws in the desire to protect Anglo property rights is discussed in Carby.

21. Though it claims to take place in the Hudson River Valley, *The Last of the Mohicans* was actually shot in California. *The Vanishing American*, however, was indeed filmed in Monument Valley, despite the widespread publicity of a later era which touted Ford's 1939 *Stagecoach* as the first film to make use of this locale.

22. In James Fennimore Cooper's original novel, Cora is revealed to be part black during the course of the story. The recent movie version of the tale with Daniel Day Lewis avoids the issue of miscegenation entirely by recreating the romance as one between Cora and Hawkeye, the Mohicans' white companion.

23. The summary of the original script of *The Vanishing American* prepared by Paramount characterizes the story as demonstrating "the difficulties in the path of any satisfactory mixing of the two races." The reader concludes, "It is difficult to see how, in view of the harrowing character of the story, it could be made available for pictures without radical revision" (*Vanishing American*). Zane Grey, author of the fictional version of the story, equated the tragic end of the interracial romance with the extermination of the Indian people by having Nophaie die of influenza, a plague visited upon the Indians by the Anglos. (The film engineers an accidental death for the Indian hero.) Grey concludes his novel with a poignant statement on the hopelessness of the Indians' position: "The broken Indians and the weary mustangs passed slowly out upon the desert" (308). Aleiss claims that in another unpublished version of the story Grey has Nophaie and Marian marry even as Nophaie recognizes the inevitable extinction of his people (472).

24. The centrality of the principle of due process to American jurisprudence is largely a phenomenon of the twentieth century. Though the phrase is employed in relation to a broad spectrum of legal issues, I am referring here to its use with respect to procedural rather than substantive matters.

25. Geertz considers his generalizations about the wide variety of judicial systems he is surveying as crude and approximate. My own extrapolations from Geertz's scheme are far cruder, and probably involve woeful distortions of significant subtleties. My purpose, however, is simply to highlight the fact that there *are* discernibly different legal principles at work in Western films, and that connections exist between these principles and the competing conceptions of the social order which the genre puts at issue.

26. For a discussion of the relationship between the written word and American legal institutions of due process, see Cover. For a more developed argument on the general connection between writing and the law in the Western genre, see Wexman.

27. One commentator has claimed that Wister's *The Virginian* was read by more Americans of its time than any other American novel (Durham vii). A stage version by Kirk LaSalle also enjoyed great popularity in its day. The characters' many lengthy debates over legal issues were thus presumably familiar to a good portion of the film's original audience. Wister's vision of his hero's racial identity is evident in an essay he wrote entitled "The Evolution of the Cowpuncher," in which he characterized the cowboy heroes as "Saxon boys of picked courage" (Durham vii).

28. Cecil B. DeMille's version of the story, released in 1914, omits the character of Spanish Ed but dresses Trampas in Mexican garb.

29. Michel Foucault has designated the eighteenth century as the time in European

law when offense against property seem to gain ascendency over crimes of violence in the minds of the public (75).

30. For a similar analysis of the Anglo-American legal tradition of property right, see MacPherson.

31. For a discussion of Indian conceptions of land, see Ward Churchill's book *Fantasies of the Master Race*. Churchill writes, "Land . . . is the absolutely essential issue defining viable conceptions of Native America, whether in the past, present or future. Contests for control of territory have also been the fundamental basis of Indian/non-Indian interaction since the moment of first contact, and underlie the virtually uninterrupted (and ongoing) pattern of genocide suffered by American Indians over the past half-millennium" (131).

32. The version of the film generally in circulation substitutes an ending added in 1925 in which Harry marries Joan, Sims's daughter, in place of the original resolution in which he relinquishes her to another suitor (Gallagher 22).

Reference List

Aleiss, Angela. "The Vanishing American: Hollywood's Compromise to Indian Reform." *Journal of American Studies* (December 1991): 467–472.

Anderson, Benedict. *Imagined Communities: Reflections on the Origin and Spread of Nationalism*. London: Verso, 1983.

Anderson, Robert. "The Role of the Western Film in Industry Competition, 1907–11." *Journal of the University Film Association* 1, no. 2 (Spring 1979).

Balibar, Etienne. "Is There a Neo-Racism?" Balibar and Wallerstein. 17–28.

———. "Racism and Nationalism." Balibar and Wallerstein. 37–68.

———, and Immanuel Wallerstein. *Race, Nation, Class: Ambiguous Identities*. New York: Verso, 1991.

Bhabha, Homi K., ed. *Nations and Narration*. New York: Routledge, 1990.

Birchard, Robert S. *King Cowboy: Tom Mix and the Movies*. Burbank, Cal.: Riverwood Press, 1993.

Boime, Albert. *The Magisterial Gaze: Manifest Destiny and American Landscape Painting c. 1830–1865*. Washington, D.C.: Smithsonian Institution Press, 1991.

Bourdieu, Pierre. "Land and Matrimonial Strategies." *The Logic of Practice*. Trans. Richard Nice. Stanford, Cal.: Stanford University Press, 1990. 147–61.

Brennan, Timothy. "The National Longing for Form." Bhabha. 44–70.

Brownlow, Kevin. *The War, the West and the Wilderness*. New York: Alfred A. Knopf, 1979.

Buscombe, Edward. *The BFI Companion to the Western*. London: The British Film Institute, 1988.

———. "Painting the Legend: Frederic Remington and the Western." *Cinema Journal* 23, no. 4 (Summer 1984): 12–27.

Carby, Hazel B. "'On the Threshold of Woman's Era': Lynching, Empire and Sexuality." *Critical Inquiry* 12, no. 1 (Autumn 1985): 262–277.

Cashmore, Ellis. *Dictionary of Race and Race Relations*. London: Routledge, 1984.

Chatterjee, Partha. "Nationalism as a Problem in the History of Political Ideas." *Nationalist Thought and the Colonial World*. London: Zed Books Ltd., 1986. 1–53.

Churchill, Ward. *Fantasies of the Master Race*. Monroe, Me.: Common Courage Press, 1992.

Cooper, James Fennimore. *The Last of the Mohicans*. Ed. William Charvat. Cambridge, Mass.: Riverside, 1958.

Cover, Robert M. "Violence and the Word." *Yale Law Journal* 95 (1986): 1,601–1,629.

Covered Wagon, The. Program Book. Academy of Motion Picture Arts and Sciences Library. Los Angeles. Microfiche.

———. Clipping File. Academy of Motion Picture Arts and Sciences Library. Los Angeles.

DeLoria, Vine, and Clifford M. Lytle. *American Indians and American Justice*. Austin: University of Texas Press, 1983.

Durham, Philip. "Introduction." Wister. v–xii.

Dyer, Richard. "White." *Screen* 29, no. 4 (Autumn 1988): 44–65.

Fenin, George N., and William Everson. *The Western: From Silents to the Seventies*. New York: Grossman Publishers, 1973.

Ferguson, Robert. *Law and Letters in American Culture*. Cambridge: Harvard University Press, 1984.

Fisher, Philip. *Hard Facts*. New York: Oxford University Press, 1985.

Foucault, Michel. *Discipline and Punish: The Birth of the Prison*. Trans. Alan Sheridan. New York: Random House, 1979.

Friedman, Lester B., ed. *Unspeakable Images: Ethnicity and the American Cinema*. Urbana: University of Illinois Press, 1991.

Gallagher, Tag. *John Ford: The Man and His Films*. Berkeley: University of California Press, 1986.

———. "Shoot-Out at the Genre Corral: Problems in the 'Evolution' of the Western." *Film Genre Reader*. Ed. Barry Keith Grant. Austin: University of Texas Press, 1986. 202–216.

Garfield, Brian. *Western Films: A Complete Guide*. New York: Rawson Associates, 1982.

Geertz, Clifford. "Local Knowledge: Fact and Law in Comparative Perspective." *Local Knowledge: Further Essays in Interpretive Anthropology*. New York: Basic Books, 1983. 167–234.

Goody, Jack. *Production and Reproduction: A Comparative Study of Domestic Domain*. New York: Cambridge University Press, 1976.

Grey, Zane. *The Vanishing American*. New York: Walter J. Black, Inc., 1925.

Hall, Stuart. "The Whites of Their Eyes: Racist Ideologies and the Media." *Silver Linings*. Ed. George Bridges and Rosalind Brent. London: Lawrence and Wishart, 1981.

Jacobs, Wilbur R. *Dispossessing the American Indian: Indians and Whites on the Colonial Frontier*. New York: Charles Scribners' Sons, 1972.

Koszarski, Diane Kaiser. *The Complete Films of William S. Hart: A Pictorial Record*. New York: Dover Publications, 1980.

Langman, Larry. *A Guide to Silent Westerns*. Westport, Conn.: Greenwood Press, 1992.

Leutrat, André. *L'Alliance brisée: le western des années 1920*. Lyon: Presses Universitaires de Lyon: Institut Lumière, 1985.

MacPherson, C. B. *The Political Theory of Possessive Individualism: Hobbes to Locke*. London: Oxford University Press, 1964.

Marx, Leo. *The Machine in the Garden: Technology and the Pastoral Ideal in America*. New York: Oxford University Press, 1964.

Miller, Angela. *The Empire of the Eye: Landscape Representation and American Cultural Politics 1825–1875*. Ithaca, N.Y.: Cornell University Press, 1993.
Mitchell, W.J.T. "Imperial Landscape." Mitchell. 5–34.
———, ed. *Landscape and Power*. Chicago: University of Chicago Press, 1994.
Nash, Roderick. *Wilderness and the American Mind*. New Haven, Conn.: Yale University Press, 1967.
Novak, Barbara. *Nature and Culture: American Landscape Painting 1825–75*. New York: Oxford University Press, 1980.
Pease, Donald, ed. *National Identities and Post-Americanist Narratives*. Durham, N.C.: Duke University Press, 1994.
Pitts, Michael R. *Western Movies: A TV and Video Guide to 4200 Genre Films*. Jefferson, N.C.: McFarland & Company, Inc., 1986.
Pocock, J.G.A. *The Machievellian Moment: Florentine Political Thought and the Atlantic Political Tradition*. Princeton, N.J.: Princeton University Press, 1975.
Pratt, Mary Louise. *Imperial Eyes: Travel Writing and Transculturation*. New York: Routledge, 1994.
Renan, Ernest. "What Is a Nation?" Bhabha. 8–22.
Rosaldo, Renato. "Cultural Citizenship and Educational Democracy." *Cultural Anthropology* 9, no. 3 (August 1994): 402–411.
Said, Edward W. *Culture and Imperialism*. New York: Alfred A. Knopf, 1993.
Shohat, Ella. "Ethnicities-in-Relation:" Friedman. 215–250.
Sinclair, Andrew. *John Ford: A Biography*. New York: The Dial Press/James Wade, 1979.
Slotkin, Richard. *Gunfighter Nation: The Myth of the Frontier in Twentieth Century America*. New York: Atheneum, 1992.
Smith, Henry Nash. *Virgin Land*. New York: Vintage Books, 1950.
Snyder, Joel. "Territorial Photography." Mitchell. 175–202.
Stanfield, Peter. "The Western 1907–14: A Cast of Villains." *Film History* 1 (1987): 97–112.
Stannard, David E. *American Holocaust: Columbus and the Conquest of the New World*. New York: Oxford, 1992.
Stocking, George W., Jr. "The Turn-of-the Century Concept of Race." *Modernism/Modernity* 1, no.1 (1993): 4–16.
Stone, Lawrence. *The Family, Sex and Marriage in England 1500–1800*. New York: Harper & Row, 1977.
Tompkins, Jane. *West of Everything: The Inner Life of Westerns*. New York: Oxford University Press, 1992.
Vanishing American, The. Production File. Academy of Motion Picture Arts and Sciences Library. Los Angeles.
Wallerstein, Immanuel. "The Ideological Tensions of Capitalism: Universalism Versus Racism and Sexism." Balibar and Wallerstein. 29–36.
Wexman, Virginia Wright. "Star and Genre: John Wayne, the Western and the American Dream of the Family on the Land." *Creating the Couple: Love, Marriage, and Hollywood Performance*. Princeton, N.J.: Princeton University Press, 1993. 67–129.
Whitehead, Neil L., and R. Brian Ferguson, eds. *War in the Tribal Zone*. School of American Research Press, 1992.
Wilson, Rob. "Techno-Euphoria and the Discourse of the American Sublime." Pease. 205–229.

Wister, Owen. *The Virginian*. Ed. Philip Durham. Boston: Riverside, 1968.
Woll, Allen. "From Bandits to President: Latin Images in American Films, 1929–39." *Journal of Mexican History* 4 (1974): 28–40.
Worseley, Peter. *The Third World*. Chicago: University of Chicago Press, 1964.
Wunder, John R. *"Retained by the People": A History of American Indians and the Bill of Rights*. New York: Oxford University Press, 1994.

Dan Streible

RACE AND THE RECEPTION OF JACK JOHNSON FIGHT FILMS

No discussion of race and early cinema in the United States would be complete without considering the impact of Jack Johnson's cinematic image on the racial order of things. During his reign as heavyweight boxing champion from 1908 to 1915 a radically new African American representation forced its way onto the screen. As the first black holder of the symbolic ring title, Johnson broke the color line that John L. Sullivan had imposed a generation earlier. Motion pictures of his daunting knockouts of white champions Tommy Burns (1908), Stanley Ketchel (1909), and—especially—Jim Jeffries (1910) helped break other racial barriers imposed in the age of Jim Crow. Highly publicized feature-film presentations showing Johnson pummeling "white hopes" offered a potent challenge to the social conceptions of race upon which segregation was built. The African American community used these films as occasions for celebration and affirmation when they played on the emerging black theater circuit. White reception of Johnson's image, after some initial curiosity and tolerance, however, was marked by alarm over this icon of black power. So great were white anxieties that many states and cities censored Johnson films in particular and the U.S. Congress banned interstate traffic in prizefight films in general.

Jack Johnson was not the first black boxer to appear in films, but his bold, confrontational persona radically contradicted prevailing racial stereotypes (Figure 1). Earlier screen caricatures portrayed black fighters as either naturally deferential to or fearful of whites. Ring mythology held that black boxers had "yellow streaks."

The myth of the "spooked" black fighter, in fact, often appeared in accounts about the first moving pictures. When champion "Gentleman" Jim Corbett sparred before Edison's kinetograph in 1894, he declined to box against the renowned West Indian boxer Peter Jackson, choosing instead to face an unknown white fall guy, Peter Courtney. Yet later biographies of Thomas Edison, repeated a spurious anecdote about "a Negro fighter" who, "paralyzed with terror," "began trembling" and ran from the film studio, frightened by Corbett and the movie camera.[1] In

1901, Ed Martin, the first black heavyweight to be filmed, also became a foil to a white boxer, Gus Ruhlin. The Edison catalogue said of its film *Ruhlin Boxing with "Denver" Ed. Martin*: "Here we present Ruhlin in a lively bout with the dusky well known 'Denver' Ed. Martin. The bout is very lively from start to finish and is ended up with a little piece of comedy by Ruhlin presenting Martin with a live chicken, which he receives in a joyful manner."[2]

Yet another forerunner of Johnson fight films, the recordings of lightweight champion Joe Gans deployed racist conventions of representation but less overtly. Press descriptions of Gans as a mild-mannered athlete made it clear that whites acknowledged his considerable boxing skills only because he had proven unthreatening. When he died in 1910, the white press contrasted him with the controversial Johnson, lauding Gans as "a model of consideration and politeness . . . [who] never sought the limelight, [and] kept among his own race."[3] White authorities therefore permitted the showing of his three filmed interracial grudge matches with Battling Nelson from 1906 to 1908—especially when Nelson won their last two fights.

The films of Jack Johnson's three title fights between 1908 and 1910 presented a dramatically different representation. Johnson's image became a symbol of opposition to white dominance and a signifier of "race pride."

Reaction to the *Johnson-Burns Fight* Film

When he defeated Tommy Burns on December 26, 1908, John Arthur Johnson assumed the undisputed world championship of boxing. A Gaumont camera crew in Sydney, Australia, recorded the event amid a crowd of 20,000 spectators. In the United States, sporting and theatrical magnate William A. Brady and others bought the rights to the films, resulting in widespread feature exhibition. When the *Johnson-Burns* films debuted on American screens in March 1909, a rancorous debate over race politics ensued. This controversy framed the grounds for the film's reception.

Even before Johnson's films were exhibited, the legitimacy and stakes of his holding the title were clearly spelled out. Author Jack London, covering the Sydney fight for the *New York Herald*, published a column widely reprinted in both the black and white American press. As a subscriber to both boxing's primitive ethos and the belief in "Caucasian" supremacy, London put into stark words what seemed to be many white

Fig. 1: Jack Johnson, heavyweight champion from 1908 to 1915, increased his problematic celebrity and his status as a hero in the African American community by being a "star" of several motion pictures during his reign. (Courtesy of the Todd-McLean Collection, University of Texas at Austin)

Americans' reaction to the historic event: "The fight, there was no fight." All reporters agreed with him that Johnson had toyed with Burns, openly taunting him, punching at will. The new champion laughed and smiled throughout the contest, talking to reporters as he demonstrated the ease of his mastery.

London depicted the new champion as an "Ethiopian" "colossus." The writer even suggested Johnson was in control of the image he would project on movie screens: "He cuffed and smiled and cuffed, and in the clinches whirled his opponent around so as to be able to assume beatific and angelic facial expressions for the cinematograph machines." In the most influential and widely quoted words of London's career, the writer concluded his account of the fight with a racial call to arms. Depending upon the editor, his appeal read: "But one thing [now] remains. Jim Jeffries must now emerge from his alfalfa farm and remove that [golden] smile from [Jack] Johnson's face. Jeff, it's up to you. [The White Man must be rescued.]"[4]

The white American public and press largely echoed London's cry. Earlier, Jeffries had retired because he had beaten all white challengers and refused to meet others. The racial logic that dictated his retirement now demanded his return. A black champion could not be abided. Raconteur Jim Corbett spurred the racial anxiety and antagonism, declaring "the white man has succumbed to a type which in the past was conceded to be his inferior in physical and mental prowess."[5] Others suggested Burns' defeat was the beginning of the end for whites about to surrender their supremacy. "A Negro is the champion pugilist," warned the *Detroit Free Press*: "[The] dark-colored peoples of the earth are threatening to ply the mischief generally with the civilization of the white man. . . . Is the Caucasian played out? Are the races we have been calling inferior about to demand to us that we must draw the color line in everything if we are to avoid being whipped individually and collectively?"[6] Such fears were not new but entirely consistent with the views expressed by the White House's bully pulpit. President Roosevelt was known for his support of boxing and the "strenuous life," advocating the "ability to fight well and breed well" as a way to prevent an impending "race suicide."[7] Rather than repudiate fisticuffs, as many white progressives did, TR's symbolic response to Johnson was to invite "the white champion of the world," Battling Nelson, to the White House in February 1909.

Conversely, black America hailed Johnson's achievement as a milepost of racial uplift. "No event in forty years has given more genuine satisfaction to the colored people of this country than has the signal victory of Jack Johnson," the *Richmond Planet* editorialized.[8] The crowning of a black champion had come at a moment as bleak as any in post-slavery America, making this rare breaker of the color line an immediate hero.

With public reaction largely polarized along racial grounds, the reception of the *Johnson-Burns Fight* films differed greatly depending upon the conditions of its exhibition. To some extent, lag time between the fight and its screening muted visceral, race-driven responses to the pictures. The American premiere took place on March 21, 1909, when the promoter of the fight, Hugh D. McIntosh, narrated the "motion pictures of the Burns-Johnson battle" during a two-week engagement at the Chicago Auditorium. The *Chicago Tribune* did not comment on the racial composition of the audience. However, in describing the show as "good pictures of a poor fight," it implied a pro-white reception of the film.[9]

In New York, theater impresario Felix Isman opposed the display of Johnson's victory. He unsuccessfully sought a court injunction prohibiting the show, saying "to produce the pictures would be to lower the dignity of the playhouse."[10] The rupture in the color line surely motivated Isman's claim, since other boxing pictures had been prominent in New York theaters for a decade. Although, as the *New York Times* put it, the *Johnson-Burns Fight* showed "the white man outclassed," white men produced the Broadway Theatre debut for a white audience. The spectators were not there to cheer the exploits of the black champ they disparaged with the nickname "Little Arthur" (or even "Li'l Arfa"). Some dedicated boxing fans no doubt wanted to appraise the boxer's performance. Others may have been out to judge Burns's claim that police stopped the fight prematurely. The "pictures show everything" he told the press. Indeed they did. "To the majority of those who witnessed the exhibition," said the *Times*, "the pictures were a disappointment on account of the miserable showing made throughout by Burns." Again the audience, by implication, was white.[11]

Moreover, for these disillusioned white spectators the screening was an opportunity to rally for Jeffries' return. The film's promoter fostered talk of a Jeffries-Johnson scenario by concluding the Chicago premiere with an offer of a $50,000 purse for such an event. The White Hope himself was in fact appearing on stage at the American Music Hall during the *Burns-Johnson Fight's* New York run. Jeffries's former manager, William Brady, appeared at the Broadway Theatre premiere, further encouraging a "dump Johnson" atmosphere. McIntosh's narration of the pictures also appropriated Jack London's call-of-the-white—that the smile be removed from Johnson's face. According to one account, McIntosh "announced from behind the canvas that some in the crowd [in Australia] yelled to knock the grin off Johnson's face. Then Johnson did grin and he could be seen replying to the request."[12] White audiences were thus urged to read Johnson's image as a grinning stereotype that merited not a championship but a rebuttal from their hero "Jeff."

Whites responded to the *Johnson-Burns Fight* in varied ways, but the prevailing opinion was that expressed by the audience of white men represented in a *New York Journal* cartoon drawn by the noted boxing journalist "Tad" Dorgan. Public outcry immediately forced Jeffries to reappear on the vaudeville stage where "the reception" was nearly univocal.[13] Further evidence that the *Johnson-Burns* pictures spurred white demand for a Jeffries-Johnson battle came that summer. Exhibitors took McIntosh's footage and appended scenes from the *Jeffries-Sharkey Fight* of 1899—the moment of Jeffries' greatest glory.[14]

Not surprisingly, black reception of the films of Johnson hammering Burns took a different tone. Particular screenings of the first set of Johnson films are difficult to document. However, anticipation of the picture's arrival was clearly great. The *Indianapolis Freeman*, a widely circulated African American weekly, kept tabs on both Johnson's activities and the *Johnson-Burns* films. Immediately after the fight in Sydney, the paper informed readers that the pictures would "arrive in the United States in two months."[15] When McIntosh arrived in England with the motion pictures, the event was noted. A follow-up article described the "English opera house" premiere, including details about the fight, training scenes, and preliminary footage of Mrs. Johnson and other celebrities.[16] The newspapers' many pictures of the dapper new champion clearly portrayed him as a symbol of race pride. Johnson's personal appearances attracted crowds of black (and some white) fans. Popular songs by black artists lionized the skilled "black gladiator."[17]

One documented showing of the *Johnson-Burns Fight* occurred in Chicago on the day of Johnson's first title defense in 1909—but was intentionally mis-billed. According to *Freeman* columnist "Juli Jones, Jr." (the pseudonym of William Foster, a Chicago-based theater manager and pioneer African American filmmaker), a bunco artist used the black community's anticipation of the new Johnson films to scam moviegoers in Chicago's black district:

> One game knight of slot houses put one over on Dehomey to show us how many suckers we have at large. . . . his bright young man rented a closed theater and put out a sign,
>
> FIRST MOVING PICTURES OF THE JOHNSON-KETCHELL [SIC] FIGHT."
>
> The funny part of it is that he opened his show at 5 o'clock on Saturday afternoon. The men did not go into the ring until 5:30. He used the Burns and Johnson fight pictures. Nobody woke up until the wise gent had loaded

up. He said that he would return next Saturday with the Jeffries and Johnson pictures.[18]

The fact that a print of the Burns bout was in ready circulation suggests there were legitimate screenings earlier. While distributors may have withheld the *Johnson-Burns* films from the black community, such was not the case with its enormously popular "sequel," the *Johnson-Ketchel Fight*. This second Johnson feature received wide distribution via the Motion Picture Patents Company's empire and separate black exhibition circuits. The proliferation of the black champion's cinematic image helped increase the racial bifurcation that surrounded his celebrity.

The Johnson-Ketchel Fight Pictures and the Buildup for Jeffries

The film of Johnson's first title defense—against Stanley Ketchel on October 16, 1909—recorded a performance which held some attraction for both white and black audiences. It also continued to feed demand for a Johnson-Jeffries showdown.

In the twelfth round of the bout, a dramatic and unexpected exchange offered a stunning climax to the fight and film. Ketchel swung a roundhouse through an opening to Johnson's head. Retreating, the champion fell to the mat—perhaps knocked down, perhaps having slipped. The crowd of white men rose to cheer the underdog's feat. Before any celebration could take hold, however, a deliberate Johnson lunged across the ring, smashing Ketchel squarely in the mouth and immediately rendering him unconscious. Johnson leaned casually on the ropes, hand on hip, as the referee counted out his victim (Figure 2).

The *Johnson-Burns Fight* had panicked many in white America who took "Caucasian" possession of the boxing crown for granted, perceiving it as confirmation of racial superiority. The pictures from Australia had at least been truncated by police so that Johnson's final downing of the bloodied Burns never reached the screen. The *Johnson-Ketchel* pictures, however, presented spectators with a sensational depiction of a fearsome, indomitable athlete. The legend surrounding Johnson's image grew as replays of his knockout artistry spread. One interpretation, possibly spurious, insisted that the film showed Johnson scraping Ketchel's teeth from his glove as the overreaching "Michigan Assassin" lay sprawled on the mat.[19] The movies, along with the widely reprinted still photos of Johnson standing over an unconscious white hope, confronted white

Fig. 2: In 1909, the Johnson-Ketchel fight pictures offered an unequivocal image of black power, as did this widely reprinted photo of Johnson standing over the unconscious "white hope." (Courtesy of the Todd-McLean Collection, University of Texas at Austin)

viewers with an historically unprecedented image of black power. For African American audiences, the same pictures offered a laudable antidote to the pervasive negative stereotypes of popular culture.

Several circumstances tempered white reaction to the film. First, many whites as well as blacks did not take a dubious tradition like prizefighting to be symbolic of the larger question of racial equality. Furthermore, even though racial prejudice prevailed, it was hardly universal. Some whites became Johnson fans. A white spectator like the socialist and painter John Sloan, who often slummed in nickelodeons and patronized Negro League baseball games, appreciated Johnson's historic performance on film. In his diary Sloan wrote that he and a friend "went up to Hammerstein's Victoria and saw the cinematograph pictures of the recent fight between Ketchel and the negro Jack Johnson. The big black spider gobbled up the small white fly—aggressive fly—wonderful to have this event repeated."[20] Second, it was precisely because so many whites envisioned Johnson as a monster—more frightening than a mere "big black spider"—that they came to see him put on display at his most ferocious. Even as the films bolstered his gladiatorial reputation, newspapers fed the public imagination with gossip, anecdotes, and fabricated quotations that made his image even more terrible. In the ring, the champion taunted and literally laughed at white hopes, whom he humiliated and dispatched in exhibitions.[21] Outside the ring he developed a reputation as a profligate spender, drinker, womanizer, and all-around disturber of the peace. Johnson kept company with white prostitutes as well as a white wife. He was frequently arrested for speeding in his automobiles, and later for more serious offenses. As all of Johnson's biographers agree, he knowingly fulfilled the role of the "Bad Nigger."[22] A braggadocio and a dandy, he gleefully and openly rebelled against white and bourgeois standards of behavior. Many white filmgoers no doubt came as curiosity seekers, wanting a glimpse of the controversial, bigger-than-life figure whose public persona had become that of a freakish monster.

A third reason the *Johnson-Ketchel* pictures played to white audiences was that Ketchel's alleged knockdown of the champion gave a glimmer of hope that the "Ethiopian colossus" could be vanquished. W. W. Naughton, dispenser of boxing's conventional wisdom, watched the filmed replay of the fight and asserted that the scene of scrappy Ketchel sending Johnson to the mat would be the focal point of the pictures: "[The knockdown] is registered in the pictures for what it is worth, and will possibly add to their value as a show asset. . . . [H]ordes of people will visit and revisit the Ketchel-Johnson pictures in order to determine whether Johnson sprawled in earnest when Ketchel nabbed him on the mastoid."[23] In reviewing the premiere of the films at Hammerstein's Victoria, despite Johnson's in-person appearance, the *New York Sun* reiterated the predominant white point of view. "According to the pictures," said the *Sun*, Johnson's knockout blow was delivered "with so much power that the crowd in the theater was quickly convinced that the only man who has a chance with the negro is Jeffries."[24] Even the staid *New York Times*, upon the release of the Ketchel pictures, demonstrated its racist impulse to see Johnson destroyed: "[We] wait in open anxiety the news that [Jeffries] has licked the—well, since it must be in print, let us say the negro, even though it is not the first word that comes to the tongue's tip."[25]

Reports in the Negro press evidenced an oppositional, pro-Johnson reading among black audiences. This was true even though African American reviewers often only had access to first-run screenings of the *Johnson-Ketchel Fight* at mainstream white theaters or at presentations presided over by white narrators.

The film, however, soon found its way onto a growing all-black movie circuit. Although the MPPC controlled the movie, Johnson used his leverage as champion to obtain prints of the film from Chicago-based distributor George Kleine.[26] Copies of the pictures then wound up in the possession of Johnson's friend, Robert T. Motts, a fellow Chicagoan who ran America's best known black owned-and-operated theater, the Pekin. So successful was the Pekin that dozens of other black-only movie and vaudeville houses across the country adopted the Pekin name.[27] As Motts traveled the country opening other theaters, the press reported his employees were "on the road with fight-moving pictures, owned by Mr. Motts."[28] Few descriptions of these screenings for African American audiences survive. Yet the pictures stayed in circulation at least until the time of the Jeffries bout. The Chicago Pekin revived the *Johnson-Ketchel* pictures on the eve of the big contest, screening them between stage acts and round-by-round announcements of the fight.

However, a *Freeman* columnist who saw an early exhibition of the pictures, summed up the ultimate importance of the *Johnson-Ketchel* fight film. "Uncle Rad Kees" thought Johnson's superiority so apparent in the filmed replay that the boxer must have staged his own knockdown:

> If this Johnson-Ketchel fight wasn't a pre-arranged affair, there was some awful clever catering to the moving picture machine. Just imagine Johnson, the cleverest man in the ring today, allowing a little fellow like Ketchel to drop him with a wild swing back of the ear . . . not in a thousand years. . . .
>
> After the supposed blow Johnson went down on his hands and toes, rolled over backward on one hand, and facing the moving picture machine all the time; then, seeing that Ketchel was waiting for his cue, he jumped up and rushed at Ketchel like a wild man. . . . The referee stood squarely over Ketchel, counting him out, and all three were in full view of the moving picture machine.[29]

The whole point of the performance, he argued, was to give birth to a Johnson versus Jeffries match. "The child was born," as Uncle Rad Kees put it, with the champion's conspicuous cinematic display.

Framing Johnson-Jeffries Battle as Proof of Racial Superiority

As soon as the *Johnson-Ketchel* films were in wide circulation, the champion inked a deal to meet the unretired Jeffries. Tex Rickard, who had made his fortune exploiting the interracial Gans-Nelson grudge match, outbid other promoters for the rights to this even bigger race battle, staking $101,000 in prize money and guaranteeing the boxers two-thirds of the expected bonanza in film receipts.[30]

As hype for the bout intensified, it was clear that Johnson versus Jeffries had become the testing ground for conflicting ideologies about race. For whites who took Negro inferiority as a governing assumption, Jeffries' victory became paramount. As boxing historian Jeffrey T. Sammons argues, for many whites destroying Johnson would be "a lesson akin to a public lynching for blacks who did not know their place."[31]

While black celebrities were usually forced to stand as representatives of their race, Jeffries—the most cherished of white hopes—became a representative of his in a way few other white people had. His image was made to bear the essence of whiteness. "Jeffries is the embodiment of all that is powerful and brutish in the white man," Corbett's newspaper column said.[32] Largely ignoring his advancing age and paunch, the white press consistently represented Jeffries as a white ideal who countered the negative traits thought inherent in his black opponent. The White Hope was sober, the "Black Menace" a drinker. Jeffries was stolid; Johnson, flashy. He was humble, not a braggart; given to discipline, not dissipation; courageous, not "yellow."[33]

While London portrayed Jeffries as a noble "brute," much misplaced white hope was pinned on the belief that superior intelligence would overcome primitive instinct in the ring. In 1910 a prevalent "scientific racism" still held that the match was a "contest of brains." As a preview in *Current Literature* put it, "science" predicted that Johnson would lose because it taught that "the superiority of the brain of the white man to that of the black . . . is undisputed by all authorities." "The white man, being intellectually superior—as he must be," also had the advantage of self-control in the ring, while "the black man's psychology" made him perform "emotionally."[34] The heavyweight crown that was at stake, as Sammons has shown, was deemed the "true test of skill, courage, intelligence, and manhood."[35]

Just as Jeffries became a "white hope," the black press and public made Johnson a signifier of race pride. Booker T. Washington staged a public meeting with him in August 1909.[36] As July 4, 1910, approached, racial solidarity increased. "Thousands of Negroes," the *Afro-American Ledger* told him, "have nailed your name to their masthead. . . . Nobody has so much to win or lose as you and the race you represent."[37] In his history of African American athletes, Arthur Ashe concurs with black scholars such as William H. Wiggins, Jr., that the Johnson-Jeffries fight represented for blacks not just a signal moment in sports history, but the most important event since Emancipation.[38]

As hype for the fight grew to unprecedented proportions, moralist groups attempted to prevent it. While public discourse on the bout keyed on racial conflict, the organized protest stressed an anti-violence theme. Protestant ministers petitioned President Taft to intervene, but the White House remained silent.[39] Taft, the gossip ran, had arranged to receive telegraph reports on the bout, and it was purported that his son was "a violent Jeffries partisan . . . betting all his money on the pride of the white race."[40]

After several setbacks, Rickard got permission from the governor of Nevada to stage the infamous battle in Reno. Massive press attention ensued. Three hundred reporters, including special contributors like Rex Beach, Jack London, Alfred Henry Lewis, and (for *Variety*) Al Jolson, poured into the small town. They painted the event as nothing less than "a staging ground for racial supremacy."[41] As the *Chicago Tribune* put it, the "absorbing question of whether a white man or a negro shall be supreme in the world of fisticuffs" in this case meant supreme "in the world at large."[42]

Filming the Reno Fight

Motion picture coverage of the Johnson-Jeffries affair far outstripped that afforded any previous prizefight. Twelve Patents Company cameras recorded the event. A panning "slave" camera followed Jeffries' movements—framing the white boxer as the protagonist and privileging white spectatorship.[43] The extensive preliminary footage inserted in the release of the *Johnson-Jeffries Fight* also signaled the white supremacy hopes of the film's producers. Scenes of Johnson clowning in his training camp were countered with pictures from Jeffries' camp that included depictions of white solidarity. Icons Sullivan and Corbett ceased their seventeen-year feud to shake hands and pose together for pictures with Jeffries.

The white-run film industry desired a Jeffries victory for more than financial reasons. As the *Moving Picture World* so bluntly put it, the purpose of the Reno fight was "to wrest the championship from the colored race, and incidentally provide crowded houses for the moving picture men."[44] Another trade assessment held:

> It is no exaggeration to say that the entire world will await a pictorial representation of the fight. . . . With good light and a battle of, say, thirty well-fought rounds, and the unmistakable victory of Jeffries, these pictures should prove in the current locution, a "gold mine." This is the wish that is father of the thoughts of hundreds of millions of white people throughout the world.
>
> [But] . . . if Johnson wins? It is commonly believed that the pictures would then be of comparatively little value, especially among the white section of the community.[45]

But Johnson did win. Regardless of white desires or the filmmakers' biases, camera angles and editing strategies could do nothing to alter the clearly photographed reality of Johnson's dominating performance. He treated the slow-footed Boilermaker much the way he had Burns and Ketchel, verbally teasing and mocking his rival as he hit him. Witnesses reported that his remarks were aimed as much at ringside observers Sullivan and Corbett (who flagrantly race-baited Johnson during the bout) as they were at Jeffries.[46] In the fifteenth round Johnson finished off the bloodied and dazed Jeffries. Three times he knocked the white hope down and into the ropes, causing referee Rickard to stop the contest. The nearly all white crowd expressed disappointment but exited without incident.[47] Elsewhere, however, reaction to the news of Jeffries' embarrassing performance and Johnson's definitive title defense was severe.

A wave of violent assaults, some fatal, broke out in many American communities when the results of the Reno fight were announced. Most of the attacks were interracial, usually conducted by vengeful white mobs. At least eighteen African Americans were killed.[48]

Reactionary Suppression of the *Johnson-Jeffries Fight* Film

Citing the potential for further race riots, local and state authorities across the nation immediately banned exhibitions of the fight film. "Within twenty-four hours," said the *San Francisco Examiner*, attempts to prohibit screenings of the fight had "assumed the proportions of a national crusade."[49] Throughout July and August 1910 newspapers offered a steady stream of front-page headlines detailing the fate of the controversial *Johnson-Jeffries* films. Many editorials affirmed the decision of municipal leaders to suppress them. What is clear from the heat generated over the issue, however, is that the moralist objections to prizefight films were intertwined with racist desires to censure this particular film precisely because it contained such an undeniable image of black power and white vincibility. Moral suasion had failed to keep previous fight films from the screen, but the injection of race at a heightened level prevented many—though not all—exhibitions of the *Johnson-Jeffries Fight.*

Much of the impetus for the censorship crusade was generated by the United Society for Christian Endeavor, a Protestant youth organization that claimed four million members. Employing a well-organized system of publicity committees, newspaper contacts, and letter-writing campaigns, the Christian Endeavor maintained an active voice in government and the press.[50] On July 5, the group "telegraphed every governor" and big city mayor in the country, advocating prohibition of the film.[51] Letters to newspapers implored officials to prevent the "evil and demoralizing influences" of the fight pictures from "tainting and brutalizing" "the minds of the young."[52] Their public opinion barrage elicited an editorial cartoon in the *New York Tribune*. It depicted two hands—labeled "Christian Endeavor" and "Public Opinion"—blocking the film image of Jeffries and Johnson from the view of children.[53]

Other voices of reform—Protestant, Catholic, and secular—condemned the pictures. The Women's Christian Temperance Union, which had spearheaded an attack on the *Corbett-Fitzsimmons Fight* film in 1897, now led a coalition of civic groups against *Johnson-Jeffries*. James Cardinal Gibbons, Archbishop of Baltimore, wrote "it would be wrong to show these horrible pictures. . . . Showing of the pictures would have a bad effect upon the men and women of the community."[54] The archbishop's statement against boxing films was rhetorically and thematically typical of the religious-based reform movement's campaign: "If the pictures of this contest were permitted, I am sure hundreds of children would see them, and what would be the result? Their morals would not only be contaminated, but they would have the wrong ideal of a true hero. After seeing the pictures a boy would naturally infer that the real American hero was a man bespattered with blood and with a swollen eye given him by another in a fistic encounter."[55] A key political endorsement of the suppression of the fight film came from Theodore Roosevelt, who said in *Outlook* that "it would be an admirable thing if some method could be devised to stop the exhibition of the moving pictures taken" in Reno.[56]

Many newspapers supported the movement as well, caricaturing the fight film interests as crude commercial exploiteers. The Hearst press

Fig. 3: When Jack Johnson defeated Jim Jeffries, the white press illustrated the immediate opposition to the prospect of having Johnson's victory replayed on movie screens across the world. (*San Francisco Examiner*, July 9, 1910, p. 1)

syndicate jumped on the anti-prizefight bandwagon immediately. In a front-page cartoon on July 7, "Real Moving Pictures, or the Return to Reno," the *San Francisco Examiner* depicted a cigar-chomping sport carrying the films around the country. Every major city and the entire South adamantly reject him. The *Examiner* cartoon "And Not a Friendly Port in Sight" followed on July 9 (Figure 3). This time the boorish promoter of the "Jeffries-Johnson Moving Pictures" is washed out on a sea of opposition and barred from ports overseas.[57] Indeed bans on the fight film were appearing abroad. In England, for example, where a major constituency for pugilism existed, Home Secretary Winston Churchill supported the restrictions enacted by local councils.[58]

As Al-Tony Gilmore details in his thorough account, "The Suppres-

EDUCATIONAL?

Fig. 4: White segregationists tied the rhetoric of progressivism to their fears of racial integration during the move to ban the Johnson-Jeffries fight pictures. (*Jackson Clarion-Ledger*, July 21, 1910)

sion of the Johnson Fight Films," it did not take long for preemptive bans on the *Johnson-Jeffries Fight* to take effect. All of the South forbade screenings, as did many Northern, Midwestern, and Western cities. Some locales barred only the Reno fight film, others all interracial fights, and still others eliminated all boxing pictures.[59]

There was an obvious gap between the moralists' rhetoric and the racist (or at least race-based) rationale often articulated by advocates of censorship. A representation of the controversy, such as the cartoon "Educational?" appearing in Jackson, Mississippi's *Clarion-Ledger*, used the words of moral uplift while implying interracial contact was the greater, unspoken concern (Figure 4). The drawing depicted a pair of boys, one black, one white, gazing at a poster for the fight film. Other censors were more blunt about keeping the races apart. In Washington, D.C., for example, police prohibited the exhibition of the *Johnson-*

Jeffries Fight following a night of racial violence they could not control.[60] Most other mayors, councils, police chiefs, and legislators cited similar concerns in initiating censorship measures. As Gilmore shows, however, "a more sufficient reason for the censure of the films" lay in the fact that Johnson had won the fight. The films had to be suppressed, many whites argued overtly, in order to prevent black empowerment.[61]

Put in historical context, censorship was traditionally seen as necessary for the protection of impressionable, childlike minds. Whether in the thinking of Southern politicians or Northern progressives, both children and non-whites were categorized as creatures in need of an Anglo-Saxon protector. The "great race problem in America" was perceived to be, as reformer Jane Addams expressed to the newly formed NAACP, caused by "a colony of colored people who have not been brought under social control."[62] Addams opposed showing the fight films. Also condoning fight film censorship in particular, one white California reformer stated that "a superior people" needed to guide and school the "childlike race": "We deny them this by encouraging them to believe that they have gained anything by having one of their own race as a champion fighter."[63] Empowering or glorifying a black figure, especially one of Johnson's audacity, was a thing to be fought against on both the "progressive" and racist agenda. For some, the desire to control what they believed to be blacks' riotous nature by removing racially inflammatory images was consistent with their view of religion, reform, and progress. For others, with a more overt white supremacy agenda, the rhetoric of moralism served as subterfuge.

Most African American opinion leaders—and many whites—saw it differently. They labeled the wildfire calls for a film ban as hypocritical and racist. Even those who favored suppressing the films (because they thought the sport barbaric, or because they feared white backlash) recognized that anti-Negro sentiment fueled the campaign. The relatively conservative *St. Paul Appeal* offered a judgment typical of black editors: "[W]e are firmly of the opinion that the apparently country-wide objection to the exhibition of the Johnson-Jeffries fight pictures comes more from race prejudice than from a moral standpoint. Who believes for one minute, that had Jeffries been the victor at Reno, there would have been any objection to showing the pictures of him bringing back 'the white man's hope?'"[64]

Two editorial cartoons drive home the intensity of feeling that the black press in both the North and South held with regard to the hypocrisy of the anti-fight film movement. The radical *Chicago Defender*

Fig. 5: The Black press decried the hypocrisy of banning films of Johnson's prize-fights while the government did little to stop real violence against Black citizens. (*Chicago Defender*, July 30, 1910, p. 1)

harshly condemned white America for criminalizing the films. Its front-page depiction, "The Strong Arm of the American Law," showed Sheriff Uncle Sam tossing a "fight picture promoter" into a paddy wagon, while several white lynchers escape (Figure 5). A similar representation appeared in the *Richmond Planet* with the caption "Hypocrisy That Shames the Devil." The "moral wave" against the *Jeffries-Johnson* film was illustrated by an angry white man standing upon a "sham platform." He invokes "the unwritten law" to condemn the "immoral, unchristian, brutal" "prize-fight business," while behind his back black men are lynched, hung, and burned. Some critics went a step further, encouraging the actual exhibition of the films. Rationales for this advocacy ranged from simple fairness to the need for black empowerment.[65]

Screenings of the *Johnson-Jeffries Fight* Film

Despite all obstacles, the *Johnson-Jeffries Fight* was screened in many places, including New York, Philadelphia, Detroit, St. Louis, Kansas

City, Buffalo, Denver, Hoboken, Pittsburgh, and smaller towns and suburbs. It even played in Peoria. Controversy contributed to its box office appeal. Submitting to legal bans where necessary, promoters proceeded with as many bookings as they could get elsewhere. Neither race riots nor any misbehavior occurred, as exhibitors practiced well-established forms of class and race controls on audiences.

Waging a publicity counteroffensive, the picture promoters rushed the film to market. J. Stuart Blackton and William T. Rock of Vitagraph arranged for speedy rail transport of the film from Nevada to New York. By the morning of July 8 the unprocessed film arrived. Blackton held news conferences and a press screening. On July 10, "a score of men, representatives of the various concerns and individuals interested in the J. & J. Co. [the film's nominal booking agency]," assembled at the Patents Company office on Fifth Avenue to examine the product.[66]

"Hundreds of offers from theaters and houses of amusement" came in, particularly after New York City's libertarian mayor, William J. Gaynor, indicated he would not bar the film. J. & J. officers sold territorial distribution rights to the *Johnson-Jeffries Fight*, passing the risk of bad box office down to the local exhibitors. The producers, who had invested hundreds of thousands of dollars, still made money. Local bans cut into their expected million-dollar profits. If the $60,000 Illinois contract, the $150,000 offered for Canadian rights, and the $12,000 bid for one New York theater were any indication, the promoters profited handsomely.[67]

To bolster theatrical play for the film, Blackton announced that the colorful vaudeville magnate Percy G. Williams would arrange all New York engagements. Williams booked two Broadway houses, as well as the Gotham and Orpheum theaters in Brooklyn; the Bronx and Colonial theaters in the Bronx; and the Alhambra (and later the Crescent) in Harlem as his first showplaces.[68] Perhaps hoping to capitalize on the black champion's popularity among African American audiences, the Alhambra was selected as the unveiling place for the fight film.

Exhibitors enforced with extra rigor the usual means of controlling and sequestering audiences on the basis of race, holding down black participation even at this high point in black cultural affirmation. As reported by New York's *Times* and *Clipper*, raised admission prices did not prevent a full house from turning out at the Harlem Alhambra on the night of July 16. With so many pundits having predicted race riots at screenings of the film, the *Times* emphasized that there was "no sign of race feeling" when the pictures were shown. However, the circumstances described also indicate an environment of *de facto* racial intimidation.

The white manager invited companies of New York and Boston firemen to the premiere. Police patrolled the theater. Given this show of force by white authorities the *Times* ought to have been less surprised that there were "fewer negroes in the audience than had been expected, and these took seats only in the upper parts of the theatre."[69]

For New York's black audiences who avoided such uninviting settings, alternative opportunities came along a month after the fight. Outdoor screenings were held nightly at Olympic Field in the heart of Harlem with fifty-cent grandstand admissions. Meyerrose Park in Brooklyn also hosted the *Johnson-Jeffries* pictures. Both exhibitions advertised to black patrons through the *New York Age*, receiving endorsements from the paper's theater critic and African American celebrities.[70]

While there is little documentation about the particular reactions of audiences at such screenings, what evidence exists confirms that African Americans remained interested in seeing Johnson's victory on film and perceived it as an affirmation of race pride. But antagonistic conditions habitually limited their access. In West Virginia, for example, a "Negro teacher" let his students out of school an hour early to see the *Johnson-Jeffries* fight pictures. "The white people" of the town, reported the *Chicago Defender*, were "threatening to tar and feather Professor Page."[71] In other towns, exhibitors who wished to curb such tensions, but still make a profit from black demand, took extra steps to segregate audiences. As early as July 7, an official in Hollidaysburg, Pennsylvania, "effected an agreement with the proprietors" of the local "motion picture places . . . for separate exhibitions of the Johnson-Jeffries prizefight." According to the *New York Tribune*, "No negroes [were] allowed to attend the performances for the white people and vice versa."[72]

In the end, public debate about the film became more important to black advancement than the film itself. Johnson won his monumental victory and African American communities celebrated the event in public congregations—at theaters, news offices, bars, churches, parks, and street corners—and read about it in newspapers. This was proof of black achievement. Lack of access to motion picture replays was secondary. In the estimation of an *Afro-American Ledger* critic, suppression of the film merely made white reactionaries look childish since it in no way denied Johnson's accomplishment.[73] For *Defender* reviewer Mildred Miller, the fact that Chicago banned the fight pictures but not racist melodramas—such as William Brady's production of "The Nigger"—indicated how unjust U.S. law was. "Why not let the Johnson-Jeffries pictures be shown?" she asked. "These show equality in every particular."[74]

Black spectators saw the *Johnson-Jeffries Fight* as a signifier of racial equality, but they remained only a small percentage of the total audience for the film. Despite the Anglo-led opposition, most fight film customers were white. Many of the film's largest crowds were exclusively so. Their motivations and reactions were less clearly articulated. One black columnist rationalized that, at least in the North, "there are thousands of white men who bet on Johnson and won, and they are the ones who would like to see the fight pictures and who feel good every time the affair is mentioned."[75] In areas where black populations were small, the film played especially well among white audiences. Without the threat of an African American constituency turning out to lend a black empowerment reading to Johnson's image, white sports fans or thrill seekers could watch Jeffries' Waterloo with more detachment. In Madison, Wisconsin, for example—a seat of Progressive reform where application of the moralist ban might have been expected—the Reno film was allowed. It played the town's main movie venue, the Fuller Opera House, and was enough of a hit to be revived for a run in 1911. (Yet even in Madison the appearance of Jack Johnson on film elicited a letter warning that "every coon in town will turn out."[76])

Because of its topicality, audiences from high and low spheres of influence sought out the film, contraband or not. Clandestine shows were held in private hotel suites and on river barges. Philadelphia's large Forrest Theater held both public and private screenings, the latter being attended by "most of the prominent city officials."[77] For a while the film even held a certain cultural caché. Philanthropist Joseph E. Widener and his wife had the film screened in the drawing room of their Newport summer home. A hundred of the Wideners' dinner guests saw the *Johnson-Jeffries* scenes, with musical accompaniment by "McLellan's Colored Singers."[78] Even the sight of a powerful black fighter thrashing the "Great White Hope" could be reconfigured as a plantation entertainment for some white viewers.

As the film circulated, the formidable scenes of Johnson in Reno continued to offer a stiff rebuttal to Jack London's racist call to arms. While making the theatrical rounds in 1910, the champion even posed for ironic photos (with his white wife and entourage) outside a theater marquee advertising "Jack Johnson" alongside a poster for London's *Call of the Wild*. But Johnson's public appearances and press representations diminished the threat that many whites initially saw in the *Johnson-Jeffries* films. As biographer Randy Roberts describes, Johnson's theatrical

Fig. 6: Jack Johnson successfully defends his heavyweight title against "great white hope" Jim Jeffries on July 4, 1910. Ad hoc censorship ordinances and segregated exhibition practices prevented much of Johnson's African American constituency from seeing motion pictures of the much-hyped racial battle, although many cities eventually permitted well-policed screenings. (Courtesy of the Todd-McLean Collection, University of Texas at Austin)

tours presented him to white audiences in a form closer to the accepted, nonthreatening stage character of "coon" stereotypy—a "smiling, happy-go-lucky black." Soon his monologues and songs were cut back and he became something of freak show display, a mere posing body on the stage.[79]

Other events of 1910–11, some even on-screen, began to diminish the impact of the *Johnson-Jeffries Fight*. A devotee of fast cars, Johnson challenged champion driver Barney Oldfield to a series of races in October 1910. Cameras filmed Oldfield's victories at Coney Island in front of five thousand spectators. The production was a minor event compared to the film taken in Reno, but it did cause the *Chicago Defender* to remark sarcastically that "white people will be able and willing to find consolation in the Johnson-Oldfield auto-pictures."[80]

It would be nearly five years before Johnson had his title taken from him by an awkward and unlikely white hope, Jess Willard. Between 1911 and his defeat in 1915, Johnson's reputation declined steadily.

Johnson's Descent and the Federal Ban on Prizefight Films

The victory over Jim Jeffries and its replay on movie screens marked a high point in Jack Johnson's career. Although most black audiences were prevented from celebrating the *Johnson-Jeffries Fight*, they lionized their champion. Black leaders, however, were always cautious to separate their pride in Johnson's accomplishment from an endorsement of the controversial individual. After 1910, black support for Johnson faded quickly and white attacks intensified. The press and public virtually ignored subsequent Johnson films—*Johnson-Flynn* (1912) and *Johnson-Moran* (1914)—as the fighter became increasingly vilified. Reports of his fast living and legal troubles were thought to adversely affect the environment in which all African Americans had to live.

More to the point, his "film career" was cut short when the United States Congress took specific action to outlaw the interstate transportation of prizefight pictures. As debate about the action made clear, the cinematic glorification of Jack Johnson was what most framers of the law specifically intended to quash. Animus for both the House and Senate bills was clearly focused on race. While the proposed act did not single out race films, the unreconstructed Southern Democrats who steered the bill did. Georgia congressman Seaborn Roddenbery linked his aversion to fight films with his racist hatred of Johnson and all other blacks. On July 19, 1912, he declared:

> It is well known that one of the chief inducements and incentives to these prize fights now is the sale of the films. . . . I call the attention of the House to the fact that the recent prize fight which was had in New Mexico presented, perhaps, the grossest instance of base fraud and bogus effort at a fair fight between a Caucasian brute and an African biped beast that has ever taken place. It was repulsive. This bill is designed to prevent the display to morbid-minded adults and susceptible youth all over the country of representations of such a disgusting exhibition.

Democratic Ohio representative William Sharp interrupted Roddenbery's tirade to ask if he really thought it was "more indefensible for a white man and black man to engage in a prize fight than for two white men to engage in such a conflict?" Roddenbery responded that "no man descended from the old Saxon race can look upon that kind of a contest without abhorrence and disgust."[81]

When Northern members challenged such grandstanding, the bill's architect, Thetus Sims of Tennessee, intervened. He cut off his political ally and merely reminded the House that there was a consensus that immoral prizefight films should be stopped. The bill was passed and signed into law July 31, 1912.[82] Fight film production ceased in the United States, truncating any discussion of the impact of Johnson's screen image. Even the 1915 motion pictures showing Willard knocking out Johnson in their fight at Havana, Cuba, could not be brought into the U.S.

Conclusion

In the opening half of his reign Jack Johnson, the world's first black heavyweight champion, had been at the center of the American public arena. The new mass availability of motion pictures of his controversial prizefights triggered white concerns and black celebrations of his image. Recordings of his first three championship fights played to broad audiences. However, the dynamics of race continually and directly affected their reception. Johnson was an important part of this period in African American film exhibition. Yet because of the enormously high stakes of the racially charged Johnson-Jeffries fight, white censors severely restricted films of Johnson's greatest moment of fame. Only a small percentage of Johnson's black constituency got to see the *Johnson-Jeffries Fight*. The 1910 film, however, became as widely discussed as any single production prior to *The Birth of a Nation*. It was therefore more than ironic that Johnson's descent culminated with motion pictures of his defeat in April 1915, a film that appeared just as *The Birth of a Nation* was creating its own firestorm of controversy about race, censorship, and cinematic representation. The black press in particular took note of the double standard that permitted exhibition of a poisonous race drama like Griffith's epic but banned an observational documentary like the *Johnson-Jeffries Fight*. In Chicago, blacks responded to the local debut of *Birth of a Nation* by putting on a tent-show revival of the *Johnson-Jeffries* pictures.[83]

"The problem of the Twentieth Century is the problem of the color-line," W.E.B. Du Bois posited in 1903.[84] The early part of the century was indeed a vicious period for race relations in the United States. New Jim Crow policies, increased lynchings of blacks by whites, and other forms of violent and coercive social control negated the seeming progress of Reconstruction. Historians such as George C. Wright characterize this "nadir period" as a "time of worsening race relations," with the Supreme Court's *Plessy* v. *Ferguson* decision (1896) officially sanctioning such regression. The civilizing reforms of the Progressive Era were largely ineffectual for black Americans, as white-led progressivism remained blind to the problems of what Du Bois called "life behind the veil."[85] For African Americans the coercion of segregation intensified in all spheres of social life. For black athletes seeking access to the ring, as well as for black filmgoers seeking out pictures of these boxing heroes, the color line drawn by white society was a pernicious barrier. Jack Johnson played a notable role in partially breaking the color line in boxing and on movie screens. His performances put the lie to the prevailing ideology of white supremacy in a forceful and dramatic way. African Americans responded to his films enthusiastically, even though a racist backlash eventually contained Johnson's disruption.

The films of Johnson knocking out Burns, Ketchel, and Jeffries constitute one of the earliest forms of an African American cinema. Black audiences, often in black theaters, rallied to see and extol an accomplished, popular, and sovereign African American celebrity to a degree never before possible. Censorship of that image and the imposing segregation of theatrical space remained a defining reminder of white rule. But the cinematic icon of Johnson cast upon the screen, before both blacks and whites, presented an undeniable challenge to the racial status quo of that era.

Notes

1. Francis Trevelyan Miller, *Thomas A. Edison: Benefactor of Mankind; The Romantic Life Story of the World's Greatest Inventor* (Chicago: John C. Winston, 1931), p. 230; Frank Lewis Dyer, et al., *Edison: His Life and Inventions*, vol. 2 (New York: Harper and Brothers, 1929), p. 543. Even Matthew Josephson's ostensibly more scholarly *Edison* (New York: McGraw-Hill, 1959), p. 393, repeats this anecdote. The "spurious tradition" is explained in Gordon Hendricks, *The Edison Motion Picture Myth* (1961), reprinted in *Origins of the American Film* (New York: Arno Press and the *New York Times*, 1972) , pp. 190–195.

2. *Edison Films*, July 1904, p. 29. An earlier copy (January 12, 1904) referred to Martin as "colored" rather than "dusky." In Charles Musser, et al., eds., *Motion Picture Catalogs by American Producers and Distributors, 1894–1908: A Microfilm Edition* (Frederick, Md.: University Publications of America, 1985).

3. "Real Champion Gone," *Washington Post*, August 11, 1910, p. 9.

4. Roberts, p. 68 (citing *New York Times*, December 28, 1908, p. 5, and Nat Fleischer, *Fighting Furies: Story of the Golden Era of Jack Johnson, Sam Langford and Their*

Contemporaries, p. 44); "Black Jack's Golden Smile," *Baltimore Afro-American Ledger*, January 2, 1909, p. 1 (citing *Baltimore Sun*); "Southern Negro is Heavyweight Champion of the World," *Richmond Planet*, January 2, 1909, p. 1 (citing *New York Herald*); London, "Jack London Says Johnson Made a Noise Like a Lullaby with His Fist," *New York Herald*, December 27, 1908 (reproduced in Lardner's *The Legendary Champions*, p. 195); Finis Farr, "Jeff, It's Up to You!" *American Heritage Magazine*, February 1964, pp. 64–77. Tony van den Bergh's book, *The Jack Johnson Story* (London: Panther, 1956, p. 83), tellingly misrepresents London as writing "wipe the golden smile off the nigger's face."

In hyping the Johnson-Jeffries fight, the *Washington Post* embellished the legend of Johnson playing to the movie camera, writing: "He would throw Burns around into a position that would permit him to grin into the gaping mouth of the moving picture machine, and would then throw Burns off with one hand and smash him with the other, acting always for the camera." "Wanderings of a Prize Ring Championship and the Result," *Washington Post*, July 3, 1910, p. 4.

The fight with Burns was not the first on-camera appearance for Jack Johnson. While following Burns to Europe in hope of getting a title bout, Johnson was filmed boxing an English fighter, Ben Taylor. An unknown British producer recorded the *Jack Johnson–Ben Taylor* pictures on July 31, 1908, at Plymouth, England. The films were not widely seen and do not survive.

5. "Johnson's Win Blow to Boxing," *Louisville Courier-Journal*, January 4, 1909, p. 6 (citing Corbett letter to *Chicago Tribune*).

6. "The Caucasian's Plight," *Detroit Free Press*, reprinted in "Afro-American Journal," *New York Age*, January 14, 1909, p. 3.

7. Albert Bushnell Hart and Herbert Ronald Ferleger, eds., *Theodore Roosevelt Cyclopedia* (New York: Roosevelt Memorial Association, 1941), pp. 498ff.

8. *Richmond Planet*, February 9, 1909, p. 4.

9. "Fight Fans See Pictures," *Chicago Tribune*, March 22, 1909, p. 14.

10. "Row on Broadway; Isman Seeks to Stop Moving Prize Fight Pictures There," *New York Times*, April 8, 1909, p. 11.

11. "Burns Would Like to Be Slaughtered by Johnson," *Indianapolis Freeman*, January 9, 1909, p. 7; "Johnson-Burns Fight Here," *New York Times*, April 13, 1909, p. 11. The *Times* description of the film also indicated something of a white bias in the editing of the pictures. Preliminary footage shot in Sydney showed Australian society feted the champ: "It was apparent from these that Burns before the contest was a big favorite, as pink teas and other entertainments attest."

12. Harry W. Jackson, "As the Fight Pictures Told the Story," *Indianapolis Freeman*, May 1, 1909, p. 7.

13. Reprinted in *Richmond Planet*, January 30, 1909, p. 1.

14. "Popular Fight Pictures," *Billboard*, August 14, 1909, p. 13.

15. *Indianapolis Freeman*, January 9, 1909, p. 7.

16. "Burns-Johnson Films," *Indianapolis Freeman*, February 20, 1909, p. 7; Jackson, May 1, 1909, p. 7.

17. The song "The Black Gladiator: Veni, Vidi, Vici—Jack Johnson," by J. "Berni" Barborn, celebrated the victory over Burns as "proof that all men are the same/in muscle, sinew, and in brain/No other blood flows through our veins/but that of Negro Ham's own strain/Master of all the world—your claim." "Back Johnson Heavily," *Freeman*, January 23, 1909, p. 7.

18. Juli Jones, "Dehomey in Peace," *Freeman*, October 23, 1909, p. 5. Dehomey was an informal term for the African American district, taken from the West African territory of Dahomey, as well as the popular black musical comedy, *In Dahomey* (Will Marion Cook, 1902).

19. Lardner, p. 177; Roberts, *Papa Jack*, p. 84; Arnold, *History of Boxing*, pp. 49, 127; Golesworthy, p. 82; William H. Wiggins, Jr., "Jack Johnson as Bad Nigger: The Folklore of His Life," *Black Scholar*, January 1971, 43–44. Wiggins lists several versions of the legend about Ketchel's teeth.

20. John Sloan, October 29, 1909, in *John Sloan's New York Scene*, ed., Bruce St. John, (New York: Harper & Row, 1965).

21. In 1909, between his filmed title bouts, Johnson fought unremarkable exhibitions against Victor McLaglen (later of Hollywood acting fame), Philadelphia Jack O'Brien, Tony Ross, and Al Kaufman.

22. Al-Tony Gilmore, *Bad Nigger! The National Impact of Jack Johnson* (Port Washington, N.Y.: Kennikat Press, 1975); Roberts, *Papa Jack*, pp. 69ff; Wiggins, pp. 4–19.

23. W. W. Naughton, "Colored Man Is Still Champion," reprinted in *Richmond Planet*, October 23, 1909, pp. 1, 5.

24. "The Johnson-Ketchel Fight Pictures," *New York Sun*, October 26, 1909, reprinted in *Richmond Planet*, October 30, 1909, p. 1.

25. *New York Times*, November 1, 1910, p. 10.

26. On December 11, 1909, Jack Johnson wired George Kleine for a print of the Ketchel film. On December 27, he confirmed receiving one set of films (four reels) from Kleine. Memos in the George Kleine Collection, Library of Congress.

27. Motts incorporated daily film shows into his popular variety house as early as 1905. By all accounts in black newspapers across the United States, the opening and sustained success of the Pekin marked a progressive shift in the state of black theatrical enterprises. Previously, African American show places had been relegated to the level of honky-tonks. But the Pekin was considered "the original and only colored legitimate house" and the "first race theater" in the nation.

The Pekin had its name franchised nationally. As Motts's stock company of performers and managers toured, the name Pekin became a signifier of African American popular culture. Pekin theaters could be found in Cincinnati, Lexington, Louisville, Memphis, Norfolk, Savannah, and dozens of other towns. By 1909, some thirty-three showplaces bore the name of Motts's original home theater—about thirty percent of all black-owned venues. When the Cincinnati Pekin, a "moving picture house," opened under the management of a Motts's protégé, the *Freeman* cast it as part of "'Pekin' fever," noting that the "Pekin Amusement Company" was building a chain.

Ultimately the Pekin influence reached into the beginnings of African American filmmaking. When Peter P. Jones, William Foster, and Hunter C. Haynes all began producing black-cast films for black audiences in 1913–14, each used cast members from "the old Pekin stock company" (including the legendary Charles Gilpin). *Freeman*, December 2, 1909; J. Hockley Smith, "Funeral of Robert T. Motts, *Defender*, July 15, 1911; "Colored Manager Dies," (*Variety*, July 15, 1911), in *Variety Obituaries* (New York: Garland, 1988), "Another Pekin Theater," *Freeman*, January 30, 1909, p. 5; "The States Theater," *Defender*, August 9, 1913, n.p.; "Foster Film Co.," *Defender*, August 30, 1913, n.p.; [William Foster is in Dayton with his photoplays], *Defender*, January 3, 1914, n.p.; "One Large Evening," *New York Age*, April 9, 1914, p. 6; [Review of "Mandy's Choice"],

Defender, May 9, 1914, n.p.; "Peter P. Jones Head Motion Picture Co.," *Defender*, June 13, 1914, p. 6. See also, Gregory A. Waller, "Another Audience: Black Moviegoing, 1907–1916," *Cinema Journal* 31, no. 2 (1992): 3–25.

28. Sylvester Russell, "Musical and Dramatic," *Defender*, April 30, 1910, p. 4.

29. Uncle Rad Kees, "Johnson Shows Physical Prowess of the Negro," *Freeman*, November 27, 1909, p. 7. Similar skepticism was voiced by white reviewers. "Right to the Jaw Puts Ketchel Out; Black Fight for Pictures," *Chicago Tribune*, October 17, 1909, sec. 3 p. 1: "If the two men had been accomplished actors they couldn't have devised anything half so good for moving pictures as the show that was put up. . . ."

30. "Tex Rickard's Bid for Fight Accepted," *New York Times*, December 3, 1909, p. 9; "Rickard Gets Fight," *New York Tribune*, December 3, 1909; Lardner, p. 180.

31. Sammons, p. 35.

32. James J. Corbett, "Tradition Factor in the Big Fight. Corbett Says Black's Fear of White in Old Times Will Count on July 4," *Chicago Tribune*, July 1, 1910, p. 13.

33. Using Jeffries' byline, in 1909, *Physical Culture* magazine published essays reminiscent of Roosevelt's warnings about "race suicide." Jeff advocated boxing as mental and moral training for a weakening nation and as a way to fight "the Great White plague" (tuberculosis). James J. Jeffries, "The Need of an Athletic Awakening," *Physical Culture*, May 1909, 397–400; "Mental and Moral Training through Boxing," August 1909, 153–157.

34. "The Psychology of the Prize Fight," *Current Literature*, July 1910, 57–58; see also "Intellectuality of the New Pugilism," *Current Opinion*, February 1913, 130–131, for further racist arguments that members of the "unhappy race" were intellectually inferior to whites. See Rhett S. Jones, "Proving Blacks Inferior: 1870–1930," *Black World*, February 1971, 4–19; Steven J. Gould, *The Mismeasure of Man* (New York: W. W. Norton, 1981); I. A. Newby, *Jim Crow's Defense: Anti-Negro Thought in America, 1900–1930* (Baton Rouge: Louisiana State University Press, 1965), pp. 19–51.

35. Sammons, p. 34, traces how the heavyweight title, since the time of John L. Sullivan, came to stand for both nation and race.

36. "Booker Washington Meets Jack Johnson," *Baltimore Afro-American Ledger*, August 21, 1909, p. 1.

37. "Now Jack!" *Baltimore Afro-American Ledger*, March 12, 1910, p. 4.

38. Arthur R. Ashe, Jr., *A Hard Road to Glory: A History of the African-American Athlete, 1619–1918*, vol. 1 (New York: Amistad, 1993), pp. 38–41; Wiggins, p. 44.

39. F. L. Goodspeed, President of the Ministerial Union to William Howard Taft, May 9, 1910. Lapsley A. McAfee, Berkeley Presbyterian Churches, to Taft, May 10–11, 1910. *The William Howard Taft Papers*, Library of Congress, microfilm edition.

40. "Taft's Dates Mixed, Asks Son About Fight," *San Francisco Examiner*, July 4, 1910, p. 1.

41. Gilmore, p. 59.

42. H. E. K. [Hugh E. Keough], "The White Man's Real Hope Is that the Better Man Is Not Cheated," *Chicago Tribune*, July 4, 1910, p. 10.

43. Reported by filmmaker Laurie Block during production of *Fit: Episodes in the History of the Body* (1991). Extant archival footage of *Johnson-Jeffries* viewed by Block was taken by a camera that panned to follow Jeffries to his corner between rounds, taking Johnson out of the shot.

44. *Moving Picture World*, July 9, 1910, pp. 80–81.

45. "Pictures of the Jeffries-Johnson Fight," *Moving Picture World*, June 18, 1910, p. 1,039.

46. Al Jolson, "The Fight at Reno," *Variety*, July 9, 1910, p. 4.

47. "Passing of Jeffries as a Fighter," *New York Tribune*, July 5, 1910, p. 1; W. W. Naughton wrote: "when Jeffries fell there was one cry, then silence held the crowd"; the "melancholy crowd filed out forlornly." "Jeffries Mastered—Whipped by Grinning, Jeering Negro," *Chicago Tribune*, July 5, 1910, pp. 1–3. Jeffries' fan Nat Goodwin described the scene: "Imagine over sixteen thousand human beings filing slowly from a cemetery where departed heroes have been put away from earthly cares!" "A Day at Reno," in *Nat Goodwin's Book*, pp. 192–196.

48. "Whites and Blacks in Many Riotous Battles," *New York Tribune*, July 5, 1910, p. 1. The violent atmosphere of the prizefight was compounded by the social license, bordering on anarchy, that typically accompanied Independence Day. Roy Rosenzweig, *Eight Hours for What We Will: Workers and Leisure in an Industrial City, 1870–1920* (Cambridge: Cambridge University Press, 1983), chaps. 3, 6.

Most of the confrontations were "street scuffles" that erupted in less segregated social settings. But even in the usually controlled environs of the theater some incidents were reported. At Atlanta's Grand Opera House a "race clash" followed when "a mixed audience heard the fight bulletins read." *New York Age* theater columnist Lester Walton reported being assaulted. "Race Clash at Atlanta," *Louisville Courier-Journal*, July 5, 1910, p. 1; Lester A. Walton, "Merit, Not Color, Won," *New York Age*, April 8, 1915, p. 6; "Ban on Negro Parade," *New York Tribune*, July 4, 1910, p. 4 [Pittsburgh police intervene to stop white gangs from stoning black paraders]; "Police on Guard in Richmond," *New York Tribune*, July 4, 1910, p. 4; "Negro Dead After Riots," and "Aftermath of Rioting," *New York Tribune*, July 6, 1910, p. 4; "Fists Stir Up a Black Crowd," *Louisville Courier-Journal*, July 5, 1910, p. 1; "Racial Bloodshed Follows Fight at Reno," *Arkansas Democrat*, July 5, 1910, pp. 1, 7.

49. "Fight Pictures Prohibited Here by Mayor," p. 1. To cite one example of the fight film legislation being passed, the Texas statute called for "an act to prohibit the exhibition of prize fights or glove contests, and any obscene, indecent or immoral show or exhibition by means of moving picture films, bioscope, magic lanterns or other devices, in moving picture shows, theaters or any other place." *Texas Laws, 1910*, H. B. No. 5, c. 8, pp. 21–22 (August 15, 1910); Elmer M. Million, "History of the Texas Prize Fight Statute," *Texas Law Review* 17 (1938): 152–159

50. Henry Warner Bowden, *Dictionary of American Religious Biography* (Westport, Conn.: Greenwood Press, 1977), pp. 99–100; *New Catholic Encyclopedia*, vol. 3 (New York: McGraw-Hill, 1967), pp. 638–639; Bert H. Davis, *Publicity Plans for Christian Endeavor* (Boston: International Society of Christian Endeavor, 1930).

51. "Fight Pictures Prohibited by Mayor," p. 1.

52. "Fight Pictures," *Louisville Courier-Journal*, July 6, 1910, p. 2; *New York Tribune*, July 7, 1910, p. 1, and July 11, p.4.

53. *New York Tribune*, July 9, 1910, p. 1. Even a year later, the Society opened their national convention, before President Taft, by "condemn[ing] the Jeffries-Johnson prizefight pictures." *New York Times*, July 7, 1911, p. 9. Not all religious groups offered condemnation. Some Dutch ministers offered support, saying there was no reason "why the record [of the fight] in pictures should not be kept and shown," since they regarded it as

"a historic struggle." "Dutch Like Fight Pictures," *Film Index*, August 13, 1910, p. 10 (graciously provided by Roberta Pearson).

54. *[Spokane] Spokesman Observer*, July 7, 1910. p. 1. (From a clipping in the *Theodore Roosevelt Papers*, microfilm edition.)

55. Allen Sinclair Will, *Life of Cardinal Gibbons* (New York: E. P. Dutton, 1922), p. 802.

56. *Outlook*, July 1910, 551.

57. Chopin, "Real Moving Pictures, of the Return to Reno," *San Francisco Examiner*, July 7, 1910, p. 1; Chopin, "And Not a Friendly Port in Sight," *San Francisco Examiner*, July 9, 1910, p. 1.

58. Churchill acknowledged that "the British government itself [had] no power to suppress the films." "Can't Bar Pictures," *Jackson Clarion-Ledger*, July 14, 1910, p. 3.

59. Gilmore, pp. 75–93.

60. *Washington Bee*, July 9, 1910, p. 9; "To Bar Fight Pictures," *New York Tribune*, July 6, 1910, p. 4; "Educational?" *Jackson Clarion-Ledger*, July 21, 1910.

61. *Moving Picture World*'s statement at the height of the boxing film furor that "there is an under-current in this matter that is working upon the simplicity and prejudices of certain people" could scarcely have been more understated. *MPW*, July 16, 1910, p. 191.

62. Jane Addams, "Social Control," *Crisis: A Record of the Darker Races*, January 1911, 23.

63. Mrs. James Crawford, Vice President of California Women's Club, quoted in *San Francisco Examiner*, July 9, 1910; reprinted in Gilmore, p. 81.

64. "The Johnson-Jeffries Fight," *St. Paul Appeal*, July 9, 1910, p. 2.

65. *Defender*, July 30, 1910, p. 1; *Planet*, August 6, 1910, p. 1.

66. "Three negatives of the big fight were reeled off" and evaluated for photographic quality. "At Stag Houses Only," p. 3; "Keith Bars Fight Film," p. 4.

67. When Vitagraph manager George [Albert?] Smith exhibited the film at London's National Sporting Club in September, he claimed the firm had already made back its investment. Promoter Jack Gleason later put the total profits at $300,000. "Keith Bars Fight Film," p. 4; H.E.K. [Hugh E. Keough], "Now Up to Jeff to Plan Battle," *Clipper*, July 16, 1910, p. 555; *Bioscope*, September 15, 1911; "Havana Fight Films Barred from U.S.," *New York Times*, April 16, 1915, p. 8.

68. "At 'Stag' Houses Only," p. 3; "Fight Pictures Liked by New York Audiences," *Clipper*, July 30, 1910, p. 603.

69. "First Fight Pictures Seen," *New York Times*, July 17, 1910, sec. 2 p. 16; "First Glimpse of the Jeffries-Johnson Pictures," *Clipper*, July 23, 1910, p. 583; "What the Pictures Show," *New York Times*, July 19, 1910, p. 5.

70. "Fight Pictures at Meyerrose Park," *New York Age*, August 4, 1910, p. 6 (Negro baseball league star Nat Strong was mentioned as an interested party); Lester A. Walton, "Music and the Stage," *New York Age*, August 11, 1910, p. 6.

71. "Fight Pictures Stop School; Negro Teacher Sends Children to See Jeffries-Johnson Show," *Defender*, October 1, 1910, p. 1.

72. "Hollidaysburg, Penn.," *New York Tribune*, July 8, 1910, p. 4.

73. N. Barnett Dodson, "Johnson the Real Victor," *Baltimore Afro-American Ledger*, July 16, 1910, p. 4.

74. Mildred Miller, "The Nigger Unmolested," *Defender*, December 10, 1910.

75. "Too Much Jack Johnson," *Richmond Planet*, August 13, 1910, p. 4.

76. Janet Staiger, lecture, University of Texas at Austin, 1988; Staiger, "The Fuller Opera House: A Transition from Theater to Cinema," unpublished MS, 1977 (citing *Wisconsin State Journal:* "Hurrah for the Pictures," September 30, 1910, p. 8; September 29, 1910, p. 7; "Many See Pictures," October 1, 1910, p. 4); "Fight Pictures in Dublin," *New York Times*, August 21, 1910, sec. 3, p. 2; "Big Hit in Ireland," *Freeman*, September 3, 1910, p. 7; [Johnson-Jeffries Fight Pictures still being shown in Paris], *MPW*, March 4, 1911, p. 486; "Jeffries-Johnson Fight," *Bioscope*, October 12, 1911, p. 143; "Fight Pictures in Ireland," *Clipper*, August 27, 1910, p. 662; [Berlin Sees Johnson-Jeffries Fight Film at leading theaters], *New York Times*, September 17, 1911, sec. 3, p. 1.

77. "Among the Picture Theaters. Philadelphia and Vicinity," *Nickelodeon*, August 1, 1910, p. 80. Philadelphia promoter William McCarney barred children but drew no color restrictions.

78. "Newport Sees Fight Films," *New York Times*, August 9, 1910, p. 9; "Mrs. Widener Entertains with Fight Pictures," *Nickelodeon*, September 1, 1910, p. 24.

79. Roberts, *Papa Jack*, p. 118; National Archives photograph, unnumbered plate.

80. *Defender*, December 3, 1910, p. 2; Roberts, *Papa Jack*, p. 120; *MPW*, March 4, 1911, p. 486.

81. *Congressional Record*, July 19, 1912, p. 9305.

82. *Congressional Record*, May 29–July 31, 1912, pp. 7408, 7501, 7887, 7890, 8234–8235, 8550–8551, 9304–9309, 9447, 9554, 9585, 9988; 62d cong., 2d sess., Chap. 263, pp. 24–41; H.R. 858, "Interstate Transportation of Pictures of Prize Fights," pp. 1–2. See also, "Senate Ban," *Motography*, September 14, 1912, p. 205; September 28, 1912, p. 234.

83. "Johnson-Jeffries Fight Pictures May Be Shown in Chicago," *Defender*, September 4, 1915, p. 1.

84. W.E.B. Du Bois, *The Souls of Black Folk* (1903; rpt. New York: New American Library, 1969), p. xi.

85. George C. Wright, *Life Behind a Veil: Blacks in Louisville, Kentucky, 1865–1930* (Baton Rouge: Louisiana State University Press, 1985), p. 45; C. Vann Woodward, *The Strange Career of Jim Crow*, 3rd rev. ed. (New York: Oxford University Press, 1974); Eric Foner, *Reconstruction: America's Unfinished Revolution*, 1863–1877 (New York: Harper & Row, 1988).

THE FEAR OF MISCEGENATON

Chon A. Noriega

BIRTH OF THE SOUTHWEST
Social Protest, Tourism, and D. W. Griffith's *Ramona*

D. W. Griffith
Producer of all great Biograph successes,
revolutionizing Motion Picture drama
and founding the modern technique of the art.

Included in the innovations which he introduced and which are now generally followed by the most advanced producers, are: The large or close-up figures, distant views as presented first in Ramona, *the "switchback," sustained suspense, the "fade-out," and restraint in expression, raising motion-picture acting to a higher plane which has won for it recognition as a genuine art.*

—*Advertisement,* The New York Dramatic Mirror,
December 31, 1913[1]

While Griffith's claims above are somewhat exaggerated, presented as an advertisement to announce his break with Biograph, it is notable that he makes reference to *Ramona: A Story of the White Man's Injustice to the Indian* (1910) with respect to "distant views" or long shots. In fact, *Ramona* is the only film cited alongside a technical innovation, even though Griffith himself had already used long shots in an earlier film, *In Old Kentucky* (1909), also starring Henry B. Walthall. But in leaving Biograph, Griffith sought to establish himself—in the words of one reviewer of *Ramona*—as a filmmaker "strongly entrenched in public confidence . . . never pandering to the baser elements of society nor catering to perverted instincts," and as someone who has "advanced a step in the evolution of a new art and blazed the way for additional, greater achievement."[2] That the reviewer (as was common) spoke of the "producers" or the production company and not Griffith per se suggests one reason why Griffith would associate himself with *Ramona* as he also laid claim to technical innovations and acting codes that established film as a "new" and "genuine" art form.

Still, by all accounts, Griffith's adaptation of *Ramona* did set a number of precedents within the emergent film industry. At Griffith's insistence, Biograph paid the publisher for the movie rights to the novel, and credited both the publisher and author on the introductory inter-title.[3] In addition, *Ramona* was the first film to identify the location where it was shot: "Camulos, Ventura County, California, the actual scenes where Mrs. Jackson placed her characters in the story." Biograph, which usually distributed weekly handbills to motion picture exhibitors, issued a special illustrated handbill for filmgoers which announced, among other things, "that *Ramona* was the most expensive film ever made."[4] On the technical front, Griffith increased the number of scenes (45), camera positions (22), and inter-titles (18—mostly, summary titles) used in his previous films.[5] The result was, according to Mrs. D. W. Griffith in *When the Movies Were Young* (1925), "Mr. Griffith's most artistic creation to date."[6]

Above all, however, Griffith's reference to *Ramona* seems intended to tap into the critical and commercial success of the film and of its more famous source, Helen Hunt Jackson's novel of 1884.[7] In addition to more than three hundred printings and numerous stage productions, *Ramona* was adapted to the screen four times in the United States between 1910 and 1936, and remains the subject of a ritual re-enactment each Spring in the Southern California Ramona Pagent—which is the longest continuously running play in the United States.[8] By one estimate, the "texts of Ramona"—novel, nonfiction publications, stage productions, film adaptations, popular song, tourist sites, product tie-ins—generated some $50 million in revenues by 1916.[9] In Southern California, a town (home of the Ramona Pioneer Historical Society), streets, businesses ("Ramona's Chile Rellenos"), and real estate developments have been named after Ramona.[10] More than anything, as Kevin Starr argues in *Inventing the Dream*, *Ramona* contributed the "mission myth" of halcyon days of the Spanish Dons to the cultural transformation of Southern California in the Booster Era (1885–1925) under the auspices of Colonel Harrison Gray Otis, owner of the *Los Angeles Times*. Pulling together a group of Eastern journalists and writers, "Otis promoted an image of Southern California that dominated the popular imagination at the turn of the century and is alive to this day: a melange of mission myth (originating in Helen Hunt Jackson's *Ramona*), obsession with climate, political conservatism (symbolized in open shop), and a thinly veiled racialism, all put to the service of boosterism and oligarchy."[11] Since then, *Ramona* has become, in Mike Davis's words, "a romance that generations of tourists and white Angelenos have confused with real history."[12]

And yet, despite its rich historical context, technical innovations, and business precedents, *Ramona* is hardly ever mentioned in recent studies of Griffith,[13] while the popular novel—a product of the "damned mob of scribbling women" (Nathaniel Hawthorne)—never attained canonical status in literary studies.[14] What explains the simultaneous popularity and critical devaluation of *Ramona*? Most often, Griffith's *Ramona* is cited as an example of his more benign treatment of "Indians" (in contrast to his other "racial portraiture"), taking his own one-line description of the film as a formula: "It most graphically illustrates the white man's injustice to the Indian."[15] That critics take Griffith at his word and look no further suggests more about the marginal role of "race" within examinations of early silent cinema than it does about Griffith himself.[16]

In the past few years, however, a critique of race and silent cinema has emerged from a group of multi-media artists in San Diego.[17] This work suggests a model for a much-needed critical discourse in film studies on the function of race, gender, class, and nation in early cinema history. David Avalos and Deborah Small have made *Ramona* the focus of a didactic "multi-disciplinary installation" titled *Mis*ce*ge*NATION* that has traveled throughout the nation since 1991. The installation, which occupies an entire gallery, includes four components: *Mes*ti*zo*NATION*, a wall of eighteenth-century Mexican *castas* paintings which provide a taxonomy of racial mixture; *Ramona's Bedroom*, a viewing and reading room in the center of the gallery in which the audience sits on a hay-and-sarape bed; *Ramona: Birth of a Mis*ce*ge*NATION*, a single-channel video on racial mixing in Hollywood films that faces Ramona's bed; and an artist's book located on the bed itself. The book takes the form of a textbook or primer, complete with multiple choice questions—itself a response to struggles over multicultural education and the fact that *Ramona* "was required reading in California schools into the 1950s."[18]

In their video, Avalos and Small suggest another line of inquiry with respect to Griffith's *Ramona*.[19] The opening sequence re-centers the discussion of *Ramona* around issues of tourism, Hollywood, and racial purity as national ideology, self-consciously situating itself at a point in time in which the earlier texts—both the novel and the silent films—have been forgotten. The female voice-over narrator, identified in the script as "a tourist guide for the multiculturally impaired," introduces Ramona as "the Pocahontas of pluralism, the Malinche of multiculturalism, California's Mother of Miscegenation." But her male "multicultural tourist," also off-screen, is confused: "I don't get it. I've never heard of this Ramona." The tourist guide reassures him: "Don't worry, you already know the story, even though you've never heard of it. It's *Last of the Mohicans*, *West Side Story* and *La Bamba* all at the same time. If you've seen 'em all you've seen one."

Interestingly, Avalos and Small never include images from Griffith's *Ramona*, which becomes codified as an absent cause, identifiable through its effects, but not present in and of itself.[20] Instead, the video proceeds to appropriate scenes from Hollywood films of the studio era in order to reveal an underlying and unchanging racial ideology. This approach requires a strategic reductionism about the representation of racial mixture in U.S. popular culture, especially insofar as the artists' stated agenda is to open up a space for bi-racial identity within the contemporary "cultural landscape." Thus, Avalos and Small's historical revisionism must mirror the same mythical function they critique: that is, it has an uncomplicated view of the past (or, here, of past representation) speak for and guide the present *in the language of the present*. This approach provides an insightful critique of tourism and Hollywood with respect to historical amnesia, but says little about bi-racial identity itself and even less about the historical permutations across the "texts of Ramona." Instead, the video blurs the boundaries between tourism, mass media, and education, establishing visual and multicultural literacy through the pedagogical tourism of an art space.

Given its present-day concerns, then, Avalos and Small's installation raises an unanswered question about the function of Griffith's *Ramona* in the United States in 1910. In the remainder of this essay, I will look at the proliferation and permutation of the "texts of Ramona" between Helen Hunt Jackson's novel and Griffith's film adaptation. It is within this historical context that Griffith's *Ramona* can be seen as a marking a shift between nineteenth and twentieth century discourses of race, class, gender, and national identity. In this period, the "texts of Ramona" follow a movement from social protest to myth of origins to tourist experience. Griffith's *Ramona* relocates and rearticulates the story within mass *visual* culture as part of a project to transform cinema into a middle class art form.

The Novel and Beyond (1884–1910)

Helen Hunt Jackson's novel *Ramona* can be taken as a "foundational fiction" for the U.S. Southwest, similar in scope and objective to Harriet Beecher Stowe's *Uncle Tom's Cabin.*[21] Jackson—a prolific and popular writer of travel sketches, essays, poetry, fiction, and children's books—became deeply concerned over the plight of Native Americans in 1879 after hearing a lecture in Boston by Standing Bear and Bright Eyes on the injustices against the Ponca Indians: "For the first time she identified herself with a national reform movement, not having written for the causes of black-white equality, temperance, and suffrage."[22] In 1881, Jackson published *Century of Dishonor*, which extensively documented the government's injustices to the indigenous population since the Revolutionary period, sending a copy to each member of the 1880 Congress, challenging them to "redeem the name of the United States from the stain of a century of dishonor." In 1882, President Chester Arthur appointed Jackson and Abbot Kinney as special commissioners of Indian Affairs, and charged them to conduct a fact-finding investigation of the Mission Indians of California. In 1883, Jackson and Kinney submitted their report, complete with ten policy recommendations, to the Department of Interior. The report was ignored. In the aftermath of these efforts, Jackson realized that she needed to change public sentiment in order to influence government policies, prompting her to write a popular novel based on the report's findings and the stories she had heard as commissioner.[23] She expressed her goals in a letter to a friend: "If I can do one-hundredth part for the Indian as Mrs. Stowe did for the Negro, I will be thankful."[24]

In the novel, Ramona is the foster child of the Moreno family who—to the dismay of the Señora—falls in love with Alessandro, a Luiseño Indian and natural leader of the men in his village who provide seasonal work on the estate. When Ramona discovers that she is not Mexican, but rather half-Indian and half-Scottish, she elopes with Alessandro. White settlers stake a legal claim to the village, and Ramona and Alessandro become landless, moving from one site to another as settlers continue to displace them.[25] In an interlude of sorts, the couple befriends the Hyer family from Tennessee, establishing common cause and mutual support across race and language on the basis of a class-bound sense of universal humanity. When their child dies, Alessandro becomes "half-crazed," mistakenly taking a White man's horse, whereupon he is pursued and shot dead. The ever-faithful Felipe—the son of the Moreno estate—arrives to rescue Ramona. In the end, they marry, relocate to Mexico, and raise a family.

Despite its focus on the "love story" of Ramona and Alessandro, the novel provides an overview of the social changes since the Mexican American War as it relates to Mexicans, Indians, and various classes of Whites, and it raises issues of the legal and bureaucratic rights of the Indian population. This comes about through the character of Ramona, who circulates within the text—between families, races, husbands, and nations—as a marker of social change and racial-cum-legal hierarchies. But, while extremely popular, Jackson's novel came under criticism from two fronts for its "feminine" sentimentalism with regard to politics. Progressives such as Theodore Roosevelt ridiculed the "foolish sentimentalists" who advocated protection of Indian rights and land claims; and more liberal critics such as Allan Nevins dismissed "sentimental reformers" because they "present only one aspect of a complex and difficult problem and thereby oversimplify and distort it," and they "offer no constructive remedy for the difficult problem they expose."[26] Equating women/femininity with emotions and men/masculinity with rationalism, both critiques acknowledge the power of the sentimental novel to appeal to the emotions, but suggest its influence is limited since political action must follow a "realist" code: "These problems can be solved only by cold, careful, sustained use of the intellect."[27]

In *Sensational Designs*, Jane Tompkins turns this criticism on its head, arguing that these novels express a "sentimental power," which she defines as "the power to work in, and change, the world,"[28] precisely on the basis of their popularity and appeal to the emotions. For Tompkins, as for many scholars of the sentimental novel, "the popular domestic novel of the nineteenth century represents a monumental effort to reorganize culture from the woman's point of view . . . offer[ing] a critique of American society far more devastating than any delivered by better-known critics such as Hawthorne and Melville."[29] Tompkins's *Sensational Designs* represents a decisive critical intervention within literary studies. Interestingly, regional and Western writers such as J. Frank Dobie and Charles F. Lummis made similar claims about *Ramona* earlier in the century, although toward much different ends.[30] Lummis, who in 1905 credited *Uncle Tom's Cabin* and *Ramona* as the two books with "the deepest and the longest influence on American public sentiment and American politics," provides an early expression of Tompkins's thesis: "great reforms are wrought, not by politicians, but by public sentiment . . .

aroused not by statistics, no matter how damning, but by a proper appeal to the emotions."[31]

But if the novel exerts "sentimental power," it does so on much different terms than Jackson's political tracts directed at a male-dominated civil society, even if the overarching goal is the same: the federal protection of Indians. Perhaps, then, Ramona's half-Scottish background provides the avenue for the novel's "sentimental power," as do other concessions to her audience's cultural frame of reference.[32] Ramona—described as the best of both races with steel blue eyes—allows the mostly White, presumably female readers to occupy the space of the Indian in a moment of "sentimental" identification. This process of identification engages yet inverts the colonial mimicry that Homi Bhabha discusses with respect to India, in which the colonized becomes almost the same as the colonizer but "not quite/not white."[33] Here, the Mexican-cum-Indian must be made "almost the same" through miscegenation and assimilation in order to engage the reader's identification, then allowed to "return" to her true "nature" in a sort of leap of faith that is all-too-similar to racial masquerade—her newfound Indian-ness is *assumed*, despite the racial, linguistic, cultural, and class differences between Ramona and the other Indians she encounters. Thus, if Ramona is "almost the same but not quite," she is also alone in this two-sided mimicry, so that she functions as the go-between (in the narrative) and the point of identification (for the reader), but cannot occupy a stable position. Bhabha's colonial binarism does not hold up in this case because Ramona's mimicry is represented within a residual Spanish colonialism in order to speak obliquely to U.S. Manifest Destiny and Progressivism.[34] Thus, as an exception within the realm of social relations, Ramona establishes the existence of differences (of race, class, culture), and, by moving between these differences, she facilitates *emotional* moments of universal identification for female readers. But, despite her potential *racial* claims to whiteness, Ramona cannot exceed her *cultural* construction within the terms of Spanish colonialism—hence, her exile to Mexico.

Here it becomes most apparent that *Ramona* works at the level of reader-text-context relations, and not those between reader and character. Jackson is not trying to change individual or personal behavior per se through one-to-one identification, but—on the other hand—neither is she speaking on behalf of tribal sovereignty or self-government. Instead, Jackson seeks to provide an emotional basis for support of *state* intervention and abjudication within social relations. In one sense, Jackson wants the state to take over the colonial paternalism she attributes to the old Spanish and Mexican social order. Thus, it is important to locate the novel and its impact on readers within contemporary debates over federal policy and reform which led up to the Dawes Act of 1887. If, as critics pointed out, the sentimental novel "offers no constructive remedy," Jackson and Kinney's earlier report was both constructive and practical, outlining policy recommendations as well as written agreements with the Catholic church and private landowners. *Ramona*, then, must be read in relation to *Century of Dishonor* and Jackson and Kinney's report.

Still, Jackson's vision operates more in terms of class than of colonialism, as is evident in the social relations she establishes between characters. Insofar as Jackson subsumes racism within a class analysis, *Ramona* represents a counter-discourse within the dominant strategy of linking working class Whites and "Indians" within a progressive politics, as represented by Teddy Roosevelt.[35] Whereas Roosevelt describes a "natural" progression beyond the influence of human agency, Jackson emphasizes the attendant violence and injustice in order to place these events within the realm of the political. Therefore, if Jackson conflates Indians and working-class Whites within a class analysis, she also maintains "whiteness" as part of a critique of the nation and its institutions—business and government. Indeed, in all her writings on Indians, Jackson uses "White" as a generic racial marker at a time when political discourse made racial distinctions within "whiteness" that conflated class and ethnicity. As historian Richard Slotkin notes: "The use of 'Anglo-Saxon' rather than 'White' signaled the emergence of a crucial distinction in the language of American racialism, a need to differentiate not only Whites from Blacks and Indians, but to distinguish between different classes of Whites."[36] Slotkin includes "Mexicans in Texas and the Far West" within this pan-ethnic Whiteness. His assertion has *legal* merit in the Treaty of Guadalupe Hidalgo, which granted Mexicans in the United States the full rights of citizenship, then limited to "free whites."[37] While the distinction is an important one vis-à-vis the concurrent legal status of Black, Indian, and Chinese populations, in social practice and popular discourse Mexicans would constitute a non-White "race," or, at best, a much inferior, antiquated class of Whites (as "Spanish"). Within Jackson's milieu, the popular formulation of Mexicans-as-Whites was removed from a contemporary binational context (Mexico-United States) and placed within the mythical past (Spanish California). Jackson, however, was an exception in that she refers to the Moreno family as "Mexican" throughout the novel, and recounts the political and economic consequences of the Mexican-American War and massive "White" immigration into Southern California.

But despite its avowed social protest on behalf of Indians, in the two decades after its initial publication, *Ramona* functioned in unexpected ways as a "foundational fiction" for California, securing the Southland to the national imagination through nostalgia or "ersatz mythology" that could be re-lived both as tourism and through the vicarious identification of racial masquerade in annual "Spanish fiestas" throughout Southern California.[38] This produced a paradox in which White Anglo-Saxon Protestants celebrated a romanticized Catholic-Mission past, masquerading as Spanish Dons. George Wharton James, in *Through Ramona's Country* (1908), places this scene within an unabashed boosterism that strangely prefigures Bhabha's formulation: "How the few old *señoritas* who remain from that time must gaze and wonder at the crowds, the excitement of it all, so like, yet so different from their own Mexican and Spanish *fiestas*."[39] In this way, *Ramona* provided a myth that both explained and elided the racial and class reorientation of the state's economic and political structure in the period *after* the novel's publication. In other words, the dispossession of Ramona and Alessandro ceased to signify in terms of a contemporary issue about Native Americans, and became instead a myth of origins for California that conformed to the progressive ideology of Social Darwinism. The appropriation and romanticization of *californio* history, then, bespoke the inevitable succession of superior "races" in the pursuit of higher forms of social organization, from nomadic to feudal to small farms to conglomerates: Mexicans over Indians, White (immigrant) settlers over Mexicans, and White (Anglo-Saxon) capitalists over White (immigrant) settlers. But, as McWilliams implies, it also removed this succession from the political sphere of struggle, resistance, and violence, turning it into an act of symbolic identification with the elites of a past social order—"to the total neglect of its realistic latter-day manifestations" in working class *barrios* and migrant farm camps.

The publication of *Ramona* coincided with the demise of the *californios* as a cultural, political, and economic force. In Southern California, Mexican families from the old ruling-class elite "were concentrated in sufficient number so that they remained an important political factor through the 1880's."[40] With the influx of Anglo-Americans into Southern California in the 1880s, "the Spanish-Mexican appearance of

Southern California towns changed overnight," dispossessing the upper classes and displacing Mexican workers.[41] This shift occurs in concert with actions by the U.S. Court of Land Claims, which, between 1891 and 1904, dispossessed Mexican Americans from the majority of the land holdings nominally guaranteed them by the Treaty of Guadalupe Hidalgo. After 1900, with the dissolution of the native *californio* social order, Mexican culture in California would be characterized by the large number of working class immigrants from Mexico, and the formation of an urban populace. Writing in 1946—at a point in which immigration had itself produced a Mexican-American generation focused on "first class citizenship" and civil rights—Carey McWilliams wryly notes, "the restored Mission is a much better, a less embarrassing, symbol of the past than the Mexican field worker or the ragamuffin pachucos of Los Angeles."[42]

The novel also provided an allegorical account of the condition of White settlers in the period after the Western frontier has been announced "closed"—a period that coincides with the texts' popularity and its adaptations to the stage, cinema, and tourism. Ironically, as Slotkin explains, "the Frontier was far from closed," with more public land brought into production between 1890 and 1920 than in the decades after the Homestead Act (1862). What had "closed," however, was not so much a material or geographical frontier, but access to public land by the working class: "Individual entrepreneurs and settlers on the new frontiers of the industrial and railroad eras had to contend (on increasingly disadvantageous terms) with large capitalist enterprises for control of the new resources."[43]

Nonetheless, Slotkin argues that by 1893 the West had "closed" within the national imagination as "a geographical place and a set of facts requiring a historical explanation[,] . . . becoming a set of symbols that *constituted* an explanation of history."[44] *Ramona* served as an "ersatz myth" that explained the racial and class transformations then underway in California within the context of "boosterism" and real estate development. The "invented dream" of California, then, shifted from open land (farm or ranch) to real estate (house) around a romantic tale of Indian dispossession.[45] Still, the myth—at least in its allegorical dimensions—was not a total one, given that mythic space often overlapped with contemporary political discourse and events. In the silent era, film Westerns (defined broadly as films set in the West) were especially marked by this tension. On the one hand, they sought to articulate a "set of symbols that *constituted* an explanation of history" through archetypal characters, locations, and plots. On the other hand, more often than not these films were set in the present, featuring contemporary technology (cars), events (The Mexican Revolution), social types (the "new woman"), and states (New Mexico, Arizona). The brief decline of the Western between 1930 and 1938—which Slotkin attributes to the Depression—would also mark the end of the West in material terms: Border conflict (1830–1930), closing of the U.S.-Mexico border, Depression-era "repatriation" programs, the rise of a "Mexican-American generation." When the Western returned in the late 1930s, the socio-economic rupture had been completed, and the "West" had become a thing of the past—a past mode of production, an old social order—that subsequent films refigured as a purely mythical space. But in the silent period, the Western spoke to its viewers from a kind of mythical present that hadn't quite passed into history, let alone mythology.

After 1900, concurrent with the rise of cinema, *Ramona* would be placed within the realm of "nonfiction" when a number of writers attempted to locate the "real" Ramona or to situate the novel's events within an historical landscape, as did D. A. Hufford in *The Real Ramona* (1900), George Wharton James in *Through Ramona's Country* (1908), Margaret V. Allen in *Ramona's Homeland* (1914), and Carlyle C. Davis and William A. Alderson in *The True Story of Ramona* (1914).[46] Whereas Jackson's goal was to use fiction for "sentimental power" within the political arena, these writers sought real-life referents for the novel, promoting tourism within Southern California by offering a "real" person or place that one could experience firsthand. In this manner, the novel became trapped within a circular logic in which it could never represent anything more than a social landscape that looked exactly like the novel itself. Once there was a "real" Ramona, the novel's character ceased to be symbolic of all Indians, and became instead a sign for a tourist exhibit.

Even James's *Through Ramona's Country*, with its extensive research and repeated insistence that Ramona and Alessandro were nothing more than fictional characters, nonetheless devotes several chapters to Ramona Lubo, a Luiseño basket weaver whose husband, Juan Diego, was shot for mistakenly taking a White man's horse. In fact, James admits that Jackson had heard this same story from a Mrs. Jordan, and he reprints her recounting of it in *Century of Dishonor* as a precursor to the novel's strikingly similar tragic events. He even identifies Diego's murderer, Sam Temple, as the model for Alessandro's murderer, and Mrs. Jordan as the model for Aunti Ri. But, in contrast to promotional pamphlets, James and other "serious" writers deny that Ramona Lubo is the model—or even one model—for Jackson's Ramona, and they do so on the basis of racialized standards of beauty: Ramona Lubo is "squat, fat, and unattractive . . . with low forehead, prominent cheek bones, wide nostrils, heavy lips."[47] Thus, if Jackson made Ramona both half-Scottish and acculturated to an elite class in order to undermine this sort of racial repulsion, the nonfiction writers studiously distinguish "the facts and fictions of Ramona," separating the character (and the reader's emotional identification with her) from the very people, history, and current injustices that she is supposed to represent. By the time of Griffith's adaptation, *Ramona* would operate as a myth of the romantic *californio* past and as a fictional narrative with "real-life" correspondences in contemporary Southern California. And, as Biograph's own inter-titles and promotion suggest, tourism would mediate between the mythical and the historical, and the past and the present. The reader was no longer moved to address the underlying issues, but, rather, to visit the "real" sites and people who now served as a marker for the past and the fictional texts.

D. W. Griffith's *Ramona*

Titled *Ramona: A Story of the White Man's Injustice to the Indian*, the 1910 film provides an outline of the novel's major scenes directly related to the "love story" of Ramona and Alessandro, from their mutual attraction to Alessandro's murder. In the film, the inter-titles provide both plot description and information about Ramona's racial character. The fact that Ramona "has Indian blood" explains her "intuition" about the events in the previous scene in which "Whites destroy Alessandro's village," and it also foretells the subsequent scenes summarized in the inter-title, "The White's Persecution: 'These lands belong to us.'" Following their elopement, Ramona and Alessandro purchase a small house, but are made "Homeless" by the arrival of two White men. They retreat to a mountaintop, where their child dies and Alessandro goes mad. The previous line, "This land belongs to us," is repeated in the inter-title before the scene in which a White settler arrives to eject them from the mountaintop, shooting a crazed Alessandro. In these last few scenes, Griffith intersperses three shots of Felipe riding in search of the couple. It is uncertain whether these shots represent cross-cutting or parallel editing, since the time scheme for each event is unclear, but the effect is to create a brief suspense, then disappointment when Felipe arrives at the murder scene—his arrival now coded as "too late."

Fig. 1: Alessandro meets Ramona.

Fig. 2: Ramona, Felipe, and Alessandro.

Fig. 3: Alessandro and Ramona evicted by local whites.
Fig. 4: Alessandro goes crazy after the death of his child.

Fig. 5: Felipe and Ramona mourn over Alessandro's body against a pictorial landscape.

Griffith's film adaptation points to a shift in *californio* narratives in the twentieth century, wherein the characters' Mexican origins are rewritten as "Spanish." The first inter-title after the credits introduces the main characters as follows: "Alessandro the Indian. And Ramona of the Great Spanish Household of Moreno." In this manner, films from *Ramona* to *Duel in the Sun*, which center on the intermarriage of Spanish creole and Indian, can be said to "deconstruct" the historical Mexican and Mexican-American subject, bifurcating a mestizo or mixed-race identity into its constituent parts. Unless viewers had read the novel, the film (and its promotion) would have given the impression that Ramona is half-Spanish and half-Indian, since she is identified with the Moreno household and "learns that she has Indian blood." Film reviews would not point out the fact of her Scottish father until the 1916 adaptation, which, at fourteen reels was some two thousand feet longer than *The Birth of a Nation*, and followed the novel in great detail.[48]

Ramona has been described as the film in which Griffith first integrates close-up with full and extreme long shots.[49] As in other discussions of Griffith's "innovations," these claims tend to focus on general formal or narrative effects, rather than the particular application around which they developed. But one might argue instead that technical "innovations" are a means of ideological encoding that have been used in highly precise ways. For instance, the use of close-up renders the half-breed protagonist as a subject within a social context of family and home (full shot), followed by her repeated dispossession and widowhood at the hands of "Whites" either in front of property (full shot) or from a mountaintop view (extreme long shot). Thus, in a strange sort of way, Griffith depicts the birth of the Mexican American and the Native American citizen at the level of technique (or form): Editing innovations identify Ramona with the land at the very moment that the film narrative depicts her loss of communal property rights (under Mexico and the Treaty of Guadalupe Hidalgo) and emplacement within a "White" economic and legal system under the United States.

Interestingly, it is Griffith himself who brings this racial discourse to the forefront, then places it within a sentimentalist discourse focused on Ramona and Alessandro alone. The novel, ostensibly about the injustices done to the Indian, ends with the reconstitution and exile of the "Mexican" hacienda, which has been disabused of its wealth, power, and fertility while in the United States. In the film, however, this all occurs off-screen or is implied, like the subsequent marriage of Felipe and Ramona and their exile to Mexico. In identifying the Moreno estate as "the great Spanish household," the film contradicts the actual decline of the *californios* that coincided with the novel's publication. But, at the same time, the other scenes reveal the Morenos' greatness to exist on another level than that of active participation in the narrative: The "Whites" destroy Alessandro's village, which provides labor for the Moreno household—evident in the first shot. And, in the end, Felipe cannot do anything to stop the violence that attends the "White" refrain that "These Lands Belong to Us." Both visually and discursively, Griffith's *Ramona* situates the Moreno household outside of the history being told (or before, perhaps during Spain's colonial control of California). It is of interest, then, that Griffith did shoot a scene depicting the marriage of Felipe and Ramona, but, more than likely, had to cut it in order to meet Biograph's standard length of one thousand feet.[50] Like the novel, such a scene would have provided narrative closure around the reconstitution of the "Great Spanish Household" rather than around the murder of Alessandro, placing Ramona within the ambiguous time frame of a residual Spanish colonialism. Even so, when combined with the "Spanish" classification of the Moreno family, this omission further removes Mexican-American history from the film narrative—or, at the very least, requires that the knowledgeable viewer "read" it into the film.

In Griffith's *Ramona*, the focus is on an old (Spanish) ruling class and an undifferentiated class of frontier "Whites," without the novel's critique of the U.S. government's neglect and of how class conflict had structured race relations. Furthermore, in the novel, the Indians are not "savages" but workers within the old (and heavily romanticized) economic system of the Mexican ranchera and Catholic missions, and are left with scant economic and political opportunities within the new social order. Thus, as I mentioned earlier, Jackson balances between a class analysis that cuts across race and a critique of the state for structuring its institutions around "whiteness." In the film, however, "Whites" are not differentiated, nor do they occupy the foreground, except in full shot scenes of dispossession. Missing are the poor Hyer family, local government and business, as well as the implacable bureaucracy of the Bureau of Indian Affairs. Stripped down to these two elements—the "Indian" couple and "White" land grabbers—the film slips from an active social protest with a race-class analysis into the nostalgia of the frontier myth. Two film reviews in *Moving Picture World* reveal the consequences of these changes or omissions in terms of viewer identification: "The love story loses nothing of its power in the picture, and one wants to do something to help the unfortunates whose property is destroyed, whose land is taken and who are persecuted and driven even farther into the wilderness. It is too late now for the reproduction of the novel to exert any influence in the rectification of a great wrong" (June 4, 1910, p. 942). Considered a faithful "reproduction," the film nonetheless creates the sense that it is "too late" to do anything for Native Americans, let alone reproduce Jackson's political agenda. The "love story" and "injustices," then, provide little more than an edifying account of what is now cast as an inevitable history: "the injustice that preceded the settlement of a considerable portion of the United States." For one earlier reviewer, the film fulfills not the novel's original call for reform, but rather the latter-day longing it instills in the reader to experience the events as tourist: that is, "to visit the scenes wherein lived the simple, patient Ramona, and the noble-hearted Alessandro" (May 28, 1910, p. 897).

The Quiet Audience

Ramona opens up a number of possible readings, depending on viewer expectations and knowledge. It is safe to assume that numerous viewers would have read the novel, known about the historical referent revealed in *Through Ramona's Country*, or been aware of the tourist industry that had built up around the novel through postcards and pamphlets. Ramona Lubo and other "Ramonas" were still alive, and at least one "Spanish" family promoted its estate as the real-life site of the novel's events. At a crucial point in the film industry's own development, *Ramona*—like other "Westerns"—spoke to the recent past (the "old" west was still just a generation removed) while it carried strong connections to the present. Thus, *Ramona* takes part in the shift from social protest to tourism/nostalgia through the implied historical referent (Ramona Lubo and the Moreno Ranch) and the erasure of the class allegory.

In a number of ways, Griffith's *Ramona* marks (if not effects) a crucial shift in the ideal audience for the "texts of Ramona" from primarily White women to businessmen. Related to this shift, reviewers and Griffith's own advertisement emphasized the role of *Ramona* in the class reorientation of cinema itself, from "unthinking elements" to "serious patrons." Louis Reeves Harrison, in an extended report in *Moving Picture World*, described a sold-out screening of a "special feature" that had attracted an "unusually large" and "quiet" audience that "was rather above than below the average in quality, and it was largely composed of men. The men were of all classes and conditions, they were uniformly earnest-looking, most of them seemed to be business men, who had possibly left the absorbing occupation of trying to do to others as they might reasonably expect to be done, in order to rest an hour or two and recuperate from brain fag." Harrison's article is important both for its description of the film's audience, but more so for its speculation about the motivations and inclinations of what was perceived to be an ideal audience, "including many who ordinarily stay away from exhibitions of motion pictures." In fact, Harrison's article is a stunning divigation on the gender and class constitution of this "new" audience, wherein "business men" were identified as the ideal viewer. Harrison provides an early prescriptive version of Laura Mulvey's thesis that narrative cinema centers on the male heterosexual gaze.[51] In essence, he argues that men act and women (and "unmanly" men) are to be looked upon: "We look to women for what beautifies existence, and, as interest in picture plays is stimulated by what is seen, it becomes centered on the heroine of the story. To suit the role, she must be lovable." Men on the screen are positioned as either a "thing of beauty" and thus "unmanly," or—more preferable—as a "creature of forceful character" and thus "unlovely." Harrison frames this mode of cinematic identification within an ascendant medical discourse on sexuality, suggesting that deviations from his model are the result of homosexuality: "*She* goes over. Any man who does not think so should send for Doctor Osler."[52] Thus, other forms of identification with Ramona, including those of women viewers, fall into the "unmanly" domain of the to-be-looked-at, whether for beauty or for pathology.

In adapting the sentimental novel to cinema, Griffith maintained its middle-class orientation, but shifted its ideal audience from domestic women to business men. In that shift, he stripped the film of the novel's "sentimental power." To be sure, Griffith's *Ramona* did invite viewers' emotional identification with the characters and their plight, although Harrison claims that "the idea of the white man's injustice to the Indian did not reach out into the sympathies of the [male] audience at all." But even when acknowledged as effective, these injustices were not seen as a contemporary political issue, perhaps, in part, because of the film's omissions of the novel's social critique. Thus, as Harrison's article reveals, the plot became an occasion for quite a different reading, one in which Ramona becomes the object of desire for "business men" who—following the dictates of natural selection—can fancy themselves better husbands than the "weakling" Alessandro.

Harrison makes an explicit connection between the "White men" who despoil, then kill Alessandro and the "business men" in the audience, who share the admirable, natural "habit of not allowing conscience to handicap business." But, in pitching his article in terms of science and evolution, Harrison is able to downplay race as a factor; in fact, the above "habit" is cited as "still in operation regardless of race." Earlier on he identifies the male audience in the widest possible terms—"of all classes and conditions"—so that the phrase "business men" refers more to a certain capitalist *culture* or code of behavior than to a *class* status or position within capitalism. In this manner, "race" is not a determinant within social relations, but rather an effect or by-product of "natural selection," defined here as a perversion of the Golden Rule and placed within a "business" ideology. That Henry B. Walthall portrays Alessandro within the verisimilar code places him within the universal and transparent "realism" that the reviewer assumes in his discussion of the narrative, serving to downplay his character's race and racial difference. Alessandro's "miserable collapse" is the one scene acted in the unchecked histrionic code, and it is this shift in codes (and behavior)—and not his race—that justifies his removal "from the face of the earth in the cold-blooded way that nature eliminates the unfit." Alessandro is "unfit" because he "submits like a weakling" and fails to make "a manly effort" in the course of "business."[53]

The goal of the "new art" is to reflect these truths from the perspective of male heterosexual desire, balancing the sacred and the profane, the proper and the prurient, business and pleasure. That Ramona is referred to throughout the article in generic terms as "the woman," leads to a slippage between the half-breed character (Ramona) and the White player (Mary Pickford), so that by the end it is somewhat unclear as to whether Harrison is speaking of the character, actor, or women in general. What is clear, however, is that within the bounds of "good taste" *she* best fulfills her role when she "stirs the irresponsible pulses of responsible men," men who do not allow "conscience to handicap business," just their relation with "ideal creatures" such as Ramona/Pickford. It is this pleasurable impact of narrative cinema on the implied white male viewer, and not the "injustice of the white man to the Indian," that reviewers argue "will linger long in the memory."[54]

Notes

I am grateful to Lisa Cartwright for her detailed and insightful comments on an earlier version of this essay.

1. Quoted in editor's introduction, Harry M. Geduld, ed., *Focus on D. W. Griffith* (Englewood Cliffs, N.J.: Prentice-Hall, 1971), p. 6; and in Terry Ramsaye, *A Million and One Nights* (New York: A Touchstone Book, 1986 [1926]), pp. 635–637.

2. Louis Reeves Harrison, in *The Moving Picture World*, June 4, 1910, p. 933. Reprinted in Anthony Slide, ed., "Reviews of *Ramona* (1910)," *Selected Film Criticism, 1896–1911* (Metuchen, N.J.: Scarecrow Press, 1982), pp. 78–80.

3. In May 1908, the U.S. Circuit Court ruled that film companies had to secure the author's permission in order to make a film based upon a story or novel. The usual payment was about twenty-five dollars, but many companies still preferred to borrow plots and characters, changing the title, instead. Griffith, however, convinced Biograph to purchase the rights for an unprecedented one hundred dollars. While the purchase contributed to the film's record high cost, it also provided an obvious promotional "hook" with the bestseller and its related texts. Robert M. Henderson, *D. W. Griffith: His Life and Work* (New York: Oxford University Press, 1972), p. 94.

4. Lewis Jacobs, *The Emergence of Film Art* (New York: Hopkinson & Blake Publishers, 1969), p. 51.

5. The information in this paragraph comes from Kemp R. Niver, *D. W. Griffith His Biograph Films in Perspective* (Los Angeles: John D. Roche, 1974), pp. 130–133. Interestingly, Griffith—under the name Lawrence Griffith—portrayed Alessandro in two stage adaptations of *Ramona*, one in San Francisco and the other in Los Angeles, before he started at Biograph. For an account of the latter, including a reprint of the review in the

Los Angeles Times, see George Wharton James, "The Staging of Ramona," *Through Ramona's Country* (Boston: Little, Brown, and Company, 1908), pp. 348–356.

6. Mrs. D.W. Griffith [Linda Arvidson], *When the Movies Were Young* (New York: Dover Publications, 1969 [1925]), p. 170.

7. Helen Hunt Jackson, *Ramona* (New York: Signet Classic, 1988 [1884]).

8. Feature-length film versions include: Lloyd Brown and Donald Crisp's *Ramona* (1916, Clune Productions); Edwine Carewe's *Ramona* (1928, United Artists), starring Dolores Del Rio; and Henry King's *Ramona* (1936, Twentieth-Century Fox), starring Loretta Young and Don Ameche. In exile in the United States, Cuban writer and revolutionary José Martí translated *Ramona* into Spanish shortly after its original publication. In Mexico, Víctor Urruchúa directed a version of *Ramona* in 1946.

9. *Ramona: A Tale of Passion and Protest* (1988), a 30-minute documentary for public television.

10. Writing in 1946, Carey McWilliams notes that "the name Ramona appears in the corporate title of fifty or more businesses currently operating in Los Angeles." Carey McWilliams, "Southern California: Ersatz Mythology," *Common Ground* (Winter 1946): 32.

11. Kevin Starr, *Inventing the Dream: California through the Progressive Era* (Oxford: Oxford University Press, 1985), p. 76. See, also, section on "The Boosters" in Mike Davis, *City of Quartz: Excavating the Future in Los Angeles* (New York: Vintage Books, 1992), pp. 24–30. As part of this promotion, on March 8, 1907, the *Los Angeles Times* gave extensive coverage to the wedding of the "real" Ramona's son. The article is reprinted in James, *Through Ramona's Country*, pp. 161–164. The phrase "texts of Ramona" is borrowed from Tony Bennett and Janet Woollacott, *Bond and Beyond: The Political Career of a Popular Hero* (New York: Methuen, 1987), to refer to the process by which the figure of Ramona overrides authorship and authorial intention as the predominant "principle of textual classification" for readers.

12. Mike Davis, *City of Quartz*, p. 330.

13. For example, Tom Gunning, *D. W. Griffith and the Origins of American Narrative Film: The Early Years at Biograph* (Urbana and Chicago: University of Illinois Press, 1991), and Scott Simmon, *The Films of D. W. Griffith* (Cambridge: Cambridge University Press, 1993).

14. See Jane Tompkins, *Sensational Designs: The Cultural Work of American Fiction, 1790–1860* (New York: Oxford University Press, 1985), especially chap. 5, "Sentimental Power: *Uncle Tom's Cabin* and the Politics of Literary History," pp. 122–146.

15. Reviewers at the time would borrow this phrase as well, one sign of the early impact of promotional items on the press. See, for example, Robert M. Henderson, *D. W. Griffith: His Life and Work* (New York: Oxford University Press, 1972), p. 94; Jack Temple Kirby, "D. W. Griffith's Racial Portraiture," *Phylon* 39, no. 2 (June 1978): 118–127; and, more recently, Gary D. Keller, *Hispanics and United States Film: An Overview and Handbook* (Tempe, Ariz.: Bilingual Press, 1994), pp. 100–101.

16. For significant examples of scholarship on race in early cinema, see Mary Carbine, "'The Finest Outside the Loop': Motion Picture Exhibition in Chicago's Black Metropolis, 1905–1928," *Camera Obscura* 23 (May 1990): 9–41; Fatimah Tobing Rony, "Those Who Squat and Those Who Sit: The Iconography of Race in the 1895 Films of Felix-Louis Regnault," *Camera Obscura* 28 (January 1992): 263–289; and Ella Shohat,

"Imaging Terra Incognita: The Disciplinary Gaze of Dire," *Public Culture* 3, no. 2 (Spring 1991): 41–70.

17. In addition to the artists discussed, Sandra Peña-Sarmiento also produced a video titled *Crónica de un ser* (1990), which appropriated a silent short on miscegenation, *Licking the Greasers* (1914), as part of her exploration of contemporary Chicana-Latina sexual and gender identity.

18. Deborah Small and David Avalos, *Ramona: Birth of a Mis*ce*ge*NATION*, a Book-in-Progress, 1993.

19. Miki Seifert and William Franco also collaborated on the video.

20. Most likely, they were unable to appropriate footage of the film, which is neither available for film rental nor included in video compilations of Griffith's work.

21. I borrow Doris Sommers's phrase for the nineteenth-century romances in Latin America in which sexual relations became allegorical of concurrent nationalist movements and nation-building projects. See *Foundational Fictions: The National Romances of Latin America* (Berkeley: University of California Press, 1991).

22. Taimi M. Ranta, "Helen Hunt Jackson," in *American Writers for Children. Before 1900*, ed. Glenn E. Estes (Detroit: Bruccoli Clark, 1985), p. 247.

23. Ibid., and Barry W. Bienstock, "Helen Hunt Jackson," *American Historians. 1866–1912*, ed. Clyde N. Wilson (Detroit: Bruccoli Clark, 1986), pp. 148–152.

24. Quoted in Ranta, "Helen Hunt Jackson," p. 249.

25. The dispossession of the Indian villages of Temecula and Saboda were based on actual experiences.

26. Allan Nevins, "Helen Hunt Jackson, Sentimentalist vs. Realist," *The American Scholar* 10, no. 3 (Summer 1941): 269–285, esp. 284. Nevins ends with an acknowledgment that sentimental literature can play a necessary propagandistic role in "great reforms." Nevins's position is similar to that of Bakhtin, who identifies sentimentalism with a limited historical perspective, locating it in the private room. Mikhail M. Bakhtin, "Discourse in the Novel," *The Dialogic Imagination*, trans. Caryl Emerson and Michael Holquist (Austin: University of Texas Press, 1981), pp. 396–398.

27. Nevins, "Helen Hunt Jackson, p. 284.

28. Tompkins, *Sensational Designs*, p. 130.

29. Tompkins, *Sensational Designs*, p. 124. In contrast to Bakhtin, Tompkins argues that the sentimental novel is not limited to the private room or domestic sphere of personal concerns. See p. 146.

30. J. Frank Dobie, "Helen Hunt Jackson and *Ramona*," *Southwest Review* (Spring 1959): 93–98.

31. Lummis's comments on *Ramona* are reprinted in James, *Through Ramona's Country*, pp. 349–353. Lummis, editor of *Out West* and one of the major promoters of the romantic myth of Spanish California, had two notions of reform: national Indian policies and restoration of Mission architecture and other tourist sites. In fact, his comments are part of the playbill for the 1905 theatrical adaptation of *Ramona* (starring Lawrence Griffith), which was intended to raise money for the restoration of El Camino Real.

32. James speculates on Jackson's use of the Italian form of the name, Alessandro, instead of the Spanish, Alejandro: "It is more than probable, however, that knowing she was writing for a large class who were not, and could not be expected to be familiar with Spanish pronunciations, and not wishing them to make clumsy attempts, or glib and incorrect 'successes,' she deliberately spelled the name in the way it is found . . . giving

to it a spelling that could not be mispronounced." *Through Ramona's Country*, pp. 81–82. In these matters of detail, as James reconfirms, Jackson was more concerned with persuasion than with description.

33. Homi K. Bhabha, "Of Mimicry and Man: The Ambivalence of Colonial Discourse," *October* 28 (1984): 125–133.

34. As I discuss later, where the destabilizing function of mimicry can be detected is in the response of writers to the claims of various Luiseño women to be the "real" Ramona.

35. Richard Slotkin, *Gunfighter Nation: The Myth of the Frontier in Twentieth-Century America* (New York: Harper Collins, 1992), p. 40: "By associating 'savages' with the class of White 'failures' under the rubric 'cumberers of the earth,' Roosevelt was working within a tradition of public discourse that dated to the newspaper editorials of the mid-1870s."

36. Ibid., p. 46.

37. See Tomás Almaguer, "Ideological Distortions in Recent Chicano Historiography: The Internal Model and Chicano Historical Interpretation, *Aztlán: A Journal of Chicano Studies* 18.1 (1987): 7–28.

38. McWilliams, "Ersatz Mythology," pp. 36–38.

39. James, *Through Ramona's Country*, p. 401. Among other things, James appears to originate Southern California's other myth, that of being able to ski in the mountains, enjoy "semi-tropic luxuriance," and swim in the Pacific Ocean all in one day! (p. 394). Within this larger framework, the *fiestas* become "only a part of the day's enjoyment."

40. Carey McWilliams, *North From Mexico: The Spanish-Speaking People of the United States*, new ed., updated by Matt S. Meier (New York: Praeger, 1990 [1948]), p. 91.

41. Ibid.

42. McWilliams, "Ersatz Mythology," p. 38. For a more indepth account of this period and its multiracial and class dimensions, see Leonard Pitt, *The Decline of the Californios: A Social History of the Spanish Speaking Californians, 1846–1890* (Berkeley: University of California Press, 1966); Douglas Monroy, *Thrown Among Strangers: The Making of Mexican Culture in Frontier California* (Berkeley: University of California Press, 1990); and Tomás Almaguer, *Racial Fault Lines: The Historical Origins of White Supremacy in California* (Berkeley: University of California Press, 1994).

43. Slotkin, *Gunfighter Nation*, p. 31.

44. Ibid., p. 61.

45. As McWilliams notes, "Both rediscoveries, that of the Indian and that of the Spaniard, occurred between 1883 and 1888, at precisely the period when the great real estate promotion of Southern California was being organized." McWilliams, "Ersatz Mythology," p. 34.

46. D. A. Hufford, *The Real Ramona of Helen Hunt Jackson's Famous Novel* (Los Angeles: D. A. Hufford & Co., 1900); George Wharton James, *Through Ramona's Country* (Boston: Little, Brown, and Company, 1908); Carlyle Channing Davis and William A. Alderson, *The True Story of "Ramona": Its Facts and Fictions. Inspiration and Purpose* (New York: Dodge Publishing Company, 1914); and Margaret V. Allen, *Ramona's Homeland* (Chula Vista, Cal.: Denrich Press, 1914). Hufford and Allen's books are more like tourist pamphlets, the former associated with the Los Angeles Chamber of Commerce, and the latter with the Pioneer Society of San Diego County. James's book is the definitive study of *Ramona* and its historical referents, from which Davis and Alderson borrow quite

heavily even as they propose to tell the "true story" for the first time. Begun as early as 1887, James's research includes phonograph interviews with Sam Temple (the model for Alessandro's murderer) and Ramona Lubo (the Luiseño widow of the man Temple murdered).

47. James, *Through Ramona's Country*, p. 161.

48. Although it was hailed as a "cinema triumph," several reviewers noted the excessive length, especially "the second act where nothing in particular keeps happening and happening in an abstracted manner." *New York Times*, April 6, 1916, p. 11.

49. A. Nicholas Vardac, "Realism and Romance: D. W. Griffith," in *Focus on D. W. Griffith*, ed. Harry M. Geduld, (Englewood Cliffs, N.J.: Prentice-Hall, 1971): pp. 70–79, esp. pp. 72–73. See, also, David A. Cook, *A History of Narrative Film* (New York: W. W. Norton & Company, 1981), p. 65; and Richard Griffith and Arthur Mayer, *The Movies* (New York: Simon and Schuster, 1957), p. 25.

50. That this and presumably other scenes were shot but not included in the film explains the discrepancy between the amount of film used (1,507 feet) and the length of the final release print (995 feet). For a brief summary of the scenes, see Mrs. D. W. Griffith, *When the Movies Were Young*, pp. 169–170.

51. Laura Mulvey, "Visual Pleasure and Narrative Cinema" (1975), reprinted in *Visual and Other Pleasures* (Bloomington: Indiana University Press, 1989), pp. 14–26.

52. William Osler was a well-known physician, professor of medicine, and administrator who created the first organized clinical unit in the United States, revolutionizing medical education in the process. While he specialized in physiology and pathology, Osler wrote and lectured on a wide range of topics, publishing a book of essays (*An Alabama Student*, 1908) and lay sermons (*Man's Redemption of Man*, 1910) in the period before Griffith's *Ramona*.

53. See the brief discussion of Walthall's performance in *Ramona* in Roberta E. Pearson, *Eloquent Gestures: The Transformation of Performance Style in the Griffith Biograph Films* (Berkeley: University of California Press, 1992), p. 117. While Pearson does not deal with race, the shift from histrionic to verisimilar performance styles provided one way of coding racial distinctions within a narrative. For an example of one such analysis, see Enrique LaMadrid, "Ig/noble Savages of New Mexico's Silent Cinema, 1912–1914," *Spectator* 13, no. 1 (Fall 1992): 12–23.

54. Harrison quotations from his review in *Moving Picture World*, June 4, 1910, p. 942.

Nick Browne

THE UNDOING OF THE *OTHER* WOMAN

Madame Butterfly in the Discourse of American Orientalism

The title character of *Madame Butterfly* is, of course, a Western figure of the Orient. She is, moreover, a cross-cultural heroine, though not explicitly a racial one, a tragic image of a Japanese woman undone from two directions, East and West. "Madame Butterfly" figures in a distinctly American dialectic of cultural and ideological power that is inseparable, at least up to the time of World War I, from both Japanese masculinity and from the musical sphere of high art in the West.[1] That is, "Madame Butterfly" is sexed as a complex cultural difference in early twentieth-century American representation of "Asia."

From Commodore Perry's "opening up" of Japan in the mid-nineteenth century to the advent of the movies, the American artistic imagination, as distinct from that of missionaries and traders, was mediated by European, in particular Italian, opera. Though originating as a musical form in which performance of royal magnificence was linked to the exhibition of forms of political absolutism, in early nineteenth-century America, opera was typically sung in Italian and hence occupied a culturally ambiguous site—as both the cultural legacy of a disenfranchised immigrant population, and as the symbolic capital of the American artistic elite.[2] The establishment of the standard form of locale, costume, and gesture for representing Japan in America followed from the enormously successful run of the English Gilbert and Sullivan production of *The Mikado* (1885). The cultural historian of opera in America, John Dizikes reports that "it produced a rage for Japanese art and for things Japanese throughout Canada and the United States"[3] The language of the production was, of course, English, and presumably, in part, the basis of its popular success was its irreverent attitude toward serious opera.[4]

By 1915, the year when Paramount released both *Madame Butterfly* and Cecil B. DeMille's *The Cheat*, Japan was not an unfamiliar subject to American movie audiences. Gregory Waller has identified over one hundred films noted in the pages of *Moving Picture World* between 1909 and 1915 that were "distributed in the United States and that took Japan as their subject or setting and/or featured characters identified as Japanese."[5] Half of the films were fictional, almost entirely melodramas; of these, Waller reports, eighteen were set in Japan with no non-Japanese characters; the bulk were produced by American companies. These, according to Waller, typically involved historical dramas of ill-fated lovers trapped in a hierarchical social system of arranged marriages, rigid class lines, and inescapable familial obligations. Imported Japanese films, like most of the genre, concluded in violence—duels, suicides, etc. *The Yellow Slave* (1913), for example, ends when the lovers "willingly fill the sleeves of their kimonos with stones and walk into the water."[6] Fully half of the thirty-five films that portray cross-cultural relations (American *and* Japanese) take the form of ill-fated romance. Though documentaries were common—frequently picturesque depictions, centered around Japanese habits, customs, and landscapes—the dominant form of fictional representation is condensed around the figure of the Japanese woman, that is, the "Madame Butterfly" situation. The English-language prototype of this Oriental figure was John Luther Long's 1896 story, *Madame Butterfly*, though Pierre Loti's novel *Madame Chrysantheme* (published in French in 1887 and made into an operetta of the same title by André Messager in 1893) anticipated its major narrative and cultural elements. Giacomo Puccini discovered the story through David Belasco's 1900 adaptation and dramatization of Long's text and employed it as the basis for his 1904 opera, *Madama Butterfly*.

The American image of Japan in the sphere of popular entertainment is a dialectical one, a dynamic composite of Japanese figures, feminine and masculine. In Waller's report on the 1914 film *Katana, Oath of the Sword*, produced by the Japanese-American Film Company, "The Japanese heroine, whose fiancee is studying in California, falls in love with a 'thorough-going scoundrel,' an American ship captain. The fiancé returns to Japan, discloses that the American has a wife in the U.S., and kills him." The heroine then commits *hara-kiri*. Likewise in the film *A Relic of Old Japan* (1914), the son of a samurai family is tricked into marriage with an American showgirl; when she deserts, he strangles her.[7] The theme here is that culturally the "Butterfly" story is *in*transitive. Though either a Japanese female or Japanese male can be deceived, it is always the Japanese that undergoes the betrayal; and it is always the woman, whether Japanese or American, who dies. But just as important in these versions is that the Japanese man, in seeking his revenge, kills Americans, male and female.

Madame Butterfly and *The Cheat*, released by Paramount within weeks of each other at the end of 1915 (*Butterfly* was made by the Famous Players Film Company; *The Cheat* by Jesse Lasky Feature Play Company) can be regarded culturally as companion pieces—contrasting images of Japanese sexual difference—Mary Pickford's Butterfly and Sessue Hayakawa's Hisuru Tori. Hayakawa had appeared in at least nineteen films prior to *The Cheat*, most notably Ince's *The Wrath of the Gods* (1914) and *The Typhoon* (1914). He was born in Japan of a Samurai family, joined the navy, was dismissed with a medical discharge, attempted *hara-kiri*, and eventually attended the University of Chicago before moving to Los Angeles as an actor.[8] In *The Typhoon*, Hayakawa plays a Japanese diplomat working on military matters in Paris. When he discovers that his French mistress has secretly taken another lover, he confronts her. She screams: "You yellow whining rat—and your Japan, a yellow blot on the ocean." He kills her, though an underling takes the blame. In the same year, Hayakawa plays a killer in *A Relic of Old Japan*, a story of his revenge against a white woman who deserted him. In these roles, Hayakawa marries and then kills a white woman. In *The Cheat*, Hayakawa enters into a contract with a rich, married, white American socialite, Edith Hardy, who needs money to avoid public embarrassment and exposure for reckless gambling with Red Cross funds. When she seeks to renege and repay the loan with a check, Hayakawa, in a sensational scene, attacks, tears away her clothes, and brands her with his personal insignia. Edith then shoots and wounds him with a pistol. The husband reports that he did the shooting. At the trial, the court is about to find the husband guilty, but "Edith makes a dramatic revelation of the truth and bares her scarred shoulder, revealing the proof. The courtroom crowd surges forth and can hardly restrain itself from attacking Hayakawa while Edith and her husband embrace as the case is dismissed."[9] In Donald Kirihara's view, "there may be a tendency to think of Hayakawa's image as brutal through an overemphasis on *The Cheat*,"[10] and he indicates a wider range of roles in the 1915–1918 period and after. The first film Hayakawa made for his own company, *His Birthright* (1918), was the story of an American naval officer who fathers an illegitimate son with a Japanese woman.[11] But a number of significant films in the 1914–1915 period dramatically point to Hayakawa as a center of violence—murder or (figurative) rape against white women.

Recent critical readings of *The Cheat* stress the threat of Japanese rape and interpret this as a white, female masochistic fantasy in which sexual relations with the non-white foreigner, entertained at one moment, are treated finally as sanction and punishment[12] and underline the impossibility of racial assimilation of non-whites in America.[13] These interpretations can be carried forward to *Madame Butterfly* and complicated by its contrast to *The Cheat*. The film *Madame Butterfly* (1915), made by Famous Players/Paramount and starring Mary Pickford, is a very different work from Puccini's opera, yet in its cultural meaning is finally inseparable from it. It is different, too, from Belasco's stage play by the same name. Indeed, Belasco, who had frequently cooperated with Famous Players, felt compelled to dissociate himself from the film by a disclaimer in *The Moving Picture World* of November 13, 1915, just before the film's release:

> The picturization of "Madame Butterfly" made by the Famous Players Company has no connection whatsoever with my dramatic version which also formed the basis of the grand opera, but only concerns the story. In dramatizing the story, I naturally invented and introduced dramatic situations and a succession of scenes that did not occur in the original, and these are my property. Since the Famous Players Film Company did not obtain from me the motion picture rights to my dramatic version, the picturization of "Madame Butterfly" naturally does not include any of my dramatic situations and inventions but has to do only with John Luther Long's story.[14]

Puccini's opera *Madama Butterfly* (1904) and the knowledge of it in America are the necessary and proximate aesthetic context for considering the form and meaning of the 1915 Paramount film. The main difference, apart from some significant aspects of the treatment of what Belasco calls the "story," is the fact that the film *Madame Butterfly* is not accompanied by Puccini's music. In this regard, the absence of this music from the film appears as something of an anomaly. The DeMille *Carmen*, for example, produced by Lasky and also released by Paramount a few weeks before *Butterfly*, was accompanied by selections from the opera arranged especially for the film, and, in fact, the arrangement was copyrighted under the imprimatur "Paramount photo play music."[15] In the period 1910–1912, standardized musical score sheets based on generic program music were first distributed with particular film releases. The score for *The Birth of a Nation* is taken by Anderson as the first original score for a film, one described as "closely synchronized and based on operatic compositional practice of leitmotifs."[16] Indeed, 1915 marks the commercial significance the industry, and presumably the audience, assigned to accompanying music. At that time, *Paramount Progress*, a weekly newsletter of distribution sent to exhibitors of Paramount films, began a section titled "Musical Selections for Paramount Releases." It advertised *Carmen* by trumpeting "smashing musical effects from the opera"[17] and went further by publishing the entire score of the arrangement. The absence of any mention of Puccini either in connection with *Madame Butterfly* or for *Girl of the Golden West*, released in the same year, or the evident existence of an original score suggests that Paramount and Puccini's musical publisher, if they tried, never reached a business accord. The score from *The Cheat*, by contrast, is in the Kliener collection at the University of Minnesota. The records of Riensenfeld's musical overtures at a flagship theater like the Rialto in New York City in the period shortly after the release of the film *Madame Butterfly* show that the most frequently played composers were Liszt, Tchaikovsky, Verdi, Wagner, and Weber.[18] There is no mention of Puccini in Anderson's account of movie music.

The Puccini operas changed the American operatic repertoire and the operatic aesthetic in the first decade of the century. At New York's Metropolitan Opera House from 1900 to 1921, *La Bohème*, *Tosca*, and *Madama Butterfly* received 341 performances. (By contrast, four Mozart operas received 65 performances.) Starting in 1906, the Met performed *Madama Butterfly* 106 times in sixteen seasons. Its 1907–1908 national tour of 112 cities with 300 performances was at the time the most comprehensive operatic tour in American history.[19] This popularity, rooted perhaps in the *verismo* aesthetic, appealed as one critic wrote, to the "rhythms of everyday hearts . . . the experiences of common people."[20] In seeking the ordinary, Puccini democratized operatic experience; its popularity of form lay not so much in dramatic construction but in the creation of memorable melody. Though often regarded as vulgar by the modernists, Puccini's combination of theatricality and singing drew famous divas to the piece, challenged by the possibility of bringing a realistic interpretation to the subjectivity of the character through vocal performance.

The notable critic of *Harper's Weekly*, Lawrence Gilman wrote on the occasion of the premiere that the opera was built on an irresolvable aesthetic contradiction—"the attempt to give lyrical and intense expression in music to a contemporary subject."[21] He added, "Under the circumstances, the music is often surprisingly successful; but it is significant that the most poetic and moving passages in the score are those which enforce emotions and occasions which have no necessary connection with time and space."[22] Reiterating a cornerstone of early twentieth-century art criticism, he argued that what is artistically successful is beyond or above the everyday. In other words, realism of manner and speech poses a problem. Two years later, in remarking on the November 1908 performance with Geraldine Farrar, Caruso, and Toscanini conducting, *The New York Times* commented that "Miss Farrar's representation of the *luckless* [my emphasis] Japanese girl was infinitely charming, not only of voice, but also of pose and action. . . . In Mr. Caruso's Pinkerton, the interesting part is the singing, for he presents a figure *far from characteristic* [my emphasis] of a Naval officer. . . . It is a *strange idea* [my emphasis] of an American officer that the composer gives him to embody."[23] There is a tension between the aesthetic and the moral/evaluative aspect of the performance, one which extends to both male and female characters. This is the basis of a critical equivocation. Though critics doubted the achievement of the music in comparison with *Tosca*[24] and with *La Bohème*,[25] *Madama Butterfly* was praised for "its subtlety of color and expressiveness . . . the weaving of its melodies and the delicacy and power of its orchestration.[26]

A few weeks before the debut of the film, the engagement of a Japanese primadonna, "Mme. Tamaki Miura" of Tokyo, for the lead role of Butterfly in a New York production gave rise to an animated debate "as to whether a woman from the West can better portray the Butterfly of Puccini's opera than a woman of her own nation."[27] The debate turned on the question of cultural authenticity. One critic asserted that, though there is an ethnographic truth in some details, "Mme Miura had to divest herself of most of the artistic traditions of her own land before she could impersonate the character imagined by an American novelist and set to music in Italy." Another, Mr. Finck, of the *New York Evening Post*, declared her performance "authoritative, as no Occidental conception can be."[28] He praised the truth and expressiveness of her acting in the final scene: "Like a true Oriental, she makes less of meeting death than other Butterflies." In Finck's account, the quality of voice, as distinct from acting and gesture is the central site of a cultural contradiction: At the lower end of the register, the voice hints at an impurity—an Oriental residue—which gradually disappears with increasing volume and warmth in the higher end. He concludes that though it would be interesting to hear her in a Western role, no part "could suit" her as Butterfly does.

Of course, the transposition of operatic story and music, with their distinctive codes of realism, to the medium of silent film constituted a profound change in the mode of expression and representation of this narrative. The opera, of course, constituted the principal horizon of expectations for the audience of the Pickford film. Indeed the star who helped establish the opera in New York, Geraldine Farrar (Farrar played the title role in *Carmen* released by Paramount the week before), was initially announced to play the title role in the film.[29] Pickford, however, "the supreme favorite of the screen" was ultimately assigned. Evidently, there was some indecision about how to adapt the Long story for the film because the synopsis printed by Paramount's publicity department the week of the film's release contained a very different version of the story and especially of the ending,[30] a version in fact much closer to the opera.

The film's adaptation of the novel took considerable liberties. Both the novel and the opera began with the marriage. However, Long simply wrote: "With the aid of a marriage broker, he found both a wife and a house in which to keep her."[31] By contrast, the entire first act of the opera dramatizes the marriage day. Fully one-third of the film is given over to a set of wholly invented sequences leading up to the marriage day present neither in the novel or the opera: the chance meeting on the road, a later meeting in the theater, and Pinkerton's visit to the parents' house. The film's basic narrative principle is to linearize the chronological sequence of events and, if only implied, to supply them. For purposes of emphasis, there are several flashbacks to events seen earlier in the film. The structure of the opera's narrative recounting, by contrast, effects a temporal and dramatic compression of events. Though there are many deletions, additions, and revisions that the film's narrative makes of the novel, the significant contrasts relate to the differing function of cultural factors in the film and the novel and the quite different scope given to the representation of character subjectivity in the opera. Principally through its commentary, as distinguished from the plot, the novel centers the depiction of social relations around the exclusion and, ultimately, ostracism of Butterfly when she marries Pinkerton. The marriage is understood by all parties to be an economic transaction—consistent with necessity and tradition, the money for Butterfly being paid, as it were, for benefit of the community. The trouble begins with an insult and follows the consequence of Pinkerton's refusal to admit Butterfly's relatives into the house on the wedding day (Figure 1). This breach of custom, the novel makes plain, leads not just to a break in the line of Japanese ancestors, but a disruption of the religious order itself, breaking

Fig. 1: Butterfly's breach with the community (courtesy of the Academy of Motion Picture Arts and Sciences).

"his wife's sole link to such eternal life as she had hoped for."[32] The breach of social custom leads to tragedy. The novel makes it plain that Pinkerton intends to establish a new religion for Butterfly—Himself (Figure 2). The opera dramatizes the break in the sacred order when, in the first act, the outraged Priest, the Bonze (Butterfly's uncle), interrupts the wedding ceremony, condemns her deceitful renunciation of the community and "her true religion," and curses her with "eternal damnation." The film, on the other hand, eliminates altogether the religious dimension explicit in the novel and opera, and treats Butterfly's "out-casting" by the community as the result of a purely social affront, a breach of hospitality and manners. It ignores, in other words, the associated implications of the transgression and condemnation.

All versions indicate that the price of Pinkerton's demand is Butterfly's forceful exclusion from her natural community, her transformation of identity into a believer in American things, a conversion carried out in the name of the marriage, and ultimately of her love. That is, the crucial structural feature which underlies the story in all its versions is the figure

Fig. 2: Pinkerton: An American god (courtesy of the Academy of Motion Picture Arts and Sciences).

of a woman between two cultures who both rejects and is rejected by one in moving toward the other. By agreeing to serve as a go-between wife, and hence to relieve the native community of a financial burden, she elects to substitute one social position, unmarried in a religious community of Japanese, for another. But under the circumstances of the new position, as wife, she is obliged and, moreover, she *elects*, to accept a new belief, personified as American by B. F. Pinkerton of the US gunboat *Abraham Lincoln*.

The action and affect of the opera are staged at the border between the two cultures and is grounded in two different principles—on the one hand religious and on the other legal, a fact made evident in the debate over the binding character of the marriage as tested by the possibility of divorce. Butterfly stands between two cultural principles: ancestor worship and military adventure. It is on this ideological axis, that is, between subjectivity within the system of historical community and the subordinated individual in the emerging, imperialistic nation-state, that both the novel and the opera work as social discourses. But this exchange of cultural positions—taken as emblems or terms of discourses between nations—dominates and erases reservations about racial difference as an obstacle to intercultural marriage and brings to the fore, and comingles, national identity and the misunderstandings of love in the cultural construction of nationalism. Romantic love in this intercultural drama is the ideological principle that converts a concrete social position into a subjectively held and lived value. It is this presentation of operatic love, in its specific ideological setting in the mediation between East and West, that has established *Madame Butterfly* in the Western operatic canon and in the American popular imagination.

Indeed the critical reception of the film turned precisely on this matter of romantic love and the representation of passion. The trade press was predictable in commending the exquisite settings, the authenticity of Pickford's performance, and so on.[33] There were also reservations, however, variously framed: "Madame Butterfly is a thing of beauty. The story interests and at time moves, but the production charms all the way,"[34] or "Miss Pickford fulfills all the expectations as to her ability to handle the part, insofar as she has been allowed to fulfill them. Sid Olcott seems to have an aversion to close-ups in which he might have caught an expression even more winsome, even more pathetic than those offered in the many scenes set at a regular distance from the camera."[35] The critic of the *New York Dramatic Mirror* wrote the most cogent critique: "The film's changes in the story of the play and the opera are responsible for the lack of emotional and dramatic intensity of the film. . . . the tragedy is so softened that it is practically eliminated. . . . In Pickford's Butterfly, all the emotions are so rigorously suppressed that it is hard to realize that they existed."[36] None of the reviewers mention accompanying music. In sum, the film lacks what the opera provides—emotion.

This contrast between the opera and the film points toward what is at stake in this tale. According to Paramount's pre-release press reports of the film, the film story is identical to that of the opera! Possibly this account was for promotional purposes, borrowing from the prestige of the opera and its theatrical adaptation (hence Belasco's disclaimer quoted earlier). Two major scenes in particular bring out the difference in interpretation. The culmination of the marriage scene of the opera, after the exit of the Bonze and guests, consists of a richly orchestrated, intensely poetic testimony of mutual love. The scene is intended precisely to move from an account of the formalities of the marriage to an expression of passionate sentiment. Pinkerton plays the masculine part aggressively and, at points, Butterfly moves away demurely, refusing his embrace. Still, she expresses her love, declares herself happy, and in spite of being "alone and renounced," gives herself to him at the very end of the scene, "yours forever." That scene, taking about sixteen minutes,[37] expresses in the strongest possible terms this emerging affiliation and illustrates above all, musically, their mutual love and affection. The corresponding scene in the film is done in three shots. In the first, he presses a kiss on her; in the second, an intertitle appears—"In the silvery moonlight of old Japan"; and finally, in the third, the couple kisses in silhouette. It is a wholly schematic figuration of large scale intensified operatic desire, one that refers to and signifies desire in a conventional way, but is far from expressing or underlining it.

The opera's conclusion begins when Butterfly learns that Pinkerton has returned to Japan with his American wife and does not intend to see her again. Butterfly agrees to hand over their son if Pinkerton promises to visit her. There is an emotional aria on the extinction of her world ("Love and life entered with him. Then he went and nothing was left to us, nothing, nothing but death"). In a passionate good-bye *to her son* ("'Tis for you, my love, 'tis for you, I'm dying, poor Butterfly, so you can go away beyond the ocean, never to feel the torment when you are older"),[38] she kills herself with her father's knife as Pinkerton arrives on the scene. In the film version, Butterfly and the American wife, Adelaide, meet accidentally in the Consul's office. Adelaide offers to care for the child and with the intervention of the Consul ("Think of your baby's future"), Butterfly gives up the child to the American wife. As Butterfly, Pickford first shows anger at Adelaide's suggestion, but then despair. Though intertitles report the request of the American wife and the advice of the Consul, even at this penultimate moment, there is no printed representation, that is intertitle, either of what Butterfly says or feels. Though she is shown speaking, the expression of her pain is rendered in silent pantomime. In the final shots of the film, Butterfly, now alone, addresses her ancestors with "O, my ancestors. Never let that honorable Pinkerton know what I am going to do for him" and steps down into the lake to drown herself. The film's concluding title, which asks, "Could one give up more for love than did little Cho Cho San!", in referring to her love for Pinkerton, underlines the film's reinterpretation of the story. Yet just before the film's release, Paramount synopsized the conclusion in a very different way: "Then Madame Butterfly staggers forth, a cloth about her bleeding throat. She has clasped the child to her breast as Pinkerton enters and embraces the dying girl whose face is illuminated with infinite happiness."[39] This is, of course, essentially the ending of the opera. In Long's original story, Butterfly begins *hara-kiri* with her father's sword when the child crawls onto her lap. She stops, the maid binds up the wound, and when the American Mrs. Pinkerton arrives at Butterfly's house the next day, it is empty. Mother and child have fled.

The filmed adaptation, drawn as much from the materials of the opera as from the novel, works a fundamental change on the "opera effect," a change that can be characterized in Roman Jakobson's terms as a shift from a metaphoric to a metonymic discourse. The linearization of story event and detail in the film replaces the opera's feeling and subjectivity; the film generally adopts a denotative system for indicating "character" in place of an expressive one. That is, a prose treatment is substituted for a poetic one. The film also effects a shift in the account it gives of the situation of the action. The difference is that both the opera and the novel show that the fracture between Butterfly and the traditional Japanese community is occasioned by a religious disaffiliation. The offense is the abandoning of Japanese tradition and the embracing through Pinkerton, as her god, of the American way of life. The film, on the other hand, assigns the blame for the split between Butterfly and the Japanese community to Pinkerton's bad manners at the wedding, that is, to a social affront—not a breach of a religious or ideological order.

In both the opera and the film, Butterfly dies by her own choice, but the meaning, purpose, and representation of the final action is different. In the opera, the suicide is performed as an assumption of a duty for the welfare of the child. Butterfly's last farewell is to her son, and dying, she embraces him. The suicide, paradoxically, will free the child from the old ways. The film shows Butterfly's maid, Suzuki, handing over the child to Mrs. Pinkerton at the Consul's office. Butterfly then returns home, prays at the shrine of the ancestors, takes out the knife, lets it drop, and walks deliberately into the lake, her white sleeves sinking beneath the surface. The meaning of this action is plainly conveyed by the intertitle: "O, my ancestors! Never let that honorable Pinkerton know what I am going to do for him." In the film, the suicide is for love lost (the husband's). The purpose of the ultimate sacrifice is different in the two versions, a difference that opens a new space onto the cultural interpretation of this figure.

American Orientalism is a discourse and a practice that links through the construction of a complex, mediated, ideological, and affective map the image of the nations—America and the Other—and links them to the identity of persons. Orientalism, like Occidentalism, is an essentializing relationship between two transitive terms, both vulnerable to a double blindness: looking out at the Other for the purpose of knowledge occludes the makeup of the observing self as the subject, not the object, of knowledge. The history of Orientalism as outlook and administrative practice subtends all the twentieth-century versions of the Butterfly figure from Long's 1898 version to *Miss Saigon*, including a succession of liberal and deconstructionist versions. In David Huang's M. *Butterfly*, the foreigner is fooled into believing that the Oriental M. Butterfly (M. is an abbreviation for Monsieur) is a woman, a belief anchored by the appearance of a child. As Huang shows in his depiction of the French Officer's job evaluating military intelligence in China, the contemporary Butterfly figure, like the earlier one, is difficult to separate from American prosecution of a war, in the contemporary case in Vietnam. Since the beginning of the century, one continuing dimension of the American popular imagination of the Orient has been linked to war—Japan, Korea, Vietnam—depictions marked by multiple valences, from self-righteous aggressiveness to sharp self-criticism. The United States is presently at some distance now from the time and place of the initial establishment of the story in the operatic canon and from the initial film versions that drew it.[40]

America and American military power in the Far East are dramatically imprinted on the opera and on succeeding filmic and dramatic versions. Pinkerton, in all versions of the story in the 1915 period—novel, opera, film—is an officer aboard an American gun-boat anchored in Nagasaki harbor observing the military situation in the Far East. Musically, in the opera, he is linked to several bars of "The Star-Spangled Banner,"[41] and in the 1904 LaScala version, during the penultimate moments, Butterfly gave her son an American flag while she covers his eyes. It is evident enough that the Madame Butterfly story stages the encounter between two nations and two cultures at the turn of the century, and that Lieutenant Pinkerton is an emblem of aggressive American supervision in the Orient. American expansion and annexation—notably in Hawaii and in the Philippines—were the dominant direction of American foreign policy at the turn of the century; economic modernization required new markets, crossing into and managing new frontiers. China in particular was thought to be an especially desirable commercial market. Under these economic-military circumstances the U.S. Navy and its importance as an agent of economic expansion were vigorously reasserted by

Alfred Mahan's *The Influence of Sea Power Upon History* (1890), an argumentative book with considerable influence on the Assistant Secretary of the Navy (Teddy Roosevelt).[42]

The Navy, in Mahan's view, was a male fraternity that wielded the potential power to "possess" and "control" territory in Asia that was occupied by weak or incompetent peoples. The assertion of an American natural right to possession of such underutilized land, linked with a theory of political freedom and an expectation of strict adherence to Anglo-Saxon law, was used as the justification for American expansion. Mahan's doctrine of "Race Patriotism," the power of territorial possession embodied in the masculinity of the Navy, would serve as the instrument for opening the new frontier.

The opera *Madama Butterfly*, which brought into conjunction an "impervious" Western military man (the adjective was supplied by Pinkerton's shipmate in Long's story) and a childlike Oriental woman, is the virtual and manifest emblem of this racial theory and its territorial implications. It is a "virtual" emblem because, in point of fact, *Japan* was also an aggressive, imperialistic power in East Asia that had defeated both China (in 1895) and Russia (in 1905) in extensive military campaigns. American domestic outlook on Asia was linked to American foreign policy; the Chinese Exclusionary Laws of 1882 were triggered by legislative anxiety over the possible displacement of American labor by Chinese. More proximately, *Madame Butterfly* can be viewed in the context of Roosevelt's Gentleman's Agreement limiting Japanese immigration, most obviously by the 1913 Alien Land Law, which severely curtailed the right of Japanese to own land in the United States. In point of fact, the number of Japanese seeking admittance was small. American fear of Japanese military power in Asia was clearly manifest *within* the nation by actions of exclusion engendered and justified by "yellow peril" literature and its chief tropes of invasion and espionage. That is, the dominant version of American Orientalism was built on a substitution of imaginary terms for real ones. Its strategy was to reconfigure this discourse on the Orient through a version of "sexual difference" operating in early twentieth-century American ideology of gender relations. American Orientalism of the Progressive Era, in other words, was built on inverting and re-evaluating a certain historical configuration of economic and sexual power and mapping them onto a racial ideology. The racial unconscious of American popular culture[43] in this period is predicated on a specific prohibition: No white woman can have sanctioned sexual relations with a non-white man. The male prerogative in this system is expressed in the asymmetrical fact that a white man can under certain circumstances (for example, when residing in a foreign, non-white, country) have relations with non-white women. This general matrix of cultural prohibitions and permissions is an historical and ideological formation operating in the years leading up to and away from *Madame Butterfly* and indeed governing the forms of American popular culture well into the 1960s.

The image of Japanese power implicit in *Madame Butterfly*—in its assertion of American masculine domination and Japanese submissiveness—is founded on a denial. It is based on an historical fiction: that the Japanese are weak. In point of fact, relations between the United States and Japan in the opera are not a reflection of actual relations of international power, but are figured on the (Italian) model of the patriarchal figure of the American male with the subordinated role of the Japanese female. Yet, in films set in the United States, domestic relations between American men and women are figured, as they are in *The Cheat*, through the mediation of the American couple by another scene, the presence of the (temporarily) dominant Japanese man. American relations with the Orient are figured, in other words, in both modalities of sexual difference, female and male, and it is necessary to pair and to interpret together *Madame Butterfly* and *The Cheat* in order to apprehend what is at stake ideologically and affectively in the undoing of this Japanese woman at the turn of the century.

American culture's conception of the Orient is routed through sexual difference of the Japanese "other": submissive femininity and aggressive masculinity (the Japanese businessman). The terms of cross-cultural affiliation, the American man with the Japanese woman (*Butterfly*), and the American woman with the Japanese man (*The Cheat*)—define the cultural tensions inherent in the Western conception and practice of miscegenation. The terms of sexual exchange are the same in *The Cheat* and in *Madame Butterfly*. Money is exchanged for sexual opportunity by a business contract in one case and a marriage in the other. The attempt at enforcement in *The Cheat* is frustrated by the American wife's attempt to buy out the contract for $10,000. In both films, there is an appeal to legal doctrine for resolution of a social impasse. In effect, in *The Cheat* the court finds Haka Arakaru's forceful branding of the body of the American woman equivalent to rape, and frees her American husband from the charge of attempted murder. In the pandemonium at the end of *The Cheat*, the American couple is reunited and the Japanese businessman narrowly escapes a symbolic lynching. By contrast, in *Madame*

Butterfly, Pinkerton's violation of the Japanese marriage contract that Butterfly believes is done according to American doctrine has no legal or public consequence. Pinkerton is free to marry a second time without sanction. The Consul does express a private, moral disapproval, but ultimately moves in both the opera and the film toward the American position. Precisely what is at issue is the legal doctrine that obtains under these cross-cultural circumstances. In both instances, the American's actions are judged justifiable, without punitive legal consequence.

Post-Vietnam cultural critique in the United States turned against American governmental, industrial, and military leadership. The situation in 1915 was somewhat different. In that instance, what was at stake in the Butterfly story was not so much the legal as the *moral* assessment of Pinkerton, the emblem of the U.S. military. The critics contemporary to the film were confronted by a difficult problem—Pinkerton's evident responsibility at some level for Butterfly's death. To be sure, Pinkerton was considered "a cad," but the critics of 1915, acting as a kind of substitute jury, focused on the beautiful death of Butterfly and let Pinkerton off. The feminist evaluation of the story in the 1990s generally aligns itself with the post-Vietnam cultural critique and brings a telling indictment on those responsible for the fate of the woman. For example, Gina Marchetti, in an excellent account of the film, argues that the 1915 film version was rooted in an ideological crisis in American gender relations and on the need to shore up American patriarchy.[44] She sees Butterfly as a martyr to that cause, namely to romantic love of a Western man. Imperialism, in other words, extends to the possession of women, and necessarily engenders femininity in a masochistic mode. On this account, Butterfly is "destroyed by Western values"[45] and *for* Western values. Yet, we must ask, what pleasure does the West take in her pain?

A closer critical look at the specifically cultural dimension of the opera, and of the image of the Japanese society of which Butterfly is a part, leads in another direction. At the time the story begins, at the turn of the century, Japan is presented as consisting principally of the remnants of a feudal society with traditional lines of lineage and family still intact. The opera, in other words, seems set at a time closer to Japan's initial encounter with the West, closer to the mid-nineteenth century, than to the actual age of emergent militaristic imperialism. Butterfly's father was evidently a wealthy samurai, formerly in the service of the emperor, but now dead. The family, impoverished and uprooted, consists only of a mother and an uncle, the Bonze, and a few possessions—principally tiny statuettes bearing the souls of her forefathers. The most important and most sacred possession is the father's sword, the one sent by the Mikado, apparently with a demand for the father's life, which he obediently gave. This sacred sword, hidden on the wedding day, is brought out at the end of the tale and its inscription pronounced: "Death with honor is better than life with dishonor." With this treasured emblem of paternal obedience, Butterfly commits *hara-kiri*. Butterfly's initial adoption of the American way gives way at the end to her re-identification with Japanese tradition and community. In this, her cultural identity marks out an arc, more exactly a circle, through the course of the opera.

Butterfly's out-casting from the Japanese community is a consequence of her renunciation of her religion. She visited the Christian mission, she later explains to Pinkerton, "in order to please you" and promises, "I shall try to forget my race and kindred." At the end of Act One of the opera, Butterfly has, in effect, been excommunicated by the Bonze and the clan. Eventually she returns to traditional religious and family allegiances, a return dramatized by her subscription to the ritual of Japanese suicide conducted in the Name of the Father. Dishonored by abandonment of the Westerner, Butterfly returns to the community of Japanese, to the concept of feudal fealty and to the code of traditional Japanese honor. Butterfly honors her father's courage by repeating his act and moves to reinscribe herself within Japanese tradition. The possibility of identification with Western individualism extinguished, her body reverts through custom to the community of ancestors. The opera makes dramatically plain that this act is a sacrificial duty done for the benefit of the male child, that is, for the continuity of ancestors and not, as in the film, for love lost.

The genealogy and politics of this penultimate gesture consists of Butterfly's tacit acknowledgment that the male child belongs with the American father. This conclusion is the point of crisis for the opera's ideological project. The act of suicide/sacrifice, of violence directed by the self against the self, is the dramatization in an emotional language of the cultural cross-over point between two different patriarchal functions. In Puccini's *Madama Butterfly*, this act is not the exclusive consequence of the imposition of Western values or of romantic love, nor is it exclusively the consequence of moral masochism, but the point of conflict and condensation between two different cultures. It is an act whose meaning belongs as much to the cultural system of Japan as to America. Mystification of the meaning of this action is crucial to the function violence plays in the opera's overall ideological import. Romantic love is a cover for imperialism and the terms of its possible critique are made evident by the actual historical relations between the two cultures in conflict—the American drive toward territorial expansion and modernization, and aggressive effort by Japan to subordinate other regions in Asia. The opera's definitive inscription of Butterfly in the natural order—a small traditional house and garden on a remote mountainside overlooking the bay—defines the traditional aesthetic order and conjoins it with the ways of the last impoverished remnants of a feudal social order. Puccini's is a nostalgic, aestheticized vision of old Japan; the new militarist order of Japan is nowhere engaged. The traditional character of Japanese social relations defined by the opera is underlined by Butterfly's relation to her father and to her uncle, the Priest. Her sacrifice fulfills a Japanese social expectation and constitutes a ritual intended to perpetuate the existence of that feudal order.

The child of marriage is normally intended to belong to the community. But which one? The Japanese social system and its attending religious ideology is like the American, based on an anti-miscegenation principle, a premise expressed in the opera that marriage of a Japanese to an American, "a barbarian," is (nearly) unthinkable. Butterfly's suicide, taking place at the borders between cultures, is the first phase of an inward-looking, archaic, Japanese defensive transformation that seeks proof of Japan's moral and cultural superiority to the West. This suicide is the cornerstone of a symbolic act of cultural resistance and consolidation; violence is necessary at the point of contact for the perpetuation of the old feudal order. The aesthetic figure of the young, dying Japanese woman, on the occasion of her culture's encounter with American military power and technology, figures at the same time the end of old Japan and the sacrifice required for an entry into modernity. Butterfly is a culturally ambiguous figure, at the same time adhering to the old ways and securing their honor and integrity with her life, and the figure most vulnerable to movement toward or from the "Other." She is staged precisely at the conjuncture between ideology (nativist and imperialist) and the body. Through her pass the misunderstandings of cross-cultural contact. She is the emblem of a conservative function, both cultural and psychological, at a time of historical transition.

The aesthetic idealization of this culturally sanctioned "undoing" and its institutionalization in the operatic canon are the specific features of the Western reception of the opera. It is a European work, yet a popular one installed in the Metropolitan's repertoire. It assumed its place in the domain of early twentieth-century American high art through the genre of romantic tragedy. It replicates, though hardly without ambiguity, the image of a powerful America, a view held and with good reason by the corporate, social, and industrial elites that sponsored the New York City Opera companies. It is *operatic form*, a certain combination of drama and symphonic music, that lifts the story from potential melodrama to high art. It is precisely the operatic idealization of this suicide, turning suicide into a sacrifice, that enables the story to transcend its realistic foundations. The medium for this transvaluation of source materials, including the conduct of Pinkerton, is the opera's intensity of emotion. These moments of affective intensity are performatively real: Butterfly's waiting, her pain, and her resolve to die with honor are readily conveyed to an audience well acquainted with the code of maternal sacrifice (Figures 3 and 4). It is not discourse, but the order of affect—its intensity, range, and scale—that legitimates operatic form. The art theories of the day, evident enough in the debates over the possibility that film might transcend photography and be considered an "art," were invested precisely in the cult of transcendental beauty that sustained the relation between this feminine figure and her audience.

The adaptation from opera to the medium of film meant not just a change in the mode of representation, but a cultural displacement of the work from the sphere of high art to the sphere of popular entertainment. This was precisely the process of cultural adaptation that Lasky, DeMille, and Paramount engaged in at this time. Their strategy was making films based on high art, European sources. The film *Madame Butterfly* (1915), though invoking a high art experience, was a derivative work in a different medium for a different audience. Culturally speaking, the film turned Butterfly's act of religious disaffiliation from the community into Pinkerton's breach of etiquette and displaced the opera's focus on the mother's sacrificial death for the child for an account based on romantic love. These two alterations put Pinkerton's conduct closer to the center of the narrative. In this regard, the film goes further, intercutting his American marriage with Butterfly's patient waiting, underscoring his callous "forgetfulness." The film puts Pinkerton's conduct more at the center of the film narratively and thematically and locates its drama through the conceit of romantic love. The erasure of Puccini's music and the singing, with their coordinated power of elevation, significantly alters the conditions of reception. It is manifestly a silent film. It turns out as a prose version of a poetic text, and the consequent realism of milieu and of behavior puts in place the terms of the critical reception of the film.

There are three distinctive features of this reception: praise for the picturesque setting and for Pickford's imitation of Japanese gesture, the

Fig. 3: Butterfly's realization: He is not coming back (courtesy of the Academy of Motion Picture Arts and Sciences).

Fig. 4: Butterfly waits through the long night (courtesy of the Academy of Motion Picture Arts and Sciences).

noticeable lack of emotional drama, and the uncertainty about how to evaluate Pinkerton's character. Notably, the reviews contemporary with the release of the film do not mention race at all. Indeed none of the reviews, either of the opera or the film, explicitly raise or address the matter of the difference of race *per se* in their account of the story or of its characters. Yet, Butterfly, in the opera, explicitly speaks about trying "to forget my race and kindred." The category of race is partly refigured as a question of nationality. Since the possibility of Butterfly returning married with Pinkerton to the United States does not arise in the story, but only the question of when or whether Pinkerton will return to Japan (it is the basis for the entire temporality of the narrative), the question of American racial policy or attitude need not and is not formulated by the work. Quite understandably the Japanese, the Priest, and the community are concerned with this question of residence, for it is, after all, a matter of a Japanese woman residing with a white man in Japan. The absence of any mention of miscegenation or associated issues in American reviews and commentary is a tacit acknowledgment of the fundamental asymmetry of sexual and racial relations between parties, evident in the conclusion of *The Cheat* and *Madame Butterfly*.[46] Though it is important, as I have argued, to see the issue of racial relations, namely the injunction against intermixing, as the fundamental structuring mechanism of American film forms, in the film at hand the racial topic is covered over, disguised, and rendered culturally inoperative by a narrative *coup de force*—by concentrating the action entirely in Japan. Both the opera and the film subordinate and submerge the question of relations of persons of different races, and the category of race *per se* by identifying racial difference with cultural difference, that is, at the level of nationality, value, and belief. National ideology ordinarily works to situate the individual citizen in the ideals of the nation. But in this film, more so than in the opera, the American Pinkerton is exposed as responsible for Butterfly's death. Though Butterfly may see Pinkerton as the ideal type, the treatment of the story shows plainly that he is not. Since Pinkerton is identified throughout as the emblem of the United States, the film version is confronted by the ideological problem of dealing with the unsavory conduct of its chief representative. Indeed, Butterfly's virtues of faith, patience, and loyalty, basic premises of audience sympathy, are supported by the actress figure, Mary Pickford, who was identified in this period as an ideal American. The image of the American father/husband is a morally dubious one. The U.S. Consul in Nagasaki ultimately finds

Pinkerton reprehensible. It is for this reason—the explicit culpability and condemnation of Pinkerton—that the view of Butterfly's suicide/sacrifice as a vehicle for the legitimization of Western, or male, domination seems to me largely untenable. This argument rests on the view that Butterfly is unambiguously a "martyr who sacrifices herself for an American god."

Madame Butterfly is a film that puts a woman's desire, so to speak, in the foreground, both as topic and as perspective. Desire for what? Though the original text of Long's story shows Pinkerton as a self-aggrandizing egoist, and describes Butterfly's love for him as a kind of worship of a new divinity, this imagery does not carry over into the body of the film itself, except in the form of a single intertitle: "Could one give up more for love than did little Cho Cho San!" In a filmic adaptation that excises the religious dimension so evident in the opera and adopts the myth of romantic love and the sense of disappointment and despair as its dramatic, generic formula, this intertitle carries only a weak religious resonance. It is difficult to see this film alone as supporting an idealization, or even as a justification of American patriarchy.

Rather, the film's ideological project lies elsewhere—with the meaning of the culturally condensed figure of the tragic "other woman." The Butterfly story is a paradigm of cultural dialectics and misunderstandings concerning figures who are specifically identified with nations and cultures. The story is an Orientalist text, a Western discourse on the Orient, a treatise on military and economic power that chooses as its poetic and narrative vehicles strongly accented gendered figures. It is a work that formulates its ideological project in terms of sexual and racial difference. The figures and personalities of *Madame Butterfly* (Pickford) and *The Cheat* (Hayakawa) compose a complementary matrix—"Asian female/Asian male"—constituting a double voiced "Asia" in the American field of racial representation in the Progressive era.

The misunderstandings or disagreements about cultural and sexual power in these films are, we might say, misrepresentations of how these relations actually worked. At the turn of the century the United States undertook two principal and related missions with regard to Asia: international expansion of American economic interests with China as its ultimate objective, and within America, the restriction of Asian immigration and property rights. The initial concern regarding China had culminated in the 1882 Exclusion Acts. In the period when *Madame Butterfly* was made, the concern was Japan. Two principal tropes, imperialistic appropriation of the beyond and the exclusion or segregation of the internalized Other, defined the Orientalism of the period. The discourse of American Orientalism was not, however, a unified one. The military discourse of economic domination of Asia was premised on a frankly racial theory of white strength and superiority; the missionary discourse focused on Christian re-education and spiritual conversion; the aesthetic discourse celebrated the East's refinement and exoticism. *Madame Butterfly* brings these three Orientalist dimensions together.

Madame Butterfly and *The Cheat* are a pair in two senses: They portray in complementary fashion an Asian man and an Asian woman, and they share a common theme of cultural invasion—the American man occupies Japan / the Japanese man occupies America. In both instances, the foreigner temporarily possesses the Other's woman. The specific ideological *misfiguration* consists of two parts—showing Japan as compliant and weak in *Madame Butterfly* by portraying an old, feudal Japan, whereas Japan was in fact militarily strong, winning notable wars in Asia, and its counterpart, showing Japanese (men) as strong and dangerous in the United States, a sexually aggressive part of American high society, whereas, in fact, the Japanese in the U.S. were mostly poor, few, and marginal. That is, in actuality, Japan was a major rival of the United States for power and domination of trading interests in China and the Japanese were reduced in the United States to non-landed non-citizens. This ideological work was accomplished in these films by intensifying Western images of gender difference and inverting the cultural values associated with them, making "Asia" in the East feminine and weak (where it was strong) and in the West masculine and strong (where it was weak). The second axis of this ideological work consists of exchanging an account of cultural difference for that of racial difference and effacing this substitution. The result is the construction of *Madame Butterfly* as a "purely aesthetic image."

The "undoing" of the Japanese woman, her self-extinction, is a Western aesthetic idealization. The sponsorship of this image began in the sphere of opera, among the elite—men and women—as a symbolic investment in aesthetic privilege, and in moving to cinema, installed itself on a broader, more popular social terrain. Adapting this material for cinema meant revising the woman's story, shifting the locus of its aesthetic capital from a cultural critique and an ethnographic appreciation of Shinto feudal order to a cultural critique of the American man in a modern cross-cultural melodrama, but one without the music. The choice of Pickford, already a notable film actress, over Geraldine Farrar, the opera performer who had established the role in New York, was a commercial decision intended to move beyond the circle of operatic authenticity to reach the widest possible movie audience. This is to say, quite simply, that *Madame Butterfly* is a woman's film "*avant la lettre*." At its foundation is the structure of maternal sacrifice. Its intended audience, the one addressed by the film, is women. The film blames Pinkerton but excuses him. That is the moral disapprobation that attends such an action as Pinkerton's is set aside for the pleasure of watching the spectacle it engenders, the "undoing" of this Oriental woman.

What pleasure might a middle-class American woman take in the ritual death of this poor dispossessed Oriental figure? What, in other words, are the collateral privileges and pleasures for American women of Western imperialism? In this instance, American women's interests may be divided between Pinkerton's two wives. The white American wife, appearing only briefly, is more a story mechanism than a figure of potential identification. The emotional center is, of course, Butterfly, even if she is presented by the film in a relatively disaffected mode. The usual answer to the account of pleasure taken with another's suffering is not masochism but sadism, and in this instance we might say sadism has an actual economic—a class—foundation. The potential for middle-class identification with the white actress, Pickford, is mediated by her characterization as an Oriental figure, poor, inarticulate, suffering, silent, and yellow. The film's simulation of racial difference—Butterfly/Pinkerton—structures a denial of the racial implication of the performances Butterfly/Pickford and, hence, of the status of racial difference in the construction and significance of the entire narrative. This alternating belief/disbelief in the substitution of white for yellow (Pickford/Butterfly) seconds the primary disbelief that structures the reception of a fiction film and complicates the possibility of a white woman's identification with the *depicted* figure. Though there may be in American women's response to this film in 1915 an element of masochistic pleasure, this possibility is predicated on cross-cultural transference. Sympathy may extend to the situation of the depicted figure, the one sold and abandoned. There is for women, of course, a potential analogy with Butterfly through the fact that the melodrama genre provides a recognizable place for the Other Woman, but this film blocks its recognition by providing an alternative and installing a white woman as culturally sanctioned custodian of the child. Rather, the film offers the audience the pleasure of cultural dominance, the pleasure of *not* being that Oriental figure, of not being so subjected, the pleasure of enjoying white, Western, middle-class women's racial privilege, and the security associated with Western imperialisms. In this way, the intended audience alternates between masochism, sadism, and class and racial condescension.

Seven years after the release of Mary Pickford's *Madame Butterfly*, the story was retold in *Toll of the Sea* (1922), with Anna May Wong in the role of a Chinese Butterfly. Indeed, the proximity and slide between Japan and China in American popular imagination implicitly operates in the earlier version. The markets, resources, and territory of China, not Japan, were the ultimate object of Western imperialisms in the nineteenth century. The British, for example, sought economic domination of China by recalculating the balance of trade through the introduction and management of the opium cartel. In the 1915 *Madame Butterfly*, however, Japan stands in for Asia generally and in particular for China as the figure of a territory susceptible to American domination. As World War II showed, Japan and the West were rivals for control of China. In this regard *Madame Butterfly*, the Western, canonical image of sacrificial, cross-cultural violence across the woman's body, works as both a symbolic act of ideological domination over the old feudal ways, and in its idealization of the traditional, loving, maternal figure, serves as a screen that hides its aggressive, masculine counterpart, the military forces of the East and West whose confrontation in the theater of the Pacific would come to dominate the century.

Notes

The author thanks Ms. L. S. Kim of UCLA for research assistance on this article and the George Eastman House for screening *Madame Butterfly*.

1. Orientalism in silent film theory and in architecture of cinema theatres is treated in Nick Browne, "Orientalism as an Ideological Form: American Film Theory in the Silent Period," *Wide Angle* 11, no. 4 (1989).

2. The late nineteenth century was dominated by German opera or German-language versions of French and Italian operas. For a general discussion of the development of "high" and "popular" culture in America, see Lawrence W. Levine, *Highbrow/Lowbrow: The Emergence of Cultural Hierarchy in America* (Cambridge, Mass.: Harvard University Press, 1988).

3. John Dizikes, *Opera in America: A Cultural History* (New Haven, Conn.: Yale University Press, 1993), p. 206.

4. In 1886, *The Mikado* inspired a parody, a minstrel show called *The Micky Doo*. An advertising poster accompanying the show (reproduced in Dizikes, p. 205), shows six African Americans, dressed in kimono and wooden sandals, doing a spirited version of the "Micky-doo." Thus impersonation of Japanese and African Americans are condensed in a common image of theatrical absurdity in nineteenth-century American entertainment.

5. Gregory Waller, "Historicizing, a Test Case: Japan on American Screens, 1909–

1915" (Paper delivered at the 1991 Society for Cinema Studies Conference at Los Angeles), p. 13.

6. Waller, Ibid., quotes from *Motion Picture World*, Dec. 6, 1913.

7. The source of this is *Moving Picture World*, June 13, 1914.

8. This brief biography is drawn from Kevin Brownlow, *Behind the Mask of Innocence* (New York: Alfred A. Knopf, 1990), p. 345.

9. Sumiko Higashi, *Cecil B. DeMille: A Guide to References and Resources* (Boston: G. K. Hall, 1985), p. 56.

10. Don Kirihara, "The Accepted Idea Replaced: Stereotype and Sessue Hayakawa," in this volume.

11. Brownlow, *Behind the Mask*, p. 350.

12. The masochistic interpretation of *The Cheat* is developed in Kevin Brownlow, *Behind the Mask*, p. 348, and in Gina Marchetti, *Romance and the "Yellow Peril": Race, Sex and Discursive Strategies in Hollywood Fiction* (Berkeley: University of California Press, 1993), p. 21.

13. Sumiko Higashi, "Ethnicity, Class, and Gender in Film: DeMille's *The Cheat*", *Unspeakable Images: Ethnicity in the American Cinema*, ed. Lester Friedman, (Urbana and Chicago: University of Illinois Press, 1991), p. 130.

14. "Not Belasco Play: Famous Players version of 'Madam Butterfly' is 'Something Else Again'." *Moving Picture World*, Nov. 13, 1915, p. 1282.

15. Gillian Anderson, *Music for Silent Films, 1894–1929* (Washington, D.C.: Library of Congress Press, 1988), p. 20.

16. Ibid., p. xiv.

17. *Paramount Progress*, Sept. 16, 1915, p. 6.

18. Anderson, *Music for Silent Films*, p. xxiv.

19. Dizikes, *Opera in America*, p. 317.

20. Ibid, p. 317.

21. Lawrence Gilman, "A New Opera and a New Conductor," *Harper's Weekly*, Nov. 24, 1906, p. 1686.

22. Ibid., p. 1686.

23. "*Madame Butterfly* at the Metropolitan: Puccini's Latest Opera Given in a Performance of Much Beauty," *New York Times*, Nov. 20, 1908.

24. Gilman, "A New Opera and a New Conductor," 1686.

25. *New York Times*, Nov. 20, 1908.

26. Ibid.

27. "A Japanese Butterfly," *The Literary Digest*, Nov. 13, 1915, p. 1083.

28. Ibid.

29. *Motion Picture News*, May 22, 1915, p. 52.

30. *Paramount Progress*, Nov. 4, 1915. p. 12.

31. John Luther Long, "Madame Butterfly," in *Madam Butterfly/Madama Butterfly*, vol. 26, English National Opera Series, ed. Nicholas John (London: John Calder Ltd, 1984), p. 26.

32. Ibid., p. 27.

33. *Moving Picture World*, Nov. 13, 1915, p. 1323; *Motion Picture News*, Nov. 20, 1915, p. 80, and Nov. 27, 1915, p. 85.

34. *Motion Picture World*, Nov. 13, 1915, p. 1323.

35. *Motion Picture News*, Nov. 20, 1915, p. 80.

36. *New York Dramatic Mirror*, Oct. 29, 1915, p. 28.

37. RM Arts/Ente Autonomo Teatro alla Scala/Radiotelevione Italiana, *Madama Butterfly*, 1986. VHS Recording.

38. Giuseppe Giacosa and Luigi Illica, "Libretto: *Madama Butterfly*," in Giacomo Puccini, *Madame Butterfly/Madama Butterfly*, No. 26, English National Opera, p. 124.

39. *Paramount Progress*, Nov. 4, 1915, p. 12.

40. The most recent film version is David Kronenberg's M. *Butterfly* with Jeremy Irons.

41. A detailed discussion on the musical relation of Orientalism and opera can be found in Ralph P. Locke (1993) and Christoph-Hellmut Mahling (1991), cited in the bibliography. The study of Puccini's knowledge and adaptation of Japanese music, in particular the use of penatonics in the creation of exotic, oriental atmosphere, is addressed in detail by J. Maehder, ed., *Esotismo e Colore Locale nell' opera di Puccini* (Pisa, 1985).

42. The analysis of the navy in the building of American empire is from Ronald Takaki's chapter "The Masculine Thrust Toward Asia," in his *Iron Cages: Race and Culture in 19th-Century America*. (New York: Oxford University, 1979). Mahan visited the Far East and actively promoted his view of the importance of Asia to America's emerging business interests.

43. Nick Browne, "Race: The Political Unconscious of American Film," *The East-West Film Journal*, vol. 6, no. 1 (1992): 5–16.

44. Marchetti, *Romance and the "Yellow Peril"*, pp. 78–89.

45. Ibid., p. 81.

46. According to an American understanding, the prohibition against intermarrying applies chiefly to the case of a white woman out-marrying. That is, the prohibition is asymmetrical: The injunction against a white man out-marrying is not enforced and is not enforceable outside the nation. The injunction did in fact obtain temporarily, however, with American military personnel, who sought after the Occupation of Japan to return home with Japanese wives. This is the subject, of course, of the 1950s *Sayonara*.

Reference List

Anderson, Gillian. *Music for Silent Films, 1894–1929*. Washington: Library of Congress Press, 1988.

Ashbrook, William. *The Operas of Puccini*. Ithaca, NY: Cornell University Press, 1968.

Blaisdell, George. "Madame Butterfly: An Atmosphere of Old Japan—Mary Pickford in Famous Players' Subject Plays Tragic Heroine of Song and Story." *Moving Picture World*, November 13, 1915, p. 1323.

Browne, Nick. "Race: The Political Unconscious of American Film." *The East-West Film Journal* 6, no. 1 (1992): 5–16.

———. "Griffith's Family Discourse: Griffith and Freud." *Quarterly Review of Film Studies: Special Issue on D. W. Griffith* 6, no. 1 (Winter 1981): 67–80.

———. "Orientalism as an Ideological Form: American Film Theory in the Silent Period." *Wide Angle* 11, no. 4 (1989): 23–31.

Brownlow, Kevin. *Behind the Mask of Innocence*. New York: Alfred A. Knopf, 1990.

Clément, Catherine. *Opera, or the Undoing of Women*. Minneapolis: University of Minnesota Press, 1988.
"Complete Madame Butterfly." *Motography*, November 6, 1915, p. 966.
Cortes, Carlos E. "Hollywood Interracial Love: Social Taboo as Screen Titillation." In *Beyond the Stars Two: Plot Conventions in American Film*, edited by Paul Loukides and Linda K. Fuller. Bowling Green, Ohio: Bowling Green State University Popular Press, 1991.
"The Darling of the Gods: A Japanese Play Criticized by Japanese." *The Critic*, Vol. 42, No. 70. pp. 70–72.
Dizikes, John. *Opera in America, A Cultural History*. New Haven, Conn.: Yale University Press, 1993.
E. "Madame Butterfly." *New York Dramatic Mirror*, October 20, 1915, p. 28.
Everson, William K. *American Silent Film*. New York: Oxford University Press, 1978.
"Famous Players Film Company Schedule." *Motion Picture News*, September 25, 1915, p. 11.
"Feature Releases—Current and Coming." *Motion Picture News*, October 16, 1915.
Flynn, Caryl. *Strains of Utopia: Nostalgia and Hollywood Film Music*. Princeton, N.J.: Princeton University Press, 1992.
Friedman, Lester D., editor. *Unspeakable Images: Ethnicity in the American Cinema*. Urbana and Chicago: University of Illinois Press, 1991.
Giacosa, Giuseppe, and Luigi Illica. "Madama Butterfly: The Italian Libretto" in *English Opera National Guide Series, No. 26*. Edited by Nicholas John. London: John Calder Publishers, 1984.
Gilman, Lawrence. "A New Opera and a New Conductor." *Harper's Weekly*, November 24, 1906, p. 1686.
———. "Madame Butterfly Again." *Harper's Weekly*, October 26, 1907, 1572.
Gorbman, Claudia. *Unheard Melodies: Narrative Film Music*. Bloomington: Indiana University Press, 1987.
Higashi, Sumiko. *Cecil B. DeMille: A Guide to References and Resources*. Boston: G. K. Hall & Co., 1985.
Horowitz, Joseph. *Understanding Toscanini: How He Became an American Culture God and Helped Create a New Audience for Old Music*. Minneapolis: University of Minnesota Press, 1987.
Jameson, Frederic. *The Political Unconscious: Narrative as a Socially Symbolic Act*. Ithaca, N.Y.: Cornell University Press, 1981.
"A Japanese Butterfly." *Literary Digest*, November 13, 1915, p. 1083.
John, Nicholas, ed., *English Opera National Guide Series, No. 26*. London: John Calder Publishers, 1984.
Jolo. "Mme. Butterfly." *Variety*, November 12, 1915.
Kalinak, Kathryn. *Settling the Score: Music and the Classic Hollywood Film*. Madison: University of Wisconsin Press, 1992.
Kennedy, Thomas C. "Madame Butterfly: A Famous Players Five Reel Drama." *Motography*, November 27, 1915.
Kinder, Marsha. *Blood Cinema: The Reconstruction of National Identity in Spain*. Berkeley: University of California Press, 1993.
Kirihara, Don. "The Accepted Idea Replaced: Stereotype and Sessue Hayakawa." Paper

read the 1994 Society for Cinema Studies Meeting at Syracuse, New York. Reprinted in this volume.

———. "Chronological Annotated Hayakawa Filmography." Unpublished Manuscript.

Leong, Russell, Editor. *Moving the Image: Independent Asian Pacific American Media Arts*. Los Angeles: UCLA Asian-American Study Center and Visual Communications, Southern California Asian American Studies Central Inc., 1991.

Levine, Lawrence W. *Highbrow, Lowbrow: The Emergence of Cultural Hierarchy in America*. Cambridge, Mass: Harvard University Press, 1988.

Locke, Ralph P. "Reflections on Orientalism in Opera and Musical Theater." *The Opera Quarterly* 10, no. 1 (Autumn 1993) 48–64.

"Long's Classic Ready: Madame Butterfly with Mary Pickford Released Next Week by Famous Players." *New York Dramatic Mirror*, November 6, 1915, p. 25.

"Madama Butterfly Again: Ms. Ferrar and Messrs. Caruso and Scotti in Puccini's Japanese Opera." *New York Times*, December 15, 1907.

"Madama Butterfly at the Metropolitan." *New York Times*, November 20, 1908.

"Madame Butterfly." *Moving Picture World*, November 13, 1915.

"Madame Butterfly at the Strand." *Moving Picture World*, November 13, 1915, p. 1294.

"Madame Butterfly: A Synopsis." *Paramount Progress*, November 4, 1915, p. 12.

Mahling, Christoph-Hellmut. "'The Japanese Image' in Opera, Operetta, and Instrumental Music at the End of the 19th and during the 20th Century." In *Tradition and Its Future in Music*, edited by Yosihiko Tokumaru, et. al. Tokyo: Mita Press, 1991.

Marchetti, Gina. *Romance and the "Yellow Peril": Race, Sex, and Discursive Strategies in Hollywood Fiction*. Berkeley: University of California Press, 1993.

"Mary Pickford in Madame Butterfly for Famous Players." *Motion Picture News*, November 6, 1915.

McClary, Susan. *Feminine Endings: Music, Gender and Sexuality*. Minneapolis: University of Minnesota Press, 1991.

Miller, Stewart Creighton. *The Unwelcome Immigrant: The American Image of the Chinese, 1785–1882*. Berkeley and Los Angeles: University of California Press, 1969.

Milne, Peter. "Madame Butterfly." *Motion Picture News*, November 20, 1915, p. 80.

"Mme. Butterfly Pleases." *New York Times*, November 8, 1915, p. 13.

Moy, James S. *Marginal Sites: Staging the Chinese in America*. Iowa City: University of Iowa Press, 1993.

Nattiez, Jean-Jaques. *Music and Discourse: Toward a Semiology of Music*. Princeton, N.J.: Princeton University Press, 1990.

"New York Papers Pay Tribute to Madame Butterfly." *Motion Picture News*, Nov. 27, 1915, p. 85.

"New Famous Players List Outshines Its Old Subject." *Motion Picture News*, August 7, 1915, p. 52.

"Not Belasco Play: Famous Players Version of Madame Butterfly is 'Something Else Again'." *Moving Picture World*, November 13, 1915.

Osborne, Charles. *The Complete Operas of Puccini: A Critical Guide*. New York: Da Capo Inc., 1981.

Plaut, Eric A. *Grand Opera: Mirror of the Western Mind*. Chicago: Ivan R. Dee Publishers, 1993.

RM Arts/Entre Autonomo Teatro alla Scala/Radiotelevisone Italiana. *Madama Butterfly*. 1986. VHS recording.

"Review of *Madame Butterfly* by John Luther Long." *The Critic*, December 1898, pp. 526–527.

"Review of *Miss Cherryblossom* by John Luther Long." *The Critic*, May 1895, p. 362.

Sandmeyer, Elmer Clarence. *The Anti-Chinese Movement in California*. Urbana: University of Illinois Press , 1973.

Sneed, Vincent. "Anna May Wong." *China Doll* 1, nos. 1 & 2 (August 1991).

Takaki, Ronald. *Iron Cages: Race and Culture in 19th Century America*. New York: Oxford University Press, 1990.

———. *Strangers From a Different Shore: The History of Asian Americans*. New York: Penguin Group, 1989.

Waller, Gregory A. "Historicizing, a Test Case: Japan on American Screens, 1909–1915." Paper read at the 1991 Society for Cinema Studies Conference at Los Angeles.

"Work on Ferrar Scenarios." *Motion Picture News*, May 22, 1915.

"Zukor Off to West Coast on Secret Errand." *Motion Picture News*, February 6, 1915, p. 74.

Gina Marchetti

TRAGIC AND TRANSCENDENT LOVE IN *THE FORBIDDEN CITY*

When images of Asia and Asians on the American silent screen come to mind, too often a mental picture of diabolical villains and yielding, exotic beauties obscures the far more complex fantasy world Hollywood actually offered viewers at that time.[1] Merging the ambivalence of rapidly changing Victorian sexual mores with America's emerging role in international affairs, fantasies about romantic liaisons involving Asian characters during the silent era can be looked at today as historical markers of a racial ideology that continues to endure. In fact, these silent films often simultaneously warn against miscegenation while celebrating romantic love, cry for the separation of the races while condemning racial intolerance, and argue for exclusionism while advocating a paternalistic role for America as Asia's "savior."

With films like *Wrath of the Gods* (1914), *The Cheat* (1915), *Madame Butterfly* (1915), and *Broken Blossoms* (1919), to name just a few examples, Hollywood began to evolve a narrative lexicon that could accommodate a variety of shifting ideological positions involving race, gender, and national identity. To achieve this, Hollywood films have used the device of the parallel love story both to uphold and condemn the racial/sexual status quo within the same narrative. Usually involving two couples, these narratives offer a dual perspective on the sexual taboos with which they deal. Death allows the first tragic couple to criticize society without changing it, perhaps leaving a sense of the inexorable workings of fate more than a genuine plea for reform. The second couple, on the other hand, absorbs the social criticism of the first, weakens it, and allows for its accommodation within a slightly modified social order. (The fact that the Asian characters were often portrayed by Caucasian performers undoubtedly helped to make these romances even more acceptable to the mainstream viewer.)

The Forbidden City (1918, dir. Sidney A. Franklin, Selznick Pictures) provides an early Hollywood example of this type of parallel love story involving Asian-Caucasian relationships. The first part of the narrative deals with the love affair between San San (Norma Talmadge), daughter of a wealthy Mandarin out of favor with the Emperor, and John Worden (Thomas Meighan), Assistant Secretary to the United States Consul in Beijing. While her father, Wong Li (E. A. Warren), plans to give his daughter to the Emperor as a concubine in an attempt to win royal favor, San San secretly marries and becomes pregnant by Worden. When Worden leaves for an assignment in Shanghai, San San's father sequesters his daughter on the country estate of one of his fellow courtiers. When San San is finally presented to the Emperor (Rogers Lytton), she brings her newborn with her. Furious, the Emperor executes Wong Li. When San San refuses to renounce her American husband, he also puts her to death.

The second part of *The Forbidden City* takes up the plot roughly eighteen years later. It deals with San San's daughter, Toy (also played by Norma Talmadge), who has been roughly raised inside the Forbidden City as a warning to others. Yuan Loo (Charles Fang), one of the Emperor's guards, helps Toy to escape. She finds asylum at the American embassy and is sent to a military hospital in Manila to train as a Red Cross nurse. There, she meets Lt. Phillip Halbert (Reed Hamilton), and they fall in love. Halbert's guardian, the Governor General of the Philippines, is none other than John Worden, Toy's father. Not recognizing his daughter when they first meet, Worden absolutely forbids Phillip and Toy's marriage, and he ships the Lieutenant off to Mindanao to assure their separation. Worden becomes seriously ill, and Toy is called to nurse him. When he calls for San San in his delirium, Toy realizes that Worden is her father and humors him by dressing up in her mother's clothes. When Phillip arrives to be at his guardian's bedside, Worden emerges from his delirium, recognizes his daughter, and joins her hand to his ward's to bless their union.

As a fairly typical silent film melodrama, *The Forbidden City* makes use of coincidence, unexpected reversals, miscommunications, mistaken identities, and spectacular emotional displays to flesh out its narrative. Also, like most melodramas, it deals with disturbances in the domestic sphere, where patriarchal rights are questioned and female sexual self-determination is raised as a troubling possibility. Although both interracial romances in the film challenge taboos against miscegenation, one relationship thrives in the narrative while the other ends disastrously. Since, like most melodramas, *The Forbidden City* provides a certain type of moral instruction to its viewers, the key to the text's moral (and ideological) vision seems to lie in the differences between these two couples. Here, the differences between San San and Toy become critical. Because women generally function in the melodrama as tokens of patriarchal power, their circulation in *The Forbidden City* between husbands, lovers, fathers, and rulers provides an entry into an understanding of the text's ambivalent treatment of interracial sexuality.

San San versus Toy

The Forbidden City begins with an ominous, shadowy drawing of a ghostly form overlaid with the title "The East is East and the West is West. And never the twain shall meet," from Kipling. This quote often figures in Hollywood films with Asian themes to represent the apparently unresolvable contradiction between Asia and the West. That impossible social contradiction is then translated into narrative terms which hint at some reconciliation through the dramatic workings of the text. As often as not, however, that reconciliation turns out to be impossible, confirming the inevitable truth of the Kipling quote.

However, its use here in *The Forbidden City* proves to be somewhat deceptive, since East and West do indeed meet, fall in love, marry, reproduce, and provide a second generation to continue the cycle. While the Kipling and a later quote on fate by Omar Khayyam would seem to prepare the viewer for an inevitably tragic resolution to the plot, the narrative discourse actually works against itself by allowing for the union of its second interracial couple at the end of the film. Thus, the narrative enigma at the beginning of the film might be articulated as: "How will this text demonstrate that East and West can never be reconciled?" However, by the film's conclusion, the question has changed to: "Under what circumstances can East and West get together?" This implies a further question: "What does this signify morally? How may it alter accepted perceptions of the racial status quo?"

As in most Hollywood melodramas, the female characters in *The Forbidden City* act at the heart of the moral universe in the film. Their fate divides the acceptable and the unacceptable within the text's ethical parameters. However, at first, the two principal female characters might seem to confuse the matter by not providing sufficient contrast in moral outlooks. Neither exceeds the boundaries delineated by the Hollywood melodrama for its heroines; that is, both San San and Toy are coded as "virtuous" in terms of costuming and deportment as well as character function. Moreover, given that San San and Toy are both portrayed by the same actress, it might, at first, be assumed that Toy somehow continues to function in the same way as San San in the narrative. Indeed, as the parallel plotlines do indicate, there are similarities—e.g., the secret love affair, the disapproval of the father, the heroines' victimization and acceptance of fate.

However, on closer examination, San San and Toy cut very different figures in terms of the narrative. While they both exist as objects of exchange among the male characters and act as signifiers of male power, San San represents an unrecuperable alterity that can potentially emasculate, while the half-American Toy functions as an emblem of both political and male empowerment through assimilation. While the existence of both raises potentially disturbing challenges to popular perceptions of racial and ethnic differences and the definition of the American mainstream as white and Anglo-Saxon, Toy somehow can function as a token of tolerance and "melting pot" ideals of assimilation, while San San cannot. By looking at each character and her function in two quite similar, parallel plotlines, we can more clearly see the ways in which ideology operates within the melodramatic narrative to reconcile these apparently irreconcilable contradictions while still salvaging the conception of American society as both open and "tolerant" as well as white defined, dominated, and controlled.

San San functions ambivalently in the text as both a transparent innocent and as an occult mystery. Her face first appears in a close-up in which it is almost completely obscured by the thick ribs of a garden fence. Her eyes are closed, furthering an impression of distance and impenetrability. However, the next shot shows her playing hide-and-seek with a group of young children in the garden near a small wooded area. While her Chinese gown signifies cultural alterity, her long braids, high collar and modestly cut outfit, her angelic, full face, and quick, lively, hopping movements create the familiar picture of the Victorian child-woman; that is, innocent, insouciant, natural, almost divinely virtuous, naive, and in need of protection.[2]

Typical of the Victorian roots of the Hollywood silent melodrama, the patriarchal family is offered as the protective environment to house the angelic child-woman. Her divinity legitimizes its existence; its strictures protect her virtue. As a microcosm for bourgeois society in general, the Victorian family, its protected, virtuous child/Madonna at its heart, acts as a legitimization of the bourgeois patriarchy's wider political, economic, and cultural rule. However, in *The Forbidden City*, the American bourgeois home does not protect female virtue. Rather, the Asian patriarchy, depicted as an incomplete, decaying institution, threatens the motherless San San as the politically impotent Wong Li plans to strengthen himself through his daughter's concubinage.

John Worden appears as an alternative to Wong Li, as well as the Emperor, and this implicitly decadent, Asian patriarchy. Male domination—the necessary protection of feminine virtue—female subordination, and passivity remain unquestioned. Only the race, potency, and legitimacy of the patriarch are at issue. In contrast to the elderly Wong Li, dressed in elaborate, implicitly effeminate, Chinese attire, Worden appears dressed in the conservative white suit and summer hat, codified in Hollywood as *the* uniform for the sprightly, young diplomat abroad, linking his masculinity with his political position.

In his first scene with San San, moreover, Worden is visually associated with Asian religious icons, underscoring the connection between Western notions of romantic love, natural virtue, and divinely sanctioned heterosexuality. Worden comes upon San San, surrounded by the children with whom she had been playing hide-and-seek earlier, at a small garden shrine. He hides behind a tree, motions the children away, and playfully sneaks up behind San San to embrace her.

The positioning of the camera in this scene underscores Worden's symbolic association with a secularized, Victorian religion of love that is associated with and then replaces San San's Buddhism. At the beginning of the scene, San San is positioned at the base of the small hill leading up to the shrine. Several reverse angle shots show her in medium close-up from a slightly high angle looking up at the shrine, adjusting her hair in preparation for her prayers. The camera, positioned to take the place of the Buddhist statue, looks down on her up-turned face, chin stuck out, lips pursed, eyes half-closed. Both sensual and virginal, an erotic suppliant appeals directly to the viewer, who literally takes on the point-of-view of a god. The positioning of the camera seems to invite the viewer to take up the moral with the physical perspective and sanction the prayer revealed by the title which follows: "Oh, Buddah [*sic*], please send love-man here to give me million sweet kisses." The quaint syntax underscores the foreign child-woman's need for paternal authority, and seems further to invite the godlike viewer to see Worden as the agent of this quasi-religious, romantically inspired, patriarchal protection.

There is a cut-away to a scene in which Wong Li plans to use San San to curry the Emperor's favor by offering a photograph of San San to stimulate the Emperor's interest. In the photo, shown in close-up, San San's pose bears a marked similarity to her posture at the shrine. Her eyes are narrowed, looking up toward the camera; her jaw is outstretched, lips pouting. The photo freezes her, for the viewer, in an ambivalent moment between abject supplication and open sensuality. Like other Victorian child-women, she is innocent, but also provocative—in need of protection because she arouses lust. Likely, the fact of her racial difference and its assumed exotic eroticism adds to the ambivalence of the image. San San, indeed, provides an image that needs to be contained by more than a picture frame.

After the cut-away, Worden and San San are again shown in the garden. Physically positioned between the shrine (off-screen right) and her American lover to her left, San San looks off to the right. The camera no longer finds itself in Buddha's place, and the statue now stands as a sign of the authority of Asian patriarchy rather than the sympathetic ear for San San's erotic yearnings. A title appears: "Wise sages say girl of East never mate with foreign man." However, having taken up the voice of moral authority, Worden counters with a pronouncement that pits his "correct," "liberal," Anglo-American voice against the excesses of Asian patriarchal despotism: "Love knows no geography or race—I love you San San, because you are the woman God made for me!" American, bourgeois, patriarchal power legitimizes itself through the religion of love. In contrast to the rational calculations of Wong Li's plans for his daughter's future as an imperial concubine, the Victorian elevation of romantic love as sacrosanct bestows on Worden the absolute right to take San San away from her "pagan," Asian father. Although Worden looks off ominously in the direction of the shrine at the scene's conclusion, San San's supplicating, adoring gaze has been turned from Buddha to her godlike, American lover.

The lovers meet on bridges in idyllic garden settings, the full moon used as a halo behind their heads. Although these images seem to visually sanction their ability to "naturally" bridge the distance between their two cultures through their physical/spiritual relationship, the couple finds no "cultural" sanctuary for their romance. They keep their relationship (referred to as a "marriage" although no ceremony is ever shown) secret from Wong Li. They never enter Wong Li's home, and Worden is never shown taking San San away from the estate gardens to his embassy or anywhere else.

San San is still a subject of Chinese patriarchy. Worden misrecognizes this completely, however. When he tells San San of his reassignment, she pleads, "San San die if love-man go 'way." However, Worden dismisses her fears and replies, "I shall bring a pretty present back for San

San." Although Worden treats San San as a child, he does not take seriously the necessity for her protection nor does he realize that his child-bride will soon become a mother. A Chinese doll, which San San uses to hide her wedding ring, acts as a token of their love, a textual recognition of the Victorian assumption that "good" women are childlike, dependent, and constantly vulnerable. It also acts as a reminder of a woman's *raison d'être*, that is, to be transformed into a virginal mother, to become a secularized Madonna for the reproduction of the bourgeois, patriarchal home.

Worden never provides this sanctified domestic haven for San San, and, thus, he breaks with more than simply the conventions that prohibit miscegenation. A title indicates his recognition of this: "At last Worden yields to the popular belief that San San has suffered a Chinese father's vengeance of death for having mated with a foreigner." Although the text seems to emphasize prohibitions against interracial sexuality, a projection of the West's own sexualization of racism onto China, there is also an implicit recognition of the violation of patriarchal right. In China, Worden proves no match for the supposedly despotic patriarchy he battles with an American notion of romantic love.

When San San is presented at court, the genuine power of this Asiatic patriarchy becomes concrete. As the embodiment of this sexual despotism, the Emperor has absolute power of life and death as well as complete control over the sexuality of his subjects (particularly the concubines of his court). However, his rule is presented as implicitly corrupt because it lacks the sanctification of a Western sense of romantic love. This dooms San San who has "given all her soul to husband." Although the Emperor at first appears to respect her constancy, he still has San San executed with the added cruelty of having her killed in sight of a door leading to her freedom. He also takes her child in as a lesson to the court on the perils of sexual expression outside his prerogatives.

Through her execution, San San becomes a martyr to this vision of beatified romantic love. Although she screams when she realizes that spearmen lurk behind the curtains on either side of her, she makes no attempt to escape from them or her fate. Rather, her willing acceptance of death over dishonor appeals to a Victorian insistence on feminine virtue as the legitimization of its patriarchal right to power. Through San San's death, Worden gains rather than loses power. Although he has failed to physically protect his bride, he has won her over to the Western religion of love and saved her "soul," which she claims belongs exclusively to her godlike husband. Thus, her death solidifies his moral rectitude and patriarchal privilege to rule in Asia. Her martyrdom, moreover, pays any residual price their breaking of patriarchal convention may have exacted; they are symbolically punished within the narrative for any threat to the status quo they may have posed. Similarly, if her provocative exoticism challenged any Victorian notion of "pure" womanhood as sexless, her death allows her to transcend that potentially disturbing eroticism and become a pure icon of the virginal Madonna, that potent paradox that lies at the heart of a Victorian rationalization of its legitimacy. A scapegoat embodying a possible challenge to the racial or sexual status quo, San San paves the way to power for the man she loves (and, implicitly, the country he represents).

If San San can legitimize Western patriarchy through the spiritual transcendence of her tragic end, then Toy further solidifies the moral right of the West to rule abroad as well as at home by socially transcending any barriers to her absorption into the American family. Toy seems to be able to function in this way because the text portrays her as a very different sort of character from San San. Half American, Toy does not represent that absolute alterity embodied by San San. However, perhaps more importantly, Toy is not depicted as the Victorian child-woman, the virgin Madonna, but rather as a transitional sort of figure who at least recognizes the emergence of a "new woman" through the Suffragette Movement.[3] A softened, American patriarchy can, thus, emerge, because this more independent, but still morally high-minded woman has become better equipped to fend for herself in the public sphere.

While San San depends completely on Worden, Wong Li, and the Emperor for her social definition and physical survival, Toy is pictured as not only less dependent, but actually rebellious. As she sits at the window of the women's quarters in the Forbidden City, she looks at a distant image of a small pavilion flying the American flag. Here, the United States functions differently than it had for San San, where it was completely equated with dreams of romantic love. In this case, the U.S. represents personal freedom from Asian despotism, an escape from her tyrannical guardian the Emperor to the benevolent protection of the United States embassy.

Whereas the childlike San San never expressed any longing to be free, Toy does. Her very appearance seems to conjure up this idea visually. Dressed in a calf-length Western dress with a revealing peasant bodice covered by a fringed shawl, with shoulder-length dark, wavy hair, and long, dangling earrings, Toy looks like the Hollywood picture of the Gypsy. Thus, her attire not only attempts to mark her as a hybrid creation of Asian and Western characteristics (just as Gypsies come from the East, but have lived for generations in the West), but her appearance also connotes a Gypsy-like desire for freedom and independence, a slightly wild, openly sensual femininity, diametrically opposed to San San's quiet submissiveness. Unlike the passive San San, Toy quite actively asserts herself. When cursed at by one of the concubines who questions her mother's virtue, Toy lashes out, strikes her tormentor across the face with her fan, and threatens, "I kill you if you speak that again!" Unlike San San, who is too meek to tell even her father of her marriage and pregnancy, Toy can stand up for herself and openly express her will.

One of the imperial guards, Yuan Loo (Charles Fang), offers to help Toy escape. He goes to Toy's bedroom where she lies on an elaborate bed with a large circular frame reminiscent of a theater's proscenium arch. It provocatively frames her body. After Yuan Loo enters and offers his help, Toy caresses his hand with her cheek as the guard looks up in pleasure. When he leaves the bedroom, he closes the door slowly in front of his face so that his gaze can linger on Toy off-screen.

With all the leering glances, sensual chinoiserie, and physical intimacy this scene entails, either a budding romance or a potential seduction and/or rape would be expected. However, after Yuan Loo sees Toy safely out of the palace, he completely disappears from the plot. One of the few Chinese characters in the film to be actually portrayed by an Asian actor, perhaps Yuan Loo exists not only to facilitate Toy's escape, but also as an icon of the potential sexual threat life within the confines of the Asian patriarchy poses to feminine virtue. He represents the outer limit of Toy's quest for personal freedom, since that freedom also means that she may be vulnerable to "dishonor." Since Toy escapes from the Forbidden City through the same passageway in which her mother was executed, the importance of female virtue within the limits of a *justified* (that is, white, American) patriarchy again comes to mind through the visual association.

Thus, when Toy is welcomed by first a sympathetic diplomat at the American Embassy in Beijing and, then, an avuncular colonel in Manila, the text takes the necessity for Toy's reincorporation into the patriarchy for granted after her flight from the palace. Her personal freedom no longer is at issue, rather her willing exchange of the "corrupt" confines of the Forbidden City for the "benevolent" protection of the United States government is simply accepted as part of the necessary workings of the plot. Its ideological shoring up of patriarchal values cleansed of "Asian" excesses remains as an unvoiced consequence of the narrative action.

The Forbidden City, however, continues to present Toy as a contradictory figure, depicted as existing somewhere between the threatening independence of the Suffragette and the total self-effacement of the Victorian virgin. In Manila, she becomes a Red Cross nurse, that is, both an educated professional and a traditionally nurturing woman subordinate to the orders of the male doctors. She dresses in the prim, Western outfit of the self-confident, professional nurse, but keeps close to her San San's clothing and the photo (shown earlier in the film) of San San in a supplicating pose almost inviting victimization, a reminder of Toy's more traditional feminine role. Although the text allows Toy a pluck associated with the Western modern woman, it does not rid her of the weight of a nostalgia for the Victorian virgin/Madonna embodied by this Hollywood fantasy of the Chinese child-bride.

The final portion of the narrative revolves around the American patriarchy's final acceptance of this compromise between races and cultures as well as gender roles. As a career woman and a vulnerable innocent, as an independent American and as a submissive Chinese, Toy must be accepted into the American family as wife and daughter. Politically with this acceptance comes a legitimization of the American right to govern outside its racial borders, that is, to look on other nations as vulnerable women in need of its protective strength and voluntarily submitting to it.

The conflation of the familial with the political is quite clear in the text. All of the principal male characters have key positions in their respective governments as well as within the domestic sphere; for example, Wong Li is both a father and an out-of-favor Qing courtier, the Emperor is both the absolute ruler of China as well as the husband of his concubines and father to their children. John Worden, a low-level diplomat in the first part of the narrative, has become the Governor General of America's only Asian colony, the Philippines. Toy's fiancé, Phillip Halbert, is a medical man serving as part of the occupation forces.

In the second generation's interracial romance, Halbert replaces the ineffectual Worden, and Worden replaces the decadent Wong Li and the cruel, corrupt Chinese Emperor. Within this "tolerant," "liberal," reconfigured patriarchy, the solidification of its right to rule rests on its ability to take in Toy as a symbol of compromise. Her character can mediate between racist exclusionism and the complete end to racial hierarchies, between an emerging, independent career woman and a Victorian infant/mother.

Worden, as representative of the State, stands as the only obstacle to this ideological compromise and narrative closure. Worden forbids Toy and Phillip to marry. Although his ward assumes the motivation to be racial prejudice, the text leaves this point ambiguous, since a desire to save Phillip from his own earlier tragic marriage could also be an apt interpretation.[4] Actually, however, in textual terms, the disturbing appearance of the Amer-Asian orphan as an independent, feminine presence outside of any clear patriarchal authority may also have something to do with Worden's initial opposition.

Worden first sees Toy in modern, Western dress, her loose skirt revealing a bit of calf, a high bodice accentuating her bustline; she breezily moves about without the official weight of her nurse's uniform or the confining modesty of traditional Chinese attire. She appears wholly as a "modern" woman—free, self-confident, self-sufficient—and a potential threat to the continuing necessity for the patriarchy. Worden, puzzled because he feels that Toy looks familiar, still cannot recognize her as his daughter, nor realize his authority over her, perhaps because of what her appearance connotes.

Worden's relationship to Toy changes as she changes her clothes. On Worden's sickbed, a recognition of his relationship to Toy can finally take place as she dons the uniform of her official, nurturing role as an American Red Cross nurse and then her mother's traditional Chinese pajamas, with blossoms in her tightly wrapped hairdo. Thus, rather than acting as a reminder of the threatening freedom of the modern American woman on the verge of getting voting rights and greater opportunities within the public sphere, Toy finally can be recognized by her father as his legitimate child when she reminds him of her continued ties to her mother's more traditionally feminine role.

Worden, at first, misrecognizes Toy as San San and says, "San San, God has sent you to me!" By equating Toy with San San, Worden symbolically recoups that sanctified essence of Victorian womanhood San San represented as part of the new, outwardly different generation of women. Indeed, Toy can mediate between the two roles and, thus, find her place as daughter and wife within the American patriarchal order. As the "new" woman, she acts as a token of its liberalism, and, as the Chinese innocent, she legitimizes the need for the continuation of the patriarchy's institutional domination of women. Worden finally blesses her union with Phillip. The tolerance of the American patriarchy proven in its ability to accommodate a degree of racial difference and a certain amount of female emancipation, Toy's union with Phillip solidifies the ascendancy of an American vision of domestic relations over its own fantastical conception of the despotism of Asian patriarchy.

The Forbidden City as Political Allegory

Produced in 1918 as World War I was coming to an end, *The Forbidden City* emerges as a text which bears the traces of the strengthened role the United States assumed in international affairs by the time of the war's conclusion. Joining the Allies rather late in the conflict, the United States had been able, in its isolation, to solidify its economic presence abroad. The film industry provides just one example of this growth as Hollywood came to dominate markets globally by the time of the war's end. Hollywood could thrive as European film production was either eclipsed by the manufacture of armaments or destroyed in military attacks on industrial centers.

It should come as no surprise, then, that a text like *The Forbidden City* uses its narrative to make an argument for American rule abroad. Exploiting the malleable melodrama to construct this political discourse, the decay of the malevolent Asian patriarch as he loses his women to the benevolent American man can be read allegorically as a necessary exchange of power through the symbolic exchange of women.

To make this point, the film both recognizes and ignores history. Given that the United States "won" the Philippines from the Spanish in the 1890s and that the Philippine-American War officially ended in 1902, Worden could only be governor of the colony after that time. The text notes that Toy is eighteen when she escapes from the Forbidden City, so that Worden's sojourn in China would have been in the 1870s at the earliest, but more likely the 1880s or later. At that time, no emperor actually ruled as an absolute monarch in China. Rather, the Empress Dowager Cixi had been regent since the death of her husband in 1861.[5] However, an aging empress likely could not provide the needed contrast between the sanctified domesticity of the American bourgeoisie and the decadent excesses of the Chinese feudal patriarchy, so a potent emperor appears.

Given the decline of imperial power after the Boxer Rebellion in 1900 and the United States' growing economic presence in China because of its "Open Door" free trade policies, American involvement there became part of an official policy of unequal international relations. Even after the fall of the Qing Dynasty in 1911, and particularly during World War I, China slipped further, continuing to lose to both Western powers and Japan. Thus, that China should be represented in *The Forbidden City* by an unsettled domestic sphere that cannot control its women's sexuality seems apropos given an American bourgeois ideology that equates domestic rule with political legitimacy. Japan may even function here as an "absent presence." The Emperor of China could just as easily represent the more potent presence of the Allies' Pacific partner, thus signifying the threat of Japan's claim to rule in Asia territory the United States coveted itself.

The Philippines, then, can be looked at as a necessary contrast to China in *The Forbidden City*. If China does not recognize American power by allowing Worden to marry San San, then the Philippines, under United States rule, must affirm the American patriarchy's right as father and husband to a feminized Asia represented by Toy. In the Philippines, America appears as the benevolent father and the attentive lover within a softened, paternalistic government. The American Red Cross underscores American concern for its "less fortunate" Asian subjects. The presence of the Red Cross in the text, topical certainly because of World War I, also displays the American patriarchy as willing to give its women a certain public presence (in keeping always, of course, with their Victorian role as nurturing mother or angelic spirit). Unlike the cloistered world of the concubines' quarters in the Forbidden City, women in the American Philippines enjoy a public presence assured by the protective rule of American men.[6]

While the Asian patriarchy remains rigid in its strict rule over female sexual self-determination, the U.S. is presented as liberalism personified. Any hints of racism disappear through the "divine" workings of romantic and paternal love. Taking these domestic relations allegorically, the U.S. becomes the "melting pot" for all races, a bastion of paternalistic tolerance, and the hope for a limited freedom for its women (and, by association, its non-white subjects are seen as functioning in a similarly subordinate, feminized role).

The Forbidden City, with its tragic and transcendent lovers, has a quite different perspective on interracial sexuality than films on the same theme that appeared just a few years before it, for example, *The Cheat*, *Madame Butterfly*. At a time when Hollywood seriously began to see itself as a global enterprise, with a need to sell its products abroad as well as at home, *The Forbidden City* provides a fantasy in which America appears as the benevolent patriarch abroad. Indeed, as a legitimization of white, male, bourgeois, American rule, *The Forbidden City* serves as a clear example of Hollywood's use of the interracial romance to recognize, domesticate, and absorb differences of various sorts in order to continue the ideological hegemony of the dominant culture. *The Forbidden City* provides appropriate "places" in its narrative hierarchy of relationships for people of color, newly independent women, American colonials, as well as the morally strengthened American patriarch within its fantasy of an American world order legitimized by the power of romantic love.

Notes

1. For more on Hollywood's depiction of Asia during the silent era, see Dorothy B. Jones, *The Portrayal of China and India on the American Screen, 1896–1958* (Cambridge, Mass.: Center for International Studies, MIT, 1955); Eugene Franklin Wong, *On Visual Media Racism: Asians in the American Motion Pictures* (New York: Arno Press, 1978); Kevin Brownlow, *Behind the Mask of Innocence* (New York: Alfred A. Knopf, 1990); and Gina Marchetti, *Romance and the "Yellow Peril": Race, Sex, and Discursive Strategies in Hollywood Fiction* (Berkeley: University of California Press, 1993).

2. For more information on Victorianism and the depiction of women in the silent film, see Sumiko Higashi, *Virgins, Vamps, and Flappers: The American Silent Movie Heroine* (Montreal: Eden Press Women's Publications, Inc., 1978); Larry May, *Screening Out the Past: The Birth of Mass Culture and the Motion Picture Industry* (Chicago: University of Chicago Press, 1980); Marjorie Rosen, *Popcorn Venus* (New York: Avon, 1973).

3. The books cited above also provide excellent information on Hollywood's response to the Suffragettes.

4. A fear of incest might provide another possible explanation, since how Phillip got to be Worden's ward remains unexplained.

5. James C. Thomson, Jr., et al., *Sentimental Imperialists: The American Experience in East Asia* (New York: Harper and Row, 1981).

6. A houseboy and a few men dressed in military uniforms are the only Filipinos shown in the film. Their presence in these subordinate roles seems to act as an implicit affirmation of American rule over them.

THE COLONIAL IMAGINATION

Roberta E. Pearson

THE REVENGE OF RAIN-IN-THE-FACE? OR, CUSTERS AND INDIANS ON THE SILENT SCREEN

In 1874, an author perceived as one of the nation's foremost authorities on Indian affairs summed up his countrymen's dichotomous vision of the native inhabitants of the Great Plains:

> Seeing them [in Washington] only, it is not surprising that by many the Indian is looked upon as a simple-minded "son of nature," desiring nothing beyond the privilege of roaming and hunting over the vast unsettled wilds of the West . . . never trespassing upon the rights of others. This view is equally erroneous with that which regards the Indian as a creature possessing the human form but divested of all other attributes of humanity, and whose traits of character, habits, modes of life, disposition, and savage customs disqualify him from the exercise of all rights and privileges, even those pertaining to life itself.

The author resisted the easy bifurcation between "savage savage" and "noble savage" that had shaped popular perceptions of native peoples since the white man first set foot in the "new world," asserting that in his book the reader would instead "discover in the Indian a subject for thoughtful study and investigation."[1] Coming from the pen of George Armstrong Custer, whose place in popular memory was secured through violent death at the hands of those very subjects for thoughtful study, the contemplative and scholarly tone of these words has a certain irony, and, indeed, the style of Custer's *My Life on the Plains*, memoirs of his "Indian fighter" days, often bears stronger resemblance to dime novel melodramatics than to ethnographic treatise.

Almost four decades after Custer's demise in 1876, the Indian had been all but evicted from the vast unsettled plains but had secured a lasting home within the small confines of the moving picture screen, where both "savage savage" and "noble savage" continued to roam freely. In 1912, two films in simultaneous production finished shooting on the same day, the New York Motion Picture Company's *Custer's Last Fight*, directed by Francis Ford and "produced under the personal supervision of Thomas H. Ince," and the Biograph Company's *The Massacre*, directed by D. W. Griffith.[2] The former climaxes with its eponymous hero's death at his famous "last stand," while the latter, considered by some a "loose interpretation of the battle" of the Little Big Horn,[3] climaxes with the valiant resistance of a small band of white settlers against an overwhelming number of hostile Indians, only a mother and small child surviving the fight. But for our purposes another scene in *The Massacre* proves more enlightening.

Title: "In the far west. The scout takes part in the surprise attack on the Indian village." Shot of a long cavalry column led by the scout and an officer with long hair, mustache and beard,[4] followed by a long shot of a peaceful Indian village. Cut to a medium interior of a tepee where a woman tries to comfort a crying baby. Cut back to cavalry column and then back to the interior of the tepee. A man enters and caresses the crying child. Cut back to cavalry column as the cavalry officer draws his sabre and the soldiers attack. Extreme long shots show the cavalry charging into the surprised Indians, who at first mill around in confusion but then begin to fight back. Closer shots show the Indians resisting, focusing upon the little family first seen in their tepee. The father, now wearing a buffalo headdress, stands in front of his tepee shooting at the invaders, but a trooper nonetheless kills the fleeing mother and child. Cut to extreme long shot from the top of a hill, as the father enters from offscreen and stands in the foreground, his back to the camera, looking down on his devastated village. The scene concludes with shots of the Indian survivors gathered in the hills watching the cavalry column leave, followed by a lingering shot of the village—dead bodies, smoldering fire, barking dog—that presages the "War's Peace" shots of *The Birth of a Nation*. Judging simply from textual evidence, the "massacre" of the polysemous title could refer equally well to the deaths of the Indians at the hand of the whites as the reverse, but, in either case, it is certainly the bereaved Indian father who later seeks revenge by leading the assault upon the settlers.

Custer's Last Fight much less readily lends itself to polysemous interpretation, as we can see by looking at *its* singular massacre. Title: "Tom Custer meets a soldiers' death—and an Indian victim's fate when later Rain [in-the-Face] wreaks vengeance by cutting out his heart." Long shot of the "last stand" with flag in the background surrounded by cavalry troopers shooting rifles, as in the foreground the fatally wounded

Tom Custer collapses in his brother George's arms. Title: "The horses stampeded with the ammunition—outnumbered twelve to one, back to back, the gallant band faces the contracting whirling circle of death." Long shot of Indians on horseback circling round the beleaguered white survivors, Custer still visible and still shooting his revolver. Cut to closer shot as Custer picks up the flag and fixes it more firmly in the ground, then walks to the foreground. Cut to medium shot of Custer shooting revolver. Title: "Rain and his brother Crow King charge with a battle-mad mass of Unkpapa Sioux, overwhelming the field in a last red wave of destruction." Cut back to medium of Custer firing revolver. Title: "In less than an hour the last soldier falls, and the gallant Custer's death is worthy of his life." Shot of Indians rushing almost directly at the camera, firing rifles. Long shot of Custer being struck by bullet, as around him Indians, including women, are scalping the dead troopers. He puts the back of his hand to his forehead, staggers back, and collapses. Title: "The braves fire volley after volley into the bodies of the fallen, and the squaws and youths swarm onto the field for the ghastly work of stripping and mutilation."

Here then are two extremely divergent representations of Native Americans dating from the silent film era—the "simple-minded "son of nature" of *The Massacre* versus the "creature possessing the human form but divested of all other attributes of humanity" of *Custer's Last Fight*. The relatively sympathetic view of the former might be perceived as anomalous by those inclined to think that silent films represented Native Americans in a monolithically negative fashion. For example, Allen L. Woll and Randall M. Miller, in their book on race and ethnicity in the American film, assert that:

> Little attempt has been made by filmmakers to understand Indian motivations for action, as virtually all activities are characterized from the white man's point of view. Hence, when Indians attack white settlers, it becomes a "massacre." When soldiers attack Indian tribes, it is for the benefit of civilization and the advance of Western culture. . . . As fictional films flourished, the Indian was quickly given the status of one of the screen's dominant villains. . . . The Indian which evolved in the silent cinema seemed to have only two functions—to kill white men and to rape their women. . . . On some occasions a "noble savage" . . . emerged, who would ally with whites when the situation demanded.[5]

Contra Woll and Miller, I would argue that the silent screen reflected and refracted the complex and contradictory position and representation of Native Americans within contemporary U.S. society and culture.

Many silent Westerns, such as *Custer's Last Fight*, may conform to Woll and Miller's characterization, but many others, such as *The Massacre*, do not.

As the Indian wars wound down during the last years of the nineteenth century, the United States government tried yet another approach to the "Indian problem," the General Allotment, or Dawes Act of 1887, which divided the commonly held land of the reservations among the individual tribe members, the goal being to "fit the Indians . . . for the habits and occupations of civilized life . . . ; to individualize them in the possession and appreciation of property."[6] Through allotment and government sponsored off-reservation boarding schools, such as the Carlisle Indian Industrial School (which sought to "kill the Indian to save the man"), U.S. authorities sought a final solution to the Indian problem not through physical extermination but through cultural assimilation: Indians who adopted the habits of the white man would, in effect, cease to become Indians, losing their sense of tribal identity and merging into the white mainstream. During the 1920s, however, attitudes began to change, partially as a result of the notion of cultural relativism emerging in anthropology, the shift in perspective culminating in the 1930s in New Deal efforts to preserve both tribal governments and tribal customs.

While the United States government had, perforce, to deal with the contemporary Indian, many producers of cultural texts, both fact and fiction, were more interested in the historical Indian or, at least, with traditional Indian lifestyles as still practiced in the present. In some of these texts, generally the more "popular" forms, such as Wild West shows and boy's fiction, the need for spectacle and/or narrative clarity often demanded that the Indians be the unambivalently negative "savage savages" who served as impediments to an advancing civilization during the period of westward expansion. Yet, as Custer suggested, myriad other texts balanced this negative representation, portraying the Indians as innocent victims who wished merely to lead the life their ancestors had before them, yet whom the white man systematically betrayed. Proponents of this position strongly condemned government policy toward the Indians, arguing that the white man had behaved with consistent bad faith in making, and then breaking, often violently, the numerous treaties which persuaded various tribes to cede more and more land.[7] Yet an inherent contradiction lay at the heart of this critique: Even the Indians' strongest advocates often believed that their only hope for survival lay in total assimilation. The majority of these "friends of the Indian," as defenders of Native Americans were often termed, accepted that the indigenous peoples would inevitably succumb to the onrushing stronger civilization and shared Custer's expressed desire to make the Indian "a subject for thoughtful study and investigation." Rather than defending the Indians' cultural autonomy or trying to improve their current living conditions, many rather strove frantically to capture the so-called "vanishing Americans" before they disappeared forever—by celebrating the exploits of their ancestors in books such as Hamlin Garland's *The Book of the American Indian* or by documenting traditional lifestyles through oral histories and photography, as in the work of Edward S. Curtis. The "vanishing American," already established as a powerful metaphor early in the nineteenth century by James Fenimore Cooper among others, became a prevalent trope of the late nineteenth and early twentieth centuries, appearing in paintings, sculptures, novels, photographs, and scholarly treatises.[8]

Silent filmmakers, working within their culture's divergent and contradictory intertextual frame, portrayed Native Americans in divergent and contradictory fashion, as becomes apparent simply by glancing at the Library of Congress's filmography on the subject.[9] Aside from the obvious Westerns, the filmography includes paper print actualities such as *Carrying Out the Snakes* (Edison, 1901), Curtis's *In the Land of the War Canoes: Kwakiutl Indian Life on the Northwest Coast* (1914), and the fascinating *The Vanishing American* (Paramount, 1925), based on the Zane Grey novel of the same name, which shows the evolutionary succession of "races," including the Caucasian, in the American Southwest.[10]

Given the plethora of representations of Native Americans in the silent cinema, as well as the rich and complex intertextual frame in which texts must be situated in order more fully to understand their conditions of production and reception, focusing on films featuring the character of George Armstrong Custer permits us to keep several variables constant, as my social scientist friends say. All the films, despite their different emphases, purport to represent the same historical events and characters. They all feature the Plains Indians, most prominently the Lakota and Cheyenne, who had, as a result of providing the most continuous and recent resistance to Westward expansion, become the archetypal Native Americans in the popular mind.[11] Just as these tribes constituted archetypal Indians, the Battle of the Little Big Horn constituted the archetypal confrontation between the white man and the red man—"perhaps the most famous engagement of frontier history," said the *New York Times* during the fiftieth anniversary celebrations of the event in 1926.[12]

And, for some, George Armstrong Custer constituted the archetypal martyr on the alter of manifest destiny, the "greatest pride and brightest ornament" of the U.S. Cavalry,[13] although others took a somewhat dimmer view.

On Sunday, June 25, 1876, in the valley of the Little Big Horn River in Montana, Lakota and Cheyenne warriors led by Crazy Horse, Gall, and Two Moons, among others, and estimated as numbering anywhere from two thousand to fifteen thousand,[14] wiped out George Armstrong Custer and his immediate command, numbering about 225 officers, troopers, and civilians, and also inflicted severe casualties upon the remaining Seventh Cavalry companies commanded by Major Marcus A. Reno. For the first half century after its occurrence, the Little Big Horn retained a central position in American popular memory, the subject of numerous works of fact and fiction: lithographs; Wild West shows; battlefield re-enactments; dime novels; historical novels; historical monographs; and, of course, motion pictures.[15]

Many of these texts took a reverential tone to an event that, despite initial controversy, had been transformed into an epic defeat, often compared to Thermopylae or the Charge of the Light Brigade. Consider the characterizations of the battle in two historical novels, later adapted to the screen. Randall Parrish, author of *Bob Hampton of Placer*, said, "No voice can ever repeat the story in its fulness, no eye penetrate into the heart of its mystery. . . . With moistened eyes and swelling hearts, we vainly strive to imagine the whole scene. This, at least, we know: no bolder, nobler deed of arms was ever done."[16] Cyrus Brady, author of *Britton of the Seventh*, adopted the same semi-mystical tone. "What is hallowed ground? It is where men have died with courage in the fulfillment of duty. There are few spots in America more sacred in our memories than that lonely ridge on that desolate upland by the side of the little river flowing gently through that valley in the heart of Montana."[17] The producers of *Custer's Last Fight* referenced this prevalent view in their publicity, calling their film a "perfect reproduction of the most heroic incident in the nation's history, eclipsing by far the famous English charge of the Light Brigade."[18]

For producers and audiences during the teens and twenties, the battle of the Little Big Horn may have had the same potent ideological resonance with contemporary problems as Pearl Harbor does for us today. In the late twentieth century, representations of Pearl Harbor, particularly during the sesquicentennial celebrations, relate to contemporary debates about the decline of American economic power and Japan's ascendance as the nation's chief competitor. In the early twentieth century, representations of the Little Big Horn related to debates about the closing of the frontier, the transformation to an industrial, urban nation, and, perhaps most importantly, the defense of "white civilization" against the "lesser" races.[19] With regard to the last, consider the title of a 1913 boy's adventure novel: *On the Plains with Custer: The Western Life and Deeds of the Chief with the Yellow Hair . . . When in the Troublous Years 1866–1876 the Fighting Seventh Cavalry Helped to Win Pioneer Kansas, Nebraska, and Dakota for White Civilization and Today's Peace.*[20] The foreword to another boy's novel of the period, Captain Ralph Bonehill's *With Custer in the Black Hills*, makes the same association, speaking of the dangers pioneers faced from "treacherous Indians" in Custer's time. "And yet this was less than thirty years ago! How marvelous have been the strides of Western civilization in that time!"[21]

The ideologically resonant incidents of June 25, 1876, were popularly known not as the "Battle of the Little Big Horn" but rather as "Custer's Last Stand," or some variant thereof, for the deceased commander of the Seventh figured prominently in the mythification of the event. As Elbridge S. Brooks, author of the boy's novel *The Master of the Strong Hearts: A Story of Custer's Last Rally*, said, "The memory of General George Armstrong Custer will live as long as the story of American heroism holds him as one of its brightest examples."[22] The defeat at the Little Big Horn shocked much of white America not only because it marred the nation's centenary celebrations, but also because it marked the demise of the famous "boy general" of the Civil War, the flamboyant twenty-three-year-old cavalryman who had led charge after charge, sabre in hand and his long yellow hair floating around his head, until, at war's end, he lost his brevet rank of major-general to become Lieutenant Colonel Custer of the newly formed Seventh Cavalry, sent West with his troops to the desolate plains where he must have feared that he would quickly be forgotten. But the country's fascination with the Indian wars, a run of good luck in pursuing and defeating his elusive foe, and his own energetic self-promotion through such venues as *My Life on the Plains* kept him in the public eye.

Immediately after the battle, as the military, the government, and the general public wondered how a mere horde of savages had managed to butcher the finest cavalry regiment in the army, Custer seemed an obvious scapegoat and hard questions arose: Had he disobeyed his orders by failing to coordinate his actions with the other forces deployed in the summer campaign; had he ensured his own defeat by dividing the regiment; had he been so eager for a glorious victory that he had acted rashly? Custer's widow Elizabeth stepped in to rescue her beloved "Autie's" reputation, persuading Frederick Whittaker, formerly cavalryman in the Union Army and, in 1876, author of dime novels for the house of Beadle and Adams, to write what we would today term an authorized biography.[23] Whittaker laid the blame for the defeat upon President Grant, whose political machinations had supposedly delayed Custer taking the field for a month, and upon Major Reno, whose cowardly failure to carry out Custer's orders had supposedly enabled the Indians to massacre his commander. Mrs. Custer put her own pen in the service of her husband's memory, her five volumes of memoirs painting a laudatory picture of the noble, generous, and brave Autie who met a hero's death in the service of his country. While dissenting opinions continued to be voiced, the Whittaker analysis generally prevailed, particularly in popular cultural forms such as boys' novels, and, to some extent, the cinema. By the fiftieth anniversary of the battle, President Calvin Coolidge valorized Custer as "the gallant General who did so much to help in winning the West" and the "officer whose courage will always be a shining example to the members of our army and navy establishments."[24] In an era marked by debates over immigration quotas, panic over white slavery, the rebirth of the Ku Klux Klan, and other indices of a generalized xenophobia, the ideological link between the "last stand" and the defense of "white civilization" may have helped to preserve Custer as a relatively unblemished popular hero, despite the sympathy expressed by many for his Indian foes.[25]

Reviewing *Custer's Last Fight* in *The Moving Picture World*, Louis Reeves Harrison, according with fairly widely held sentiment, referred to Custer as one "who gave his life to the preservation of what was best in this fair country of ours" and as one whom "the nation has crowned a martyr."[26] Despite the ambivalent status of Native Americans in United States society and culture, Custer's iconic status and the centrality of the "last stand" to American national identity during the silent film era might lead us to expect the casting of the Indian foes as villains, as stereotypical "savage savages." While *Custer's Last Fight* certainly does this, other period Custer films do not and the remainder of this essay seeks to explain these differing representational strategies. The silent film period produced at least nine, and perhaps more, films featuring the "hero" of the Little Big Horn.[27] *On the Little Big Horn; or, Custer's Last Stand* (Selig, 1909) was probably the first of the silent Custer films, while the sesquicentennial, taking place a year before the transition to sound ensued, produced two of the last, *The Flaming Frontier* (Universal Pictures, 1926) and *General Custer at Little Big Horn* (Sunset Productions, 1926). I have located a print of this last, together with prints of *Custer's Last Fight*, released in three reels in 1912 and re-issued in a five-reel expanded version in 1925 (the re-issue the surviving copy), and of another Ince film, *Custer's Last Scout* (New York Motion Picture Company, 1915). In addition, two "lost" Custer films, *Britton of the Seventh* (Vitagraph, 1916) and *Bob Hampton of Placer* (First National, 1921) were based on novels of the same name and, according to reviews, seem to have adhered fairly closely to their sources, justifying the inclusion of the original sources in the analysis to some extent.

Custer: Hero or Supporting Player

Of the three extant films, only one text, *Custer's Last Fight*, features Custer as the central protagonist and focuses primarily upon the battle of the Little Big Horn and antecedent events, while *Custer's Last Scout* and *General Custer At Little Big Horn* individualize history in the fashion typical of the Hollywood cinema, featuring fictional characters whose lives and loves are set against the backdrop of the 1876 Indian wars. Of the three, *Custer's Last Fight* constitutes the most iconic representation of Custer and his last stand, and, perhaps not coincidentally, the most negative representation of the Indian foe. The film displays its initial credits alongside an oval portrait of Custer that bears a strong resemblance to the engraving in the frontispiece of the laudatory Whittaker biography from which it borrows other elements as well. An intertitle preceding the introduction of the title figure speaks of his "brilliant services in the Civil War" and describes him as "a fighter of fighters of the Indians," although nothing in the film upholds this assessment. The next shot shows Custer in his iconographically correct buckskins and long hair, while the following title tells us that the general's men called him "Old Curley" and his Indian foes "The White Chief with the Yellow Hair" or "Long Hair." The film concludes with a contemporary (fictional) sequence showing the dedication of the Little Big Horn battlefield monument to Custer, the shot of the unveiling preceded by the following intertitle: "The noble Custer fell, bequeathing to the nation his sword; to his comrades an example; to his friends a memory; and to his beloved a Hero's name." These are the last lines of the epilogue of the Whittaker biography, reminiscences of Custer written by Lawrence Barrett, prominent actor-manager and his best friend.[28]

In *Custer's Last Scout* and *General Custer At Little Big Horn* the fictional characters take central stage, reducing Custer to supporting player, albeit one with a boffo death scene. The first film concerns the adventures of "Alfred L. Chapman the only living white witness to the famous massacre of General George Armstrong Custer and soldiers of the 7th US Cavalry," although so many tales feature "only survivors" that Custer's troops would have overpowered the enemy by sheer force of numbers had all these fictional characters participated in the battle. While Chapman and his fictional rival for the fictional heroine's hand play at "cowboys and Indians," Custer sits in his office and issues orders. Custer even loses his customary iconographic distinction, both he and Chapman appearing in practically identical buckskins, hats, hair, and mustaches (the similarity contributing to the film's already considerable narrative confusion). Surprisingly, Custer does not even stand out much at his own "last stand." Chapman watches the curiously undramatic climactic scene from a nearby hilltop, the extreme long shots of his point-of-view intercut with closer, but still fairly long, shots of the battlefield action. In fact, not until all the others have fallen does Custer become distinguishable, as he stands next to his horse shooting two pistols until several Indians simultaneously shoot him. As we shall see, the Indians in this film are curiously neutral, seeming more like narrative functions than characters.

The hero of *General Custer at Little Big Horn*, Lem Hawks, described as "soldier of Fortune" and "official scout attached to Custer's staff," competes with an army officer for the hand of the fair heroine, as does Chapman in *Custer's Last Scout*. Unlike Chapman, however, Hawk's sartorial splendor far outstrips that of his commander, for in his standard Hollywood cowboy outfit—fringed leather gauntlets, complete with painted decorations, fringed shirt, and bandanna—he cuts a much more glamorous figure than the rather short and scrawny Custer, whose not particularly blond hair remains short throughout the film and whose trademark buckskins do not appear until the conclusion. In keeping with the relative importance accorded its characters, this film's "last stand" focuses more on Hawks and his rival, Page, than on Custer. In fact, the film does not even show its titular character's death! And while an intertitle during the "last stand" sequence refers to the Indians as "the naked savage," the film has earlier established strong motivation for their actions and seems on the whole fairly positively disposed toward them.

The above analysis seems to indicate an inverse correlation between the deification of Custer and the demonization of his foes, but further explanation of the contradictory representations of the Native American characters in the extant Custer films can derive only from reference to the period's extensive intertexts concerning Custer, his Indian opponents, and the Little Big Horn battle. Taking this intertextual approach, I shall not continue to treat each film as a separate entity and engage in extensive textual analysis, but shall instead treat the films thematically, situating each within three primary components of the period's intertextual frame: the general representation of Native Americans; the representation of the Sioux sub-chief Rain-in-the-Face; and the representation of the Sioux holy man Sitting Bull. How did the filmmakers select from the rich repertoire of available representations to fashion their own interpretations of historical events and peoples?

General Representation of Native Americans

In 1877, Henry Wadsworth Longfellow commemorated the battle of the Little Big Horn in his poem "The Revenge of Rain-in-the-Face," from which, for reasons that will shortly become apparent, I take my title. The last lines place the blame for the disaster not upon the eponymous villain but upon the United States government:

> And say that our broken faith
> Wrought all this ruin and scathe,
> In the Year of a Hundred Years.

In the silent film period, when many texts valorized the "vanishing American," being "a friend of the Indian" could have many possible manifestations, from striving for the accurate rendition of Native American lifestyles to praising Native American lifestyles as superior to that of the white man, to casting Native American actors as Native American characters, which, despite the valorization of *Dances with Wolves*, seems to have been fairly standard practice during much of the silent film era.[29] For my purposes, however, I want to narrow the focus to the issue that has always been at the center of white/Indian conflict and that the conclusion of Longfellow's poem implicitly invokes—the land and the white man's "broken faith" in constantly reneging on solemnly executed treaties guaranteeing the original inhabitants their rights. All "friends of the Indian" lamented the government's bad dealings, while even many of those who resisted the sentimentalization of the "vanishing American" admitted that Indians had justifiable grievances. For example, Cyrus Brady, author of *Britton of the Seventh* as well as the earlier *Indian*

Fights and Fighters, said that "putting aside all questions of their cruelty and brutality . . . they were patriots fighting for the possession of their native land."[30] In fact, that noted authority on and fighter of Indians, with whose opinions this article commenced, also commented on the land issue. Said Custer, "When the soil which [the Indian] has claimed and hunted over for so long a time is demanded by this to him insatiable monster [civilization], there is no appeal; he must yield, or . . . it will roll mercilessly over him, destroying as it advances."[31]

In the days after the news of the defeat at the Little Big Horn spread through the nation, as many in a "homicidal frenzy" clamored "for the instant extermination of the savages," the *New York Times* counseled moderation, speaking against those who accorded with the "frontier theory that the only use to which an Indian can be put is to kill him." Rather, said the *Times*, the Indians had exhibited long forbearance in the face of repeated treaty violations, the most egregious of which occurred in 1873 when Custer's exploratory expedition to the Black Hills, the Lakota's most sacred site and supposedly "ceded to them forever" by the Fort Laramie treaty of 1868, led to a "rush of reckless gold hunters." As did Longfellow, the *Times* blamed the white man, not the red, for the Little Big Horn: "It was not until after we . . . had openly abandoned all pretense of observing our treaty obligations, that the Indians . . . with the aid of outlying clans like the band of Sitting Bull renewed the fight of centuries against white aggression."[32] Even Whittaker's hagiography identified the 1873 expedition as the primary cause of the Little Big Horn and Custer's death, albeit exonerating his hero in the process: "Strange, but an illustration of poetic justice, that the very man who, in obeying his orders, became the instrument of injustice towards the Indians, should fall a victim in the contest which ensued."[33]

General Custer at Little Big Horn permits the Native American characters to articulate their claims upon the land, thereby to some extent justifying their actions at the Little Big Horn. Titles identify the main Indian characters as "Sitting Bull, Medicine Man and Chieftain," "Chief Little Horse, Cheyenne warrior, who would join with Sitting Bull and create an Indian Empire," and "Chief Gall, Sioux warrior, for whom the government has offered a reward, dead or alive." Long shots show the chiefs as an impressive group, attired in their full regalia—warbonnets with beaded headbands and fur strips dangling down, decorated buckskin jackets and bead necklaces—noble savages indeed. Medium shots single out each man as he speaks to the others in sign language, intertitles then translating his words into English. Chief Little Horse says, "Soon will there be no Buffalo—no lands for the red man—soon will the red man die. The White man wants Indians to live on reservation—prisoners!" Sitting Bull and Gall agree, the former saying that they will need many warriors and Gall saying that he will go to the reservation to recruit. Immediately preceding the Little Big Horn, the film shows "the war council of the Sioux and Cheyennes in the camp of Sitting Bull." Say the chiefs: "When we drive away the whites, the Indian will once more roam the plains, a free man" and "We must fight for what is ours." The film's sympathetic representation extends to discrediting the only explicitly anti-Indian character. Captain Page, the army officer who is the hero's rival in love, is ordered by Custer to capture Chief Gall, but disobeys, instead instructing his sergeant to kill the Indian leader. Lem Hawks, our hero, disapproves, calling Page "a disgrace to the uniform," the assessment confirmed when the captain flirts with another officer's wife. When this cad explains his disobedience to his commander by reference to what the *New York Times* in 1876 referred to as the "frontier theory"—saying, "A good Indian is a dead Indian"—his words do not persuade Custer and should not have persuaded the contemporary viewer.

Custer's Last Fight, which does in the main hold to the "frontier theory," still has to acknowledge Indian claims to the land, even if only to buttress its negative representation by providing a counter-argument. The opening series of titles sets up the conflict. The introductory title reads, "From the Missouri River to the Rocky Mountains . . . ranged the wildest and most powerful of the Plains Indians—the Sioux. They and their allies, the Cheyennes, bitterly opposed the advance of the white man and civilization." This is followed by a close-up of an Indian warrior in full headdress and then by another title, this showing a drawing of an Indian with his hand raised and saying, "Keep Out! Ours are these plains where the buffalo roams." Shot of buffalo follows then another title: "Ours are the hillsides where the deer is found." Shot of deer on hillside, then another title: "Ours the lakes and streams where the fish abound—Keep out!" Shot of lakes and streams.

Since a viewer sympathetic to the Native Americans' plight might well have interpreted these initial shots and titles as an endorsement of Indian land claims, the text moves to contain the potential polysemy. The next title reads, "Continually alert to surprise and overwhelm the pale-face these hostile Indians overlooked no opportunity to do their deadly work." Shot of three Indians lurking behind bush. Another title: "Most determined were they to keep the white man out of that rich hunting ground on the slopes of the Black Hill Mountains in Wyoming and Montana." Cut back to the three Indians and then another title: "And the immigrants and forts on the Bozeman wagon trail to Montana were subject to constant attack." In the following sequence, a cavalry column arrives in the nick of time to rescue the beleaguered defenders of a fort. Another title: "Their warfare was so persistent and savage and their entreaty so earnest, that in 1868 Congress ordered the three forts . . . abandoned and granted to the Sioux for their *exclusive* use a vast territory—thus filling them with pride and insolence." The film returns to the title card of the Indian holding up his hand to halt the white man. It now reads, "But the westward flow of civilization cannot be dammed, and in 1873 a survey is made under military guard for the Northern Pacific Railroad." The title card illustration changes from the forbidding Indian to a white man holding a surveying instrument. George Armstrong Custer and his Seventh Cavalry provided the military guard the title mentions, and, as previously noted, both Whittaker and *The New York Times* identified this expedition as the first in a chain of events leading to the Little Big Horn.

In its introductory sequence, *Custer's Last Fight* first implicitly acknowledges Indian claims to the land and then implicitly invokes a common legitimation for Westward expansion; that Native Americans had *de facto* forfeited their rights by not exploiting the land in accordance with Euro-American economic practices. No need to invoke the raw "frontier theory" equating "good Indians" with "dead Indians," for the more respectable discourses of Social Darwinism and teleological historiography demanded that a few half-naked hunter/gatherers make way for the farmers, miners, ranchers, and other enterprising white men who would much more efficiently use the vast tracts of "empty" Western land than could their current inhabitants. Even Whittaker lambasted this casuistry with an uncharacteristic hyperbolic irony, as he spoke of the reasons for the 1873 exploratory expedition: "The treaty with the Northern Indians became irksome. It was all well enough to *promise* a lot of naked savages to give them up so much land, but it could not be expected that such a promise should be *kept* a moment longer than was necessary to secure a quiet building of the railroad. It was now time to break the treaty."[34] For one holding this view, the opening shots of nature's bounty in *Custer's Last Fight*—buffalo, deer, fish—could be read not as upholding Indian land claims but as demanding westward expansion.

Those who hewed more closely to the "frontier theory" represented Native Americans not as occupants of the lower rungs of the evolutionary ladder, and thus perhaps deserving of salvation, but rather as simply inhuman—evil supernatural beings, or devastating natural forces or predatory animals—and thus deserving only of extermination. Such characterizations were part of a widespread popular discourse. Immediately after the battle of the Little Big Horn, the surviving enlisted men of the Seventh petitioned General Sheridan for Major Reno's and Captain Benteen's promotions, saying that, but for their actions, the enemy would have occupied a more strategically advantageous position: "behind those heights the Indian demons would have swarmed in hundreds."[35] Whittaker melodramatically describes the flight for life of the young Lieutenant Kidder and his eleven troopers: "A mere handful of brave men struggling to escape the bloody clutches of the hundreds of red-visaged demons who . . . were straining every nerve and muscle to steep their hands in the life-blood of their victims. . . ."[36] In *Bob Hampton of Placer*, Randall Parrish pictures the last moments of the "last stand": "Like a whirlwind those red demons came,—howling wolves now certain of their prey."[37] Earlier in the book, the initial encounter with the Indians had occasioned a fuller deployment of the non-human imagery:

> The narrow defile echoed to wild screeches and became instantly crowded with weird, leaping figures. It was like a plunge from heaven into hell. . . . these first volleys . . . proved sufficient to check the howling demons. . . . and those dark figures . . . suddenly melted from sight, slinking . . . into holes among the rocks, like so many vanishing prairie dogs. . . . Yet the experienced frontiersmen knew that eyes as keen as those of any wild animal of the jungle were murderously watching their slightest movement.[38]

This kind of imagery appears in industry discourse concerning Custer films. The Selig Company's description of its 1909 *On The Little Big Horn* refers to a "band of naked, painted devils" and to the "yelling, red fiends."[39] Vitagraph's description of *Britton of the Seventh* refers to Rain-in-the-Face as "the red devil."[40] As one might expect, *Custer's Last Fight* is the extant Custer film adhering most closely to the non-human characterization. Recall these key phrases from the intertitles describing the "last stand": "a battle-mad mass of Unkpapa Sioux, overwhelming the field in a last red wave of destruction," and "the braves fire volley after volley into the bodies of the fallen, and the squaws and youths swarm onto the field for the ghastly work of stripping and mutilation." Louis Reeves Harrison, perhaps implicitly responding to the "noble savage" imagery so often deployed in the silent cinema, reinforces the non-human theme in his *Moving Picture World* review of the film:

> The Sioux Indians in the battle of the Little Big Horn were terrible fighters, but aside from their bravery were as destitute of nobility as other savage races. They were merciless to the weak, inhuman in their outrages upon white women and children and were as incapable of gratitude as any body of grafters now supported by the Government. The real heroes were on the other side.[41]

As the above illustrates, the Custer films' representation of Native Americans must be understood within the context of the period's extensive "pro-Indian" and "anti-Indian" intertexts. Reference to the intertextual frames concerning Rain-in-the-Face and Sitting Bull, the two Native American leaders featured most prominently in contemporary popular discourse about Custer and the Little Big Horn, further illuminates the Custer films' representational strategies.[42] Sitting Bull appears in *Custer's Last Fight* and *General Custer at the Little Big Horn*, but not in *Custer's Last Scout*, and Rain-in-the-Face appears in *Custer's Last Fight* and *Custer's Last Scout*, but not in *General Custer at Little Big Horn*.

Rain-in-the-Face and Sitting Bull

In his commemorative poem "The Revenge of Rain-in-the-Face," Longfellow has his titular character cry, "Revenge upon all the race, Of the White Chief with yellow hair!" In the next stanza he wreaks his vengeance, ripping the heart from Custer's body:

> But the foemen fled in the night,
> And Rain-in-the-Face, in his flight,
> Uplifted high in air,
> As a ghastly trophy, bore
> The brave heart, that beat no more,
> Of the White Chief with yellow hair.

Longfellow here repeats one of the many variants of Rain-in-the-Face's actions at the Little Big Horn. In what seems to be the most prevalent version, Rain-in-the-Face had sworn to cut out, and perhaps eat, *Tom* Custer's heart, not George's. According to several accounts, "fact" and fiction, during the 1873 Black Hills expedition, Rain-in-the-Face ambushed and killed two harmless civilians, a veterinarian and sutler, attached to the column. After the sub-chief was overheard boasting about the "murders," George Custer dispatched his brother Tom to arrest him.

Rain-in-the-Face managed to escape from the guardhouse in which he was confined but swore vengeance upon Captain Custer, in some versions even sending him a bloody heart drawn upon buffalo hide. Rain-in-the-Face did indeed keep his threat, cutting the still beating heart from Tom's prostrate body and biting out a piece of it. In other versions, however, the sub-chief kills *George* Custer, sometimes cutting out *his* heart, as Longfellow suggests.

Whittaker's biography devotes an entire chapter to Rain-in-the-Face. Speaking of his supposed victims during the 1873 expedition, Whittaker says that "these two men were remotely the cause of Custer's own death, three years later."[43] In a melodramatic climax (and a somewhat questionable syntax) worthy of his dime novels, Whittaker actually has Rain-in-the-Face kill *George* Custer, although the culinary feast does not follow. "When only a few of the officers were left alive, the Indians made a hand to hand charge, in which Custer fought like a tiger with his sabre when his last shot was gone, that he killed or wounded three Indians with the sabre, and that as he ran the last man through, *Rain-in-the-Face kept his oath and shot Custer*."[44] Selig's *On the Little Big Horn*, perhaps the first Custer film, also seems to have accorded Rain-in-the-Face and his revenge narrative centrality. The film apparently began with "the arrest of 'Rain-in-the-Face' by young Tom Custer . . . in our first three scenes." Later the sub-chief led "Custer's cavalry into a trap," and at the film's climactic "last stand," "the red circle of death closes in about them and Rain-in-the-Face is avenged."[45]

Perhaps indebted to the Whittaker biography and the Selig film, *Custer's Last Fight* structures its entire narrative around Rain-in-the-Face and the revenge he exacts (or, in this case, literally extracts) from Tom Custer. As described above, the film opens with the 1873 exploratory expedition into the Black Hills. After a shot of the veterinarian and the sutler, a title introduces Rain-in-the-Face, "a young Sioux buck . . . eager to prove his prowess." We see two feathers sticking up over a hill and then Rain-in-the-Face emerges beneath them, looking directly at the camera and talking to himself. A title declares, "This is a good opportunity—two unsuspecting civilians," although the words could be attributed either to Rain-in-the-Face or the heavy handed irony of the narrating agency. Rain-in-the-Face kills the two white men and returns to the Indian village where he "proudly displays his trophies [scalps]." The film then follows the version of the story recounted by Cyrus Brady in his *Indian Fights and Fighters*: the sub-chief is overheard boasting of the "murders"; Custer sends his brother to arrest him; the sub-chief escapes and, as an intertitle puts it, "Captain Tom Custer gains the undying enmity of Rain-in-the-Face." During the last stand, another intertitle tells us, "Tom Custer meets a soldiers' death—and an Indian victim's fate when later the sub-chief wreaks vengeance by cutting out his heart." Louis Reeves Harrison's review of the film gives a more graphic description, supposedly quoting from Rain-in-the-Face himself: "I leaped from my pony and cut out his heart. I bit a piece out of it and spit it in his face."[46]

The characterization of Rain-in-the-Face in *Custer's Last Fight* and many other popular Custer texts fulfills what might be termed an ideological displacement function that helps to resolve the contradiction posed by having at least covertly to acknowledge Indian land claims. Consider the sub-chief's role in the Whittaker biography. The book purports to be "history," but its narrative structure and prose style bear strong resemblance to melodramatic dime novels, a contradiction that results in competing explanatory paradigms for the Little Big Horn battle. First, Whittaker refers to larger structural causes by saying that "all the subsequent trouble of the Sioux war really sprang from the deliberate violation by the United States Government of its own freely plighted faith," an implicit allusion to the 1873 depression that put pressure upon the government to support Westward expansion. Subsequently, however, Whittaker shifts explanatory paradigms, devoting a chapter to the 1873 expedition and giving prominence not to economic forces but rather to Rain-in-the-Face's attack upon the two civilians whose deaths "were remotely the cause of Custer's own death, three years later."[47] An historical analysis of the cause of the 1876 Plains Indian Wars might well emphasize the role of the United States government and entrepreneurs such as railroad and mining magnates, while many popular texts up through the silent film era instead place the blame upon a sole Indian "villain," Rain-in-the-Face, shifting responsibility from the white man to the red. This ascription of historical agency to an individual villain rather than to the economic demands that motivated repeated treaty violations seems common to many Custer texts. The Longfellow poem clearly displays this contradiction, the title blaming the individual agent, but the last line (quoted above) pointing to larger structural forces. This raises a fascinating chicken/egg question: Do ideological constraints demand that popular narratives individualize historical agency in order to resolve/disguise contradictions, or does the narrative structure of popular texts demand that individual agents be substituted for larger structural forces?

While fully addressing this question lies outside the scope of this essay, looking more closely at *Custer's Last Scout*, a text that does not use the character of Rain-in-the-Face to resolve an ideological contradiction, will provide another perspective on the issue of textual mediation—that is, how texts refract and rework, rather than simply reflect, a culture's ideological assumptions. In this film, a title introduces Rain-in-the-Face as "Custer's bitter enemy," but no previous narrative developments have motivated Rain-in-the-Face's enmity, perhaps because the viewer was presumed to be familiar with the numerous intertexts that had previously established the antagonism between the two. Nor does the sub-chief participate in his usual actions. Rather than being the sole killer of two civilians, he is one of a party of Indians that attacks and kills several army officers on a hunting expedition. Rather than being overheard boasting of his exploits, Rain-in-the-Face's arrest results from his being found with a watch belonging to one of the dead officers. And rather than the sub-chief seeking vengeance at the Little Big Horn, a title tells us that "enraged over the arrest of Rain-in-the-Face, his people plan to attack the white settlers." Rain-in-the-Face does not even appear during the "last stand" sequence.

This film, as opposed to *Custer's Last Fight*, neither explicitly nor implicitly raises the issue of Indian land rights and, hence, does not require the character of Rain-in-the-Face to serve the ideological displacement function. The character's function is instead almost wholly narratological—he provides a "bad Indian" for a plot in need of a villain, and the contemporary audience may have been intertextually predisposed to conceive of him as the "bad guy." Otherwise the film does not take a particularly malignant view of the Indian characters, who even speak their own language in a few intertitles. *Custer's Last Scout* therefore provides a good example of the relative autonomy of some fictional forms from ideology.

The Lakota holy man Sitting Bull also makes frequent appearances in Custer texts, eliciting more negative characterizations than any other Indian including Rain-in-the-Face, who, no matter his other "faults," is usually represented as a courageous warrior, while Sitting Bull is frequently depicted as cowardly. The hostility directed toward Sitting Bull may derive precisely from the fact that his role as a spiritual rather than a military leader rendered him potentially more subversive and harder to combat than war chiefs who could be decisively defeated in battle and subsequently valorized for their bravery in terms understandable to white culture—they were patriots fighting for their native land. War chiefs could also be persuaded to become peace chiefs, as in the case of Red Cloud, who had battled the white man until forcing the Laramie Treaty but subsequently proved reluctant to take to the war path again. But Sitting Bull, representing the "other" in its purest form, engaged in a *cultural* opposition that his white opponents could neither easily comprehend nor diffuse and posed a threat to the assimilationist agenda espoused even by "friends of the Indian."[48]

The Spirit Trail, a 1910 novel that advocates assimilation through Christianization, identifies Sitting Bull and his like as the white man's primary adversaries. Says the missionary character, "It is not the braves who are the stumbling block in the way of civilization and Christianity among the Dakotas, but the medicine men. I see Sitting Bull's wily and malevolent influence . . . his and that of others of his vicious pretensions to occult knowledge of the mysteries. Theirs is the evil genius that keeps in active ferment resistance to the white man's ways and the white man's God."[49] The conclusion of the boy's adventure novel *The Master of the Strong Hearts* makes much the same point. The now-adult white hero receives a visit from his now adult Lakota friend, who protected him from Sitting Bull at the time of the Little Big Horn and has subsequently been thoroughly assimilated, attending government schools and becoming a doctor. The doctor recites Longfellow's "The Revenge of Rain-in-the-Face" and comments:

> "Whose was the right and wrong?" The years must decide. I am of the vanishing race. But if we vanish as a race to become real Americans . . . even the "ruin and scathe" that hurled my brothers and your comrades to death have not been in vain. I am of the future; the past is forgotten. The Indian farm-lands that dot the valleys of my native West are to do more for my race than all the dreaming and all the medicine of [Sitting Bull].[50]

As if to disparage Sitting Bull by giving credit for the Indian victory solely to the more easily assimilable war chiefs, a repertoire of apocryphal tales circulated concerning his cowardly behavior at the battle of the Little Big Horn (being primarily a spiritual leader, he most probably did not participate in the actual fighting). In 1892, Edward S. Godfrey, a lieutenant with the Seventh at the time of the Little Big Horn, wrote a detailed description of the battle, saying of Sitting Bull: "He took no active part in the battle, but, as was his custom in time of danger, remained in the village 'making medicine.' Personally he was regarded as a great coward and a very great liar, 'a man with a big head and a little heart.'"[51] Others did not even credit Sitting Bull with having the courage to remain in the village, but rather asserted that he fled for safety to the hills, returning only when an Indian victory seemed assured. In 1903, W. Kent Thomas published what purported to be an interview with Rain-in-the-Face, who was by then performing at Coney Island. Rain-in-the-Face claims that "Sitting Bull went away to make more medicine and didn't come back till the fight was over" and that, while most Indians "gave him the credit of winning the fight because his medicine had won it," others such as the war chief Gall disagreed, saying, "We did the fighting, you only made medicine."[52] Still others further defamed Sitting Bull, reporting that he not only fled the village, but abandoned one of his twin sons in his haste to escape danger. This story appears, among other places, in Frederick Dellenbaugh's 1917 Custer biography, which is otherwise surprisingly sympathetic to the Indian cause: "Sitting Bull, not being physically very brave, was thoroughly frightened, and believing the day to be lost, he packed his effects hastily, losing one of his twin boys in the hurry, and, with his beloved family, scurried away on his horses for the safer, distant hills."[53]

Custer's Last Fight includes many of these apocryphal stories in constructing a very negative representation of Sitting Bull in the central narrative, somewhat balanced by a curiously ambivalent coda that may have been added for the 1925 re-issue. An intertitle introduces "Sitting Bull, the high chief and great medicine man of the Sioux and allied tribes—'big head but little heart'—cowardly, but crafty and capable to command dauntless war chiefs,—an implacable enemy of the white man." His followers consist of "ambitious bucks, outlaws, and disaffected braves from the agencies, who raid the country in savage bands, robbing and murdering the defenseless." When Major Reno attacks the village, "The Indians at first are thrown into a panic—Sitting Bull shares the general alarm." Shot of Sitting Bull and a very large woman in a tepee with a child. "And in his haste to evade danger leaves one of his twins." Shot of Sitting Bull and family in the hills. "Sitting Bull 'Makes medicine' for victory at a safe distance." The film's coda briefly reprises Sitting Bull's life from the Little Big Horn to his death, although not including the massacre at Wounded Knee that took place shortly thereafter. A title tells us, "Always defending the rights of his people he causes much trouble, and in 1890 he starts the Ghost Dance." Further titles explain the purpose of the Ghost Dance (to bring back all the dead Indians and drive the whites away) and assert that the arrest of Sitting Bull was ordered "to prevent an outbreak." After the film shows Sitting Bull's death at the hands of the Indian police, a title declares, "Thus ends ingloriously the life of Sitting Bull—patriot of the Sioux, to whose great generalship the monument on the battlefield of the Little Big Horn bears witness." Since the monument commemorated the fallen white soldiers, not the fallen Indian warriors, this constitutes a somewhat backhanded compliment that seems favorable only by contrast with the starkly negative representation of the main body of the film.

Although most popular-culture texts circulating in the silent film period seem to have portrayed Sitting Bull in overwhelmingly negative terms, some few offered more positive representations, ranging from grudging admiration to outright adulation. Said Whittaker, "He is an Indian of unusual powers of mind, and a warrior whose talent amounts to genius, while his stubborn heroism in defense of the last of his race is undeniable. . . . a general of the first natural order he must be, to have set the United States at defiance as he has for the last ten years."[54] In his "The Story of the Little Big Horn: Told from the Indian Standpoint by One of Their Race," Charles Eastman, a widely known Lakota who became a doctor and may have provided the model for the Indian doctor character quoted above, asserts that Sitting Bull, far from fleeing to the hills at the start of the battle, rallied his people with stirring oratory: "In the midst of the confusion, Sitting Bull stood by his teepee and addressed his people thus: 'Warriors, we have everything to fight for, and if we are defeated we shall have nothing to live for; therefore let us fight like brave men.'"[55] But Sitting Bull had his white admirers as well. In Hamlin Garland's short story "The Silent Eaters," an unnamed Lakota narrates the Little Big Horn and subsequent events, specifically countering the many negative representations in circulation: "You have heard those who now deride my chief and say that he was no warrior, that he was a coward, a man of no account; but they are ignorant fools who say this." Instead, says the narrator, Sitting Bull by an early age had "already attained rank as a valiant but not reckless warrior. . . . But his fame as a peacemaker had already far outrun his renown as a warrior. . . . He was a natural leader and a persuasive orator. A chief among my people . . . is a peacemaker and Sitting Bull was always gentle of voice." This Sitting Bull desires peace so strongly that, upon hearing that Custer is marching to find him, he proposes that his people move to land that the white man can not possibly want. "To show them that we do not care to fight I will move camp. Let us go deep into the West where the soil is too hard for the plow . . . and there live in peace."[56]

In *General Custer at Little Big Horn*, Sitting Bull is not sanctified to this extent, but neither is he demonized as in *Custer's Last Fight*. As noted above, the sequence in which the assembled chiefs relate their grievances against the white man revels in the visual spectacle of these "noble savages." The scene fades out on a medium close-up of Sitting Bull in right profile, as if in a portrait by George Catlin, a photograph by Edward S. Curtis, or an Indian head nickel by the United States mint, all poses resonant of the sentimentalized "vanishing American." Not only does the film permit the Indian leaders to protest the injustices the white man has perpetrated against them, it provides Sitting Bull with additional motivation for taking up arms. The reader may recall that the caddish army officer instructs his sergeant to kill rather than capture Chief Gall, but the soldier bungles his assignment, merely wounding his target. And an intertitle tells us that "Chief Gall did not die. His near-death was the cause of hundreds of Indians rallying to the call of Sitting Bull." Not until this point in the film do the Indians attack a wagon train and a settlement.

As should by now be amply apparent, Custer films represented Native Americans in contradictory and complex fashion. Modern critics should not assume a "natural" movement toward more "accurate," "authentic," or "balanced" representations, automatically valorizing more recent Custer films such as *Little Big Man* (Arthur Penn, 1970) over their silent predecessors. Such an assumption entails both the teleological fallacy that our culture has progressed toward a "fairer" representation of oppressed peoples—while we have seen that the representation of Native Americans in silent films was by no means monolithically negative—and the reflective fallacy that texts simply embody the culture's ideological tropes—while we have seen that one must account for textual mediations. Full understanding of the representation of Native Americans in silent Custer films must entail consideration not only of the contemporary cultural position of Native Americans, but also the relevant intertextual frames concerning key figures such as Custer, Rain-in-the-Face, and Sitting Bull, specific textual factors such as narrative structure and the general ideological climate of xenophobia.

Notes

I would like to thank my research assistants, Mika Emori and Andrea MacDonald, for their invaluable help, and the University of Pennsylvania Research Foundation for financial support.

1. George Armstrong Custer, *My Life on the Plains, or, Personal Experiences with Indians* (Norman: University of Oklahoma Press, 1976), p. 14.

2. Kevin Brownlow, *The War, the West and the Wilderness* (New York: Alfred A. Knopf, 1979), p. 257.

3. Paul Andrew Hutton describes the film this way in his essay "From Little Bighorn to Little Big Man," in Paul Andrew Hutton, ed., *The Custer Reader* (Lincoln: University of Nebraska Press, 1992), p. 404, and *The Massacre* often appears in Custer filmographies as do such other "loose interpretations" as *Fort Apache*. Provisionally accepting *The Massacre* into the Custer "canon" seems appropriate since any 1912 film in which a group of white defenders was killed to the last man would undoubtedly have reminded the audience of the most famous of all "last stands."

4. The only aspect of the officer's appearance that conforms to the standard Custer iconography is his long hair, and even that is not blond. Nor does he wear Custer's famous buckskins. The fact that the scout carries a cavalry guidon emblazoned with an "eight" for Eighth Cavalry also distances this fictional unit from Custer and the Seventh Cavalry. Hence, I shall not continue to include this film in my analysis.

5. Allen L. Woll and Randall M. Miller, *Ethnic and Racial Images in American Film and Television* (New York: Garland, 1987), pp. 327, 328.

6. Carl Schurz, "Present Aspects of the Indian Problem," *North American Review*, July 1881, p. 6, quoted in Brian Dippie, *The Vanishing American: White Attitudes and U.S. Indian Policy* (Lawrence: University Press of Kansas, 1982), p. 161.

7. One of the strongest condemnations of United States policy was Helen Hunt Jackson's *A Century of Dishonor: A Sketch of the United States Government's Dealing with Some of the Indian Tribes*. Published in 1880, a mere four years after the Little Big Horn, the book chronicled the white man's mistreatment of the Indian from colonial times down to the present day. Four years later, in 1884, Jackson wrote the best-selling novel *Ramona*, focusing on California Indians. D. W. Griffith adapted the novel to the screen in 1910, this film, like *The Massacre*, featuring white men destroying an Indian village.

8. For information on the social and cultural position of Native Americans during this period, see Brian W. Dippie, *Custer's Last Stand: The Anatomy of an American Myth* (Missoula: University of Montana Publications in History, 1976), and Robert F. Berkhofer, Jr., *The White Man's Indian: Images of the American Indian from Columbus to the Present* (New York: Alfred A. Knopf, 1978).

9. Karen C. Lund, *American Indians in Silent Film: Motion Pictures in the Library of Congress*, (Washington, D.C.: Library of Congress, August 1992).

10. The best discussion of Native Americans in the silent film, as well as of silent Westerns generally, is in Brownlow, *The War, the West*.

11. On this see John C. Ewers, "The Emergence of the Plains Indian as the Symbol of the North American Indian," *Annual Report of the Smithsonian Institute for 1964* (Washington, D.C.: Government Printing Office, 1965) pp. 531–545. The United States government itself legitimated the representational dominance of the Plains Indians through the 1913 issuance of the buffalo nickel, with an Indian profile on the obverse, and the 1923 issuance of the "American Indian" stamp.

12. "To Honor Indian Battle," *The New York Times*, June 22, 1926, p. 7.

13. Dedication to Frederick Whittaker's *A Complete Life of George Armstrong Custer* (Lincoln: University of Nebraska Press, 1993).

14. Charles Eastman, "The Story of the Little Big Horn: Told from the Indian Standpoint by One of Their Race," *Chautaqua*, July 1900, dedication page. The precise, or even approximate number of Indians participating has been endlessly debated, with many other issues, for more than a century. Eastman, a full-blooded Sioux, gives his estimate in this intriguing article.

15. For an excellent overview of "Custeriana," see Dippie, *Custer's Last Stand.*

16. Randall Parrish, *Bob Hampton of Placer* (Chicago: A. C. McClurg, 1906), p. 367.

17. Cyrus Townsend Brady, *Britton of the Seventh: A Romance of Custer and the Great Northwest* (Chicago: A. C. McClurg & Co., 1914), p. 368.

18. Program for *Custer's Last Fight*, New York Motion Picture Company, 1912 (reprinted by The Old Army Press, Fort Collins, Colorado, to accompany the videotape of the film), p. 7.

19. For an analysis of the ideological resonance of the "last stand" during the final years of the nineteenth century, see Richard Slotkin, *The Fatal Environment: The Myth of the Frontier in the Age of Industrialization, 1800–1890* (Middletown, Conn.: Wesleyan University Press, 1985).

20. Edwin L. Sabin, *On the Plains with Custer: The Western Life and Deeds of the Chief with the Yellow Hair . . . When in the Troublous Years 1866–1876 the Fighting Seventh Cavalry Helped to Win Pioneer Kansas, Nebraska, and Dakota for White Civilization and Today's Peace* (Philadelphia: J. B. Lippincott Company, 1913).

21. Ralph Bonehill, *With Custer in the Black Hills, or, a Young Scout among the Indians* (New York: The Mershon Company, 1902), p. iii.

22. Elbridge S. Brooks, *The Master of the Strong Hearts: A Story of Custer's Last Rally* (New York: E. P. Dutton and Company, 1898), p. 314.

23. For information on Whittaker and Elizabeth Custer's influence upon him, see Gregory J. W. Urwin, "Introduction," in Frederick Whittaker, *A Complete Life of General George A. Custer: Volume 1: Through the Civil War* (Lincoln: University of Nebraska Press, 1993).

24. "Coolidge Lauds Custer's Memory," *New York Times*, June 27, 1926, p. 10.

25. The first major revisionist biography of Custer that seriously questioned both his character and his military prowess did not appear until 1934 (Frederic Franklyn Van de Water, *Glory Hunter: A life of General Custer* [Indianapolis, Ind.: The Boggs-Merrill Company, 1934]).

26. Louis Reeves Harrison, "Custer's Last Fight," *The Moving Picture World*, June 22, 1912, p. 1118.

27. In his article, "'Correct in Every Detail': General Custer in Hollywood" (*Montana: The Magazine of Western History*, Winter 1991, pp. 28–57), Paul Andrew Hutton includes several more silent films in his filmography but suggests that some may be variant titles. The following is a list of films that I have seen or for which reviews indicate that Custer was indeed a character, if only a minor one: *Bob Hampton of Placer* (First National, 1921); *Britton of the Seventh* (Vitagraph, 1916); *Custer's Last Fight* (New York Motion Picture Company, three reels, 1912, reissued in five reels in 1925) (print of the 1925 re-release is at the Library of Congress); *Custer's Last Scout* (New York Motion Picture Company, 1915) (print at the National Film Archive, London); *The Flaming Frontier* (Universal Pictures, 1926); *General Custer At Little Big Horn* (Sunset Productions, 1926) (print at the Library of Congress); *On the Little Big Horn; or, Custer's Last*

Stand (Selig, 1909); *The Scarlet West* (First National Pictures, 1925) (trailer only at the Library of Congress); *Wild Bill Hickok* (Paramount, 1923). I would appreciate hearing from readers who may know the whereabouts of prints of the "missing" films.

28. Whittaker, *Complete Life*, p. 643.

29. In fact, in the three films under consideration, all the native American characters are played by Native Americans. The two produced by the New York Motion Picture Company employed a troop commonly known as the "Inceville Sioux" (Brownlow, *The War, the West*, p. 261). Of course, major roles in major films usually went to white actors in "red" face, as in *The Vanishing American*, in which Richard Dix plays the Navajo hero.

30. Cyrus T. Brady, *Indian Fights and Fighters: The Soldier and the Sioux* (New York: McClure Phillips and Co., 1904), p. 185.

31. Custer, *My Life*, pp. 22–23.

32. "Extermination," *The New York Times*, July 12, 1876, p. 4.

33. Frederick Whittaker, *A Complete Life of Gen. George A. Custer: Major-General of Volunteers; Brevet Major-General, U.S. Army; and Lieutenant-Colonel, Seventh U.S. Cavalry* (New York: Sheldon, 1876), p. 512.

34. Whittaker, 1876 ed., p. 478 (emphasis in the original).

35. "The Indian War," *The New York Times*, July 29, 1876, p. 1.

36. Whittaker, 1876 ed., p. 391.

37. Parrish, *Bob Hampton*, p. 373.

38. Ibid., pp. 14–15.

39. "On the Little Big Horn," *Moving Picture World*, Nov. 27, 1909, p. 773.

40. "Britton of the Seventh," *The Moving Picture World*, May 20, 1916, p. 1,406.

41. Harrison, "Custer's Last Fight," p. 1,118. Harrison seems to have been an atavistic adherent of the "frontier theory," unrelenting in his negative characterizations of Native Americans. See Brownlow, *The War, the West*, p. 334.

42. Crazy Horse, who has during the past few decades become, next to Sitting Bull, perhaps the most well known of all Indian leaders, plays a fairly minor role in most of the material that I read for this article. In fact, several sources, both fiction and nonfiction, mention that Crazy Horse headed a force of Cheyennes during the Little Big Horn Battle, while the chief in fact was a leader of the Oglala Sioux.

43. Whittaker, 1876 ed., p. 496.

44. Ibid., p. 601 (emphasis in original).

45. "On the Little Big Horn," *Moving Picture World*, Nov. 27, 1909, p. 773.

46. Harrison, "Custer's Last Fight," p. 1,118.

47. Whittaker, 1876 ed., p. 496.

48. "Medicine men" often seem to function as the villains in narratives authored by whites that are otherwise very sympathetic toward the Indian characters: e.g., Curtis's *In the Land of the War Canoes* and the 1890 novel *Wanneta, The Sioux* by Warren K. Moorehead (New York: Dodd Mead and Company).

49. Kate and Virgil D. Boyles, *The Spirit Trail* (Chicago: A. C. McClurg, 1910), p. 48.

50. Brooks, *Master of Strong Hearts*, p. 313.

51. "Custer's Last Battle," *The Century Magazine*, January 1892, p. 363.

52. "The Personal Story of Rain-in-the-Face," *Outdoor Life*, March 1903, reprinted in Brady, *Indians Fights*, pp. 286, 288.

53. Frederick S. Dellenbaugh, *George Armstrong Custer*, (New York: The MacMillan Company, 1917), p. 178.

54. Whittaker, 1876 ed., p. 535.

55. Charles Eastman, "The Story of the Little Big Horn: Told from the Indian Standpoint by One of Their Race," *Chautaqua*, July 1900, p. 357.

56. Hamlin Garland, *The Book of the American Indian* (New York: Harper and Brothers, 1923).

Fatimah Tobing Rony

ROBERT FLAHERTY'S *NANOOK OF THE NORTH*
The Politics of Taxidermy and Romantic Ethnography

Nanook of the North (1922), a film that focuses on the daily activities of a family of Itivimuit, a group of Quebec Inuit, is considered by many to be one of the great works of art of independent cinema (Figure 1). It is seen as a point of origin: It has been called the first documentary film, the first ethnographic film, as well as the first art film. The writings about *Nanook* are inextricably wound up with the image of its director, Robert J. Flaherty. There is an aura around the Flaherty name: he is praised as the father of documentary and ethnographic cinema, as a great storyteller and humanitarian, and as the first maverick independent artist uncorrupted by Hollywood. Unlike other white filmmakers of indigenous peoples, it is claimed that he never exploited his subjects. Flaherty embronzed his own myth when he declared: "First I was an explorer; then I was an artist."[1]

Nanook is also an artifact of popular culture. When it was released and distributed by Pathé in 1922 in both the United States and Europe, it fed upon an already established craze in those countries for the Inuit as a kind of cuddly "primitive" man. The writer Joseph E. Senungetuk, an Innupiat from Northwest Alaska, summarized this stereotype: "a people without technology, without a culture, lacking intelligence, living in igloos, and at best, a sort of simplistic 'native boy' type of subhuman arctic being."[2] *Nanook* was extremely popular when it was released worldwide, and spawned what ethnographic filmmaker Asen Balikci has called "Nanookmania."[3] Many writers consider *Nanook* as the high point of the *age d'or* of ethnographic cinema, the period from 1922 to 1932, which also saw the release of Flaherty's *Moana* (1926) and his collaboration with F. W. Murnau, *Tabu* (1931).[4] Revived on numerous occasions, *Nanook* remains a staple for high school and university courses in anthropology and ethnographic film.

The academic discourse on *Nanook of the North* centers on questions of authenticity. Some have argued that because the scenes of everyday Quebec Inuit life were reconstructed to enhance the film's visual and narrative impact, it cannot be considered true science. Other anthropologists contend that cinematic representation can never fully be objective—thus both Flaherty's innovative "flow of life" style, as Siegfried Kracauer termed it, and the purported participation of the Inuit people filmed are hailed as markers of Flaherty's pioneering genius. Still others add that the documentary value of the film lies in its portrayal of essential humanity. Ethnographic filmmaker Luc De Heusch is representative of this last school of thought. De Heusch exclaimed that *Nanook* was "a family portrait . . . the epic of a man, of a society frantically struggling to survive. . . . Family life, the human condition, are conquests from which animals are excluded. Such, in essence, is the theme of the film. Nanook, the hero of the first ethnographic film, is also the symbol of all civilization.[5]

The focus of this essay will be on an overlooked aspect of the film: what the film and the discourse surrounding it can tell us about the nature of anthropological knowledge and the role of visual media in legitimating that knowledge and other regimes of truth. *Nanook* was praised as a film of universal reality, and Flaherty was held up to be a "real" filmmaker, untainted by commercial concerns. Conversely the Oedipal slaying of this great father-figure in recent criticism has focused on Flaherty as forger of the reality of the Quebec Inuit. In both cases, what is ignored is how *Nanook* emerges from a web of discourses which constructed the Inuit as Primitive man, and which considered cinema, and particularly Flaherty's form of cinema, to be a mode of representation that could only be truthful. I am not so much interested in whether or not Flaherty was an artist or a liar, but in taxidermy, and how the discourse of authenticity has created the film.

I take inspiration from the subtitle of Leprohon's fine book on the ethnographic cinema of travel and exploration: *L'exotisme et le cinéma: Les "chasseurs d'images" à la conquete du monde . . .* (1945), and examine *Nanook of the North* as the product of a *hunt* for images, as a kind of taxidermic display. First I show how the film represents a paradigm for a mode of representing indigenous peoples that parallels the romantic primitivism of modern anthropology. Second, I examine the discourse around the Inuit, a discourse which has been largely ignored: Nanookmania was preceded by a historical fascination for Inuit performers in

Fig. 1: Nanook of the North (courtesy of the Museum of Modern Art)

exhibitions, zoos, fairs, museums and early cinema. Finally, I examine the discourse on Flaherty as explorer/artist, a discourse which has painted him as either the great artist, or, like the Wizard of Oz, the Great Humbug or falsifier of reality. There are thus three hunts (and therefore three acts of taxidermy): the history of the hunt for representations of the Inuit for science and popular culture, the hunt for cinematic images of the Inuit for the film *Nanook*, and cinema's hunt for Flaherty as great artist and/or great liar.

Taxidermy, Salvage Ethnography, and Slight Narrative

Nanook of the North is often seen as a film without a scripted narrative. Filmed on location at Inukjuak (formerly Port Harrison), at the Inukjuak River in Quebec, Canada, the family of Quebec Inuit represented in the film consists of the hunter Nanook the Bear (played by Allakariallak); the wife and mother of his children Nyla (played by Alice [?] Nuvalinga), who is always shown caring for and carrying the baby Rainbow;

another woman Cunayoo; and various children including Nanook's son Allegoo (played by Phillipoosie).[6] The narrative of Flaherty's film seems to ramble: it begins with the introduction of the family, the repair of kayaks and making of fuel; the family then trades furs at the trading post of the fur company; Nanook fishes and then hunts walrus; the family builds an igloo and goes to sleep; they then wake up and go off in their dog sleds, a scene culminating in the famous seal hunt so beloved by film theorist André Bazin.[7] The film ends with the arrival of a storm and the family taking shelter in an abandoned igloo.

Significantly, although it was not intended as a scientific research film, Franz Boas of Columbia University in New York City, perhaps the leading anthropologist of the period, also praised *Nanook*. Boas was known as the founder of cultural anthropology in the United States and a proponent of the use of film for recording "isolable actions" of the body. In 1933, Boas wrote a letter to Will Hays, the president of the Motion Picture Producers and Distributors of America, about the possibility of film collaborations between anthropologists and Hollywood on "the primitive races." Footage could be used and recycled for films of scientific, educational, as well as entertainment purposes. Boas explained that commercial films like Flaherty's *Moana* (1926) and Merian C. Cooper and Ernest B. Schoedsack's *Grass* (1925) and *Chang* (1927) (the team who would later direct *King Kong* [1933]), although of some scientific value, would have been better if a trained anthropologist had been on site in an advisory capacity.[8]

I am interested in Boas' use of the word "picturesque" in his letter to Hays:

> Assuming . . . that a man who knows Eskimo life in and out, had been at hand to direct a film like NANOOK, many exceedingly picturesque and interesting features of native life might have been brought in which would not only have improved the quality of the film but would have also made it more attractive to the general audiences. . . . most of the material of this kind has to be collected now because each year sees native cultures breaking down and disappearing under the onslaught of White civilization.[9]

Native cultures, Boas contended, were vanishing "from a pictorial point of view," and the anthropologist's task was to record as much of the pictorial and the picturesque as possible.[10]

The picturesque, as invoked directly by Boas, consists of scenes such as rituals, dance, food preparation, indigenous technology (pottery-making, for example) and so on—all that is replete with "authentic" detail and without the influence of European culture. Boas' notion of the picturesque went hand in hand with what George W. Stocking, Jr., has described as the "ethnographicization" of anthropology, a process in which the empiricism and epistemological underpinnings of anthropological notions of evolutionary time were overlaid with an increasingly romantic Rousseauesque study of "surviving primitive peoples."[11] During the "classic period" of modern anthropology, the term Stocking uses to label the period from the 1920s to the 1960s, the influence of Franz Boas and the school of American culturalism made ethnographic film and other visual media an increasingly important tool for assembling data for description. If Boas feared the "pictorial breakdown" of "primitive cultures," he chose to defy their "death" through recording and reconstructing them.[12]

I call the mode of representation of the Ethnographic which emerged from this impulse *taxidermy*. Taxidermy seeks to make that which is dead look as if it were still living. In order to explain the applicability of the term to early ethnographic cinema, I would like to borrow from Stephen Bann's description of the nineteenth-century practice of taxidermy.[13] Bann writes that as "the restoration of the life-like," taxidermy "is itself postulated as a response to a sense of loss. In other words, the Utopia of life-like reproduction depends upon, and reacts to, the fact of death. It is a strenuous attempt to recover, by means which must exceed those of convention, a state which is (and must be) recognized as lost."[14] Donna Haraway, in her marvelous article on Carl Akeley's early twentieth-century dioramas, taxidermy, photography, and film at the American Museum of Natural History, likewise speaks of taxidermy as a means to protect against loss, in order that the body may be transcended: "Taxidermy fulfills the fatal desire to represent, to be whole; it is a politics of reproduction."[15] Since indigenous peoples were assumed to be already dying if not dead, the ethnographic "taxidermist" turned to artifice, seeking an image more true to the posited original. When Flaherty stated, "One often has to distort a thing to catch its true spirit," he was not just referring to his own artistry, but to the preconditions for the effective, "true" representation of so-called vanishing culture.[16]

It is a paradox of this cinema of romantic preservationism that the reaction—"That person is alive!"—is most easily elicited if the subjects filmed are represented as existing in a former epoch. As Johannes Fabian has pointed out, the specificity of anthropology is that the subjects of its inquiry are represented as existing in an earlier age. Fabian explains the significance of the use in modern anthropology of the "ethnographic present," the practice of writing in the present tense about the people whom the anthropologist studied. The dominant pronoun/verb form is: "They are (do, have, etc.)." This form of rhetoric presupposes that the people studied are timeless, and establishes the anthropologist as hidden observer, akin to the natural historian—in that he or she stands at the peephole into the distant past.[17] As Flaherty himself explained, he did not want to show the Inuit as they were at the time of the making of the film, but as (he thought) they *had been*. The ethnographic present also obfuscates the dialogue and the encounters that took place between the anthropologist and the people studied. In other words, as Fabian writes, "pronouns and verb forms in the third person mark an Other outside the dialogue."[18]

The cinema of Flaherty worked in the same way: Nanook and his family were represented in a cinematic "ethnographic present" in which intertitles establish the camera, and thus the filmmaker, as observer. In the trading post sequence, for example, the viewer is posited as objective voyeur, enjoying the erotics of the vanishing race myth.[19] Against a wall of the white fur pelts, Nyla sits in the background rocking with her baby, and Nanook, crouched in the left foreground with the trader at the right in a higher position, gazes at the gramophone in the center (Figure 2). Nanook touches the gramophone; intertitles explain that he does not understand where the sound comes from or how it is made. He then is shown biting the record three times while laughing at the camera. This conceit of the indigenous person who does not understand Western technology was and is common to ethnographic cinema. It allows for real voyeuristic pleasure and reassures the viewer of the contrast between the Primitive and the Modern: it engrains the notion that the people are not really acting. Their naiveté—they do not understand this foreign technology—is another sign of authenticity. This conceit, of course, obscures the Inuit's own appropriation of new technology: the Inuit, after all, served as Flaherty's film crew.

This scene of abundant furs, puppies, and a constructed primitive naiveté—Nanook biting the record, Inuit women likened to female dogs, and infantile gorging of biscuits—reveals the way that genocide is made erotic, an evolutionary inevitability.[20] Furthermore, if the indigenous man, Nanook, is constructed as a being without artifice, as referent, the indigenous woman is there to be uncovered, her body—and this is true of ethnographic cinema in general—to be scopically possessed by the camera/filmmaker and the audience as well. As intended, however, this form of ethnographic film, infused with the notion of death and the

Fig. 2: Nanook of the North (courtesy of the Museum of Modern Art)

idea of vanishing races, is a cinema of archetypal moments endlessly repeated.[21] In *Nanook*, the archetypal moment is that of a society ignorant of guns or gramophones: a society of man the hunter, man against nature, man the eater of raw flesh. *Nanook of the North* was a cinema of origins in many ways: Its appeal was the myth of authentic first man.

These themes are prevalent in ethnographic cinema and, until recently, in anthropological discourse in general. Whether one examines photographic images or drawings accompanying the racial typologies of turn-of-the-century medical anthropology, or the more romanticized visual images of mid-twentieth-century anthropology, two characteristics are nearly always present: 1) a focus on the indigenous body (since the subjects of study were seen as being without sophisticated, i.e., written, language abilities, the body became the privileged site of investigation), and 2) a situating of the filmed subject in a displaced *temporal* realm (as an exemplar of an earlier epoch in evolutionary history). The viewer is conditioned to see these characteristics whenever confronted with an image of the Ethnographic. This is why, borrowing a phrase from the writer and critic V. Y. Mudimbe, I like to say that the viewer of the ethnographic film is not simply seeing indigenous culture; rather, he or she is "*seeing anthropology*."[22]

What has been called Flaherty's "slight narrative" thus fits perfectly with a racializing representation of the Inuit, which situates indigenous peoples outside modern history. *Nanook*, however, is structured as a film about the daily life of the Inuit, its novelty deriving from the fact that it was neither a scientific expedition film meant to serve as a positivist record, nor a travelogue of jokey tourism. As mentioned above, Siegfried Kracauer described Flaherty as a filmmaker of the "flow of life." Kracauer writes, "Flaherty's 'slight narratives' portray or resuscitate modes of existence that obtain among primitive peoples. . . . Most Flaherty films are expressive of his romantic desire to summon, and preserve for posterity, the purity and 'majesty' [Flaherty's word] of a way of life not yet spoiled by the advance of civilization."[23] Flaherty explained this best when he described film as "a very simple form." For Flaherty, the medium made simple was well-suited to the subject matter: films

> are very well-suited to portraying the lives of primitive people whose lives are simply lived and who feel strongly, but whose activities are external and dramatic rather than internal and complicated. I don't think you can make a good film of the love affairs of the Eskimo . . . because they never show much feeling in their faces, but you can make a very good film of Eskimos spearing a walrus.[24]

The "ethnographic" is without intellect: He or she is best represented as merely existing. It is the camera of the explorer/artist who will capture the reality of their "simply lived" lives. Hence the notion (and myth) that the actors in *Nanook* were "non-actors."

The desire of Euro-American audiences and critics to perceive Nanook as authentic Primitive man, as an unmediated referent, is evident in the fact that until the 1970s, no one bothered to ask members of the Inuit community in which the film was made for their opinions of the film. Only then was it learned that the name of the actor who played Nanook was Allakariallak. The same applies to all the other characters in the film. Although it was typical for explorers to "nickname" the Inuit they encountered, Flaherty's innovation was in giving the Inuit nicknames that sounded Inuit. Hence Nanook (the Bear) was a better and more easily marketable name than Allakariallak, because of its seeming genuineness and its dual connotations of cuddly like a teddy bear, and wild like a savage beast.

At the end of the film there is a haunting shot of Nanook sleeping, a close-up of his head. He appears to be asleep, but his absolute stillness reminds us of a waxwork or a corpse. Taxidermy is also deeply religious: When Bazin writes that the mummy complex is the impulse behind the evolution of technologies of realism—"To preserve, artificially, his bodily appearance is to snatch it from the flow of time, to stow it away neatly, so to speak, in the hold of life"—one is reminded of the image of the sleeping Nanook.[25] In ethnographic cinema, the narrative of the film hinges upon the body of the native—plugged into the narrative of evolution and the myth of vanishing races. It is this body, and not that of an Oedipal father or mother which must be slain and upon which the narrative rests.[26] That Allakariallak died two years after the film was released, of either starvation or disease, only enhanced the film's status as a work of authenticity.

The Hunt for the Inuit and the Alaskan Eskimo: Explorers, Museums, Fairs, and Films

The trail of contact between Arctic peoples and whites was already littered with corpses by the time of *Nanook*. The appetite for the Inuit—specifically for images of their bodies—by both scientists and the public began in 1577 when the explorer Martin Frobisher presented Queen Elizabeth I with a man, woman, and child from Baffinland.[27] The representation of the Inuit began with explorers' accounts: the belief that the word "Eskimo" means "eater of raw meat" reveals what the public found most interesting about them. Because of their diet of raw meat, they were described as animal-like, savage and cannibalistic. They also would be repeatedly compared to their sled dogs, and this canine metaphor was used in *Nanook*.[28]

Arctic explorers brought back more than just maps, furs, and ivory. It was common for explorers to bring back Inuit. It was also a "tradition" that these Inuit rarely returned to their homelands: they frequently died from diseases for which they had no immunity. Like the West Africans and Malagasy whom Félix-Louis Regnault filmed in exhibitions, the Inuit were extremely popular performers in exhibitions, zoos, and museums.[29] They were treated as specimens and objects of curiosity.

Some of the Inuit left behind written records of their experiences as performers. One such account is that of a man named Abraham, one of eight Labrador Inuit brought over by J. Adrian Jacobsen to perform in the Hagenbeck Zoo in Berlin. Abraham kept a diary where he described how one member of the group was beaten by a dog whip and how they performed at the zoo in freezing conditions. Like the climax of *Nanook*, the climax of these performers' acts at the zoo was a seal hunt. Within three months, however, all had died from smallpox.[30] Their bones immediately were used for anthropological research.

Explorers like Robert Peary were dependent on the good will and money of industrialists and museum philanthropists to fund their expeditions. To increase their own fame, and to make some profit, explorers brought back Inuit and Alaskan Eskimo to be exhibited. Peary was notorious for his cruelty and arrogance toward the Inuit who worked for him, often treating them no better than dogs. When they died, often from diseases which his ships inadvertently brought, he would exhume their bodies and sell them to museums. Explorers also made most of their fortunes through the furs and ivory they received from the Inuit.[31]

In 1896, Franz Boas, who was then assistant curator of the American Museum of Natural History, pleaded with Peary to bring back an Inuit for the museum. It is surprising that Boas, who in 1893 had worked on anthropological exhibits at the World's Columbian Exhibition in Chicago where many performers, including Inuit, had died (their bodies were later used in the Field Museum), apparently did not consider the danger of exposing the Inuit to disease as an obstacle.[32] Of the six Inuit from Smith Sound who were brought by Peary and housed in the American Museum of Natural History, only one did not immediately die of pneumonia, a little boy known as Minik Wallace. Abandoned by Peary and by Boas and the museum scientists who had brought him to the United States, Wallace was adopted and grew up in New York, only to discover as a teenager that when his father had died the scientists had staged a fake burial, and that indeed his father's bones were at the museum. As Wallace explained in a letter to a friend:

> You can't know the sad feelings I have. . . . No one can know unless they have been taken from their home and had their father die and put on exhibition, and be left to starve in a strange land where the men insult you when you ask for your own dear father's body to bury or to be sent home.
>
> These are the civilized men who steal, and murder, and torture, and pray and say "Science."[33]

Not surprisingly, the Inuit were popular subjects for museum models in dioramas. For example, the first museum models at the Smithsonian Institution's United States National Museum (now the National Museum of Natural History), made in 1873, represented two Inuit named "Joe" and "Hanna," flanking the figure of the explorer Dr. Elisha Kent Kane. Museum displays of life groups—depicting cultures in nuclear family units performing rituals or subsistence activities—are another characteristic form of the "taxidermic" mode of salvage ethnography.[34]

In the nineteenth century, the image of the Eskimo acquired nuances in addition to that of "wild Savage." As Ann Fienup-Riordan notes, the Eskimo were made into the mirror image of the explorers. Like the explorers, the Eskimo were represented as noble, brave, independent, persevering, and incorruptible. But ideas about the relatively lofty status of the Eskimo did not mean that the Eskimo were perceived as able to undergo their own "independent progress" without white intervention.[35] In a sense, the Eskimo were seen as Primitive success stories of an Arctic "survival of the fittest." Fienup-Riordan explains:

> The publicity these arctic representatives received marked the progressive transformation of the image of Eskimos from subhuman to superhuman. Displayed along with their sophisticated hunting tools and wearing polar bear skins, these living specimens came to represent the ultimate survivors, intrepid and courageous individualists who through sheer cunning were able to best their rivals in the free market place of the arctic world. Happy, peaceful, hardworking, independent, and adaptable—these were the images most often used to clothe the Eskimos in the twentieth century. The nuances of Eskimo reality dimmed in comparison to this dramatically staged representation, an image increasingly acceptable because of its incorporation of traits Westerners valued in themselves.[36]

This notion of the Eskimo as an uncorrupt example of all the values of the West—independence and perseverance and patriarchy—reached its epitome in the cinematic character of Nanook.[37] In both the United States and Europe, the 1920s were characterized by a pervasive fear of racial mixing: the white was constructed as the Nordic—pale, blond, blue-eyed, from the North. The term "Nordic" was used in popular culture to refer to whites of Northern European descent. The fear was that the Nordic was being annihilated by racial mixing. At best, the Inuit or Alaskan Eskimo was the primitive Nordic, or as Asen Balikci termed it, a "primitive Protestant."[38] I would like to suggest that the character Nanook was thus something of a mirror for the white audience: he too was from the North, and, as Balikci's comment suggests, like the Nordic, was seen as embodying the Protestant values of patriarchy, industriousness, independence and courage. But the character Nanook is still the subject of voyeuristic observation, not acknowledged as coequal of the adventurer/anthropologist.

As I have argued elsewhere, cinema took over from the world's fair many of the functions of the native village exhibition.[39] Indeed one of the earliest cinematic depictions of the Inuit is a body of film by Thomas Edison in 1901 of the "Esquimaux Village" at the Pan-American Exposition in Buffalo. Edison produced footage of the Inuit as happy gamesters in dog sleds amidst papier maché igloo environments with painted backdrops of snowy mountains and fake ice floes.[40]

But the appetite for the "real" and the "unexplored" was insatiable, and numerous films about Arctic exploration that include footage of or relating to the Inuit and Alaskan Eskimo were made before *Nanook*. In almost all these films, the narrative centers on a whaling expedition or arctic exploration. Footage of Inuit and Alaskan Eskimo hunting polar bear and paddling in kayaks were "picturesque" details, which lent an air of authenticity to these filmed journeys.[41]

The use of film to enhance lectures on expeditions and Arctic peoples was also common. The indigenous people served as "picturesque," elements of the landscape, marking the exotic and primitive past through which the modern white explorers were passing. In William Van Valin's films of Point Barrow, Alaska (1912–1918) there is a comparatively interesting seal hunting scene, by now a staple of films relating to the Inuit or Alaskan Eskimo. The style of the scene approaches that of the seal hunt in *Nanook*: one lone Alaskan Eskimo in an empty landscape seal hunts a long time, the intertitles explaining "thought of hungry wife and kiddies urges weary hunter on." Because this title is followed by a pan of the landscape, it allows the viewer for a moment to see with the hunter's eyes.[42]

As in *Nanook*, the emphasis in Van Valin's footage is on the hunt and the ensuing butchering of the carcass. But whereas Flaherty used intercutting shots of howling hungry dogs as a metaphor for Nanook's family's struggle, Van Valin uses catchy kitsch-y rifles like "Dog eat dog" for a scene in which a dog eats raw meat. In Van Valin's films, the Alaskan Eskimo are portrayed as carefree, playful, dancing, and instinctive: "old Eskimo smell whale through twelve feet of ice." The Alaskan Eskimo filmed tend to line up and stare, laughing at the camera; similarly, in *Nanook*, the actors often look up at the camera and laugh after they have performed a particular act.

Like most arctic exploration films, death suffuses Van Valin's film. There is a tremendous amount of footage of the bones of Alaskan Eskimo, skeletons scattered everywhere in an empty landscape, with the accompanying intertitle: "Where solitude now reigns supreme, except when the wind whistles through the eye orbits and nasal cavities of these empties."[43]

There are several aspects that *Nanook* shares with its predecessors. In both, there is an emphasis on hunting and the eating of raw meat by people and dogs. As I have suggested, the seal hunt scene is all but obligatory. To the extent that Western contact is portrayed, it is as benign, even amusing trade—the Inuit get novelties and the Euro-Americans get fur. In both *Nanook of the North* and the expedition film, moreover, the Inuit and Alaskan Eskimo are portrayed as playful, with the use of nicknames common, but in both death is always lurking.[44] The close-ups in *Nanook* also borrow from the expedition genre: the laughing Inuit holds up the fish for the camera; other portraits in Flaherty's film are infused with the dreamlike Pictorialist style akin to Edward Sheriff Curtis's work.[45]

Despite these many similarities, Flaherty's film stands out. As I argue in the next section, the innovation is not only in Flaherty's distinctive film style as in the creation of the myth that Flaherty had produced for the first time a form of cinema paralleling participant observation.

Nanook of the North and Salvage Ethnography

In the same year that Nanook was released, the anthropologist Bronislaw Malinowski wrote his pioneering ethnography, *Argonauts of the Western Pacific* (1922) about the inhabitants of the Trobriand Islands, off the coast of what is now Papua New Guinea. If *Nanook* is the archetypal documentary/ethnographic/art film, *Argonauts* is without a doubt the archetypal written ethnography. The many common aspects of Malinowski's new conception of the anthropologist as fieldworker and Flaherty's notion of the filmmaker as "explorer/artist" show that the film and the book were made and received in a similar climate of ideas about indigenous peoples and truthful representation. Malinowski wrote, "The final goal, of which an Ethnographer should never lose sight . . . is, briefly, to grasp the natives' point of view, his relation to life, to realize *his* vision of *his* world."[46] The product of this ideal of the anthropologist entering the "field" as a solitary observer was to be a written ethnography, a cultural description of "a people," rather than an historical account of an encounter, a description meant to convince the reader that the anthropologist "had been there" as both all-knowing insider and as scrupulously objective observer.

But participant observation, notes Fabian, "was not canonized to promote participation but to improve observation." Like the time machine of cinema, anthropology as participant observation involved an oscillation between the positions of distance and closeness, subject and object. Anthropology's visualism, its "ideological bias toward vision," meant that knowledge was "based upon, and validated by, *observation*."[47]

Part of the appeal of participant observation is that it purportedly enables the Ethnographer, to show not how the anthropologist sees the native, but how the native sees himself. Flaherty encouraged the belief that he was doing just that. He explained, "I wanted to show the Innuit [*sic*]. And I wanted to show them, not from the civilized point of view, but as they saw themselves, as 'we the people.'"[48]

Nanook is perhaps the first example in film of a mode of representation which incorporates the participant observation ideal. Flaherty claimed to be a long-time explorer in the area, and his admirers even said that he had been adopted by Nanook and his family (this point was never proven). Because Flaherty showed rushes to his Inuit crew, and because Inuit contributed to all aspects of filmmaking (from acting, to the repair of his cameras, to the printing and developing of the film, to the suggestion of scenes to film), critics from the art world as well as anthropology have claimed that *Nanook* represents true collaboration, the native acting out his or her own self-conception (Figure 3).[49]

As James Clifford and Clifford Geertz have pointed out, the myth of "participant observation" was fashioned out of rhetorical devices creating the impression of "being there." Although Flaherty wanted to create this impression, it would be hasty to assume that *Nanook* was the product of collaboration. The very fact that we do not have any Inuit accounts of the filmmaking process would appear to deny the "collaborative" nature of the film. Since we do not know to what degree Flaherty was "intimate" with the actors (his writings boast of an intimacy which Inuit eyewitnesses do not seem to recall), since we do not know whether he asked them to play themselves, and since we do not have an indigenous point of view to compare the film against, it is more fruitful to view the claims of collaboration as evidence of the "romantic" ideal of the ethnographer/artist than as an essential aspect of the film.[50]

In *Nanook of the North*, participant observation is achieved by the erasure of almost all signs of white contact. Thus the spectator views the

Fig. 3: Eskimo drawing of Flaherty and camera (courtesy of the Museum of Modern Art).

landscape with Nanook; but he also views Nanook. The spectator becomes both participant (seeing with the eyes of Nanook) and observer (an omnipotent eye viewing Nanook). The viewers of *Nanook* thus become participant observers themselves: the audience participates in the hunt for the seal and the walrus along with Nanook. A white viewer may identify with the Nordic qualities of Nanook, but still participate in the "hunt" for the body of Nanook, as vanishing race, as First Man. The issue then is not "whether Flaherty was a legitimate anthropologist" but how the public was led to believe that they were *seeing anthropology* in a manner that allowed them to play with the boundary between viewer and viewed as vicarious participant observers, while reaffirming the boundaries between representation and reality.

Those who have praised Flaherty see him as a great artist and observer, or as Calder-Marshall called him, "an innocent eye," a man who filmed out of love not greed. As Richard Corliss said, Flaherty "simply saw the truth and brought it home."[51] Many have complained, however, that *Nanook of the North* did not present a true representation of Inuit life. Only seven years after *Nanook* was released, the explorer Vilhjalmur Stefannson claimed that *Nanook* was as authentic as Santa Claus.[52] But there were many rebuttals to the critics' denunciations of *Nanook* as staged. Flaherty's statement, "One often has to distort a thing to catch its true spirit," was seen to prove that Flaherty was an artist who portrayed "felt experience," and so was not a mere mechanical recorder.[53] Forty years after *Nanook*, ethnographic filmmakers Luc de Heusch and Jean Rouch, as well as Asen Balikci, praised *Nanook* as the first example of participatory cinema. Unlike early ethnographic filmmakers like Baldwin Spencer, or later filmmakers like Boas and Mead, de Heusch and Rouch did not believe that cinema is objective, that one can take "cinematographic notes." De Heusch in particular pointed out that films of everyday life in real time are usually quite boring and only of interest for the anthropologist. The irony—and this irony is at the heart of taxidermy as well—is that "reality" filmed does not appear real. The filmmaker must use artifice to convey truth. One way he or she can do this is by inviting the indigenous people who are the subjects in the film to act out their lives.[54]

The image of Flaherty was that of the ideal Ethnographic Filmmaker: one who produces his work only after having lived in an area for a long time, observed the people and then collaborated with them.[55] Luc de Heusch explained that the Inuit actors willingly play-acted for the camera, a technique which he emphasized is ethnographically sound, using French anthropologist Marcel Griaule's use of role-play as an example. De Heusch wrote:

> The authenticity of this sort of "documentary" ultimately depends entirely on the honesty of the director, who, through his work, asserts that "This is what I saw." In fact he has not seen exactly this or that aspect of what he shows, he has not always seen these things in the way he shows them, since that way is a language which he invents in cooperation with actors whose roles are authentic. The documentary is a work of art imbued with rationality and truth.[56]

De Heusch continued:

> Flaherty, more than anyone, had the gift of entering into conversation, *on our* behalf, with the Stranger. Through "Nanook" we "grasp" to the fullest extent, that is emotionally and rationally, the essential condition of Eskimo man left to himself: he is no longer a phantasmal shadow moving across the snow, an anonymous creature whose body and real presence can only be imperfectly imagined from the reading of learned treatises.[57]

In a sense, then, what Flaherty was doing was opposing mere inscription (the objective of early ethnographic footage) to that which I term taxidermy, and which Bazin praised as ontological realism. Much has been written and lauded about Flaherty's innovative cinematography and editing. Flaherty's use of long takes, re-framing, and depth-of-field cinematography using deep-focus lenses constituted a new style which Bazin describes as more moving, more realistic than what had gone before:

> The camera cannot see everything at once but it makes sure not to lose any part of what it chooses to see. What matters to Flaherty, confronted with Nanook hunting the seal, is the relation between Nanook and the animal; the actual length of the waiting period. Montage could suggest the time involved. Flaherty however confines himself to showing the actual waiting period; the length of the hunt is the very substance of the image, its true object.[58]

I do not contest the great influence of Flaherty's film style on documentary and realist forms of filmmaking. However, I am interested here in how his style is coded as closer to the real. Intrinsic to this coding of *Nanook* as a work of truth, a work of great art, was the construction of the image of Flaherty as explorer/artist, an image which Flaherty himself helped to construct through his various writings. It is to Flaherty's self-fashioned self that I will now turn.

Flaherty as Explorer: Heart of Whiteness

Ethnographic filmmaker Asen Balikci has summed up the image of the explorer/ ethnographic filmmaker from the time of Nanook:

> the ethnographer from Paris, London or New York, had usually gone to an extremely remote and exotic place where he studied the people and wrote books about them. The literature of exploration in exotic regions had further contributed to the popular perception of the ethnographer as hero. Building upon this reputation, the ethnocinematographer had the added advantage of showing to a large audience a film about strange and fascinating peoples—this was a demonstration that he was actually there, that the strange people liked him and that he liked them, otherwise how could the film have been made? His was a lonely and daring adventure, an exploration into the unknown, and so on.[59]

Because of the idea that the ethnographic filmmaker must have been friends with the natives—the film being the proof of the relationship—Flaherty's image as authentic communicator of the life of the natives was always intact, even as critics complained of inaccuracies in the film.

Like Malinowski, who constructed "the Ethnographer" through rhetorical devices like the ethnographic present, Flaherty contributed to the notion that his film was authentic through his own writings. Flaherty's self-image was that of the explorer penetrating the wilderness, meeting "primitive" natives and finding treasures to take back home. In his autobiographical *My Eskimo Friends: "Nanook of the North"* (1924), the treasures he describes include his mineral discoveries and maps, as well as the film and photographs shot.[60]

My Eskimo Friends is an account of Flaherty's career as explorer and filmmaker in the Arctic. Like all great explorers, he attributes the "discovery" of an island archipelago to himself. The Inuit he meets are depicted as grateful natives, although foul-smelling, and often "primitive looking"; he, on the other hand, is a kind of explorer Santa Claus who at Christmas gives them tobacco, needles, and candy. Tellingly, he claims they call him Angarooka, "the white master."[61] He calls them "my Eskimos," and often uses animal-metaphors to describe them.[62]

The story constitutive of the relationship between Nanook (never referred to by his real name) and Flaherty is that of Nanook's devotion to the "aggie" (film). Flaherty asks Nanook if he understands that in filling the walrus hunt, the film is more important than the hunt. Nanook replies, "Yes, yes, the aggie will come first. . . . Not a man will stir, not a harpoon will be thrown until you give the sign. It is my word." Flaherty recalls, "We shook hands and agreed to start the next day."[63]

It is this anecdote that is so treasured by the critics, for it meant that the film was a *real* ethnographic film, a film without voyeurism, the product of complete collaboration. The image of the devoted native is underlined by another anecdote about how the Inuit who worked for Flaherty gave up food so that Flaherty could eat. This prepares us for Flaherty's final words of reminiscence on Nanook's death. According to Flaherty, on his departure from Inukjuak, Nanook was sad to see him go and begged him to stay:[64] "The kablunak's movie igloo, into which thousands came, was utterly beyond his comprehension. They were many, I used to say, like the little stones along the shore. 'And will all these kablunaks see our "big aggie?"' he would ask. There was never need to answer, for incredulity was written large upon his face."[65]

My Eskimo Friends was a celebration of Flaherty as great humanist explorer, beloved by the natives, privy to the essence of native life. The book is dedicated to Flaherty's father, also an explorer. Flaherty's later novel *The Captain's Chair* (1938) provides us with an even greater understanding of what being an explorer meant to him. Told in first person, it is the story of a young man like himself who goes to look for minerals in the Hudson Bay area of Canada, but who throughout his years of travels in Northern Canada is searching above all for the great explorer and trader Captain Grant, the first man to trade with the Inuit. The narrator explains that it is a story of a captain and a ship penetrating into the heart of the Hudson's Bay Company's domain on Hudson Bay. It is also a search for a "father" hero by a young explorer:[66]

> During his exploration expeditions the narrator learns of the terrible disaster that had befallen Grant. He had left England on top of the world. The Company had given him all the means in their power to let him go ahead and open up the north . . . rich not only in furs but perhaps in gold, silver, copper, and who knew what other ores? They had given him also this wonderful new ship.[67]

The book is thus an Arctic *Heart of Darkness*, or perhaps *Heart of Whiteness* is the better term. For where Joseph Conrad revealed the dark and evil side of colonialism, Flaherty only writes about its good side. Like Marlow who in *The Heart of Darkness* hears stories about Kurz's exploits, Flaherty hears stories about Grant's hardships, his noble sacrifices, how he had to lash himself to the crow's nest to fight storms. Like Kurtz in *Heart of Darkness*, Grant has confronted "the horror." The narrator muses: "I thought of the hardship, the horror, the strain of it."[68] The horror here, however, is not the heart of darkness within, but the horror of Nature's tide rips, blinding squalls, and burning cold.

Much has been written about how the anthropologist Malinowski identified with Kurtz, the mad company officer in *Heart of Darkness*, who the narrator Marlow sets out to find. In one section of his diary, Malinowski explicitly invokes Kurtz when he describes his anger at the people he is studying—the Trobrianders—for not posing long enough for adequate time exposures for his photographs, even after his bribe of tobacco: "On the whole my feelings toward the natives are decidedly tending to 'Exterminate the brutes.'"[69] When Malinowski's diary was published, it destroyed some of the most cherished conceptions of the empathetic, value-neutral anthropologist.[70] Unlike Conrad's novel in which Kurtz's "heart of darkness" can be linked to the horror of colonialism and the desire to "exterminate the brutes," Flaherty's character of Grant remains a hero explorer who "penetrates" and opens up the North for the good of the company. The Inuit are again portrayed as faithful guides, and the Indians of the region are seen as crafty. Moreover, the Indians and the Inuit are in awe of the great Explorer: "To the Indians . . . Captain Grant was a fabulous figure—chief of the biggest canoe that surely was ever in the world. Among the Eskimos in the north, too, he was a legend, he with his monster omiak [boat] with its long black tall and a voice that re-echoed among the hills."[71] Like Kurtz, Grant's nerves are frayed after his harrowing experience aboard his ship (tellingly named the "Eskimo"), but he is no Kurz, for the novel ends when the narrator finally meets Grant in person and discovers: "He looked more like a scholar than a seaman."[72] As Frances Flaherty commented, those who decry Flaherty's films for being too romantic do not realize how much Flaherty was really interested in the machine, in the emergence therefore of the Historical Same, the Civilized Self; in *The Captain's Chair*, the young explorer is not really looking for adventure and material treasure but for a mirror of his own masculine self in Grant, the Great White Explorer, his father surrogate.[73] And later ethnographic filmmakers like Rouch and De Heusch will find the mirror of their own selves in the myth of the father-figure Flaherty. In the history of documentary and ethnographic film, it is Flaherty who is kept reverently alive, the mode of taxidermy here serving the filmmaker, through the aura preserved around his name.

Conclusion: *Nanook Revisited*

In Claude Massot's documentary film *Nanook Revisited* (1988), a few of the Inuit residents of Inukjuak and of the Belcher Islands—including descendents of one of the Inuit sons fathered and left behind by Flaherty—are interviewed about their memories of Robert Flaherty and the making of *Nanook*.[74] The interviews reveal a remarkable tension between the Western reception of the film as a great work of art and the desire of the local Inuit to see records of their ancestors and their land, their recognition of the fictional quality of many of the scenes, a number of which they find ludicrous. At a screening of *Nanook*, the audience of Inuit community members of Inukjuak is shown convulsed with laughter over the famous seal hunting scene so beloved by Bazin and usually received with solemnity by Western audiences.

The inaccuracies in Flaherty's *Nanook of the North* are pointed out by Moses Nowkawalk (sp?), the manager of the local television station, and Charles Nayoumealuk (sp?), whose father was a friend of Allakariallak's. Flaherty, explained Nowkawalk, "doctored" scenes, including costuming the Inuit actors in polar bear skins, using an igloo set, and falsifying to a ridiculous extent (in the locals' eyes) the seal hunt, "so that the image would fit the Southern [i.e., non-Inuit or white] imagination." The scene with the gramophone was staged. As Nowkawalk succinctly phrases his reaction as he watches the film, "This scene [the gramophone scene] here is sort of . . . I'm not so crazy about this scene."

Explaining that Nanook's real name was Allakariallak, Nayoumealuk comments, "Nanook seemed to suit the whites better." He also points out that the two women in Nanook—Nyla (Alice (?) Nuvalinga) and Cunayoo (whose name we do not know)—were not Allakariallak's wives, but were in fact common-law wives of Flaherty. The intended audience, as Nayoumealuk explains, was meant to be white. Nayoumealuk declares, "It was a film for white people, Inuit customs alone were to be shown. It was forbidden to see white men's tools. Flaherty wanted only Inuit objects." The reception of a film as "authentic" is dependent upon the audience and its already established notions of the characteristics of "real" people. The smile of Allakariallak/Nanook is almost an icon of ethnographic cinema, and it is frequently described as unforgettable, yet Charlie Nayoumealuk explains that part of the reason for the smile is that Allakariallak found what he was told to do in front of the camera quite funny: "each time a scene was shot, as soon as the camera was starting to shoot, he would burst out laughing. He couldn't help it. Flaherty would tell him—'Be serious.' He couldn't do it. He laughed each time."

The Inuit who Flaherty encountered became quite adept at all aspects of filmmaking; their descendents also have a passion and a command for visual media. Contemporary Inuit have embraced video, realizing that the power of white media can only be combated with Inuit media. In 1981, the Inuit began the Inuit Broadcasting Corporation, the first native broadcasting corporation in North America.[75] Inuit media producers believe that knowing the history of how they were represented by whites and understanding the image-making processes themselves will serve to empower their own communities. As the Inukjuak television station manager, Nowkawalk, said about *Nanook*: "Despite all the faults that I pointed out about this film this movie is a very important movie and the photographs that Robert [Flaherty] took, because they're . . . these pictures and the still shots are the only pictures of that time in this region. . . . Cause it's everybody else proclaiming it as a great film." Both Nowkawalk and Nayoumealuk's comments reveal how early ethnographic cinema is not always received by the indigenous audience in the same manner as it is received by a Western audience. Neither art nor empirical document, it is nevertheless of value because it evokes history and memory.

Fig. 4: Qaggiq/the Gathering Place

Canadian Inuit videomaker Zacharias Kunuk uses reconstruction practices which, though on the surface similar to Flaherty's, are not used to further the kind of redemptive narrative or the taxidermic salvage ethnography of Flaherty. With his actors—members of his own community—Kunuk collaborated to make video reconstructions of Inuit life before World War II in *Qaggiq/the Gathering Place* (1988) (Figure 4), depicting the building of a community house or *qaggiq*, and *Nunaqpa/Going Inland* (1991), which depicts a hunt. Like Flaherty, Kunuk shot on location, with the actors wearing traditional seal-skin clothes. However, unlike Allakariallak in *Nanook of the North*, these Inuit actors are shown hunting with guns and using tea kettles. Outsiders to the culture are given no taxonomic devices such as a map with which to situate the events portrayed in the video: Many culturally specific details will only be understandable to members of the community themselves. Made from an insider's point of view, without the conceit of any "ethnographic present," *Qaggiq* and *Nunaqpa* have no subtitles, no voice-over narrative, just the voices of the people themselves and their laughter at their own rustiness in trying to use old equipment. Older actors recount the games they used to play and chide younger actors on their clumsiness in performing tasks—Kunuk does not camouflage the fact that the actors are present-day community members reconstructing a remembered past.

Reconstruction can be used to different ends: Kunuk collaboratively reconstructs the recent past across generations in order to foreground the vital importance of collective history, whereas Flaherty removed signs of Inuit encounter with whites in order to sustain the myth of the Inuit as archetypal Primitive man. My purpose has not been to prove whether *Nanook* was a truthful document of Quebec Inuit life in the 1920s or whether Flaherty staged scenes. Instead, my goal has been to excavate the levels of discourse around the notion of authenticity, salvage ethnography, the history of the media cannibalism of the Inuit, the film's historical and intellectual context, and the style and content of the film. I have also attempted to show how a reading of the film is inextricably connected with the cult of the Ethnographic Filmmaker in ways that other film genres are not. Flaherty's awe for the figure of the great explorer and his own similar self-fashioning reveal the underlying narrative around his persona: Flaherty is the father of a men's club of explorer/artists. Like his fictional character Grant, Flaherty was the first to "penetrate" and open up ethnographic cinema for other *chasseurs d'images*, those many independent U.S. and European filmmakers like Jean Rouch and Richard Leacock who admire him. The awe that he is granted emerges from the myth of his relationship with Nanook: it is an ideal relationship between ethnographer and his faithful, loyal, simple subject. Unlike the Trobrianders who were resistant at times to Malinowski's image-making, the Inuit who worked for Flaherty did so out of love, so the myth goes.

This is why *Nanook of the North* is seen as a point of origin for art film, documentary film, and ethnographic film: it represents the Garden of Eden, the perfect relationship between filmmaker and subject, the "innocent eye," a search for realism that was not just inscription, but which made the dead look alive and the living look dead.

Notes

1. Arthur Calder-Marshall, *The Innocent Eye: The Life of Robert J. Flaherty* (New York: Harcourt, Brace & World, Inc., 1963), p. 72.

2. Joseph E. Senungetuk, *Give or Take a Century: An Eskimo Chronicle* (San Francisco: The Indian Historian Press, 1971), p. 25.

3. Asen Balikci, "Anthropology, Film and the Arctic Peoples," *Anthropology Today* 5, no. 2 (April 1989): 7. Among the popular culture items *Nanook* spawned were ice

cream bars (in Germany) and a song (Erik Barnouw, *Documentary: A History of the Non-Fiction Film* [Oxford and New York: Oxford University Press, 1983], p. 43).

4. André F. Liotard, et al., *Cinéma d'exploration: Cinéma au long cours* (Paris: P.-A. Chavane et Cie., 1950), p. 43, and André Bazin, "The Evolution of the Language of Cinema," *What is Cinema?* Trans. and ed. Hugh Gray, vol. 1 (Berkeley, Los Angeles, and London: University of California Press, 1967), pp. 23–40.

5. Luc de Heusch, *The Cinema and Social Science: A Survey of Ethnographic and Sociological Films*, vol. 16, *Reports and Papers in the Social Sciences* (Paris: UNESCO, 1962), p. 37.

6. Jo-Anne Birnie Danzker writes: "Research with Inuit participants in *Nanook of the North* is in its initial stages. It would appear, however, that none of the leading characters were identified by their actual names; that Allakariallak's (Nanook's) clothing was not indigenous to the region; that the contrived sequences were highly amusing to the Inuit; that the seal hunt was contrived. It is also possible that the walrus hunting sequence had been shot in 1914 or 1916 as part of Flaherty's earlier films, either in the Ottawa or Belcher Islands. It was from all available accounts, an authentic record of a walrus hunt" (Danzker, ed., *Robert Flaherty Photographer/Filmmaker: The Inuit 1910–1922* [Vancouver: The Vancouver Art Gallery, 1980], p. 62).

7. Bazin, "The Ontology of the Photographic Image," *What is Cinema?*, p. 27.

8. Ira Jacknis, "The Picturesque and the Scientific: Franz Boas's Plan for Anthropological Filmmaking," *Visual Anthropology* 1, no. 1 (1987): 59–64.

9. Ibid., 61.

10. Ibid.

11. George W. Stocking, Jr., *Victorian Anthropology* (New York and London: The Free Press, 1987), p. 289.

12. Jacknis, "Picturesque," pp. 59–64.

13. The nineteenth-century British taxidermist Charles Waterton, Bann explains, complained that the reality of dead beasts was "a mere dried specimen, shrunk too much in this part, or too bloated in that; a mummy, a distortion, an hideous spectacle." Waterton explains that in order to reconstruct life, the taxidermist must accept the fact of death, and use art as well as artifice: "It now depends upon the skill and anatomical knowledge of the operator (perhaps I ought to call him artist at this stage of the process), to do such complete justice to the skin before him, that, when a visitor shall gaze upon it afterwards, he will exclaim, 'That animal is alive!'" (Charles Waterton, *Essays on Natural History Chiefly Ornithology* [London, 1838], pp. 300–304, quoted in Stephen Bann, *The Clothing of Clio: A Study of the Representation of History in Nineteenth-Century Britain and France* [Cambridge: Cambridge University Press, 1984], pp. 16–17.)

14. Bann, *Clothing of Clio*, p. 14.

15. Donna Haraway, "Teddy Bear Patriarchy: Taxidermy in the Garden of Eden, New York City, 1908–1936," *Social Text: Theory/Culture/Ideology* 11 (Winter 1984/5): 25.

16. Robert Flaherty, quoted in Richard Corliss, "Robert Flaherty: The Man in the Iron Myth," *Nonfiction Film Theory and Criticism*, ed. Richard Meran Barsam (New York: E. P. Dutton & Co., Inc., 1973), p. 234.

17. Johannes Fabian, *Time and the Other: How Anthropology Makes Its Object* (New York: Columbia University Press, 1983), pp. 84–87.

18. Ibid., p. 85.

19. Even though Allakariallak is shown repeatedly smiling for the camera, an act which may appear to preclude voyeurism, the fact that he is shown ignorant of technology such as the gramophone encourages the viewer to believe that he is ignorant of moving picture technology as well.

20. James R. Kincaid, "Who Gets To Tell Their Stories?" *The New York Times Book Review*, May 3, 1992, pp. 26–27.

21. I am borrowing here Naomi Greene's insight on Mircea Eliade's description of the mythic for her analysis of Pier Paolo Pasolini's films of the 1960s. She quotes Eliade on the sacrifice which "repeats the initial sacrifice and coincides with it. . . . And the same holds true for all repetitions, i.e. all imitations of archetypes; through such imitations, man is projected into the mythical epoch in which the archetypes were first revealed. Thus we perceive a second aspect of primitive ontology: insofar as an act (or an object) acquires a certain reality through the repetition of certain paradigmatic gestures, and acquires it through that alone, there is an implicit abolition of profane time, of duration, of "history"; and he who reproduces the exemplary gesture thus finds himself transported into the mythical epoch in which its revelation took place" (*The Myth of the Eternal Return*, trans. Willard Trask [London: Routledge & Kegan Paul, 1955], p. 35, quoted in Naomi Greene, *Pier Paolo Pasolini: Cinema as Heresy* [Princeton, N.J.: Princeton University Press, 1990], p. 167).

22. "Explorers do not reveal otherness. They comment upon 'anthropology,' that is, the distance separating savagery from civilization on the diachronic line of progress." V.Y. Mudimbe, *The Invention of Africa: Gnosis, Philosophy and the Order of Knowledge* (Bloomington and Indianapolis: Indiana University Press, 1988), p. 15 (citing R. I. Rotberg, *Africa and Its Explorers* [Cambridge: Harvard University Press, 1970]).

23. Siegfried Kracauer, *Theory of Film: The Redemption of Physical Reality* (New York: Oxford University Press, 1960), pp. 273–274.

24. Robert Flaherty, Recorded BBC Talks, London, 14 June, 25 July, 5 September 1949, quoted in Jay Ruby, "A Reexamination of the Early Career of Robert J. Flaherty," *Quarterly Review of Film Studies* 5, no. 4 (Fall 1980): 448.

25. Bazin, "The Ontology of the Photographic Image," p. 9.

26. I am referring here to Teresa de Lauretis' description of the Oedipal logic of narrative in "Desire in Narrative," *Alice Doesn't: Feminism, Semiotics, Cinema*, (Bloomington: Indiana University Press, 1984), pp. 103–157. De Lauretis writes, "what is femininity, acts precisely as the impulse, the desire that will generate a narrative" (111). It is, of course, not only the female body which must be slain, but that of the indigenous person, male or female.

27. For an excellent summary of the representation of the Inuit and Alaskan Eskimo by Euro-Americans, see Ann Fienup-Riordan, *Eskimo Essays: Yup'ik Lives and How We See Them* (New Brunswick, N.J., and London: Rutgers University Press, 1990), pp. 11–23.

28. Richard Hakluyt, *The Principal Navigations, Voyages, Traffiques and Discoveries of the English Nation in Twelve Volumes*, vol. 7 (1589; repr., New York: Augustus M. Kelley, 1969), p. 305, quoted in Ibid., p. 12. Another example was a newspaper account which explained that Minik Wallace, who returned to Smith Sound after many years in the U.S., soon became again a "full-fledged 'huskie'" (Kenn Harper, *Give Me My Father's Body: The Life of Minik the New York Eskimo* [Frobisher Bay, NWT: Blacklead Books, 1986], p. 149.

29. Fatimah Tobing Rony, "Those Who Squat and Those Who Sit: The Iconography of Race in the 1895 Films of Felix-Louis Regnault," *Camera Obscura* 28 (1992): 263–289.

30. J. Garth Taylor, "An Eskimo Abroad, 1880: His Diary and Death," *Canadian Geographic* 101, no. 5 (October/November 1981): 38–43. The intersection between anthropology and popular culture is quite interesting in the case of Franz Boas. Jacobsen's collection of ethnographic artifacts would become the core of the collections at the Berlin Royal Ethnographic Museum, where Franz Boas later worked. In 1881, Jacobsen collected Kwakiutl artifacts in the same part of Canada where Boas studied. In 1883, Boas went to Baffinland himself to collect Inuit artifacts and exhume bones from graves surreptitiously. In 1886, Jacobsen brought a group of Bella Coola Indians to Berlin, an occasion which sparked Boas' own interest in Northwest Coast Indians.

31. Harper, *Give Me My Father's Body*, pp. 4, 12–33. This book contains many of Minik's letters. Minik's family was also studied by anthropologist Alfred Kroeber who later wrote about Ishi, a Yahi Indian forced to live in a museum. See Theodora Kroeber, *Ishi In Two Worlds: A Biography of the Last Wild Indian in North America* (Berkeley and Los Angeles: University of California Press, 1961).

32. Harper, *Give Me My Father's Body*, p. 99.

33. Minik Wallace, quoted in Ibid., p. 132.

34. Thomas W. Kavanaugh, "A Brief Illustrated History of the Manikins, Statues, Lay-Figures, and Life-Groups Illustrating American Ethnology in the National Museum of Natural History," unpublished paper (16 June 1990).

35. Stocking points out that the anthropologist John Lubbock in his *Origin of Civilisation* (1870) suggested that Eskimos fended well for themselves considering the environment, but that they could not achieve progress without civilized intervention (Stocking, *Victorian Anthropology*, p. 154).

36. Fienup-Riordan, *Eskimo Essays*, p. 16.

37. It is a characterization which may be found in anthropological literature as well. In 1982, the French anthropologist Jean Malaurie explained that going to study the Inuit of Thule, Greenland "a return to the Stone Age" (Jean Malaurie, *The Last Kings of Thule*, trans. Adrienne Foulke [Chicago: University of Chicago Press, 1982], p. 19, quoted in Ibid., p. 21).

38. Balikci, "Anthropology, Film and the Arctic Peoples," p. 7.

39. Rony, "Those Who Squat," pp. 273–374.

40. These films are *Esquimaux Game of Snap-The-Whip*, *Esquimaux Leap Frog*, and *Esquimaux Village*, and are at the Library of Congress. The camera operators were Edwin S. Porter and Arthur White.

To give an example of what the Alaskan Eskimo image at the exhibition fair was like, at the 1909 Alaska-Yukon-Pacific Exposition in Seattle, the promotion blurb read: "These strange people, existing only on the products of the icy North, half civilized in their nature, knowing no god, having no laws, no government, unable to read or write, with no history of their antecedents, give continuous performances of skill, marksmanship, canoeing, dancing, singing and seal catching never before seen." ("The Alaska-Yukon-Pacific Exposition of 1909: Photographs by Frank Howell," *Alaska Journal*, Summer 1984, p. 14, as quoted in Fienup-Riordan, *Eskimo Essays*, pp. 16–17).

41. Films with Inuit of U.S., British, Italian, German, and French origin include: *Wellman Polar Expedition*. *The Nordpol Expedition* (Charles Urban Trading Co., 1906), A

Dash to the North Pole (Kineto, 1909), *Fangen Junger Eisbären* (Hunting for Young Polar Bears) (Imperium Film, 1914), *Eine Forschungsexpedition durch das Nördliche* Eismeer Nach Grönland (Mefster, 1911), and *Islands of New Zembla* (Gaumont, 1913). The above films are located at the National Film Archives in London.

42. At the Human Studies Film Archives at the National Museum of Natural History. For information on the film I consulted the correspondence file of the Human Studies Film Archives.

43. These bones said to be prehistoric Eskimo were taken to the Wistar Institute of Anatomy at the University of Pennsylvania, Philadelphia.

44. Flaherty was said to have admired *Jack London in the South Seas* by Martin Johnson (1912), which was also an expedition film. (Richard Barsam, *The Vision of Robert Flaherty: The Artist as Myth and Filmmaker* [Bloomington and Indianapolis: Indiana University Press, 1988], p. 16).

45. For more on Curtis and Flaherty, see Brian Winston, "Before Grierson, Before Flaherty. The Documentary Film in 1914," *Sight and Sound* 57, no. 4 (Autumn 1988): 277–279, and Bill Holm and George Irving Quimby, *Edward S. Curtis in the Land of the War Canoes: A Pioneer Cinematographer in the Pacific Northwest* (Seattle and London: University of Washington Press, 1980), p. 30. Both Holm and Quimby believe that Flaherty, who saw *In the Land of the Headhunters* and asked Curtis for advice, was influenced by Curtis in his choice to film only what appeared traditional, i.e., salvage ethnography. For the complete diary entry of Robert and Frances Flaherty's visit to Curtis, see Jay Ruby, "A Reexamination of the Early Career of Robert J. Flaherty," *Quarterly Review of Film Studies* 5, no. 4 (Fall 1980): 455–456.

Two famous expedition films to the South Pole are that of Sir Ernest Shackleton's 1914–1917 polar expedition, *South: Sir Ernest Shackleton's Glorious Epic of the Antarctic* (1919), filmed by Frank Hurley, which focuses on the expedition members and their camp life as well as their rescue, and Herbert G. Ponting's *With Captain Scott to the South Pole* (1911–12, British Gaumont), released later as *The Great White Silence* (1924), of Captain Robert Falcon Scott's expedition to the South Pole. Both films are at the National Film Archives, London. For more on polar expeditions see Lisa Bloom, *Gender on Ice: American Ideologies of Polar Expeditions* (Minneapolis and London: University of Minnesota Press, 1993).

46. Bronislaw Malinowski, *Argonauts of the Western Pacific* (New York: E. P. Dutton and Co., Inc., 1961), p. 25.

47. Fabian, *Time and the Other*, p. 95, 106.

48. Richard Griffith, *The World of Robert Flaherty* (New York: Duell, Sloan and Pearce, 1953, 1970), p. 36.

49. See Danzker, for attribution. Thanks to the vision of the Arctic environment of the artist Noogooshoweetok, and of later Inuit camera operators who worked for Flaherty, *Nanook* has some of the most beautiful landscape scenes ever filmed. Flaherty's use of drawings shows that he learned from the art of the Inuit (Danzker, *Robert Flaherty*, pp. 53–54). See also Peter Pitseolak, *People From Our Side: An Inuit Record of Seekooseelak, the Land of the People of Cape Dorset, Baffin Land, a Life Story with Photographs* (Edmonton: Hurtig Press, 1975), pp. 87–88.

50. If Margaret Mead's image of Polynesian society in her ethnography *Coming of Age in Samoa* (1928) was offered as a counterpoint to U.S. society which she saw as puritan, repressive, and patriarchal, Flaherty's image of the Inuit was a foil for a romantic critique

of technology and the machine. See George W. Stocking, Jr., "The Ethnographic Sensibility of the 1920s and the Dualism of the Anthropological Tradition," *Romantic Motives. Essays on Anthropological Sensibility*, ed. George W. Stocking, Jr., vol. 6, *History of Anthropology* (Madison and London: University of Wisconsin Press, 1989), pp. 208–276.

51. Corliss, "Robert Flaherty," p. 231. For a more recent study of Robert Flaherty's films, see Richard Barsam, *The Vision of Robert Flaherty: The Artist as Myth and Filmmaker* (Bloomington and Indianapolis: Indiana University Press, 1988).

52. Vilhjalmur Stefansson argued that the Inuit used guns, did not hunt seals through the ice, and that the seal in the film was obviously already dead. He also decried the fake igloo and the accompanying intertitle which explained that the igloo must be colder than freezing. (Vilhjalmur Stefansson, *The Standardization of Error* [London: Kegan Paul, Trench, Trubner, 1929], pp. 86–92, quoted in Paul Rotha, with assistance of Basil Wright, "Nanook and the North," *Studies in Visual Communication* 6, no. 2 (Summer 1980): 50).

53. Robert Flaherty, quoted in Corliss, "Robert Flaherty," p. 234.

54. De Heusch, *Cinema and Social Science*, pp. 16–28.

55. Jean Rouch, "Le film ethnographique," *Ethnologie générale*, ed. Jean Poirier, vol. 24, *Encyclopédie de la Pleiade* (Paris: Éditions Gallimard, 1968), pp. 452–453.

56. De Heusch, *Cinema and Social Science*, p. 35.

57. Ibid., p. 64.

58. Bazin, "The Ontology of the Photographic Image," p. 27.

59. Balikci, "Anthropology, Film, and the Arctic Peoples," p. 6.

60. Robert J. Flaherty, in collaboration with Frances Hubbard Flaherty, *My Eskimo Friends: "Nanook of the North"* (Garden City and New York: Doubleday, Page & Company, 1924).

For information on Flaherty's work as a prospector and cartographer, see Robert Flaherty, "The Belcher Islands of Hudson Bay: Their Discovery and Exploration," *Geographical Review* 5, no. 6 (1918): 433–458; and Robert Flaherty, "Two Traverses Across Ungava Peninsula, Labrador," *Geographic Review* 6, no. 2 (1918): 116–132.

61. Charlie Nayoumealuk (sp?) in the documentary *Nanook Revisited* (directed by Claude Massot, 1988) remembers the filming of Nanook, and that the Inuit called Flaherty "Songneoluk" (sp?) meaning "tall, left-handedman."

In Frances Flaherty's account of the filming of *Elephant Boy*, she refers to Flaherty as Borah Sahib or "Great White Chief" (Barsam, *Vision*, p. 131).

62. Flaherty and Flaherty, *My Eskimo Friends*, p. 126.

63. Ibid., p. 134.

64. Danzker points out the section in which Nanook protests all the bother of making the "big aggie" of him is almost identical to that attributed to another man, "Old Atchaweek," concerning Flaherty's 1914 film in Flaherty's *Early Account of the Film* (Danzker, *Robert Flaherty*, p. 57).

65. Flaherty and Flaherty, *My Eskimo Friends*, p. 169.

66. Another book by Flaherty about a great explorer in the Arctic who is helped by the Inuit was conspicuously titled *White Master* (London: George Routledge & Sons, LTD., 1939).

67. Robert J. Flaherty, *The Captain's Chair: A Story of the North* (New York: Scribner's, 1938), p. 290.

68. Ibid., p. 291.

69. Bronislaw Malinowski, *A Diary in the Strict Sense of the Term* (Stanford, Cal.: Stanford University Press, 1989, orig. pub. 1967), p. 69.

70. James Clifford, "On Ethnographic Self-Fashioning: Conrad and Malinowski," *The Predicament of Culture: Twentieth-Century Ethnography, Literature, and Art* (Cambridge, Mass. and London: Harvard University Press, 1988), p. 110.

71. Flaherty, *The Captain's Chair*, p. 15.

72. Ibid., p. 312.

73. Frances Flaherty, "Robert Flaherty: Explorer and Film Maker: The Film of Discovery and Revelation" (mimeographed c. 1958), pp. 14–15, quoted in Jack C. Ellis, *The Documentary Idea: A Critical History of English-Language Documentary Film and Video* (Englewood Cliffs, N.J.: Prentice Hall, 1989).

74. *Nanook Revisited* contains interviews of Inuit from the areas in which Flaherty filmed and photographed, but it quickly becomes a film about a man portrayed as a kind of latter-day Flaherty, John Johnson, the white school principal. It is his voice which dominates the second half of the film, as he discusses the erosion of Inuit values and the need to build up these values. Unlike the interview of Mary, the wife of one of Flaherty's Inuit sons, in which Mary quite tellingly answers their questions about Flaherty and *Nanook* with non-answers, Johnson is eager to explain Inuit culture to the camera. The other Inuit whom Johnson encounters in the course of the film—such as his Inuit hunting partner, or the Inuit schoolteacher—are neither named nor interviewed. *Nanook Revisited* is aptly titled: It becomes a film dominated by a white point of view.

75. Laura U. Marks, "Reconfigured Nationhood: A Partisan History of the Inuit Broadcasting Corporation," *Afterimage* 21, no. 8 (March 1994): 4–7.

Sumiko Higashi

TOURING THE ORIENT WITH LAFCADIO HEARN AND CECIL B. DEMILLE

Highbrow versus Lowbrow in a Consumer Culture

> *Orientalism is a style of thought based upon an ontological and epistemological distinction made between "the Orient" and . . . "the Occident."*
>
> —*Edward W. Said*

The Orient Express: Racial Difference as Spectacle

An advertisement addressed to consumers of highbrow culture intent on acquiring possessions signifying refinement, the Boston Museum of Fine Arts gift catalog, like other catalogs issued in an attempt to capitalize on brisk sales in gift shops, has two pages on Oriental art objects. A category labeled "Legendary *Netsuke*," a small ivory carving attached to the cord of pouches tucked away in Japanese kimono sleeves, shows reproductions of these precious objets d'art. Among the brief descriptions of a few *netsuke*, representative of a far more impressive collection on permanent display at the Los Angeles County Museum of Art, are the following: "Sambaso Dancer. In A.D. 807 in the temple of Nara, a priest first performed the Sambaso dance to placate the gods against earthquake"; or "Snake. The sign for the sixth year of the Japanese zodiac. Those born during the year of the snake are meditative and attractive people who attain their goals."[1] As was true of the artifacts that introduced crowds of visitors to Japanese culture at the New Orleans world's fair over a century ago—an event described for the highbrow readers of *Harper's Weekly* by journalist Lafcadio Hearn—the Boston Museum of Fine Arts catalog represents a fantastic world filled with gods, spirits, and demons personifying the superstitions of the mysterious "Other."[2] Orientalism as a hegemonic discourse, according to Edward W. Said, requires the theatricalization of foreign peoples for Western consumption.[3]

Although highbrow culture constructed for genteel middle-class consumers purchasing emblems of refinement, as well as serious high art, has remained fascinated with Japanese objets d'art expressing an exquisite sensibility, that sensibility is still characterized as strange, mysterious, and, finally, unknowable.[4] Unlike China, Japan, which had long been closed to foreigners, exerted significant control of American exposure to its civilization through a series of world's fair exhibitions staged in major cities in the United States (1876–1916). Yet despite the favorable impression the Japanese created with displays including porcelains, lacquerware, and bronzes, Americans still regarded them as "little brown men who were expected to make Asia safe for democracy and capitalism."[5] The United States was in fact unwilling to confer more than a token honorary status upon Japan and regarded the Far East, as did other Western powers, as a site of territorial aggrandizement.[6] The Japanese, despite successful Westernization that included military victories over China (1895) and Russia (1904), were still ranked as an inferior race. Americans were insistent, in other words, on categorizing non-white racial groups on the basis of fixed and unchanging values. A pseudo-scientific buttress for such beliefs was articulated in Spencerian evolutionism and Social Darwinism, especially the eugenicist variant of the latter, during an era of unprecedented immigration and imperialistic adventures like the Spanish-American War.[7]

Attentive to the sameness of language used to assess race and money in nineteenth-century discourse on the political economy, Michael O'Malley, following Michel Foucault, offers an explanation for American intransigence: "the freer a market society becomes, the more it would imagine differences—such as racial or sexual difference—that resist renegotiation because of 'intrinsic' character." An inverse relationship existed therefore between the volatility of the marketplace on the one hand, and the demand for a stable currency and a fixed valuation placed on race and gender on the other.[8] Granted, successive theories of racial and sexual differences based on essentialism had been endemic in American thought, but in practice such differences also intersected and reinforced each other with respect to peoples of color. Americans were disinclined, moreover, to accept cultural diversity because urban demographic change represented by the migration of former slaves and new immigrants like Italians and Jews—not to mention "new women" active in the public sphere—required an identity firmly anchored in a subject-object dichotomy that commodified the "Other."[9] Any attempt to redefine such a dichotomy in terms of intersubjectivity, that is, to introduce a fluid spectrum of colors in a pluralistic culture as opposed to a strict bifurcation of races into white and non-white categories, was threatening to the status quo. Hence, the single-minded effort of the Japanese to define their national identity for the West at successive world's fairs, especially during an era of increased expenditures and sustained inflation, was doomed to failure. Indeed, the sensational publicity about precious Oriental objets d'art displayed at the expositions testified to the belief that consumption and accumulation were Western prerogatives.

A historic transformation that occurred in the late nineteenth and early twentieth centuries, the decline of Protestant self-denial and the burgeoning of consumer capitalism reinforced a national insistence on racial, ethnic, and class as well as gender differences. To put it another way, middle-class spending on goods was a sign of cultivation that delineated existing social hierarchies and, moreover, required a release from psychic repression in genteel society or a projection of sensuality onto exotic peoples as the "Other."[10] Among the latter, the Japanese—whose naval victories in the Pacific challenged visions of the Orient as the eternal feminine—were stereotyped, like the Chinese, as sexually corrupt and depraved. At a time when an unprecedented arrival of seemingly unassimilable new immigrants provoked a resurgence of nativism and xenophobia among the elite as well as the working class, racial difference between Anglo-Saxon and Asian peoples was perceived as sexual difference that not only served to titillate but also reinforced the political, cultural, and moral superiority of the West.[11] Asian men, in particular, were either feminized and desexualized as in D. W. Griffith's *Broken Blossoms* (1919), in which white actors in yellowface denied intersubjectivity between racially different peoples, or demonized as in Cecil B. DeMille's *The Cheat* (1915).[12] Unfortunately, such psychological projections onto Asians still express irrational and virulent emotions that, despite the coinage of terms like "multiculturalism" today, remain overdetermined in an era of global economic competition. "Psychologically," as Said argues, "Orientalism is a form of paranoia."[13]

The representation of Oriental sexual depravity as the dark underside of Western fascination with exquisite Japanese artifacts may be traced back in early feature films to *The Cheat*, a production that was acclaimed at the time of its release, especially by Parisian intellectuals, as canonical silent cinema. The Japanese protagonist in the film (Sessue Hayakawa) is, not coincidentally, a merchant and art collector whose mansion replicates Oriental displays in shopping emporiums, art museums, and world's fair pavilions. As he conducts a tour of the exotic Shoji Room for a beautiful white socialite—a "new woman" who is a self-indulgent and extravagant consumer—he attempts to seduce her with rare and expensive curios. Japanaiserie, or highbrow consumption of Oriental artifacts at Tiffany's, was in effect not unrelated to paranoia expressed in popular culture about sexually perverted Asians, especially men who usurped the territorial prerogative of Western colonialists. The female body, in other words, served as a metaphor in public discourse for the body politic and was thus subject to increasing restrictions during periods of rapid social change and instability.[14] Yet sumptuous bazaars in fashionable department stores enticed privatized middle-class women, otherwise repressed by a traditional Protestant ethos, and ultimately promoted consumer values in the Americanization of newly arrived immigrants.[15] DeMille and the Jesse L. Lasky Feature Play Company, which he cofounded in 1913, were thus prescient in developing a strategy to legitimate cinema for "better" audiences and to appeal as well to the aspiring masses by demonstrating the intertextuality of cultural forms as spectacle in genteel society: the motion picture screen was congruent with elegant parlor rituals scripted according to etiquette manuals and exotic displays in fashionable emporiums. After he established his credentials as an artistic director, however, DeMille became preoccupied with sexually perverse forms of spectacle for the masses as commodity fetishism that retained Orientalism at its core.

Critics as diverse as Edward W. Said and Miles Orvell argue that the dominant cultural forms of the nineteenth century enabled the elite to represent and thereby contain the "Other" within a frame.[16] Aestheticized frameworks in genteel culture included—in addition to department stores, museums, and world's fairs—spectacles such as stage melodramas, civic pageants, panoramas and dioramas, lantern slide lectures, stereographs, and downtown movie palaces, as well as literary texts such as illustrated manuals and travel books. Containment of an urban pluralistic society was in fact legislated into economic and political terms as well. Chinese and Japanese immigration, for example, was prohibited well before Congress enacted quota laws affecting all immigrants in the 1920s, and Asians, concentrated on the West coast and subject to irrational hatred, were denied land ownership and citizenship.[17] Significantly, at a time when increased immigration and labor unrest lead to violent confrontations in a chaotic urban environment,

Orientalism as a discursive practice reinforced the construction of the urban "Other" as yet another spectacle framed for visual appropriation. Preoccupation with exotic scenery, in other words, did not require overseas travel because native sites such as New York's Lower East Side, documented by nineteenth-century journalists like George G. Foster and Jacob Riis, served to define immigrants and workers as inferior to the respectable middle class.[18] The term "colony" rather than "ghetto," not coincidentally, was then used to denote areas inhabited by subjugated peoples both at home and abroad.[19]

To sum up, a "hegemonic way of seeing" became an integral aspect of genteel culture as it was transformed by consumer capitalism. Such a privileging of sight to define an increasingly commodified self, in contrast to an objectified and appropriated "Other," not only reinforced the status quo but exemplified what Guy Debord, following Georg Lukács on the reification of social relations, calls the "society of the spectacle." The spectacle in bourgeois existence is "a social relation among people, mediated by images," and "occupies the main part of the time lived outside of modern production."[20] As the working class began to enter the world of recreation and leisure previously denied them, they, too, became enthralled by amazing sights.[21] An attempt to clarify the social and cultural dynamics of Orientalism as the basis of spectacle in consumer capitalism, this essay will focus on the lines of transmission between sacrosanct highbrow culture addressed to a cultivated middle class, and popular culture constructed for a wider audience.[22] Contrary to the Arnoldian standards of the elite, significant interpenetration between levels of cultural forms demonstrated the difficulty of sustaining a hierarchy of aesthetic tastes in an era of commercialized amusement. For example, the literary texts of Lafcadio Hearn, the most influential writer to interpret Japanese culture for genteel readers, informed the visual texts of Cecil B. DeMille, an auteur who courted "better" audiences with his early feature films but also attracted a mass spectatorship transcending class and ethnic barriers. Himself a descendant of a distinguished theatrical family, DeMille first exploited the intertextuality of established cultural forms to legitimate cinema, and then proceeded to conflate visions of the Orient in vulgar spectacles to preach unambiguous messages about white supremacy. As such, his feature films about unbridled consumer fantasies in the 1920s constitute popular culture texts, with antecedents in Arnoldian highbrow culture, that generated referential power not only on an intertextual basis but in American society as a whole.[23]

Lafcadio Hearn: Touring Japan as an Exhibition Site for Genteel Consumers

Although he himself was an immigrant of Greek and Anglo-Irish heritage and was handicapped with an eye blinded in a freak playground accident, Lafcadio Hearn was nevertheless a product of privileged society. Indeed, he personified the intense and inexhaustible quest for aestheticized and exotic experience characteristic of turn-of-the-century genteel culture. An essential component of antimodernism, or nostalgia for an idealized past eroded by the rationalizing processes of modernization, the constant preoccupation of the elite with the picturesque manifested itself in fascination with Orientalist spectacle. Credited with "powers of description . . . almost unparalleled in the America of his day," Hearn was particularly equipped as an indefatigable flaneur to recount his scenic travels for voyeuristic middle-class readers.[24] Hence, he provided a significant intertext in the form of travel books for directors like DeMille, who inserted shots of foreign countries in films with exotic settings. As a matter of fact, actuality footage like *Scenes of Japan* and *Nihonbashi Street Tokio*, produced at the turn-of-the-century, were not only scenic visualizations of Hearn's texts but antecedents of travelogs interpolated in fiction films. Such use of travel films, accepted by audiences as realistic representations, was instrumental in legitimating stereotyped and racist characterizations in fictional narratives.

Significantly, Hearn began his career as a journalist in Cincinnati in the 1870s and achieved renown overnight with a harrowing story of a sensational murder victim in the *Enquirer*. Undaunted by the sordidness of poverty and crime, he proceeded to investigate stories reported at police stations as if he were conducting a tour of exotic urban sights in the realist tradition of newsman George G. Foster.[25] The journalist appealed to highbrow readers with a brand of realism in which a lifelong penchant for the supernatural merged with voyeuristic, colorful, and detailed descriptions—a particularly arresting style for an Orientalist aesthetic. After exhaustive reporting in the metropolitan environs of Cincinnati, Hearn pursued his quest for the exotic in New Orleans, where he frequented the French Quarter, promoted the work of Southern local colorists, and met the Japanese official in charge of the world's fair exhibit. During his years as a reporter for the New Orleans *Times-Democrat*, he became preoccupied with publishing studies of Arabic culture and, since he was fluent in French, translated several works, including canonical

Orientalist texts such as Gustave Flaubert's *The Temptation of Saint Anthony* and *Salammbô*. Given French preoccupation with the Middle East as a site of Orientalism, the relationship between Hearn's translations of French literature and the publication of his Arabesques was hardly coincidental.[26] Always in pursuit of the esoteric, enchanting, and picturesque, Hearn decided to leave the United States in 1887 and spent two years amidst tropical settings in Martinique. In 1890 he undertook an even further journey to Japan to write a series of articles for *Harper's Magazine* and resituated Orientalism as discourse on the Far rather than the Middle East. An adventure typical of his restless peregrinations became a permanent stay, however, as he acquired a reputation teaching English literature, married a Japanese woman, and was legally adopted by her family as Koizumi Yakumo.

During the remaining years of his short life, Hearn published an astonishing number of works that introduced Western readers to Japanese culture, works that continued to sell even more briskly after his death in 1904. Attesting to his reputation for descriptions of artifacts, architectural wonders, and natural scenery, as well as for hypnotic accounts of strange customs, religious beliefs, and charming folk tales, critics repeatedly stressed his "ability to *see* clearly . . . imaginatively" and praised his "achievements in narrative and *word-painting* (my emphasis)." As a matter of fact, Stefan Zweig remarked that "reading Hearn . . . ranked second only to visiting the country."[27] A century later, his works about Japan still resonate with passages that impress the reader as a foreshadowing of cinematic experience. Consider, for example, this description from his *Harper's Weekly* article "The New Orleans Exposition: The Japanese Exhibit," in which he guides the reader on a tour of strange and wondrous artifacts:

> The display of bronzes and ceramics—in which the antique art of Nippon is largely represented—dazzles and deceives the inexperienced eye. Great incense-burners, with double-headed and triple-clawed dragons interlinked about them in monstrous contortion, seem to be wrought in fine bronze; but they are only faience-ware dexterously metal-tinted. Delicate vases of porcelain aspect, covered with grotesque paintings, and surmounted by a cover on which a frog, a tiger, or a gargoyle-shaped creature is sitting, turn out to be made of the finest and hardest statue metal.[28]

Or, consider this passage, which might have described a tracking shot in a film, from his first two volumes about his adopted country, *Glimpses of*

Unfamiliar Japan, a title denoting a fleeting and voyeuristic look at a strange land:

> Parallel with Tenjinmachi runs the great street of the Buddhist temples, or Teramachi, of which the eastern side is one unbroken succession of temples,—a solid front of court walls tile-capped, with imposing gateways at regular intervals. Above this long stretch of tile-capped wall rise the beautiful tilted massive lines of gray-blue temple roofs against the sky.[29]

Although the reading of Hearn in this essay is mostly confined to the two-volume work that constituted the first of many books about Japan, it is clear that the author expanded his vision at the New Orleans exposition so that the Japanese islands became a vast museum or shopping emporium. The author's commodification of images occurred, not coincidentally, within the context of a burgeoning consumer culture in which retail merchants built spectacular displays of goods that linked luxury and sensuality with exoticism. Such an association not only appealed to the erotic fantasies of consumers, but also implied that accumulation was a Western prerogative. As Hearn himself wrote, "to dare to look at anything in Japan is to want to buy it. So I buy, and buy, and buy!"[30] Addressing his readers in second person, he attests not only to the seduction of consumption, but to its expression in imperialistic form as an impulse to accumulate peoples and territories:

> What you really want to buy is not the contents of a shop; you want the shop and the shopkeeper, and streets of shops with their draperies and their habitants, the whole city and the bay and the mountains begirding it, and Fujiyama's white witchery . . . all Japan, . . . with its magical trees and luminous atmosphere, with all its cities and towns and temples, and forty millions of the most lovable people in the universe.[31]

Granted, Hearn comments from time to time on the moral character of the Japanese: "Gentler and kindlier faces I have never beheld; and they reflect the souls behind them"; or "they are still the best people in the world to live among." And he even suspects that he himself may be the barbarian as he informs his readers about floral arrangements: "you are yet a savage in such matters compared with the commonest coolies among you . . . despite your Occidental idea of self-superiority, you will feel humbled by the discovery that all flower displays you have ever seen . . . were only monstrosities." Yet, like his genteel readers, Hearn was mostly interested in touring Japan as a soul-searching exercise that led, however circuitously, back to himself. Americans like Hearn projected their dissatisfaction with the relentless experience of modernization onto Japan, as Neil Harris argues, in antimodernist discourse that emphasized exquisite arts and crafts untouched by modern manufacturing methods. Hearn wrote, for example, "whenever to-day in Japan one sees something totally uninteresting in porcelain or metal, something commonplace and ugly, one may be almost sure that detestable something has been shaped under foreign influence."[32] Not surprisingly, the author fled from unwelcome signs of Westernization in Meiji Japan. According to Robert Rosenstone, "Hearn is too canny ever to forget that only a certain kind of Japan suits his literary talent and his audience." Such is still the case. Eighty years after the first publication of *Glimpses of Unfamiliar Japan* in 1894, the Charles E. Tuttle Company issued a reprint with a foreword that testified to the lasting influence of the author: "Here are the customs, the superstitions, the charming scenery, the revelations of Japanese character . . . that Hearn found so bewitching." As Said reminds us, travel books as texts "acquire a greater authority, and use, even than the actuality it describes."[33] Cinema, by virtue of its powerful reality effect, would generate even more such authority.

Given the cultural and social context in which Hearn popularized Japan, he personified the antimodernist search for aestheticized experience even as urbanization, bureaucratization, and rationalization developed in both the West and East. Aesthetic sights appealing to the genteel sensibility were foregrounded as opposed to discussion of geopolitical, political, or constitutional issues, especially in the earlier works. Hearn was so preoccupied with legends, folk tales, and religious stories populated by spectral figures that these narratives render tenuous the line between past and present, myth and history, fantasy and reality. To put it another way, history remains a Western discourse, whereas Japan exists in a timeless vacuum as the eternal feminine. Small wonder that Western powers resented Japan's intrusion on the stage of global politics in the late nineteenth century, as signified by its victories in the Sino-Japanese and Russo-Japanese wars. Americans much preferred Hearn's characterization of an elfish fairy-tale land with gods and goddesses inhabiting exotic shrines, temples, and palaces. The author's narrative is peppered with locutions like strange, quaint, queer, weird, grotesque, monstrous, phantasmal, apparitional, ghostly, liliputian, and so forth. But he also expresses the ennui that lurks beneath his endless sightseeing trips—which necessitated the labors of a *kuruma*-runner as a beast of burden—and the boredom implicit in Western consumer culture. So he complains that he has "become so accustomed to surprises, to interesting or extraordinary sights, that when a day happens to pass during which nothing remarkable has been heard or seen . . . [he feels] vaguely discontented."[34] Decades later, DeMille experiences a similar ennui that goads him into escalating his production budgets and orchestrating ever more bizarre forms of spectacle.

Due to a history of profound misunderstanding between Japan and the United States—a historical development that Hearn may have influenced with his writings—the author has become the subject of contentiousness among critics. Matthew Josephson, for example, titled a perceptive essay about the expatriate "An Enemy of the West," whereas Arthur E. Kunst lacerates Hearn as a racial "bigot" and "propagandist" whose writings constitute "pseudo-Buddhist frauds upon . . . [the] American public." Surely, the truth lies somewhere in between. As a matter of fact, Hearn himself was most insightful about the nature of his explorations of Japan. Toward the end of his life, he began a series of lectures that he intended to deliver at Cornell University with the admission, "I cannot understand the Japanese at all." Indeed, the most revealing moment in *Glimpses of Unfamiliar Japan* occurs when he wanders into an ancient shrine only to confront his own reflection in a mirror—in a scenario prefiguring Lacanian thought about the role of vision in the formation of the human subject and spectatorship. As he contemplates the meaning of this incident, he confesses, "I am beginning to wonder whether I shall ever be able to discover that which I seek—outside myself! That is, outside my own imagination."[35] Japan, in other words, existed as a template for his own spectral visions, but such a projection was typical of Orientalist experience. At the base of Orientalism, then, was not only a reification of the mysterious "Other" as a means of defining the self, but a way of representing non-Western culture that reduced it to a curiosity, at best, and to imperialistic adventure, at worst. Yet travel books such as Hearn's that were addressed to highbrow readers were nevertheless complex representations of the Orient. When the spectacle of the Far East was recycled as travelogs in DeMille's feature films, stereotyped visions began to prevail over more ambiguous studies of peoples abroad.

Cecil B. DeMille: Orchestrating Roadshow Spectacles as Commodity Fetishism

During an era when Arnoldian culture was still sacrosanct, the cultivated elite had expressed concern about the "deverbalization of the forum," or the inversion of the semiotic ratio between words and pictures as exemplified in mass cultural forms such as advertisements and silent film with intertitles.[36] Granted, DeMille's fascination with consumption as an exotic fantasy had antecedents in highbrow culture and became overblown within a context shaped by writers like Hearn. But the worst fears of the elite were realized. The director, heretofore praised for artistic achievement in the cinema, proceeded to vulgarize Orientalist discourse that in genteel texts retained elegant phrasing and ambiguous thought. Further, he articulated blatant racism unmitigated by philosophical speculation such as Hearn's attempt to reconcile Spencerian evolutionism with Buddhism.[37] Such a debasement of genteel forms of Orientalism surely did not augur well for the politics of race relations in a pluralistic culture. Yet DeMille's indebtedness to representations of the Orient in travel books addressed to the sophisticated reader remains. Consider, for example, the only two extant silent features in which he represents the Far East, *The Whispering Chorus* (1918) and *Fool's Paradise* (1922).[38]

The Whispering Chorus is a transitional work in DeMille's silent film career and remains an interesting contrast to the trendsetting Jazz Age picture that followed it, *Old Wives for New* (1918). Significantly, consumption is still weighted down with moral issues rather than construed as a pleasurable pursuit signifying modernity, as is the case in the later sex comedies and melodramas. An adaptation of a short story, *The Whispering Chorus* traces the downward spiral of John Tremble (Raymond Hatton), a lowly bookkeeper who embezzles funds from his employer—himself involved in graft—because a meager salary barely meets the needs of his long-suffering wife, Jane, and his devoted, elderly mother. After a pitiful Christmas season, when commodities displayed behind plate glass windows appeared especially enticing, he falsifies accounting entries. Fearful that an investigation will disclose his theft, John disappears, plants his identification papers on a corpse, and becomes a deckhand on a merchant ship. Jane (Kathlyn Williams), meanwhile, assumes that he is dead and finds employment as well as romance in the office of a Progressive Era reformer (Elliott Dexter). The depth of John's physical and moral decay is shown, not coincidentally, in a sequence that occurs in China. DeMille contrasts the whorehouses of Shanghai with the superior morality of the Anglo-Saxon West through parallel editing. Shots of Jane's marriage to the reformer in an Episcopal church are intercut with shots of John being seduced by an Asian prostitute in yellowface (Julia Faye).[39] These symbolic events take place as the Chinese celebrate a new year. Shanghai festivities in effect provide the director with an opportunity to orchestrate an Orientalist spectacle in breathtaking color, complete with fireworks and a parade featuring a gigantic dragon. Albeit intended to be picturesque for the edification of film spectators, these scenes are more revealing with respect to racial attitudes as described in the script:

> Scene 142
> Exterior. Street in Shanghai—New Year's Night
> Wonderful lanterns both large and small hung from houses across street. Individual lanterns carried on poles by Orientals who throng streets in native costumes and holiday mood. Gigantic fire crackers strung across street from one balcony to another. . . . From the balconies red, blue and green colored fire is burning. The flower wreathed populace come gaily down the street with lanterns and chattering as they go. . . . among the crowd are a small group of 2 Chinamen—3 Chinese girls—"Sam-Sen" players, and Tremble. . . . At this point a gorgeously dressed "Mandarin" . . . rides indifferently along in his sedan chair, carried on the backs of six coolies. . . . Next the "Sacred Dragon" carried on poles by ten eunuchs. . . . Nostrils of Dragon spout colored fire . . . (CUT TO)
>
> Scene 143
> Exterior Street in Shanghai (Night)
> (Close Up)
> Of Tremble and one of the Chinamen in his party and one of the "Sam-Sen" players (NOTE: These must be real Orientals)[40]

Tremble's moral degradation is complete as he next enters the "Hop Joint," where a translucent scrim is rolled up to reveal a prostitute, dressed in a floral brocaded gown with kimono sleeves and lounging on a bed covered with floral drapery (Figure 1). DeMille's scene recalls Matisse's sensual and colorful paintings of reclining odalisques in the Middle East as an expression of French Orientalism. A spray of orange blossoms fancied by the prostitute motivates the film's cut back to the wedding scene, in which Jane marches down the aisle of a church to be wed in front of an altar with the stars and stripes, a symbol of American supremacy, visible to the right.

The script and mise-en-scène of *The Whispering Chorus* both represent the Chinese as exotic, morally decadent, and racially inferior. Such derogatory terms as "Chinamen" and "coolies" used in the script attest to the existence in American society of racial hierarchies not subject to renegotiation. Furthermore, the Chinese—whose (mis)recognition as the "Other" is so threatening that except for minor characters white

Fig. 1: Julia Faye in yellowface as a Chinese prostitute who lures Raymond Hatton during a stop in Shanghai. (Courtesy of George Eastman House)

actress appear in 'yellow'face—are objectified as spectacle to gratify voyeuristic consumers. As *Variety* affirmed, "There are several thrills . . . but it is the lighting of the celebration of the Chinese New Year in Shanghai that is the most effective work."[41] Such thrills were staged for didactic purposes, however, according to the tradition of spiritual uplift in pictorial realism that DeMille exemplified. Edward Weitzel remarked in *Motion Picture News* in the pedantic tone characteristic of genteel culture: "the keen artistic sense of the picture lifts . . . portions of the story above the merely sensational and dignifies them with a moral force." The critic, interestingly, bespoke the condescending attitude of the middle class toward the lower orders by commenting that if "the most superficial observer" found "nothing of interest in such a spectacle, there are still garish cabarets where his sort of entertainment is to be had." With respect to the film's reception, the uneducated classes most likely enjoyed the Shanghai spectacle, even if they were not uplifted by the redemptive message, as Weitzel observed that "Alvin Wyckoff, chief Lasky cameraman has worked in some excellent color effects."[42] The custodians of culture, it should be noted, had already expressed misgivings regarding the use of color to pander to mass tastes, as they had earlier been opposed to the proliferation of halftones diluting literary texts.

DeMille probably employed the Wyckoff two-color process, also known as the Handshiegl process, that he had used to great effect in several films starring Metropolitan Opera diva Geraldine Farrar. Indeed, the expensive use of color processes to differentiate non-white peoples from Anglo-Saxon actors was hardly coincidental. In 1922, the first two-step Technicolor film was used to film *Toll of the Sea*, a Madame Butterfly scenario starring Anna May Wong.[43]

DeMille's brief tour of Shanghai as the scene of John Tremble's greatest moral degradation foreshadows an even more bizarre voyage in *Fool's Paradise*. In contrast to the earlier film, which features an exotic journey related to the narrative, *Fool's Paradise* consists of two parts seemingly unrelated in terms of plot but echoing the same thematics about white supremacy. The first part is the narrative of an impoverished and wounded veteran named Arthur Phelps (Conrad Nagel) who settles in a Texas boom town. As indicated by an intertitle that signifies exotic fantasies, "The Arabian Nights—offers no magic compared to a new oil town on the Mexican Border." A hegemonic discourse and practice that contain the "Other" within a frame, Orientalism is threatened not only by Mexicans who cross geographical boundaries at will, but also by African Americans and workers who strike it rich and themselves become consumers. An early scene in the film, which represents Arthur's point of view, shows wealthy blacks in an expensive limousine. According to the intertitle, "In a topsy-turvy Oil Town, where you see your Boob-black in an automobile de Luxe—and your Garbage Man in diamonds, it is poor consolation to live in a shack built of Packing Cases, Tin Cans—and Dreams."

DeMille's first spectacle as a tour de force in the film focuses on a theatrical performance by a globe-trotting French dancer, Rosa Duchene (Mildred Harris), with whom Arthur fell in love while he was in a veteran's hospital in France. She appears on stage as "The Snow Queen," costumed in white drapery and ropes of pearls, and exclaims to her earthly lover, "Leave zis stupid, mortal Love, and come wiz me upon my Magic Carpet—I will show you ze World at your feet!" After striking it rich himself, Arthur abandons the woman who loves him, Poll Patchouli (Dorothy Dalton), and follows the ballerina's siren call not to the Middle East, as the magic carpet implies, but to the Far East. In fact, American preoccupation with Asia rather than Arabia as the site of Orientalism, as defined by Said, dated back to the profitable China trade (briefly alluded to in *The Whispering Chorus*) and became more urgent as Western powers and Japan carved up the decaying Manchu empire.[44] An art title

Fig. 2: Cecil B. DeMille posing with Mildred Harris on an Orientalist set in *Fool's Paradise*. (Courtesy of Brigham Young University)

with a sketch of a Buddha in the upper left-hand corner informs us: "Beyond the Turquoise Blue of Tropic Seas—ages distant from the bustling Oil Fields—Duchene has paused in her triumphal progress round the World, to make a study of the ancient Temple Dances of Siam."

Already in *The Whispering Chorus*, DeMille confuses the Chinese with the Japanese by referring to "Sam-Sen" players and costuming the prostitute in a gown with kimono sleeves. Although the *samsen* is indeed a stringed Chinese instrument, the *shamisen* is a similar musical device that kimono-clad women play in Japan.[45] As he conflates bizarre and vulgarized representations of Africa, the Middle East, and the Far East in *Fool's Paradise*, the director's imagination runs riot. Actuality footage of Siamese architecture and boats in a lagoon precede shots of a turbaned man leading an elephant, a scene that would appear to belong in India rather than Thailand (formerly Siam). Western tourists then enter a temple in which Siamese dancers are performing before Rosa Duchene, seated in lotus position on an elevated platform inside a sculpted niche (Figure 2). According to the script, "In her pose she suggests an Eastern goddess."[46] A blond ballerina has in fact eclipsed the Buddha in the earlier art title. Another title informs the audience that Rosa has had a hypnotic effect on the Siamese prince who, not surprisingly, is portrayed

Fig. 3: Cecil B. DeMille photographed with a peacock used to create an exotic setting in *Fool's Paradise*. (Courtesy of Brigham Young University)

by a white actor, John Davidson: "Prince Talat-Noi—whose Heart has become so tangled in the strands of Duchene's Golden Hair that he gives her full freedom of the Temple." Complicating the romantic plot even further, "the Almond Eyes of the Prince's chief Wife [also played by a white actress, Julia Faye], grow dark as she watches the Blue-Eyed Woman." The princess, wearing a spectacular headdress with dragon tails emerging from either side of her head, descends from a platform bordered with palm trees and guarded by black men in loin cloths as African imports.

When Arthur visits Rosa later that evening, the audience sees a mansion with Mediterranean, Spanish colonial, and Southern Californian motifs. A peacock perches on an iron railing at the perimeter of an estate graced by palm trees (Figure 3). As she lounges indoors, the ballerina plays with a monkey and a Thai doll against a background of leopard skin draped on a wall, a conflation of Asia and Africa that becomes even more preposterous in the following sequence. An event that promises to fend

Fig. 4: John Davidson in yellowface with Mildred Harris and Conrad Nagel as they peer into an alligator pit in *Fool's Paradise*. (Courtesy of George Eastman House)

off Rosa's boredom with her lackluster American suitor, a "ceremony of the Living Sacrifice to the Sacred Reptiles" is staged after she arrives at the temple with the prince (Figure 4). Seated near the throne of the Siamese prince and princess are two women wearing Egyptian costumes. DeMille intercuts scenes of Buddhist priests with shaven heads preparing to sacrifice a lamb (which in Christian iconography symbolizes Christ) with shots of teeming alligators in a pit below. Outraged by such a pagan ritual, Arthur rescues the innocent lamb, fights off a crowd of protesters, and, standing in front of a statue of the Buddha that he displaces, sneers, "You fellows have *some* idea of Sport!" Rosa has an even more dangerous idea of sport as she throws her glove in the alligator pit and commands the prince to retrieve it. Arthur rescues his hapless rival by fighting off hungry reptiles with a wooden stick and a dinner jacket.

A spectacle often repeated today in such box-office winners as *Indiana Jones and the Temple of Doom*, *Fool's Paradise* is a naked assertion of white supremacy that conflates representations of peoples around the globe to show them as exotic, mysterious, pagan, culturally backward, and racially inferior. The Orient, in other words, is the subject of a voyeuristic tour that reifies foreigners so that they are reduced to the level of curios produced in consumer capitalism and, more to the point, assigned a low rate of exchange favorable to Anglo-Saxon spectators. Accordingly, the script enumerates the "types" that populate Siam: "temple-bonzes; beggars; men, women, and children with offerings for the gods; vendors of fruit, flowers and jewels; pariah dogs; sacred monkeys; [and] pheasants," as if they were interchangeable commodities.[47] Such a bazaar, though located in the Far East, exemplifies Lukács argument that the process of reification pervasive in bourgeois society results in objects invested with human qualities and human beings construed as objects.[48] Asians (as well as Arabs and Africans) are specifically represented at a low premium in terms of exchange value because Americans, having anchored their identity in a subject-object dichotomy rather than in intersubjectivity, perceive the "Other" as being the same. The script thus specifies, "People move about on the promenade—Siamese types and with perhaps a few Chinese and Japanese."[49] The Siamese prince, furthermore, is married to a Javanese woman.

A vulgarized form of Orientalism as a cultural practice of the elite, *Fool's Paradise* attests that film as popular culture had antecedents in Arnoldian culture as "the best that has been thought and said in the world."[50] DeMille's spectacle for the masses was a motion picture version of scenic tours that authors like Hearn had popularized for a genteel readership. Indeed, travel books dazzled readers with a cinematic quality that a director like DeMille actualized in his production of images constituting the "society of the spectacle." Significantly, trade journal and fan magazine critics, who were undoubtedly middle class in their social origins, expressed disapproval of the director's pandering to a mass audience with bread and circuses. A perceived difference existed between spectacle that was uplifting and vulgar shows that appealed to the base instincts of the lower orders. Laurence Reid, for example, complained in *Motion Picture News* that the sightseeing tour of *Fool's Paradise* was a "Barnum and Bailey show" that bore little relation to the narrative: "DeMille . . . takes the spectator on a journey to Siam. . . . These scenes are lavish in the extreme, but they serve no purpose in advancing the story. They merely dazzle the eye. The simple structure of the early sequence is lost in a maze of Oriental trappings." Similarly, *Motion Picture Magazine* commented: "This latest . . . production is a feature production and a travelog all in one. As a matter of fact, someone said, there was just everything in "A Fool's Paradise" [*sic*] but the Siamese twins. . . .

There was . . . a short episode which found the characters in India or some far Eastern [*sic*] clime." After being touted as one of the most artistic filmmakers in the industry, DeMille squandered his reputation and was seduced by film production as commodity fetishism or an expression of displaced emotions and desires. As Frederick James Smith warned in *Motion Picture Classic* with reference to yet another cheap amusement for the working class: "Cecil DeMille is fast slipping from his luxuriously upholstered seat as one of our foremost directors. . . . The production is as tinselly and unreal as the Coney Island midway."[51] Significantly, Paramount's program for the film emphasized the very sensational and voyeuristic qualities of the film that critics labeled inauthentic and tawdry:

> See the wonderful Ice-ballet and the flight of the magic carpet
> See the marvelous growth of a Mexican border oil-town and its colorful cantina
> See the great thrill of the pit of sacred reptiles and the fight for life against man-eating alligators
> See the spectacular Siam Soo dances by natives and the attempt at living sacrifice
> See the great theatre scenes, the cigar explosion, the knife throwing villain, the sacrifice of a woman's soul for the man she loves and a thousand other elements of a marvelous story[52]

As noted by critics, *Fool's Paradise* represented a decline in DeMille's considerable cultural capital. That is to say, the director became obsessed with filmmaking as a form of commodity fetishism rather than adhering to middle-class cultural practice that dictated realistic narrative for didactic ends. Starting with his early Jazz Age films, the director's production budgets escalated at such an astonishing rate that he was constantly involved in disputes and contract renegotiations with the front office in New York. Usually, Jesse L. Lasky, a longtime business associate and the corporation's vice-president, ran interference between him and the president, Adolph Zukor. In June 1921, however, Zukor himself wrote Cecil B. DeMille Productions—a partnership that the director established to share profits with Famous Players–Lasky—regarding the cost of *Fool's Paradise*: "We again ratify the expenditure to date . . . on the production . . . ; such cost of production having exceeded . . . the sum of $290,000, the amount referred to in paragraph four of the aforesaid contract." Famous Players-Lasky's strategy to recoup production costs was to premiere the film at first-run theaters such as the Criterion in New York and to charge top admission prices ranging from $1.50 to $2.20. As expected, *Fool's Paradise*, promoted as a series of lavish and breathtaking spectacles, proved to be a moneymaker at the box office. Critics did not fail to comment on the obvious expense involved in its production. *Variety*, for example, remarked that "as a production it speaks of unlimited expenditure in the making. . . . while here and there a slight suggestion of overproduction slips in, . . . only those interested technically and from the standpoint of the finances will take notice."[53]

DeMille has mostly been forgotten as an artist who played an important role in legitimating early feature film and is remembered instead as a showman who produced kitsch spectacles. Ultimately, his obsession with filmmaking as a form of Orientalist consumption has left the more lasting impact on American consumer culture. Significantly, his acclaimed silent biblical epics, *The Ten Commandments* (1923) and *The King of Kings* (1927), foreshadowed the Orientalism of his sound films by representing sexual excess in female stereotypes such as Mary Magdalene, draped in a scarlet gown and lounging with a pet leopard in stunning Technicolor. Although the director began his career in an era that was seduced by realistic representations of the "Other" as spectacle, Orientalist fantasies in the form of outré flashbacks or fantasy sequences increasingly displaced the tradition of pictorial realism in the 1920s. A form of commodity fetishism that reinforced the consumer ethos and validated accumulation and display as a Western franchise, the director's vulgar spectacles conflated exotic scenery, architecture, peoples, animals, and artifacts. Such eclecticism, which represented a looting of the world's iconography, had antecedents in travel narratives published by highbrow authors like Hearn, but soon became the stock in trade of amusement park freak shows. Since Americans invested their national identity in a subject-object dichotomy that precluded differentiation among the "Other," the fixed division of the races into white and nonwhite categories justified visual appropriation and imperialistic conquest alike. Attempts by the Japanese, who Westernized, to define themselves as unique for American spectators at world's fair exhibitions were thus unequal to the practice of Orientalism as a totalizing discourse. To this day, the Orient remains a travel book illustration haunted by spectral visions that, depending on the dictates of the political economy, are either aestheticized or demonized for consumption by the West.

Notes

I wish to thank Edward E. Stratmann at George Eastman House; Ned Comstock at the Cinema-TV Library, University of Southern California; and James V. D'Arc at Harold B.

Lee Library, Brigham Young University for their assistance with research for this essay. Also, thanks go to Robert Rosenstone for information about Lafcadio Hearn.

1. Museum of Fine Arts, Boston, Gift Catalog (Fall 1994), pp. 40–41. The *netsuke* are offered in collaboration with the Peabody Essex Museum in Salem, Mass. Robert Rosenstone writes about the experience of William Elliot Griffis, Edward S. Morse, and Lafcadio Hearn as Westerners who popularized Japan during the nineteenth century. Edward S. Morse, interestingly, stored enormous collections of Japanese artifacts at both the Boston Museum of Fine Arts and the Peabody Museum. See Rosenstone, *Mirror in the Shrine* (Cambridge: Harvard University Press, 1988). Consistent with representations of Japan as a fairy-tale land, cartographers visualized the island nation as being surrounded by sea monsters even as late as the seventeenth century. See Lutz Walker, ed., *Japan: A Cartographic Vision* (New York: Prestel, 1994), a catalog issued in conjunction with an exhibit held at the Japan Society.

2. Lafcadio Hearn, "The New Orleans Exposition," *Harper's Weekly*, 31 March 1885, p. 71; "The East at New Orleans," *Harper's Weekly* 7 March 1885, p. 155; reprinted in Lafcadio Hearn, *Occidental Gleanings*, ed. by Albert Mordell (Freeport: Books for Libraries Press, Inc., 1925), pp. 209–219.

3. Edward W. Said, *Orientalism* (New York: Pantheon, 1978), p. 63.

4. For the sake of accuracy, I refer to highbrow culture in terms of the cultural consumption of the genteel middle-class rather than focusing on questions of aesthetics.

5. Neil Harris, "All the World a Melting Pot? Japan at American Fairs, 1876–1904," in *Cultural Excursions: Marketing Appetites and Cultural Tastes in Modern America* (Chicago: University of Chicago Press, 1990), pp. 29–55; Robert W. Rydell, *All the World's a Fair: Visions of Empire at American International Expositions, 1876–1916* (Chicago: University of Chicago Press, 1984), p. 205. See also Rydell, "The Culture of Imperial Abundance: World's Fairs in the Making of American Culture," in Simon J. Bronner, ed., *Consuming Visions: Accumulation and Display of Goods in America, 1880–1929* (New York: W. W. Norton, 1989), pp. 191–216.

6. According to Western cartography, the world consists of the West as privileged vantage point and a non-Western sphere designated as the Near, Middle, and Far East.

7. See John Higham, *Strangers in the Land: Patterns of American Nativism 1860–1925* (New York: Atheneum, 1981; New Brunswick: Rutgers University Press, 1955).

8. Michael O'Malley, "Specie and Species: Race and the Money Question in Nineteenth-Century America," *American Historical Review* 99 (June 1994):391.

9. On reification, see Georg Lukács, *History and Consciousness: Studies in Marxist Dialectics*, trans. Rodney Livingstone (Cambridge: MIT Press, 1971); Martin Jay, *Marxism and Totality: The Adventures of a Concept from Lukács to Habermas* (Berkeley: University of California Press, 1984); Fredric Jameson, "Reification and Utopia in Mass Culture," *Social Text* 1 (1979):130–148.

10. On the repressive social practices of elite society, see Edith Wharton, *The Age of Innocence* (New York: Charles Scribner's Sons, 1968; New York: D. Appleton & Co., 1920).

11. See Higham, *Strangers*. See also Richard Hofstadter, *Social Darwinism in American Thought* (Philadelphia: University of Pennsylvania Press, 1944).

12. On *Broken Blossoms*, see Nick Browne, "Griffith's Family Discourse: Griffith and Freud," *Quarterly Review of Film Studies* 6 (Winter 1981):67–80; reprinted in Christine Gledhill, ed., *Home Is Where the Heart Is* (London: British Film Institute, 1987), pp.

223–234; Dudley Andrew, "Broken Blossoms: The Art and Eros of a Perverse Text," *QRFS*, 81–90; Julia Lesage, "Artful Racism, Artful Rape," *Jump Cut* 26 (1981):51–55; reprinted in Gledhill, ed., *Home Is Where the Heart Is*, pp. 235–254; Robert Lang, *American Melodrama: Griffith, Vidor, Minnelli* (Princeton, N.J.: Princeton University Press, 1989), pp. 90–104; Gina Marchetti, *Romance and the "Yellow Peril": Race, Sex, and Discursive Strategies in Hollywood Fiction* (Berkeley: University of California Press, 1993), chap. 2. On *The Cheat*, see my *Cecil B. DeMille and American Culture: The Silent Era* (Berkeley: University of California Press, 1994), chap. 4; see also my "Ethnicity, Class, and Gender in Film: DeMille's *The Cheat*," in Lester Friedman, *Unspeakable Images: Ethnicity and the American Cinema* (Urbana: University of Illinois Press, 1991): pp. 112–130; Marchetti, *Romance and the "Yellow Peril,"* chap. 2.; Judith Mayne, *The Woman at the Keyhole: Feminism and Women's Cinema* (Bloomington: Indiana University Press, 1990), pp. 33–36; Mayne, "The Limits of Spectacle," *Wide Angle* 5 (1989):6–9. On Hayakawa, see Donald Kirihara, "The Accepted Idea Displaced: Stereotype and Sessue Hayakawa," in this volume.

13. Said, *Orientalism*, p. 72. Witness the recent cinematic version of Michael Crichton's best-seller *Rising Sun* (1993), a box-office success praised by some critics as a toned-down version of the paranoid conspiratorial plot of the Japan-bashing novel. Director Phillip Kauffman, however, represents the Japanese as menacing corporate figures who presume to appropriate not only the Western prerogative of Foucauldian panoptic surveillance with advanced high-tech gadgetry, but also disport themselves in sexual perversions with white blond prostitutes. The relationship between technological advancements that enhanced perception and pornography, let alone surveillance, is nothing new, but it is particularly sinister among Japanese plotting global economic warfare.

14. See Carroll Smith-Rosenberg, *Disorderly Conduct: Visions of Gender in Victorian America* (New York: Alfred A. Knopf, 1985). See also n. 18 below.

15. See Michael B. Miller, *The Bon Marché: Bourgeois Culture and the Department Store, 1869–1920* (Princeton: Princeton University Press, 1981): pp. 166–178; Rosalind H. Williams, *Dream Worlds: Mass Consumption in Late Nineteenth-Century France* (Berkeley: University of California Press, 1982), chap. 3; William Leach, *Land of Desire: Merchants, Power, and the Rise of a New American Culture* (New York: Pantheon, 1993), pp. 104–111. See also Emile Zola, *The Ladies' Paradise* (Berkeley: University of California Press, 1992), a translation of *Au bonheur des dames*; Rachel Bowlby, *Just Looking: Consumer Culture in Dreiser, Gissing, and Zola* (New York: Methuen, 1985), chap. 5.

16. Said, *Orientalism*, pp. 40–41; Miles Orvell, *The Real Thing: Imitation and Authenticity in American Culture, 1880–1940* (Chapel Hill: University of North Carolina Press, 1989), 35–36.

17. Yuji Ichioka, *The Issei: The World of the First Generation Japanese-American Immigrants, 1885–1924* (New York: The Free Press, 1988), pp. 71–72; Harry L. Kitano, *Japanese Americans: The Evolution of a Subculture* (Englewood Cliffs: Prentice-Hall, 1969), chap. 2; Roger Daniels, *Concentration Camps USA* (New York: Holt, Rinehart & Winston, 1971), chap. 1.

18. See George G. Foster, *New York by Gaslight and Other Urban Sketches*, ed. with an introduction by Stuart Blumin (Berkeley: University of California Press, 1990); Jacob Riis, *How the Other Half Lives: Studies among the Tenements of New York* (New York: Charles Scribner's Sons, 1890; Minneola: Dover Publications, 1971). On Riis, see Maren Stange, *Symbols of Ideal Life: Social Documentary Photography in America 1890–1950*

(Cambridge: Cambridge University Press, 1989), Peter B. Hales, *Silver Cities: The Photography of American Urbanization* (Philadelphia: Temple University Press, 1984), chap. 2; Alexander Alland, Sr., *Jacob A. Riis: Photographer and Citizen* (Millerton: Aperture, 1974).

19. David Ward, *Poverty, Ethnicity, and the American City, 1840–1925: Changing Conceptions of the Slum and the Ghetto* (Cambridge: Cambridge University Press, 1989), p. 12.

20. See T. J. Jackson Lears and Richard Wightman Fox's introduction to *The Culture of Consumption* (New York: Pantheon, 1983), p. x. On hegemony, see Raymond Williams, "Base and Superstructure in Marxist Cultural Theory," *Problems in Materialism and Culture* (London: Verso, 1980), pp. 31–49; Williams, *Marxism and Literature* (New York: Oxford University Press, 1977), chap. 8; Guy Debord, *Society of the Spectacle* (Detroit: Black & Red, 1977), pp. 4, 6. On reification, see Lukács, *History and Class Consciousness*.

21. On the working class and commercialized amusement, see Roy Rosenzweig, *Eight Hours for What We Will: Workers and Leisure in an Industrial City, 1870–1920* (Cambridge: Cambridge University Press, 1983); Francis G. Couvares, *The Remaking of Pittsburgh (Albany: State University of New York Press*, 1984); Elizabeth Ewen, *Immigrant Women in the Land of Dollars: Life and Culture on the Lower East Side 1890–1925* (New York: Monthly Review Press, 1985); Kathy Peiss, *Cheap Amusements: Working Women and Leisure in Turn-of-the-Century New York* (Philadelphia: Temple University Press, 1986); Lizabeth Cohen, *Making a New Deal: Industrial Workers in Chicago, 1919–1939* (Cambridge: Cambridge University Press, 1990), chap. 3; Miriam Hansen, *Babel and Babylon: Spectatorship and Silent Cinema* (Cambridge: Harvard University Press, 1991). The working class, unlike the middle class, competed with new immigrants for employment so that they were undoubtedly very receptive to the demonization of the alien "Other."

22. See Lawrence W. Levine, *Highbrow/Lowbrow: The Emergence of Cultural Hierarchy in America* (Cambridge: Harvard University Press, 1988); Neil Harris, "Four Stages of Cultural Growth: The American City," in *Cultural Excursions* (Chicago: University of Chicago Press, 1990), 12–28; Paul DiMaggio, "Cultural Entrepreneurship in Nineteenth-Century Boston: The Creation of an Organizational Base for High Culture in America," *Media, Culture and Society* 4 (January 1982):33–50.

23. For a fuller discussion of these issues, see my *Cecil B. DeMille and American Culture*.

24. Albert Mordell, "Introduction," in Lafcadio Hearn, *Occidental Gleanings* (Freeport: Books for Libraries Press, 1925), vol. 1, p. xv. The title of Hearn's work, by the way, has an Orientalist connotation. For an excellent biography of Hearn, see Elizabeth Stevenson, *Lafcadio Hearn* (New York: Macmillan, 1961).

25. See O. W. Frost, *Young Hearn* (Tokyo: Hokuseido Press, 1958); Edward Larocque Tinker, *Lafcadio Hearn's American Days* (Detroit: Gale Research Co., 1970; New York: Dodd, Mead & Co., 1924); Stevenson, *Lafcadio Hearn*. On realism, see Alfred Habegger, *Gender, Fantasy, and Realism in American Literature* (New York: Columbia University Press, 1982), chaps. 7, 11. See also Amy Kaplan, *The Social Construction of American Realism* (Chicago: University of Chicago Press, 1988).

26. For interpretations of Hearn's works, see Carl Dawson, *Lafcadio Hearn and the Vision of Japan* (Baltimore: Johns Hopkins University Press, 1992); Arthur E. Kunst, *Lafcadio Hearn* (New York: Twayne, 1969); Beongcheon Yu, *An Ape of Gods: The Art and Thought of Lafcadio Hearn* (Detroit: Wayne State University Press, 1964), a work whose title has obviously been influenced by Hearn's Orientalist vision; Matthew Joseph-

son, "An Enemy of the West: Lafcadio Hearn," in *Portrait of the Artist as American* (New York: Octagon Books, 1964), pp. 199–231; Malcolm Cowley, Introduction, in Henry Goodman, ed., *The Selected Writings of Lafcadio Hearn* (New York: Citadel Press, 1949). On French Orientalists, see Said, *Orientalism*.

27. Kunst, *Lafcadio Hearn*, p. 122; Dawson, *Lafcadio Hearn and the Vision of Japan*, p. xiv.

28. Hearn, "The New Orleans Exposition," p. 71.

29. Lafcadio Hearn, *Glimpses of Unfamiliar Japan* (Tokyo: Charles E. Tuttle Co. 1976; Boston: Houghton Mifflin, 1894), p. 155.

30. Ibid., p. 86.

31. Ibid., p. 9.

32. Ibid., pp. 123, 674, 168, 129.

33. Robert Rosenstone, *Mirror in the Shrine*, p. 227; Publisher's Foreword, Hearn, *Glimpses of Unfamiliar Japan*, p. x; Said, *Orientalism*, p. 93. On American response to modernization and Japan, see Harris, "All the World a Melting Pot," in *Cultural Excursions*, pp. 53–55; T. J. Jackson Lears, *No Place of Grace: Antimodernism and the Transformation of American Culture 1880–1920* (New York: Pantheon, 1981), pp. 148–49, 175–177.

34. Hearn, *Glimpses of Unfamiliar Japan*, p. 158.

35. Josephson, "An Enemy of the West"; Kunst, *Lafcadio Hearn*, p. 89; Lafcadio Hearn, *Japan: An Attempt at Interpretation* (Tokyo: Charles E. Tuttle Co., 1955), p. 6; Hearn, *Glimpses of Unfamiliar Japan*, p. 24.

36. See Levine, *Highbrow/Lowbrow*, pp. 47–48; Harris, "Iconography and Intellectual History: The Halftone Effect," in *Cultural Excursions*, pp. 304–317.

37. Yu, *An Ape of Gods*, chap. 13.

38. Unfortunately, there is no surviving print of an earlier film situated in the Middle East and titled *The Arab* (1914).

39. Julia Faye, interestingly, was also DeMille's mistress and assigned bit parts in his films for decades after their relationship ended.

40. Script of *The Whispering Chorus*, Cinema-TV Library, USC.

41. *The Whispering Chorus*, *Variety Film Reviews, 1907–1980* (New York: Garland, 1983), 5 April 1918.

42. Edward Weitzel, "The Whispering Chorus," *Motion Picture News*, 6 April 1918, p. 128.

43. I discussed this point in a presentation on *Toll of the Sea* at the Asian American Film Festival held at American University, Washington, D.C., September 1988. I am grateful to Gina Marchetti for inviting me to the festival and to David Parker of the Library of Congress, who was on the same panel, for explaining the details of the Handschiegl and Technicolor processes to me. For a discussion of the reaction of the cultural elite to the use of color, see Harris, "Color and Media: Some Comparisons and Speculations," in *Cultural Excursions*, pp. 318–336. See also Paolo Cherchi Usai, "The Color of Nitrate," *Image* 34 (Spring/Summer 1991):29–38.

44. John Kuo Wei Tchen, "New York before Chinatown," PhD diss., New York University, 1992.

45. I wish to thank Esther Yau for information regarding Chinese musical instruments.

46. Script of *Fool's Paradise*, USC.

47. Ibid.

48. Lukács, *History and Class Consciousness*, pp. 83–103.

49. Script of *Fool's Paradise*, USC.

50. Edward W. Said points out in *Culture and Imperialism* (New York: Alfred A. Knopf, 1993) that critics tend to overlook the fact that Arnold, who celebrated culture, was in fact racist and imperialist (pp. 130–131).

51. Laurence Reid, "Fool's Paradise," *Motion Picture News*, 24 December 1921, p. 123; "A Fool's Paradise," *Motion Picture Magazine*, 22 March 1222, p. 118; Frederick James Smith, *Motion Picture Classic*, April 1922, p. 92. On Siamese twins as a circus spectacle, see Tchen, "New York before Chinatown."

52. Souvenir program, in *Fool's Paradise* clipping file, Margaret Herrick Library, Academy of Motion Picture Arts and Sciences, Los Angeles.

53. Adolph Zukor to Cecil B. DeMille, 22 June 1921, Jesse L. Lasky folder, Lasky Co./Famous Players-Lasky, Cecil B. DeMille Archives, Harold B. Lee Library, Brigham Young University; *Fool's Paradise*, *Variety Film Reviews*, 16 December 1921. *Fool's Paradise* cost $291,367.56 and grossed $906,937.79. See David Pierce, "Success with a Dollar Sign: Cost and Grosses for the Early Films of DeMille," in Paolo Cherchi Usai and Lorenzo Codelli, eds., *The DeMille Legacy* (Pordenone: Edizioni Biblioteca dell'Immagine, 1991), pp. 308–317. Due to the fact that DeMille Productions split profits with Famous Players-Lasky and to ongoing litigation between the director and the IRS, Pierce's figures, derived from a list dated April 1927 at the DeMille Archives in BYU, is difficult to interpret. As he himself indicates, a number of variables including whether the grosses included foreign as well as domestic rentals cannot be ascertained. For a fuller discussion of DeMille's production budgets and film production as commodity fetishism, see my *Cecil B. DeMille and American Culture*, chap. 7.

Selected Bibliography

Compiled by Daniel Bernardi

This bibliography is not exhaustive. It includes the major books and articles cited by the contributors, as well as some sources from a reading list I complied, with the help of Don Kirihara and Lahn S. Kim, over the last few years. The emphasis is on studies that have appeared since the 1980s, though some earlier works are included.

Whiteness

Dyer, Richard. "White." *Screen* 29, no. 4 (Autumn, 1988): 44–64.

Frankenberg, Ruth. *White Women, Race Matters: The Social Construction of Whiteness.* Minneapolis: University of Minnesota Press, 1993.

hooks, bell. "Representing Whiteness in the Black Imagination." In *Cultural Studies*, edited by Lawrence Grossberg et al. New York: Routledge, 1992.

Morrison, Toni. *Playing in the Dark: Whiteness and the Literary Imagination.* Cambridge: Harvard University Press, 1992.

Roediger, David R. *The Wages of Whiteness: Race and the Making of the American Working Class.* New York: Verso, 1991.

———. *Towards the Abolition of Whiteness: Essays on Race, Politics, and Working Class History.* New York: Verso, 1994.

Saxton, Alexander. *The Rise and Fall of the White Republic: Class Politics and Mass Culture in Nineteenth-Century America.* New York: Verso, 1990.

Race in Early Cinema

Aleiss, Angela. "*The Vanishing American*: Hollywood's Compromise to Indian Reform." *Journal of American Studies* (December 1991): 467–72.

Browne, Nick. "Orientalism as an Ideological Form: American Film Theory in the Silent Period." *Wide Angle* 11, no. 4 (1989): 23–31.

Brownlow, Kevin. *Behind the Mask of Innocence.* London: Cape, 1990.

———. *The War, The West and the Wilderness.* New York: Alfred A. Knopf, 1978.

Carbine, Mary. "'The Finest Outside the Loop': Motion Picture Exhibition in Chicago's Black Metropolis, 1905–1928." *Camera Obscura* 23 (May 1990): 8–41.

Cripps, Thomas. "Oscar Micheaux: The Story Continues." In *Black American Cinema*, edited by Manthia Diawara. New York: Routledge, 1993.

———. "'Race Movies' as Voices of the Black Bourgeoisie: *The Scar of Shame* (1927)." *American History/American Film: Interpreting the Hollywood Image.* Expanded ed., edited by John E. O'Connor and Martin A. Jackson. New York: Unger, 1988.

———. *Slow Fade to Black: The Negro in American Film, 1900–1942.* New York: Oxford University Press, 1977.

Gaines, Jane. "Fire and Desire: Race, Melodrama, and Oscar Micheaux." In *Black American Cinema*, edited by Manthia Diawara. New York: Routledge, 1993.

———. "The Scar of Shame: Skin Color and Caste in Black Silent Melodrama." *Cinema Journal* 26, no. 4 (Summer 1987): 3–21.

Green, Ronald J. "'Twoness' in the Style of Oscar Micheaux." In *Black American Cinema*, edited by Manthia Diawara. New York: Routledge, 1993.

Green, Ronald J., and Horace Neal, Jr. "Oscar Micheaux and Racial Slur: A Response to 'The Rediscovery of Oscar Micheaux'." *Journal of Film and Video* 40, no. 4 (Fall 1988): 66–71.

Higashi, Sumiko. *Cecil B. DeMille and American Culture: The Silent Era*. Berkeley and Los Angeles: University of California Press, 1994. See pp. 100–112.

———. "Ethnicity, Class, and Gender in Film: DeMille's *The Cheat*." In *Unspeakable Images: Ethnicity and the American Cinema*, edited by Lester D. Friedman. Chicago: University of Illinois Press, 1991.

Keil, Charlie. "Reframing the Italian: Questions of Audience Address in Early Cinema." *Journal of Film and Video* 42, no. 1 (Spring 1990): 36–48.

Lamadrid, Enrique R. "Ig/noble Savages of New Mexico's Silent Cinema, 1912–1914." *Spectator* 13 no. 1 (Fall 1992): 12–23.

Lamb, Blain P. "The Convenient Villain: The Early Cinema Views the Mexican-American." *Journal of the West* 14 (October 1975): 75–89.

Lang, Robert, ed. *The Birth of a Nation: D. W. Griffith, Director*. New Brunswick, N.J.: Rutgers University Press, 1994.

Lesage, Julia. "*Broken Blossoms*: Artful Racism, Artful Rape." *Jump Cut* 26 (December 1981): 51–55.

Lund, Karen C. *American Indians in Silent Film: Motion Pictures in the Library of Congress*. Washington, D.C.: Library of Congress, August 1992. Updated April 1995.

Marchetti, Gina. "The Rape Fantasy: *The Cheat* and *Broken Blossoms*." In *Romance and the "Yellow Peril": Race, Sex, and Discursive Strategies in Hollywood Fiction*. Berkeley and Los Angeles: University of California Press, 1993.

May, Larry. "Apocalyptic Cinema: D. W. Griffith and the Aesthetics of Reform." In *Screening Out the Past: The Birth of Mass Culture and the Motion Picture Industry*. New York: Oxford University Press, 1980.

Merritt, Russell. "D. W. Griffith's *The Birth of a Nation*: Going after Little Sister." In *Close Viewings: An Anthology of New Film Criticism*, edited by Peter Lehman. Tallahassee: Florida State University Press, 1990.

Moy, James S. *Marginal Sights: Staging the Chinese in America*. Iowa City: University of Iowa Press, 1993. See chap. 7.

Musser, Charles. "Ethnicity, Role-playing, and American Film Comedy: From *Chinese Laundry Scene* to *Whoopee* (1894–1930)." In *Unspeakable Images: Ethnicity and the American Cinema*, edited by Lester D. Friedman. Chicago: University of Illinois Press, 1991.

Oehling, Richard A. "The Yellow Menace: Asian Images in American Film." In *The Kaleidoscopic Lens: How Hollywood Views Ethnic Groups*, edited by Randall M. Miller. Englewood, N.J.: Jerome S. Ozer, 1980.

Orellana, Margarita De. "The Circular Look: The Incursion of North American Fictional Cinema, 1911–1917, into the Mexican Revolution." In *Mediating Two Worlds*, edited by John King et al. London: BFI Publishing, 1993.

Reid, Mark A. "Early African-American Film Companies." In *Redefining Black Film*. Berkeley and Los Angeles: University of California Press, 1993.

Rogin, Michael. "Making America Home: Racial Masquerade and Ethnic Assimilation in the Transition to Talking Pictures." *Journal of American History* 79 (December 1992): 1,050–1,077.

———. "'The Sword Became a Flashing Vision': D. W. Griffith's *The Birth of a Nation*." *Representations* 9 (Winter 1985): 150–195.

Rios-Bustamante, Antonio. "Latino Participation in the Hollywood Film Industry, 1911–1945." In *Chicanos and Film: Representation and Resistance*, edited by Chon A. Noriega. Minneapolis: University of Minnesota Press, 1992.

Rony, Fatimah Tobing. "Those Who Squat and Those Who Sit: The Iconography of Race in the 1895 Films of Felix-Louis Regnault." *Camera Obscura* 28 (January 1992): 262–289.

Simmon, Scott. "Mr. Griffith's Civil War: The Birth of a Nation and Family Honor." In *The Films of D. W. Griffith*. New York: Cambridge University Press, 1993.

Snead, James. "*Birth of a Nation*." In *White Screens/Black Images: Hollywood form the Dark Side*, edited by Colin MacCabe and Cornel West. New York: Routledge, 1994.

Staiger, Janet. "Class, Ethnicity, and Gender: Explaining the Development of Early American Film Narrative." *Iris* 11 (Summer 1990): 13–25.

———. "Rethinking 'Primitive' Cinema: Intertextuality, the Middle-Class Audience, and Reception Studies" and "*The Birth of a Nation*: Reconsidering Its Reception." In *Interpreting Films: Studies in the Historical Reception of American Cinema*. Princeton, N.J.: Princeton University Press, 1992.

Streible, Dan. "A History of the Boxing Film, 1894–1915: Social Control and Social Reform in the Progressive Era." *Film History* 3, no. 3 (1987): 235–257.

Waller, Gregory A. "Another Audience: Black Moviegoing, 1907–1916." *Cinema Journal* 31, no. 2 (1992): 3–25.

Race and Classical and Contemporary Cinema

Books with significant work on early cinema can be found in the previous section. Essays on race and classical/contemporary cinema in anthologies such as Manthia Diawara's *Black American Cinema* and Chon Noriega's *Chicanos and Film*, listed separately in the above section, are not cross-listed listed in this section.

Aleiss, Angela. "Prelude to World War II: Racial Unity and the Hollywood Indian." *Journal of American Culture* 18, no. 2 (Summer 1995): 27–36.

———. "A Race Divided: The Indian Westerns of John Ford." *American Indian Culture and Research* 18, no. 3 (Summer 1994): 167–186.

Baker, Houston A., Jr. "Spike Lee and the Commerce of Culture." *Black American Literature Forum* 25, no. 2 (Summer 1991): 237–252.

Berg, Charles Ramirez. "Immigrants, Aliens and Extraterrestrials: Science Fiction's Alien 'Other' as (Among Other Things) New Hispanic Imagery." *CineAction!* 18 (Fall 1989): 3–17.

———. "Stereotyping in Films in General and of the Hispanic in Particular." *The Howard Journal of Communications* 2, no. 3 (Summer 1990): 286–300.

Bobo, Jacqueline. "The Color Purple: Black Women as Cultural Readers." In *Female Spectators Looking at Film and Television*, edited by E. Deidre Pribram. London: Verso, 1988.

Bogle, Donald. *Toms, Coons, Mulattoes, Mammies & Bucks: An Interpretive History of Blacks in American Films*. New expanded ed. New York: Continuum, 1989.

Browne, Nick. "Race: The Political Unconscious of American Film." *The East West Film Journal* 6, no. 1 (1992): 5–16.

Buscombe, Edward. "*The Magnificent Seven*." In *Mediating Two Worlds*, edited by John King et al. London: BFI Publishing, 1993.

Cham, Mbye D., ed. *Critical Perspectives on Black Independent Cinema*. Cambridge, Mass.: MIT Press, 1988.

Cortes, Carlos E. "Hollywood Interracial Love: Social Taboo as Screen Titillation." In *Beyond the Stars: Plot Conventions in American Film*, edited by Paul Loukides and Linda K. Fuller. Bowling Green, Ohio: Bowling Green State University Popular Press, 1990.

Cripps, Thomas. *Black Film as Genre*. Bloomington: Indiana University Press, 1978.

———. *Making Movies Black: The Hollywood Message Movie from World War II to the Civil Rights Era*. New York: Oxford University Press, 1993.

———. "*Sweet Sweetback's Baadasssss Song* and the Changing Politics of Genre Film." In *Close Viewings: An Anthology of New Film Criticism*, edited by Peter Lehman. Tallahassee: Florida State University Press, 1990.

DelGaudio, Sybil. "The Mammy in Hollywood Film, I'd Walk a Million Miles for One of Her Smiles." *Jump Cut* 28 (April 1983): 23–25.

Diawara, Manthia, ed. *Black American Cinema: Aesthetics and Spectatorship*. New York: Routledge, 1993.

———. "The Absent One: The Avant-Garde and the Black Imaginary in *Looking for Langston*." *Wide Angle* 13, nos. 3 and 4 (July-October 1991): 96–109.

Dyer, Richard. "The Colour of Virtue: Lillian Gish, Whiteness and Femininity." In *Women and Film: A Sight and Sound Reader*, edited by Pam Cook and Philip Dodd. Philadelphia: Temple University Press, 1993.

———. "Paul Robeson: Crossing Over." In *Heavenly Bodies: Film Stars and Society*. New York: St. Martin's Press, 1986.

Dunkerley, James. "'All That Trouble Down There': Hollywood and Central America." In *Mediating Two Worlds*, edited by John King et al. London: BFI Publishing, 1993.

Film & History 23, nos. 1–4 (1993). Special issue on the Hollywood Indian.

Fregoso, Rosa Linda. *The Bronze Screen: Chicano and Chicana Film Culture*. Minneapolis: University of Minnesota Press, 1993.

Friedman, Lester D., ed. *Unspeakable Images: Ethnicity and the American Cinema*. Chicago: University of Illinois Press, 1991.

Gaines, Jane. "White Privilege and Looking Relations: Race and Gender in Feminist Film Theory." *Cultural Critique* 4 (Winter 1986): 13–27.

Guerrero, Edward. *Framing Blackness: The African American Image in Film*. Philadelphia: Temple University Press, 1993.

———. "Spike Lee and the Fever in the Racial Jungle." In *Film Theory Goes to the Movies: Cultural Analysis of Contemporary Film*, edited by Jim Collins et al. New York: Routledge, 1993.

Hall, Stuart. "The Whites of Their Eyes: Racist Ideologies and the Media." In *Silver Linings*, edited by George Bridges and Rosalind Brent. London: Lawrence and Wishart, 1981.

———. "Cultural Identity and Cinematic Representation." *Framework* 36 (1989): 68–81.

Heung, Marina. "'What's the Matter with Sara Jane?' Daughters and Mothers in Douglas Sirk's *Imitation of Life*." *Cinema Journal* 26, no. 3 (Spring 1987): 21–43.

hooks, bell. *Black Looks: Race and Representation*. Boston: South End Press, 1992.

Julien, Isaac, and Kobena Mercer, eds. "The Last 'Special' Issue on Race?" *Screen* 29 (1988).

Keller, Gary D. *Hispanics and United States Film: An Overview and Handbook*. Tempe, Ariz.: Bilingual Press, 1994.

Klottman, Phyllis Rauch. *Frame by Frame: A Black Filmography*. Bloomington: Indiana University Press, 1979.

Leab, Daniel J. *From Sambo to Superspade: The Black Experience in Motion Pictures*. Boston: Houghton Mifflin, 1975.

Lopez, Ana M. "Are All Latinas from Manhattan? Hollywood, Ethnography, and Cultural Colonialism." In *Unspeakable Images: Ethnicity and the American Cinema*, edited by Lester D. Friedman. Chicago: University of Illinois Press, 1991.

Lott, Tommy L. "A No-Theory Theory of Contemporary Black Cinema." *Black American Literature Forum* 25, no. 2 (Summer 1991): 221–236.

Marchetti, Gina. *Romance and the "Yellow Peril": Race, Sex, and Discursive Strategies in Hollywood Fiction*. Berkeley and Los Angeles: University of California Press, 1994.

Noriega, Chon, ed. *Chicanos and Film: Representation and Resistance*. Minneapolis: University of Minnesota Press, 1992.

———. "Internal 'Others'; Hollywood Narratives 'about' Mexican-Americans." In *Mediating Two Worlds*, edited by John King et al. London: BFI Publishing, 1993.

———. "'Waas Sappening?': Narrative Structure and Iconography in Born in East L.A." *Studies in Latin American Popular Culture*, 14 (1995): 107–128.

Pines, Jim. *Blacks in Film*. London: Studio Vista, 1975.

Reid, Mark A. *Redefining Black Film*. Berkeley and Los Angeles: University of California Press, 1993.

Roberts, Shari. "The Lady in the Tutti-Frutti Hat": Carmen Miranda, a Spectacle of Ethnicity." *Cinema Journal* 32, no. 3 (Spring 1993): 3–23.

Rogin, Michael. "Blackface, White Noise: The Jewish Jazz Singer Finds His Voice." *Critical Inquiry* 18 (Spring 1992): 417–453.

Shohat, Ella. "Imaging Terra Incognito: The Disciplinary Gaze of Empire." *Public Culture* 3, no. 2 (Spring 1991): 41–70.

Shohat, Ella, and Robert Stam. *Unthinking Eurocentrism: Multiculturalism and the Media*. New York: Routledge, 1994.

Snead, James. "Images of Blacks in Black Independent Films: A Brief Survey." In *Blackframes, Critical Perspectives on Black Independent Cinema*, edited by Mbye D. Cham and Claire Andrade-Watkins. Cambridge, Mass.: MIT Press, 1988.

———. *White Screens/Black Images: Hollywood from the Dark Side*, edited by Colin MacCabe and Cornel West. New York: Routledge, 1994.

Studlar, Gaylyn. "Discourses of Gender and Ethnicity: The Construction and De-(con)struction of Rudolph Valentino as Other." *Film Criticism* 13, no. 2 (Winter 1989): 18–35.

Taylor, Clyde. "Black Film in Search of a Home." *Freedomways* 23, no. 4 (1983): 226–233.

———. "The Colonialist Subtext in *Platoon*." In *From Hanoi to Hollywood: The Vietnam*

War in American Film, edited by Linda Dittmar and Gene Michaud. New Brunswick, N.J.: Rutgers University Press, 1990.

———. "Decolonizing the Image: New U.S. Black Cinema." In *Jumpcut: Hollywood, Politics and Counter-Cinema*, edited by Peter Steven. Toronto: Between the Lines, 1985.

———. "New U.S. Black Cinema." *Jump Cut* 28 (1983): 46–48.

———. "We Don't Need Another Hero: Anti-Theses on Aesthetics." In *Critical Perspectives on Black Independent Cinema*, edited by Mbye D. Cham. Cambridge, Mass.: MIT Press, 1988.

Winokur, Mark. "Black Is White/White Is Black: 'Passing' as a Strategy of Racial Compatibility in Contemporary Hollywood Comedy." In *Unspeakable Images: Ethnicity and the American Cinema*, edited by Lester D. Friedman. Chicago: University of Illinois Press, 1991.

Woll, Allen L. "From Bandits to President: Latin Images in American Films, 1929–39." *Journal of Mexican American History* 4 (1974): 28–40.

Woll, Allen L., and Randall M. Miller, *Ethnic and Racial Images in American Film and Television*. New York: Garland, 1987.

Wong, Eugene Franklin. *On Visual Media Racism: Asians in the American Motion Pictures*. New York: Arno Press, 1978.

Early Cinema

Allen, Robert C. *Vaudeville and Film, 1895–1915: A Study in Media Interaction*. New York: Arno Press, 1980.

Altman, Rick. "*The Lonely Villa* and Griffith's Paradigmatic Style." *Quarterly Review of Film Studies* 6, no. 2 (Spring 1981): 123–134.

Anderson, Gillian. *Music for Silent Films, 1894–1929*. Washington, D.C.: Library of Congress, 1988.

Berg, Charles Merrell. *An Investigation of the Motives for and Realization of Music to Accompany the American Silent Film (1896–1927)*. New York: Arno Press, 1973.

Bordwell, David, et al. *The Classical Hollywood Cinema: Film Style & Modes of Production to 1960*. New York: Columbia University Press, 1985.

Bordwell, David, and Kristin Thompson. "Linearity, Materialism and the Study of the Early American Cinema." *Wide Angle* 5, no. 3 (1983): 4–15.

Bowser, Eileen. *The Biograph Bulletins: 1908–1912*. New York: Farrar, Strauss and Giroux, 1973.

———. *The Transformation of Cinema* (1907–1915). New York: Charles Scribner's Sons, 1990.

Browne, Nick. "Griffith's Family Discourse: Griffith and Freud." *Quarterly Review of Film Studies* 6, no. 1 (Winter 1981): 67–80.

DeCordova, Richard. *Picture Personalities: The Emergence of the Star System in America*. Chicago: University of Illinois Press, 1990.

Eisenstein, Sergei. "Dickens, Griffith and the Film Today." *Film Form*, edited and translated by Jay Leyda. New York: Harcourt, Brace, Javonich, 1949.

Elsaesser, Thomas, and Adam Barker. *Early Cinema: Space, Frame, Narrative*. London: BFI Publishing, 1990.

Everson, William K. *American Silent Film*. New York: Oxford University Press, 1978.

Fell, John L., ed. *Film before Griffith*. Berkeley and Los Angeles: University of California Press, 1983.

Gunning, Tom. "The Cinema of Attraction: Early Film, Its Spectator and the Avant-Garde." *Wide Angle* 8, nos. 3 and 4 (1986): 63–70.

———. *D. W. Griffith and the Origins of American Narrative Film: The Early Years at Biograph*. Chicago: University of Illinois Press, 1991.

———. "Weaving a Narrative: Style and Economic Background in Griffith's Biograph Films." *Quarterly Review of Film Studies* (Winter 1981): 10–25.

Hansen, Miriam. *Babel and Babylon: Spectatorship in American Silent Film*. Cambridge: Harvard University Press, 1991.

———. "Early Silent Cinema: Whose Public Sphere?" *New German Critique* 29 (Spring/Summer 1983): 147–184.

———. "The Mother and the Whore." *South Atlantic Quarterly* 88, no. 2 (Spring 1989): 368–388.

Henderson, Robert M. *D. W. Griffith: His Life and Work*. New York: Oxford University Press, 1972.

Jesionowski, Joyce E. *Thinking in Pictures: Dramatic Structure in D. W. Griffith's Biograph Films*. Berkeley and Los Angeles: University of California Press, 1987.

Keil, Charlie. "Transition through Tension: Stylistic Diversity in the Late Griffith Biographs." *Cinema Journal* 28, no. 3 (Spring 1989): 22–40.

Musser, Charles. "Another Look at the Chaser Theory." *Studies in Visual Communications* 10, no. 4 (Fall 1984): 24–44.

———. *Before the Nickelodeon: Edwin S. Porter and the Edison Manufacturing Company*. Berkeley and Los Angeles: University of California Press, 1991.

———. *High-Class Moving Pictures: Lyman H. Howe and the Forgotten Era of Traveling Exhibition, 1880–1920*. Princeton, N.J.: Princeton University Press, 1991.

———. *The Emergence of Cinema: The American Screen to 1907*. New York: Charles Scribner's Sons, 1990.

Niver, Kemp R. *Motion Pictures from the Library of Congress Paper Print Collection, 1894–1912*, edited by Bebe Bergsten. Berkeley and Los Angeles: University of California Press, 1967.

———. *D. W. Griffith: His Biograph Films in Perspective*. Los Angeles: John D. Roche, 1974.

Quarterly Review of Film Studies 6, no. 1 (Winter 1981). Special issue on D. W. Griffith.

Pearson, Roberta E. *Eloquent Gestures: The Transformation of Performance Style in the Griffith Biograph Films*. Berkeley and Los Angeles: University of California Press, 1992.

Ramsaye, Terry. *A Million and One Nights*. New York: Simon and Schuster, 1986 [1926].

Ruby, Jay. "A Reexamination of the Early Career of Robert J. Flaherty," *Quarterly Review of Film Studies* 5, no. 4 (Fall 1980): 431–457.

Salt, Barry. "The Unknown Ince." *Sight and Sound* 57, no. 4 (Autumn 1988): 268–272.

———. "What Can We Learn from the First Twenty Years of Cinema." *Iris* 2, no. 1 (1984): 83–90.

Singer, Ben. "Manhattan Nickelodeons: New Data on Audiences and Exhibitors." *Cinema Journal* 34, no. 3 (1995): 5–35.

Slide, Anthony. *The Big V: A History of the Vitagraph Company*. Metuchen, N.J.: Scarecrow Press, 1987.

Urrichio, William, and Roberta E. Pearson. *Reframing Culture: The Case of the Vitagraph Quality Films*. Princeton, N.J.: Princeton University Press, 1993.

Wide Angle 3, no. 1 (1979). Special issue on Silent Film.

Winston, Brian. "Before Grierson, Before Flaherty. The Documentary Film in 1914." *Sight and Sound* 57, no. 4 (Autumn 1988): 277–279.

Contributors

Daniel Bernardi is a University of California President's Postdoctoral Fellow in the Department of Film and Television at UCLA. His dissertation, *The Wrath of Whiteness: The Meaning of Race in the Generation of* Star Trek (Rutgers University Press, forthcoming), traces the articulation of race across the *Star Trek* phenomenon: from the television shows of the late 1960s to the films of the mid-1980s to the spin-off programs of the late 1980s and early 1990s. He is currently putting together an anthology on the meaning of race in classical Hollywood cinema.

Nick Browne is Professor of Critical Studies in the Department of Film and Television at UCLA. He is the editor of books on American television, French film theory, Chinese cinema, American film genre and Francis Ford Coppola. He is the author of books on the history of film theory and on narration in film. He is currently working on a study of the representation of violence in American film.

Pearl Bowser is an independent scholar and filmmaker. She is the founder and director of African Diaspora Images, a collection of historical and contemporary black films and memorabilia. The collection was one of the primary resources for material in the 1993 production of the documentary *Midnight Ramble: Oscar Micheaux and the Story of Race Movies*, which she also co-directed. She has curated exhibitions on Black Cinema at universities, museums, and community centers around the country. She has worked with Louise Spence on several oral history projects and is currently collaborating with her on the soon-to-be-published book *In Search of Oscar Micheaux*. Their joint research and collection of oral histories for the book has been supported by The Ford Foundation and the National Endowment for the Humanities grants and artists' fellowships at MacDowell Colony, Blue Mountain Center, and the Virginia Center for Creative Arts.

Thomas Cripps is University Distinguished Professor at Morgan State University. He has written numerous articles, two of which have won literary prizes, and several books, the latest of which is *Making Movies Black* (Oxford, 1993). He has also written numerous television scripts, among them *Black Shadows on a Silver Screen* (Post-Newsweek TV, 1976), which won gold medals in several international festivals. He has been a fellow of the National Humanities Center, the Guggenheim Foundation, the Woodrow Wilson International Center for Scholars, and other scholarly foundations.

Sumiko Higashi teaches American history, film, and women's studies at SUNY Brockport. She rewrote film history as cultural history in *Cecil B. DeMille and American Culture: The Silent Era* (University of California Press, 1994). A frequent film reviewer for the *American Historical Review*, she has published essays in anthologies such as *Re-visioning History: Film and the Construction of the Past*, *Unspeakable Images: Ethnicity and the American Cinema*, *From Hanoi to Hollywood: The Vietnam War in American Film* and *The Persistence of History: Cinema, Television, and the Modern Event*.

Donald Kirihara teaches film history, criticism, and theory at the University of Arizona. He has written about film in *Film Criticism*, *Film Quarterly*, *The Journal of Film and Video*, and *Film Reader*, and is the former editor of *The Velvet Light Trap* and *Wide Angle*. He is also the author of *Patterns of Time: Mizoguchi in the 1930's* (University of Wisconsin Press, 1992).

Gina Marchetti is Associate Professor at the University of Maryland, College Park. She recently completed *Romance and the "Yellow Peril": Race, Sex, and Discursive Strategies in Hollywood Fiction* (University of California Press, 1994).

Chon A. Noriega is Assistant Professor in the UCLA Department of Film and Television. In addition to writing numerous articles and book chapters, he is editor of *Chicanos and Film: Representation and Resistance* (University of Minnesota Press, 1992) and special issues of *Spectator* (Fall 1992) and *Jump Cut* (June 1993; June 1994). He is co-editor of *The Mexican Cinema Project* (UCLA Film and Television Archive, 1994) and *The Ethnic Eye: Latino Media Arts* (University of Minnesota Press, 1996). In addition, he served as a consultant on media and the visual arts, and has curated exhibitions for the Whitney Museum, the Robert Flaherty Seminar, and the American Museum of the Moving Image, among others. He is currently curating an exhibition on Chicano narrative photography and the American West for the Mexican Museum in San Francisco, and preparing a forty-year retrospective on Puerto Rican multimedia artist Raphael Montañez Ortiz.

Roberta E. Pearson is Assistant Professor at the Annenberg School for Communication at the University of Pennsylvania. She is the author of *Eloquent Gestures: The Transformation of Performance Style in the Griffith Biograph Films* (University of California Press, 1992), the co-author of *Reframing Culture: The Case of the Vitagraph Quality Films* (Princeton University Press, 1993) and the co-editor of *The Many Lives of Batman: Critical Approaches to a Superhero and His Media* (Routledge/BFI, 1991). She is currently working on a manuscript concerning the representation of race, gender, and history in Custer texts, tentatively titled *Custer's Last Scene*.

Fatimah Tobing Rony is a film and art historian and a filmmaker. She teaches Asian American Studies and World Arts and Cultures at UCLA. Her forthcoming book, *The Third Eye: Race, Cinema, and Ethnographic Spectacle*, will be published by Duke University Press. Her recent video, *On Cannibalism*, is distributed by NAATA and Women Make Movies, and she is currently working on a documentary entitled *Tondi*.

Louise Spence teaches media and cultural studies at Sacred Heart University, Fairfield, Connecticut. She has published articles in such academic journals as *Screen*, *Cinema è Cinema*, *Quarterly Review of Film and Video*, *Journal of Film and Video*, and several anthologies. She is currently collaborating with Pearl Bowser on an examination of "Race movies" and the career of African American independent filmmaker Oscar Micheaux, soon to be published by Rutgers University Press. Work on this book has been supported by an American Council of Learned Societies Fellowship, a Ford Foundation grant, and the National Endowment for the Humanities.

Dan Streible is an Assistant Professor in Radio-Television-Film at the University of Wisconsin–Oshkosh. He has also taught at the University of Texas and Austin Community College. He has published essays on the history of American cinema and is a regular contributor to the *Motion Picture Guide*. He is the author of a forthcoming book on the history of prizefight films. He is also co-editing a reader on Emile de Antonio. A native of Louisville, he marched behind Muhammad Ali in the 1979 Kentucky governor's inaugural parade. Correspondence welcome: streible @ vaxa.cis.uwosh.edu.

Clyde Taylor is Professor of literature and film in the English Department, Tufts University. He has taught at Howard University; California State University, Long Beach; University of California, Los Angeles; University of California, Berkeley; Stanford; and Mills College. His publications include *Vietnam and Black America* (editor), essays and reviews in *Black World, Africa Now, The Black Scholar, American Film, Screen, Framework, Jumpcut, Blackframes: Critical Perspectives on Black Independent Cinema, Questions of Third Cinema*, and *Black American Cinema*, among many others. Taylor has lectured widely on themes of Black world cinema. Among the exhibitions he has organized is the much cited "L.A. Rebellion," which he curated for the Whitney Museum of American Art and Brooklyn Museum. Taylor wrote the script for *Midnight Ramble: The Life and Legacy of Oscar Micheaux*, a documentary film completed in 1993. He is currently completing a study of the politics of representation in cinema and literature, entitled *Breaking the Aesthetic Contract* (University of Minnesota Press, forthcoming).

Virginia Wright Wexman teaches courses in film, literature, cultural studies, and women's studies at the University of Illinois at Chicago, where she is Professor of English. She received her B.A., M.A., and Ph.D. from the University of Chicago and was Visiting Associate Professor of English there in 1990. She is the author of numerous books and articles on film and cultural studies, including *Robert Altman: A Guide to References and Resources* (G. K. Hall, 1976; co-authored with Gretchen Bisplinghoff), *Roman Polanski* (Twayne, 1984), *Letter from an Unknown Woman* (Rutgers University Press, 1986; co-authored with Karen Hollinger), and *Creating the Couple: Love, Marriage and Hollywood Performance* (Princeton University Press, 1993). A past President of the Society for Cinema Studies, she also edited the Society's quarterly *Cinema Journal* from 1982 to 1987.

Index

Addams, Jane, 18, 186
Adventures of Dollie, The, 108
aesthetic(s), 16, 17, 18, 22; discrimination, 22; Orientalist, 334; theory, 35
aestheticism, 29
African American filmmaking, 5, 15, 105, 186
Africanism, 34
Afro-American Ledger, 181, 189
Agee, James, 19
Aiken, George L., 110
Akeley, Carl, 304
Alaska, 300
Alderson, William A., 213
Alhambra Theater, Harlem, N.Y., 188
Alien Souls, 89, 91
Allakariallak, 302, 307, 319, 320, 321
allegory, national, 15–36
Allen, Margaret V., 213
America, 24
American Biograph Company, 124, 274
American Biograph Films, 8, 93, 104, 107, 108
American culturalism, school of, 304
American Film Manufacturing Company, 109
American Museum of Natural History, 304, 309
American Music Hall, New York, 174
Amossy, Ruth, 81, 82
Anderson, Benedict, 130
Anderson, Gillian, 230
"Anglo-Saxons," 4
Argonauts of the Western Pacific, 312
Arizona, 2
Arthur, President Chester A., 207
Ashe, Arthur, 181
assimilation, 209, 230, 260, 276
Australia, 176
authenticity, 131, 133, 232, 250, 301, 308
Avalos, David, 205
Avenging a Crime, 110

Baffinland, Canada, 308
Baker, Houston A., 66
Baker Ranch, Snake Valley, Nev., 142
Balikci, Asen, 300, 310, 315, 316
Baltimore, Md., 62
Bann, Stephen, 304
Barrett, Lawrence, 281
Bazin, André, 303, 308, 316, 319
Beach, Rex, 181
Behind the Mask of Innocence (Brownlow), 6
Belasco, David, 85, 228, 230, 236
Belcher Islands, Canada, 319
Bennett, Tony, 70
Benteen, Captain, 287
Betrayal, The, 65, 72
Bhabha, Homi K., 131, 209, 211
Bierstadt, Alfred, 141
Biograph Bulletin, 118, 121
biological classification/subdivision, 1, 4
biological determinism, 4, 7, 8
Birth of a Nation, The, 5, 7, 8, 15–36, 122, 193, 274, 230
Birth of a Race, The, 7, 38–53
Birthright, 57
Bison 101 Productions, 129, 140
Black American Cinema (Diawara), 5
black: empowerment, 187; inferiority, 65; representation, 72
Black Hills, Wyo., 284, 285
Black Hills expedition, 288
blackness, 26, 34, 65, 67, 70, 106; perception of, 64
Blackton, J. Stuart, 188
Boas, Franz, 303, 309, 315
Bob Hampton of Placer, 278, 281
Body and Soul, 57, 66, 71
Bonehill, Capt. Ralph, 279
Book of the American Indian, The (Garland), 277
Booster Era (1885–1925), 204
Boston, Mass., 189
Boston Museum of Fine Arts, 329
Bourdieu, Pierre, 130, 131
Bowser, Pearl, 7
Brady, Cyrus, 278, 283, 289
Brady, William, 171, 174, 189
Bravest Way, The, 90, 92
Bridge over the River Kwai, The, 81

Britton of the Seventh, 278, 281, 283, 287
Broadway Theater, New York, 174
Broken Blossoms, 8, 24, 103, 257, 331
Broncho Billy Anderson, 133
Broncho Billy and the Baby, 153
Bronx, N.Y., 188
Bronze Screen: Chicana and Chicano Film Culture, The (Fregoso), 5
Brooklyn, N.Y., 188
Brooks, Elbridge S., 279
Browne, Nick, 8, 119
Brownlow, Kevin, 6, 7
Brute, The, 57
Buffalo, N.Y., 188, 311
Buffalo Bill, 109
Buffalo Bill's Wild West Show, 109, 131, 206
Buffalo Dance, 109
Bureau of Indian Affairs, 207, 219
Burns, Thomas, 170
Buscombe, Edward, 140

Cashmore, Ellis, 130
Calder-Marshall, Arthur, 314
California, 89, 143; immigration into, 211; Southern, 140, 204
Call of the East, The, 92, 94
Call of the Wild, The, 118–119
Camulos, Ventura County, Calif., 204
capitalism, consumer, 331, 333
Captain's, Chair, The (Flaherty), 317
Caribbean, 7
Carlisle Indian Industrial School, 276
Carmen, 230, 231, 233
Carrying Out the Snakes, 277
Caruso, Enrico, 232
Catholic Church, 210
Catlin, George, 295
"Caucasians," 4
Cecil B. DeMille and American Culture: The Silent Era (Higashi), 6
Century of Dishonor (Jackson), 207, 213
Chang, 303
Chaplin, Charlie, 9
Chapman, Alfred L., 282
Charge of the Light Brigade, the, 278
Charles E. Tuttle Company, 337
Cheat, The, 81, 91, 94, 227, 229, 257, 331
Chenault, Lawrence, 63, 68, 71
Chesnutt, C. W., 69–70
Chesnutt, Helen M., 69
Chicago, Ill., 57, 59
Chicago Defender, 56, 66, 73, 186, 189, 191
Chicago Tribune, 174, 181
Chicago Whip, The, 62
Chicana/o filmmaking, 6
Chicanos and Film: Representation and Resistance (Noriega), 5
Chicken Thief, The, 111
China, 84, 239, 240, 330
Chinese Exclusionary Laws, 240
Chinese Laundry Scene, 5, 109
Chisholm, Cheryl, 23
Churchill, Ward, 131
Churchill, Winston, 184
Cincinnati, Ohio, 334
Cinémathèque Royale/Koninklijk Filmarchief, Belgium, 56
cinematic processes, 104
City of Dim Faces, The, 92
Civil War, 129, 279, 281; Confederacy, 19, 24; Reconstruction era, 17, 19, 20, 29, 31; Union, 19
Clarion Ledger, 185
class, 8, 206, 220, 331
Classical Hollywood Cinema: Film Style and Modes of Production to 1960 (Bordwell et al.), 6
Clifford, James, 313
Cole, Thomas, 141
Collier's, 89
colonialism, 4, 9, 209, 218, 332
Colonial Theater, Bronx, N.Y., 188
Columbia University, 303
Competitor, The, 69
Coney Island, N.Y., 191, 293
Conquest, The, 59, 66, 68, 74
Conquest: The Story of a Negro Pioneer by the Pioneer, The (Micheaux), 59
Conrad, Joseph, 318
Coolidge, President Calvin, 280
Cooper, James Fenimore, 277
Cooper, Merian C., 303
Corbett, Jim, 170, 180, 181, 182
Cornell University, 338
Corner in Wheat, A, 93
Courtney, Peter, 170
Courtship of O San, The, 85
Covered Wagon, The, 133, 142
Crazy Horse, 278
Crescent Films, 110
Cripps, Thomas, 5, 7, 103
Cruze, James, 143

Cullen, Countee, 56
cultural critique, 242, 249
cultural diversity, 330
culture, 1, 4, 206, 209, 250, 270, 277, 341, 346; American, 158; consumer, 336, 337; and contradiction, 232; cross-cultural relations, 228; difference, 86; indigenous, 307; Japanese, 9, 329, 335; mass, 15, 339; Mexican, 212; native, 303; oppositional, 292; pluralistic, 331, 339; popular, 332, 333, 346, 347; and resistance, 244; and superiority, 244; white, 292
Cunayoo, 303
Curtis, Edward S., 277, 312
Custer, George Armstrong, 9, 273–295
Custer's Last Fight, 274, 280, 281

Daily Ohio State Journal, The, 69
Dalton, Dorothy, 342
Dances with Wolves, 283
Darwin, Charles, 132
Davidson, John, 344
Davis, Carlyle C., 213
Davis, Mike, 205
Dawes Act, 210, 276
Dawn Maker, The, 133
Debord, Guy, 333
Deceit, 57
Dellenbaugh, Frederick, 293
Delluc, Louis, 91
DeMille, Cecil B., 9, 227, 245, 332–333, 339–348
Denver, Colo., 188
Department of the Interior, Bureau of Indian Affairs, 207, 219
Deserter, The, 129
Detroit, Mich., 56, 62, 187
Detroit Free Press, 173
Dexter, Elliot, 339
dialectics, 227, 248
Diawara, Manthia, 5
discourse, 1, 2, 104, 130, 131, 133, 235, 238, 333; academic, 301; aesthetic, 17, 24, 33, 36; American Orientalism, 249; anthropological, 306; antimodernist, 337; and authenticity, 9, 301; class, 8, 206; colonialist, 4; counter-, 210; gender, 8, 206; hegemonic, 329, 342; imperialist, 4; narrative, 112, 117, 259; nationalist, 130; Orientalist, 339; political, 210, 212, 268; popular, 210, 288; public, 332; on race, 4, 7, 8, 169, 206, 218; sentimentalist, 218; on sexuality, 221; social Darwinism, 286; totalizing, 348; Western, 248, 337; on whiteness, 104
Dixon, Thomas, 21, 24, 25, 28, 31
Dizikes, John, 227
Doctor Faustus, 33
documentary, 315
domination, colonial, 105
Dorgan, "Tad," 175
Dubie, J. Frank, 208
Du Bois, W.E.B., 193
Duchene, Rose, 343
Duel in the Sun, 217
Dungeon, The, 57
D. W. Griffith and the Origins of American Narrative Film (Gunning), 103
Dyer, Richard, 106
Dyer anti-lynching bill, 57

Eastman, Charles, 294
Eaton, Winnifred, 88, 94
Edison, Thomas, 109, 170, 311
Edison Manufacturing Company, 110, 125
Eisenstein, Sergei, 29, 103
Elizabeth I, 308
empowerment, political and male, 260
Engle, David, 152
enlightenment, 157
Cincinnati Enquirer, 334
eschatology, Christian, 20
"Esquimaux Village," Pan-American Exposition, 311
Essanay, 109
ethnicity, 3, 260, 331
ethnographic cinema, 300, 304, 306, 308; makers of, 300, 316
eugenics, 1, 4, 106
Eurocentrism, 3, 4, 5, 29
Europe, 4, 96
Exile, The, 59, 64
exoticism, 262, 336

Fabian, Johannes, 305, 313
false consciousness, 36
Famous Players/Famous Players–Lasky Company, 229, 230, 347
Fang, Charles, 258, 265
fantasy, masochistic, 230
Farrar, Geraldine, 232, 233, 249, 342
fascism, 29

Fatal Hour, The, 124
Faye, Julia, 339, 344
Felton, William Mack, 70
femme ideal, 24
Ferguson, Robert, 152
fetishism, 27, 332; commodity, 347, 348
Fienup-Riordan, Ann, 310
Fifty-ninth Street Theatre, New York, 70
Fighting Blood, 129
Film Art: An Introduction (Bordwell and Thompson), 6
Film History: Theory and Practice (Allen and Gomery), 6
Fisher, Philip, 129
Flaherty, Robert, 9, 300–322
Flaming Frontier, The, 281
Flaubert, Gustave, 335
Fool's Paradise, 339, 342, 345–346
Forbidden City, The, 9
Forbidden Paths, 92
Ford, Francis, 274
Ford, John, 30, 136, 158
Forged Note, The, 60, 67
formation: hegemonic, 6; historical, 241; ideological, 241; racial, 3, 4, 6, 9; social, 1, 3
Forrest Theater, Philadelphia, 190
Fort Laramie treaty, 284, 292
Foster, George G., 333, 334
Foster, William, 175
Foucault, Michel, 330
Framing Blackness: The African American Image in Film (Guerrero), 5
Frank, Leo M., 58
Franklin, Sidney A., 257
Fregoso, Linda, 5
French Quarter, New Orleans, 334
Frobisher, Martin, 308
Frontier, The, 61
frontier theory, 285
Fujiyama, Mt., 336
Fuller Opera House, Madison, Wisc., 190

Gall, Sioux chief, 278, 284, 293
Gans, Joe, 171
Gans-Nelson fight, 180
Garland, Hamlin, 277, 294
Gates, Henry Louis, 1
Gaynor, William J., 188
gaze, male, heterosexual, 220
Geertz, Clifford, 152, 313
gender, 8, 206, 240, 257, 331
General Custer at the Little Big Horn, 281
Gennette, Gérard, 111
genocide, 305
genre, expedition, 312
Gentlemen's Agreement, 240
Gibbons, James Cardinal, 183
Gilman, Lawrence, 231
Gilmore, Al-Tony, 184, 186
Girls and Daddy, The, 122–123
Gish, Lillian, 7, 26
Glimpses of Unfamiliar Japan (Hearn), 337, 338
Godfrey, Edward S., 292
God's Stepchildren, 65, 69, 71
Gone With the Wind, 15
Gotham Theater, Brooklyn, N.Y., 188
Grant, President Ulysses S., 280
Grass, 303
"greaser" films, 7, 9
Great K and A Train Robbery, The, 133
Great Plains, 59
Greece, ancient, 35
Greeley, Horace, 61
Gregory County, S.D., 61
Grey, Zane, 277
Griaule, Marcel, 315
Griffith, D. W., 7, 8, 15–36, 129, 158, 274, 331
Guerrero, Ed, 5
Gunning, Tom, 9, 93, 103, 104, 108, 109, 112
Gunsaulus Mystery, The, 57

Hagenbeck Zoo, Berlin, 309
Half-Century Magazine, 56
Hall, Iris, 64, 71
Hall, Stuart, 3
Hamilton, Reed, 258
Haraway, Donna, 304
Hardy, Edith, 229
Harlem, New York City, 188
Harper's Magazine, 335
Harper's Weekly, 231, 329
Harris, Mildred, 342
Harris, Neil, 84, 337
Harrison, Louis Reeves, 220, 221, 280, 287, 290
Hart, William S., 62, 131, 133, 158, 162
Harvard University, 18
Hatton, Raymond, 339
Havana, Cuba, 193
Hawaii, 239

Haworth Pictures, 96
Hawthorne, Nathaniel, 208
Hayakawa, Sessue, 7, 8, 81–96, 229, 331
Hays, Will, 303
Hearn, Lafcadio, 9, 329–338
Hearst newspapers, 84, 183
Heart of Darkness (Conrad), 318
Hearts of the World, 24
hegemony, 333; ideological, 270; racist practices, 105
Hell's Hinges, 158
Henry, Edward, 62
heteroglossic voices, 151
Heusch, Luc de, 301, 315, 319
Hidden Pearls, 92
hierarchies: racial, 266, 340; social, 331
Higashi, Sumiko, 6, 9
Hiroshima, Japan, 33
His Birthright, 229
His Trust, 115–117
His Trust Fulfilled, 115–117
historiography, teleological, 286
history: experience of, 2; industrial, 5
History of Narrative Film, A (Cook), 6
Hoboken, N.J., 188
Hodges, John, 70
Hollidaysburg, Pa., 189
Hollywood, 26, 96, 132, 140, 257, 261, 268, 300, 303; cowboy movies, 282; fantasies, 266; films, 27, 205, 206, 257, 259, 264, 281; financiers, 7; functionaries, 30; genres, 130; melodramas, 259; style, 103, 125
Homestead Act (1862), 212
Homesteader, The (Micheaux), 59, 74
Homo sapiens, 1, 132
Honorable Friend, The, 89, 92
hooks, bell, 72
House Behind the Cedars, The, 57, 70, 71
Howard, Shingzie, 71
Huang, David, 239
Hudson Bay, Canada, 318
Hudson River School, 141
Hudson River Valley, 147
Hudson's Bay Company, 318
Hufford, D. A., 213
Hughes, Langston, 67
Hurston, Zora Neale, 67
hybridity, 131

icon(s), 9, 194, 261, 280, 282, 320
iconography, 345
identification: in cinema, 220; sentimental, 209; symbolic, 211
identity, 1, 2, 3, 4, 8, 9, 58, 112, 234, 260, 346; "Anglo-Saxon," 210; bi-racial, 206; cultural, 113; ethnic, 135; European American, 105; gender, 257; national, 8, 130, 131, 146, 151, 205, 206, 247, 257, 280, 331; racial, 75, 104, 206, 240, 257; tribal, 276; white, 209, 210, 219
ideology, 10, 18, 27, 235, 278; axis of, 235; bourgeois, 88, 269; and contradiction, 291; crisis of, 242; determination of, 17; dominant, 96; and gender relations, 240; national, 130; political, 33; racial, 9; reciprocal, 105; religious, 244; white supremacist, 194
image, 333; black power, 177, 183; cinematic, 9, 302; commodification of, 336; racially inflammatory, 186; visual, 19
imperialism, 141; and gaze, 141; and nation-state, 235; Western, 250, 251
Ince, Thomas H., 85, 274
Ince Studio, 83
India, 343
Indian, 38, 273; archetypal, 277; Indianness, 209; Mission Indians, California, 207; Plains, 277; rights, 208; as vanishing American, 295
Indian tribes: Cherokee, 158; Cheyenne, 277, 278; Crow, 135; Dakota, 292; Lakota, 277, 278; Luise–o, 207; Ponca, 207; Shoshone, 145; Tiano, 3; Unkpapa Sioux, 275
Indiana Jones and the Temple of Doom, 345
Indianapolis Freeman, 175, 179
Indian Fights and Fighters (Brady), 283–284
Indian War Council, 109
individual, subordinated, 235
Influence of Sea Power Upon History, The (Mahan), 240
Innupiat Inuit, 300
interracial love stories, 8
Interrupted Crap Game, 110
intersubjectivity, 331, 346
intertextuality, 332
Inuit Broadcasting Company, 320
Inukjuak (Port Harrison), Canada, 302, 317
Inukjuk television station, 320
Inventing the Dream (Starr), 204

Iron Horse, The, 136
Irwin, Wallace, 89
Isman, Felix, 174
Italy, 30

Jackson, Helen Hunt, 8, 204, 207
Jackson, Peter, 170
Jackson, Miss., 62, 185
Jackson-Kinney report on Indians, 207
Jacob, Lewis, 15
Jacobson, J. Adrian, 308
Jaguar's Claws, The, 92
Jakobson, Roman, 238
James, George Wharton, 211, 213
J & J Company, 188
Japan, 18, 84, 86, 96, 239, 241, 330
Japanese-American Film Company, 228
Japanese Nightingale, A, 88
Jazz Singer, The, 15
Jeffries, Jim, 170, 173, 192
Jeffries-Sharkey Fight, 175
Jennings, Al, 133
Jesse L. Lasky Feature Play Company, 81, 83, 90, 93, 96, 229, 332
Jim Crow laws, 107, 124, 170
Johnson, George P., 60
Johnson, Jack, 9, 10, 108, 170–194
Johnson, Noble, 60
Johnson-Burns Fight, 174–176
Johnson-Flynn Fight, 192
Johnson-Jeffries Fight, 181–193
Johnson-Ketchel Fight, 176, 178–179
Johnson-Moran Fight, 192
Jolson, Al, 7, 181
Josephson, Matthew, 338
Julian, Col. Hubert Fauntleroy, 75

Kane, Dr. Elisha Kent, 310
Kansas City, Mo., 187
Katana, Oath of the Sword, 228
Keaton, Buster, 9
Keats, John, 34
Ketchel, Stanley, 170, 176, 182
Khayyam, Omar, 259
Kidder, Lieutenant, 287
King of Kings, The, 348
Kinney, Abbot, 207, 210
Kipling, Rudyard, 259
Kirihara, Donald, 8, 229
Kleine, George, 179
Kliener Collection, 231
knowledge, 1
Korea, 239
Kracauer, Siegfried, 301, 307
Ku Klux Klan (KKK), 8, 18, 21, 25, 27, 29, 57, 62, 63, 68, 103, 280
Kunst, Arthur E., 338
Kunuk, Zacharias, 321, 322

La Bamba, 206
La Bohème, 231, 232
Lafayette Theater, New York, 63
Lamarkian evolutionary theory, 132
landowners, 210
Lang, Robert, 103
La Scala, Milan, 239
Lasky, Jesse, 230, 245, 347
Lasky Studios, 81, 83, 90, 93, 96, 229, 332
Last Drop of Water, The, 122, 129
Last of the Mohicans, The, 147, 206
Latino films, 5
Leacock, Richard, 322
Leather Stockings, 122
Lee, Charlie, 113–114
Leerseen, Jeop, 82
leitmotifs, 231
Lengyel, Menyhért, 85
Leopard's Spots, The, 25
Leprohon, Pierre, 301
Lesage, Julia, 103
Letters of a Japanese Schoolboy (Irwin), 89, 93
Lévi-Strauss, Claude, 26
Lewis, Alfred Henry, 181
L'exotisme et le cinéma: Les "chasseurs d'images" à la conquete du monde (Leprohon), 301
Library of Congress, 277
Life of a Cowboy, 111
Lincoln Motion Picture Company, 60
Lindsay, Vachel, 86
Ling, Amy, 88
Lippman, Walter, 82
Liszt, Franz, 231
Little Big Horn River, Mont., 278
Little Big Horn, Battle of, 274, 277, 281
Little Big Man, 295
Little Horse, Cheyenne chief, 278, 284
Locke, Alain, 67
Locke, John, 158
London, Jack, 171, 181
Long, John Luther, 85, 228, 230
Longfellow, Henry Wadsworth, 283, 292

Los Angeles, Calif., 26, 229
Los Angeles County Museum of Art, 329
Los Angeles Times, 204
Loti, Pierre, 228
Lubin, Siegmund, 110, 124
Lukács, Georg, 333, 346
Lummis, Charles F., 208
Lusitania, 7
Lying Lips, 75
lynching, 57; symbolic, 241
Lytton, Rogers, 258

McCoy, Tim, 133
McIntosh, Hugh D., 174
McLellan's Colored Singers, 190
McWilliams, Carey, 211, 212
Madame Butterfly (story, play, opera), 85, 257, 342
Madame Butterfly (film), 8, 85, 227–251
Madame Chrysantheme, 228
Madison, Wisc., 190
Mahan, Alfred, 240
Mahon, Carl, 71
Making Movies Black (Cripps), 5
Malinowski, Bronislaw, 312, 316, 318, 322
Manchu empire, 342
Manila, Philippines, 258, 266
Mann, Thomas, 33
Marchetti, Gina, 6, 9, 242
"Mario the Magician" (Mann), 33
Martin, Ed, 171
Martinique, 335
mass media, 22
Massacre, The, 274
Massot, Claude, 319
Mast, Gerald, 18, 22
Master of the Strong Hearts: A Story of Custer's Last Rally, The (Brooks), 279, 292
Matisse, Henri, 340
Maynard, Ken, 133
M. *Butterfly* (Huang), 239
Mead, Margaret, 315
Meighan, Thomas, 258
Meiji Japan, 337
Melville, Herman, 208
*Mes*ti*zo*NATION* (Avalos and Small), 205
Messager, André, 228
Metropolitan Opera, New York, 231, 342
Mexican Americans, dispossessed, 212
Mexican American War, 208, 211
Mexican's Gratitude, A, 109
Mexico, 105
Meyerrose Park, Brooklyn, N.Y., 189
Micheaux, Oscar, 7, 8, 56–75
Micheaux Book and Film Company, 61
Mikado, The (Gilbert and Sullivan), 227
Miller, Mildred, 189
Miller, Randall M., 275
Millionaire, The, 66
Mindanao, Philippines, 258
minstrel shows, 28
miscegenation, 8, 22, 26, 209, 241, 247, 257, 258, 263; anti-miscegenation, 244; stereotype of, 95
*Mis*ce*ge*NATION* (Avalos and Small), 205
Miss Saigon, 239
Mitchell, W.J.T., 141
Miura, Mme. Tamaki, 232
Mix, Tom, 133
Moana, 300
Modell, John, 89
Mohawk's Way, A, 122
"Mongoloids," 4
Montana, 278
Monument Valley, Ariz., 147
Morrison, Toni, 34, 65
motif, 155, 344; cultural, 131
Motion Picture Classic, 347
Motion Picture Magazine, 346
Motion Picture News, 341, 346
Motion Picture Patents Company (MPPC), 108, 124, 179, 188
Motion Picture Producers and Distributors of America (MPPDA), 303
Motts, Robert T., 179
Moving Picture World, 181, 219, 220, 228, 230, 280, 288
Moy, James, 85
Mudimbe, V. Y., 307
Mukařovský, Jan, 83
multiculturalism, 331
Mulvey, Laura, 220
Murnau, F. W., 300
Musser, Charles, 91, 110
Mussolini, Benito, 30
My Eskimo Friends: "Nanook of the North" (Flaherty), 317
My Life on the Plains (Custer), 279
mystification, 34, 243
myth: fabric of, 21; mission of, 204; of national origin, 130

NAACP, 18, 108, 186
Nagasaki, Japan, 239, 247
Nagel, Conrad, 342
Nanook of the North, 9, 300–322
Nanook Revisited, 319–322
Nara, temple of, 329
narration, narrative, 104, 133, 266, 308; classical mode of, 95; cinematic, 220, 222; economy, 88; function, 282; hierarchy, 270; history, 5; structure, 290; as a system, 103, 112, 117
national: allegory, 15–36; identity, 162; origin, 130, 131, 132
National Board of Review, 108, 124
National Museum of Natural History, 309–310
nationalism, 8; White American, 21
nationality, 247
Native American genocide, 105
Naughton, W. W., 178
Nayoumealuk, Charles, 319, 320
Nebraska, 60
negrophilia, 27
negrophobia, 7, 17, 27
netsuke, 329
Nevins, Allan, 208
New Deal, 276
New England, 21
Newhall, Calif., 158
New Orleans, La., 57, 329, 334
New Orleans Times-Democrat, 334
Newport, R.I., 190
Newsome, Carmen, 71
New World, 153
New York Age, 63, 70, 189, 309
New York City, 231, 249, 333, 347
New York Clipper, 188
New York Dramatic Mirror, 236
New York Evening Post, 232
New York Herald, 171
New York Journal, 175
New York Motion Picture Company, 274
New York Sun, 178
New York Times, 174, 178, 188, 232, 277, 284, 285, 286
New York Tribune, 183, 189
Nigger in the Woodpile, 111
Night in Blackville, 110
Nihonbashi Street Tokio, 334
Noriega, Chon, 5, 8
Northern Pacific Railroad, 286
Nowkawalk, Moses, 319, 320
Nunaqpa/Going Inland, 321
Nuvalinga, Alice, 302, 320
Nuyoricans, 3

objectivity, 313, 315
Occidentalism, 239
Ododo Theater, Tucson, Ariz., 3
Olcott, Sid, 236
Oldfield, Barney, 191
Old Wives for New, 339
Old World, 154
Olympic Field, Harlem, N.Y., 189
Omaha, Neb., 57
Omi, Michael, 3, 4, 105
101 Ranch Wild West Show, 140
On the Little Big Horn; or, Custer's Last Stand, 280, 289
On the Plains with Custer (Sabin), 279
On Visual Media Racism (Wong), 5
oppression, structure of, 2
oral history, 277
order: ideological, 238; patriarchal, 267; religious, 238
Oregon Trail, 142
Oriental figure, 228; mannerisms of, 86
Orientalism, 239, 331–348; American, 238, 240; history of, 239
Orpheum Theater, Brooklyn, N.Y., 188
Orvell, Miles, 332
Other, 3, 106, 141, 153, 329–348; internalized, 249
Otis, Col. Harrison Gray, 204
Outlook, 183

Paine, Thomas, 151
Paley, William, 110, 124
Pan-American Exposition, 311
Papua New Guinea, 312
Paramount, 142, 227, 229, 230, 231, 233, 236, 245, 347
Paramount Progress newsletter, 231
Parrish, Randall, 278, 287
participant observation, 312, 313
Pathé, 300
patriarchy, 310; American, 242, 247, 264, 265; Asian, 261, 262, 265, and authority, 262, 267; bourgeois, 260; Chinese, 262; and despotism, 262; institutions of, 267; Western, 263
Pearl Harbor, Hawaii, 278
Pearson, Roberta E., 9
Peary, Robert, 309

Pekin Theater, Chicago, 179
Penn, Arthur, 295
Peoria, Ill., 188
Philadelphia, Pa., 187
Philippines, 239, 269
Phillipoosie, 303
Pickford, Mary, 7, 85, 222, 229, 230, 233
Plains Indian Wars, 290
Platte River, 143
Plessy v. Ferguson, 107, 194
Pocock, J.G.A., 157
Point Barrow, Alaska, 311
Poisoned Flume, The, 109
popular culture, 3, 177, 206, 280, 294, 300, 302; American, 240, 241; discourse, 133; narratives, 290
popular imagination, 85, 236, 273, 277, 278
Porter, Edwin S., 7, 35, 110, 111, 124
power: cultural, 227; ideological, 227; patriarchal, 259; sentimental, 208–213
practice: Orientalist, 238; racist, 105; social, 210
Pratt, Mary Louise, 142
Preer, Evelyn, 71
prejudice, racial, 266
primitive man, 307
privilege, social, 3
Prize Fight in Coontown, 110
Progressive Era, 194, 240
protest, social, 220
Puccini, Giacomo, 8, 85, 228, 230, 231, 244, 245
Puerto Ricans, 3

Qaggia/the Gathering Place, 321
Qing dynasty, 269
Quebec Inuit, 322

radicalism, 31
race: articulation of, 3; biological subdivision of, 1; categories, 247; classification of, 1; construction of, 1–3; and determinism, 1; and difference, 247, 248, 249, 250, 260, 262, 268, 329, 330, 331; illusion of, 1; and inferiority, 330, 346; myth of, 305; and patriotism, 240; policy, 247; purity, 205; and social Darwinism, 1, 4; trope of, 1; vanishing, 306
racial characterizations: borders of, 17, 266; and hierarchies, 105; as Other, 9; and politics, 7; practice of, 5, 7; and privilege, 250; relations among, 247; representation of, 23, 27, 83; theory of, 249
racialism, 210
racism, 4, 6, 107, 269; agenda of, 186; cinematic, 6; and exclusionism, 266; as group psychosis, 25; ideology of, 17; passive, 7; practices of, 107; punitive, 125; sexualization of, 263; white, 106, 108
racist images and narratives, 5, 7, 18
Rain-in-the-Face, 288–293
Ramona, 8, 203–222
Ramona's Bedroom (Avalos and Small), 205
*Ramona: Birth of a Mis*se*ge*NATION* (Avalos and Small), 205
Ramona's Homeland (Allen), 213
Ramona Pagent, 204
reality, universal, 301
Real Ramona, The (Hufford), 213
Reconstruction, 194
Red Cloud, 292
Red Raiders, 133
Redefining Black Film (Reid), 5
Regnault, Félix-Louis, 308
Reid, Laurence, 346
Reid, Mark A., 5
re-identification, 243
Relic of Old Japan, A, 228, 229
Remington, Frederic, 141
Renan, Ernest, 129
Reno, Maj. Marcus A., 278, 280, 289, 293
Reno, Nev., 181, 182, 183, 186, 190, 191
representation, 4, 5, 9, 85, 108, 110, 141, 153–155, 170, 182, 228, 244, 294, 302, 331, 345; aesthetic, 22; of Africa, 343; American, 9; of Asia, 227, 343; authentic, 293; black, 22; of blackness, 106; of character's subjectivity, 233; cinematic, 193, 301; of Middle East, 343; media, 17; mode of, 301, 304, 313; of Native Americans, 275, 277, 283, 288; of narrative space, 66; negative, 276; political, 33; politics of, 22, 104; racial, 248; of racial mixture, 206; racialist, 7; racist, 108; strategies of, 131; visual, 141; white American, 22; of whiteness, 106
resistance, 9, 141, 142, 151, 274; power of, 132
Return of Draw Egan, The, 162
Rhinelander, Alice Jones, 70

Rhinelander, Leonard Kip, 70
Rialto Theater, New York, 231
Richmond Planet, 173, 186
Rickard, Tex, 180, 181
Riensenfeld (musical arranger), 231
right, patriarchal, 258, 263
Riis, Jacob, 333
Roberts, Randy, 190
Robeson, Paul, 71
Rock, William T., 188
Rocky Mountains, 144
Rocky Mountain School, 141
Roddenberry, Congressman Seaborn, 192
Rogin, Michael, 103
romance, interracial, 258, 266
Romance and the "Yellow Peril" (Marchetti), 6
Romance of the Western Hills, A, 117–118
Rony, Fatimah Tobing, 9
Roosevelt, President Theodore, 84, 132, 174, 183, 208, 210, 240
Roots, 15
Rosebud Reservation, S.D., 59, 60
Rosenstone, Robert, 337
Rouch, Jean, 315, 310, 322
Rousseau, Jean-Jacques, 129
Ruhlin, Gus, 171
Ruhlin Boxing with "Denver" Ed Martin Catalogue, 171
Russia, 84, 240, 330

Said, Edward, 131, 332–348
St. Louis, Mo., 187
St. Paul Appeal, 186
Salammbô (Flaubert), 335
salvage ethnography, 302–303
Sambaso Dancer, 329
Sammons, Jeffrey T., 180
San Diego, Calif., 205
San Francisco, Calif., 84
San Francisco Examiner, 182, 184
Santa Ynez Canyon, Calif., 140
Scenes of Japan, 334
Schickel, Richard, 23, 30
Schoedsack, Ernest B., 303
Scorsese, Martin, 30
Searchers, The, 5, 30
segregation, spacial, 115
Seitz, George B., 148
self-superiority, 336
Selig, William, 109, 124, 289
Selig Company, 287
Selznick Pictures, 257
Sensational Designs (Tompkins), 208
sentimentalism, feminine, 208
sentimental power, 208, 209, 221; reformers, 208
Senungetuk, Joseph E., 300
sexual difference, 230, 247–248, 330, 331
sexuality, interracial, 259, 263, 269
Shanghai, China, 339–341
Sharp, William, 192
Sheridan, Gen. Philip, 287
Shohat, Ella, 4, 6, 131, 136
Short History of the Movies, A (Mast), 18
signifier, cultural, 106; of male power, 260; of race pride, 171
Sims, Congressman Thetus, 193
Sioux City, Iowa, 60
Sioux Ghost Dance, 109
Sitting Bull, 278, 284, 291, 292
Sloan, John, 177
Slotkin, Richard, 133, 210, 212
Slow Fade to Black (Cripps), 5
Small, Deborah, 205
Smith, Frederick James, 347
Smith Sound, Canada, 309
Snake Valley, Nev., 142
social change, 208
social Darwinism, 106, 107, 108, 211, 330
social history, 2
social order, 210, 244
social relations, 333
society, pluralistic, 332; U.S., 208
socio-historical process, 4
Son of Satan, A, 65
Song of the South, 15
South Dakota, 60, 68, 72
Spanish-American War, 330
Spence, Louise, 7
Spencer, Baldwin, 315
Spencerian evolutionism, 330, 339
Spirit Trail, The, 292
Staiger, Janet, 110
Stam, Robert, 4, 6
Starr, Kevin, 204
status, racial/sexual, 257
Stefannson, Vilhjalmur, 314
Steiner, William F., 110
stereotypes, Asian, 92
Stevens, Congressman Thaddeus, 21
Stocking, George W. Jr., 132, 304
Story of Dorothy Stanfield, The (Micheaux), 72

Stowe, Harriet Beecher, 66, 110, 206
Straight Shooting, 158
strategies: representaional, 280, 288; visual, 151
Streible, Dan, 9
structure: economic, 211; political, 211
Studlar, Gaylyn, 92
style, cinematic, 104, 310
subjectivity, 235
Sullivan, John L., 170, 181, 182
superiority: cultural, 331; moral, 331; political, 331
supremacy: American, 340; white, 333, 342, 345
Survivors, The, 33
Sydney, Australia, 171
symbolism, collective cultural, 26
Symbol of the Unconquered, The, 8, 65, 71

Tabu, 300
Taft, President William Howard, 181
Talmadge, Norma, 258
Tatum, E. G., 67
taxidermy, 302, 304, 308, 310, 316, 321; display, 301
Taxi Driver, 30
Taylor, Clyde, 6, 7, 103
Tchaikovsky, Peter Ilich, 231
Temporary Truce, A, 124
Temptation of Saint Anthony, The (Flaubert), 335
Ten Commandments, The (1923), 348
Texas, 342
Thailand, 343
That Chink at Golden Gulch, 113–115
"The Nigger" (Brady), 189
Thermopylae, 278
Thirty Years Later, 65
Thomas, Kent W., 293
Thompson, Walter, 63, 71
Thread of Destiny, The, 122
Through Ramona's Country (James), 220
Time magazine, 75
Todorov, Tzvetan, 111
Togo, Hashimura, 89
Tokyo, Japan, 232
Toll of the Sea, 251, 342
Tomashevsky, Boris, 58
Tompkins, Jane, 133, 208
Toomer, Jean, 67
Tosca (Puccini), 231, 232
Toscanini, Arturo, 232
tourism, 205
Tourneur, Maurice, 148
transformation: class, 212; historical, 331; racial, 212
Treaty of Guadelupe Hidalgo, 210
Tremble, John, 342
tribal governments, 276
Triumph of the Will, 29, 33
Trobriand Islands, 312, 318, 322
trope(s), 1, 2; of the body, 131; dangerous, 1, 2; espionage, 240; invasion, 240; vanishing American, 277; visual, 144; Western, 9
True Story of Ramona, The (Alderson), 213
Tucker, Lorenzo, 71
Tucson, Ariz., 3
Tumbleweeds, 158
Two Moons, 278
Typhoon, The, 85, 94, 92, 229

"Uncle Rad Kees," 179
Uncle Tom's Cabin (Stowe), 66, 207; film, 110
Union Army, 280
United Society for Christian Endeavor, 183
United States, 4, 7, 8, 16, 31; capitalism in, 105; filmmaking in, 32; government, 83, 219, 265, 276, 283, 290; history, 105, 231; law, 189; plays in, 204; race relations, 193
U.S. Cavalry, 277, 278
U.S. Congress, 84, 170, 192, 286, 332
U.S. Court of Land and Claims, 212
U.S. Supreme Court, 107
University of Chicago, 229
University of Minnesota, 231
Unkpapa Sioux, 287
Unthinking Eurocentrism (Shohat and Stam), 6
Up from Slavery (Washington), 73
Urban League, 108

Valentino, Rudolph, 7
values, patriarchal, 265
Vanishing American, The, 147, 277
Van Valin, William, 311
Variety, 341, 348
Vaudette Theater, Detroit, 56
Veblen, Thorstein, 19
Veiled Aristocrats, 65

Vendome Theater, Chicago, 56
Verdi, Giuseppe, 231
Vietnam, 5, 239
Virgina State Board of Motion Picture Censors, 57
Virginian, The, 153–157
Vitagraph, 188
voyeurism, 311, 317, 341, 346

Wagner, Richard, 231
Wallace, Minik, 308
Waller, Gregory, 84, 227
Walthall, Henry B., 203, 221
Walton, Lester, 70
war: Russo-Japanese, 337; Sino-Japanese, 337
War (Griffith), 24
War, the West and the Wilderness, The (Brownlow), 6
Warren, E. A., 258
Washington, Booker T., 66, 73, 180
Washington, D.C., 185
Watanna, Onoto, 88, 91
Watermelon Patch, The, 110
Weber, Max, 231
Weitzel, Edward, 341
West, the, 4
West, Cornel, 1
Western Book Supply Company, 60
Westernization, 330
West Side Story, 206
West Virginia, 189
Wexman, Virginia Wright, 8
When the Movies Were Young (Griffith), 204
Whispering Chorus, The, 339, 340
whites, 3, 4, 8; civilization of, 279; as class, 210; culture of, 4; as filmmakers, 300; and nationalism, 8; solidarity of, 181; supremacy of, 6, 7, 9, 20, 30, 35, 65, 105, 181, 186
White House, 173
White Man's Law, The, 92
whiteness, 5, 6, 8, 9, 10, 26, 35, 65, 68, 104, 106, 109, 110, 111, 113, 114, 115, 117, 118, 180, 210; as biological classification, 105; discourse of, 105, 111, 112; genealogy of, 104; hierarchy of, 113; historical formation of, 105; ideology of, 118; and racial morality, 122; and racist ideals, 115; superiority of, 113; voice of, 113, 119, 121
Whittaker, Frederick, 280, 281, 284, 286, 289
Widener, Joseph E., 190
Wiggins, William H. Jr., 181
Wilderness Trail, The, 75
Wilkerson, Chief Justice Charles F., 129
Willard, Jess, 192, 193
Williams, Kathlyn, 339
Williams, Percy G., 188
Williamson, Joel, 24, 31, 32
Williams v. Mississippi, 107
Wilson, President Woodrow, 107
Winant, Howard, 3, 4, 105
Wind from Nowhere, The (Micheaux), 65
Winner, S.D., 59
Wister, Owen, 153
With Custer in the Black Hills (Bonehill), 279
Within Our Gates, 57, 63, 71
Woll, Allen L., 275
Women's Christian Temperance Union, 183
Wong, Anna May, 7, 251
Wong, Eugene Franklin, 5
Woodward, C. Vann, 108
Woollacott, Janet, 70
World's Colombian Exhibition, Chicago, 309
World War I, 84, 89, 227, 268, 269
World War II, 7, 321
Wounded Knee massacre, 293
Wrath of the Gods, The, 229, 257
Wright, George C., 194
Wunder, John, 152
Wyckoff, Alvin, 341
Wyeth, Sidney, 72

xenophobia, 89, 280, 295, 331

Yakumo, Koizumi, 335
"yellow peril," 240
Yellow Slave, The, 228

Zukor, Adolph, 347
Zulu's Heart, The, 120–122
Zweig, Stefan, 335